STUDIES
IN THE PENTATEUCH

SUPPLEMENTS

TO

VETUS TESTAMENTUM

EDITED BY
THE BOARD OF THE QUARTERLY

J.A. EMERTON – W.L. HOLLADAY – A. LEMAIRE
R.E. MURPHY – E. NIELSEN – R. SMEND
J.A. SOGGIN – M. WEINFELD

VOLUME XLI

STUDIES
IN THE PENTATEUCH

EDITED BY

J.A. EMERTON

E.J. BRILL
LEIDEN · NEW YORK · KØBENHAVN · KÖLN
1990

ISSN 0083–5889
ISBN 90 04 09195 5

PHOTOSET BY INTERPRINT LTD, MALTA
PRINTED IN THE NETHERLANDS

CONTENTS

Preface VII

R.S. HESS, Splitting the Adam: the usage of ꜥādām in Genesis
i–v 1
H.N. WALLACE, The Toledot of Adam 17
W. HOROWITZ, The isles of the nations: Genesis x and
Babylonian geography 35
J.A. EMERTON, The site of Salem, the city of Melchizedek
(Genesis xiv 18) 45
J.A. EMERTON, Some problems in Genesis xiv 73
R.W.L. MOBERLY, Abraham's righteousness (Genesis xv 6) 103
T.D. ALEXANDER, The Hagar traditions in Genesis xvi and
xxi 131
Marsha WHITE, The Elohistic depiction of Aaron: a study in
the Levite-Zadokite controversy 149
G.I. DAVIES, The wilderness itineraries and recent archaeo-
logical research 161
E. FIRMAGE, The biblical dietary laws and the concept of
holiness 177
R.W.L. MOBERLY, "Yahweh is one": the translation of the
Shema 209
D.J. REIMER, Concerning return to Egypt: Deuteronomy
xvii 16 and xxviii 68 reconsidered 217
D.R. DANIELS, The creed of Deuteronomy xxvi revisited . 231

Indexes
Authors cited 243
References 247

PREFACE

Like several earlier volumes in the series *Supplements to Vetus Testamentum* – most recently *Studies in the Historical Books of the Old Testament, SVT* 30 (1979) — this book brings together a number of essays, most of which were submitted for publication in *Vetus Testamentum*. It will be evident to readers that no attempt has been made to secure uniformity of opinion among the contributors.

J.A. EMERTON

SPLITTING THE ADAM:
THE USAGE OF ʾĀDĀM IN GENESIS I-V[1]

by

RICHARD S. HESS

Glasgow

1. ʾdm in Genesis i-v

ʾdm occurs 34 times in Gen. i-v. Of these occurrences, only 5 should be identified as personal names. The remainder of the occurrences appear to be generic expressions for mankind in general or the male in particular. 22 of the occurrences are preceded by the article, and this suggests that the forms should not be understood as personal names.[2] In fact, all the articular occurrences appear within the narrative. The occurrence in i 27 requires an understanding of the term which includes both male and female, i.e. a generic sense referring to the whole of humanity.[3] Although there is an initial ambiguity in ch. ii, v. 22 requires hʾdm to be understood as a male, in contrast to the female who is created. V. 25 designates hʾdm as one of two figures, along with his wife, who are naked. If we assume the consistency of the narrative in ch. ii, the designation of hʾdm is different from that in ch. i. In ch. i it refers to humanity in general, while in ch. ii it refers to one male

---

[1] The research for this article was done at Tyndale House, Cambridge, as part of the Genesis 1–11 Project.

[2] The passages are: i 27, ii 7 (twice), 8, 15, 16, 18, 19 (twice), 20, 21, 22 (twice), 23, 25, iii 8, 9, 12, 20, 22, 24, iv 1.

[3] Cf. "von dem Menschen in gattungsbegrifflichen Sinne gemeint ist", in Franz Delitzsch, *Neuer Commentar über die Genesis* (Leipzig, 1887), p. 65; "den Menschen" in H. Gunkel, *Genesis* (Göttingen, ²1902), pp. 97–8; " the human race" in J. Skinner, *A Critical and Exegetical Commentary on Genesis* (Edinburgh, ²1930), pp. 32–3; "ein kollektivum" in G. von Rad, *Das erste Buch Mose. Genesis Kapitel 1–12, 9* (Göttingen, ³1953), p. 44; "mensen" in W.H. Gispen, *Schepping en paradijs. Verklaring van Genesis 1–3* (Kampen 1966), pp. 73, 81; "den Menschen" in C. Westermann, *Genesis 1–11* (Neukirchen-Vluyn, 1974), p. 108; "human race" in his *Genesis 1–11. A Commentary* (E. tr. by J.J. Scullion; Minneapolis and London, 1984), pp. 77. Cf. the rabbinic view that "man was created with two faces, that is, a hermaphrodite", in U. Cassuto, *A Commentary on the Book of Genesis. Part I. From Adam to Noah* (Jerusalem, 1961), p. 57.

individual, i.e. "the Man".[4] Such a usage may be best understood as titular, in which the title possesses the sense of a male with the function of caring for the garden and also the reference to (in this case) a single individual who is a focus of attention in chs. ii and iii.[5] The articular occurrences in ch. iii continue the meaning of $h^{\circ}dm$ as a single male. Although the final two appearances of $h^{\circ}dm$ in *vv.* 22 and 24 may refer to a collective term, i.e. humanity in general, in the context of the narrative of ch. iii it is more likely that they refer to the single male of the preceding section.[6] Ch. iv has one articular occurrence, in *v*, 1.[7] In context, this occurrence is clearly that of the single male individual of chs ii and iii.

There are several non-articular occurrences of $^{\circ}dm$ whose appearance within these chapters suggests a meaning similar to the articular ones. The occurrence of $^{\circ}dm$ in i 26 is parallel to its usage in i 27, as a reference to humanity in general. In ii 5 $^{\circ}dm$ may refer to any human being who is not present to till the soil.[8] However, given the context of

---

[4] A.M. Grant, "*adam* and ^{c}ish", *Australian Biblical Review* 25 (1977), pp. 2–11 (esp. pp. 5–6, 10–11), argues that, while an individual is intended for the first time with the appearance of $h\bar{a}^{\circ}\bar{a}d\bar{a}m$ in ii 21ff., the use of $^{\circ}\bar{a}d\bar{a}m$ throughout the chapter is intended to refer to the whole of humanity, represented in one individual. The particular focus suggested by Grant is supported by the titular usage suggested here, although this article would argue that it begins earlier in ch. ii. This meets the requirement of a more general usage (cf. also the discussion below under "$^{\circ}dm$ among the theologians") which is particularized in a single individual. Cf. Delitzsch, p. 75; von Rad, p. 61. E. Lussier, "$^{\circ}ADAM$ in Genesis 1, 1–4, 24", *CBQ* 18 (1956), pp. 137–9, finds four senses in which $^{\circ}dm$ is used in the opening chapters of Genesis. He follows two of the categories suggested here, but divides what is identified here as the titular usage of "the Man" into two "senses": (1) that of the first man created by God in ii 5, 7 (twice), 8,15,16,18,19 (twice), 20 (twice), 21, iii 9, 22, 24, iv 1; (2) a particular "man" in relation to "woman", the first man's wife in all the other occurrences in chs ii and iii. The analysis proposed here would understand these two "senses" as two aspects of a single usage.

[5] In that the title has sense it is to be distinguished from the personal name in iv 25 and v 1a, 3–5. In that it has reference it is to be distinguished from the generic term in ch. i. Cf. further below under "$^{\circ}dm$ among the linguists".

[6] So Delitzsch, p. 113; Gunkel, pp. 19–20; S.R. Driver, *The Book of Genesis* (London, [12]1926), pp. 50–1; Cassuto, pp. 172–7; E.A. Speiser, *Genesis* (Garden City, New York, 1964), p. 23, Gispen, pp. 195, 201. For *vv.* 22, 24 as a conclusion separate from and independent of *v.* 23, cf. Westermann, pp. 368–73; E. tr., pp. 271–4.

[7] Of the commentators noted, only Cassuto, p. 196, translates the personal name "Adam" here. Elsewhere, they distinguish between non-articular and articular appearances of $^{\circ}dm$, assigning the personal name to the non-articular and the common noun to the articular occurrences. Yet, the occurrence in iv 1 is articular. Although no rationale for this departure from custom is given in either commentary, it presumabley has to do with the formulaic similarity with iv 25 where the personal name does occur.

[8] On the importance of this concept for the understanding of the human's role in Gen. ii–iii, cf. B.D. Naidoff, "A Man to Work the Soil: A New Interpretation of Genesis 2–3", *JSOT 5* (1978), pp. 2–14. For the concept in relation to the curse and to Gen. ii–ix, cf. P.R. Davies, "Sons of Cain", in J.D. Martin and P.R. Davies (ed.), *A Word in Season. Essays in Honour of William McKane* (Sheffield, 1986), pp. 35–56. For

the narrative in ii 5ff. and the unique reponsibility of the male to work the soil in ii 15, it seems that *ʾdm* here refers to "the Man" of the narrative throughout ch. ii. The lack of a partner for the *ʾdm* of v. 20 also supports the same intepretation for this non-articular form.[9] After pronouncing a curse on the woman, God turns to (*ûlᵉ*) *ʾādām* in order to pronounce a curse on this figure (iii 17). In iii 21 God makes animal skin tunics *lᵉʾādām* and for his wife.[10] Although the occurrences in ii 20 (second occurrence), iii 17, and iii 21 could be personal names (they are not articular in the MT), it is better to see in all of them the title which is found in the articular forms scattered throughout these two chapters. These latter are not personal names, or they would not be articular, and there is no reason within the narrative for sudden switches in the three places mentioned to have occurred. Further, ii 20, iii 17, and iii 21 may all have been articular at one time. Since each of the three is preceded by the inseparable preposition, *l*, if they were articular there would be no change in the consonantal text. The *shewāʾ* under the *lamedh* would become a *qāmeṣ* − a slight change in pronunciation which could easily have occurred during the centuries before the oral tradition of reading was written into the text in the form of the vowel pointing. Indeed, the apparatus to *BHS* calls for such a change in vowel pointing.[11]

---

a deconstructionist reading of the text with tilling the soil as a focus, cf. D. Jobling, "Myth and Its Limits in Genesis 2.4b–3.4", in *The Sense of Biblical Narrative: Structural Analyses in the Hebrew Bible II* (Sheffield, 1986), pp. 17–43.

[9] Delitzsch, p. 93, identifies here a qualitative usage of the non-articular form. In this he is followed by Gunkel, p. 9; and by Westermann, p. 253; E. tr., p. 185. Such a distinctively qualitiative usage of *ʾdm* has not been established, however. Nor, even if it were, would the use or absence of the article be thereby determined. It is therefore better to follow Skinner, p. 68; Driver, p. 42; and Speiser, p. 18.

[10] *lᵉʾištô* appears here. It corresponds to *lᵉʾādām* and is marked as definite.

[11] So also for iii 17, 21: Gunkel, p. 18; Skinner, pp. 83, 87; Speiser, p. 24; Westermann, p. 254; E. tr., p. 186. Driver, pp. 49–50, translates the occurrences as "Adam" without comment. Delitzsch, p. 109, argues that such a repointing would be arbitrary, but fails to establish a reason why the personal name is introduced in these places for the first time. For ii 20, cf. the preceding note. Cassuto, pp. 126, 133, 166–7, 171, rejects all the above interpretations for ii 20, iii 17, and iii 21. Instead, he argues from the analogy of *ʾĕlōhîm*, which takes a prepositional suffix pointed with a *ṣērē* and not with a *qāmeṣ*. Likewise, *ʾdm*, when used as a proper name, is pointed only with a *shewāʾ*, and not with a *qāmeṣ*. This argument appears to be one of special pleading using a unique case to establish a generalization. Yet, even if that is granted, the *shewāʾ* is a different vowel from the *ṣērē*, and there is no basis for arguing that the two function similarly in similar cases. J.A. Soggin, *Old Testament and Oriental Studies* (Rome, 1975), p. 177, also objects to the change in vowel pointing proposed here: "why, in fact, would the Massoretes have chosen the less obvious reading in the present context if they had a better one at hand?" This appears to ignore the repeated occurrence of the phenomenon in three places in the chapter, where the change in vowel pointing would suit each case; and to disregard the degree to which the tradition of the vowel pointing was held to be sacred by the Massoretes and thus not open to choice on their part.

In Gen. iv 25 ʾ*dm* occurs without an article. Although there is a clear parallel with iv 1, the lack of an article in iv 25, coupled with certain differences in the material that follows in the remainder of the verse and in ch. v, suggests that this is not the same title as was used before, but that here for the first time ʾ*dm* is used as a personal name.[12] Despite the suggestion of *BHS* to place *h* in front of ʾ*dm* and thereby to read an article,[13] there is no evidence in the Hebrew text for this, and it would require a change of the consonantal text.[14] Instead, as the emphasis is on naming in *vv.* 25 and 26, as well as in ch.v, and as this is in contrast to the preceding genealogy of ch. iv where personal names are given but there is no mention of the process of naming, then the ʾ*dm* of iv 25 should be understood as the personal name Adam. This shift from the use of ʾ*dm* as a title to its use as a personal name may reflect the movement of the text from the narrative of the first three chapters to the genealogy in ch. v. If so, the section from iv 1 to v 2 represents a transition from titles and figures to persons and their names as part of a genealogy. Thus it is only near the end of ch. iii that the first personal name appears, that of *ḥwh*. With chs iv and v the focus shifts to personal names. But the transition is not abrupt, nor does there seem to be great concern for distinguishing between title and personal name in the opening verses of ch. v. Thus the first ʾ*dm* of v 1 may well be a personal name as the *twldwt* formulae of all succeeding genealogies use personal names.[15] But the second occurrence of ʾ*dm* in v 1 is not a personal name, for it is couched in the phrasing of the earlier narrative, especially i 26–7.[16] The same is true of v 2. Here the phrasing is that of i 27. In these two occurrences lies the change from the common noun to the personal name as observed in the texts themselves. Although ʾ*dm* is best understood as a common noun, its usage in v 2, with the formula of giving someone a name, points in the direction of a personal name.[17] It is an example of

---

[12] Delitzsch, p. 132; Skinner, p. 125.

[13] Cf. also Gunkel, p. 48, who makes his argument on the basis of sources: P alone can use the personal name. However, since this is J it probably is not a personal name and should have the article in front of it.

[14] Westermann, p. 459; E. tr., p. 338.

[15] Cf. M.D. Johnson, *The Purpose of the Biblical Genealogies with Special Reference to the Setting of the Genealogies of Jesus* (Cambridge, 1969), p. 16.

[16] Cf. Cassuto, p. 275; R.R. Wilson, *Genealogy and History in the Biblical World* (New Haven, Conn., and London, 1977), pp. 158–9, 164.

[17] Delitzsch, pp. 140–1, uses the personal name for all occurrences in *vv.* 1–2. The other commentators follow the proposal set forth here, to understand the personal name in *v.* 1a and the common noun in *vv.* 1b and 2. Cf. Gunkel, pp. 119–20; Driver, p. 75; Skinner, p. 130 ("we may suppose the writer's aim to have been to explain how ʾ*dm*, from being a generic term, came to be a proper name"); Cassuto, pp. 275–6;

ambiguity (see below under "ᵓdm among the linguists"), in which the text moves the reader from the common noun to the personal name which will henceforth be used when referring to ᵓdm. Both of these occurrences of ᵓdm refer back to the generic use of the term in ch. i. With their phrasing, they form an inclusio to the narrative materials of the first four chapters, bringing to an end the story of the very first generations of mankind on the earth.[18] v 3, 4, and 5 plunge into the genealogy with its common formula. The use of the non-articular ᵓdm in such a context confirms its meaning as a personal name.[19]

2. ᵓdm as a title elsewhere

An examination of the biblical and ancient Near Eastern context of the titular use of ᵓdm in the opening chapters of Genesis provides a control for understanding better what such a usage may imply. The use of ᵓdm as a title is not found elsewhere in the Hebrew Bible. However, the synonymous ᵓyš does have such a usage. When placed in construct with a following noun, it can be used to designate offices, professions, and nationalities: ᵓîš kōhēn, "priest" (Lev. xxi 9); ᵓîš śar, "prince" (Exod. ii 14); ᵓîš milḥāmâ, "fighter" (Joel ii 7); ᵓîš miṣrî, "Egyptian" (Gen. xxxix 1).[20] Of special interest is the use of ᵓîš as a term for a ruler in charge of a city or region. This may occur in 2 Sam. x 6, 8, where the Ammonites obtain help from ᵓîš ṭôb. Although

Speiser, pp. 39–40. Westermann, pp. 481–3; E. tr., pp. 355–6, also understands the occurrrences in this way.

[18] Cf. the comment of R.B. Robinson, "Literary Functions of the Genealogies of Genesis", *CBQ* 48 (1986), pp. 595–608 (esp. p. 600).

[19] It may be of interest to compare the LXX's translation of ᵓdm in these opening chapters of Genesis. From the occurrences of i 26 through ii 15, the Hebrew is followed closely with a translation of ᵓdm by ἄνθρωπος, with the Greek article, exactly as in the Hebrew. At ii 16, however, the LXX introduces the dative form, τῷ᾽ Αδὰμ, an articular personal name not found in Hebrew but occurring in Greek. τὸν ἄνθρωπον reappears in verse 18, but is then replaced by the personal name in all other occurrences of ᵓdm for the remainder of ch. ii and chs iii and iv. It appears with an article except in ii 19 (second occurrence), 20 (first occurrence), 23, iii 12, 20, iv 1, 25. Significantly, the personal name appears with an article in the three places noted above where an article is lacking in the vowel pointing but is permitted by the consonantal Hebrew texts (i.e. ii 20 [second occurrence], iii 17, and iii 21). In v 1 the first occurrence is ἄνθρωπον while the second occurrence is the personal name with a definite article. This is the opposite of the interpretation suggested here, but not surprising considering the consistent use of the personal name in chs ii, iii, and iv. The occurrences in *vv.* 2, 3, 4, and 5 are all personal names. The text used is J.W. Wevers, *Genesis* (Göttingen, 1974).

[20] L. Koehler and W. Baumgartner, *Hebräisches und aramäisches Lexikon zum alten Testament* 1 (Leiden, ³1967), p. 42; N.P. Bratsiots, "ᵓîš", in G.J. Botterweck and H. Ringgren (ed.), *Theologisches Wörterbuch zum Alten Testament* 1 (Stuttgart, Berlin, Köln, Mainz, 1973), cols 238–52 (239–40).

this has been understood as a personal name,[21] or as a generic reference to the "warriors" of the land of Tob,[22] the simplest way to interpret it, in the light of the parallel references in the verse, is as a reference to the ruler of Tob, who provides military aid.[23]

This same usage is attested among Semitic rulers in the ancient Near East in textual evidence from the second millennium B.C. The logographic sign for "man, human being" is the lú sign. In Akkadian texts, this sign is used in syllabic cuneiform before names of offices and functions which individuals or groups might hold or perform.[24] In this respect it is similar to the usage of ʾiš as a gentilic noted above ("the Egyptian"). As in 2 Sam. x, the logogram can also be used to indicate the ruler of a particular city or geographic region. Thus lú may precede the name of a city and function as a means of indicating the ruler of that city. Although a common phenomenon, it is of special interest to observe this usage in the Western peripheral Akkadian dialects of the second millennium, i.e. in the texts from Mari, Alalakh, and Amarna (*CAD* A1, p. 57).

For example, this phenomenon occurs with some 34 different individuals in the Amarna texts. In EA 198.4–5, a figure named *a-ra[-wa]-na* is given the title, lú uru *ku-mi-di*^ki, i.e. leader of the city of Kumidi. This title is used by rulers of numerous cities and regions throughout Canaan in the 14th century B.C. Included are the leaders of Beirut, Amurru, Byblos, Sidon, Lachish, Gezer, Megiddo, Ashkelon, Acco, and other cities.[25] There is no doubt that the usage in these

---

[21] *BHS;* J. Wellhausen, *Der Text der Bücher Samuelis untersucht* (Göttingen, 1871), p. 179; A. Klostermann, *Die Bücher Samuelis und der Könige* (Nördlingen, 1887), p. 171; H. Winckler, *Geschichte Israels in Einzeldarstellung* (Leipzig, 1895–1900) 1, p. 140; K. Budde, *Die Bücher Samuel erklärt* (Tübingen and Leipzig, 1902), p. 248; H.P. Smith, *A Critical and Exegetical Commentary on the Books of Samuel* (Edinburgh, 1912), p. 315.

[22] K.A. Leimbach, *Die Bücher Samuel übersetzt und erklärt* (Bonn, 1936), p. 166; H.W. Hertzberg, *Die Samuelbücher* (Göttingen, 1956) p. 242 = E. tr. *I & II Samuel* (London, 1964), p. 302; F. Stolz, *Das erste und zweite Buch Samuel* (Zürich, 1981), pp. 231, 233; P.K. McCarter, *II Samuel* (Garden City, New York, 1984), pp. 268, 271–2. McCarter's refutation of the interpretation of the expression as "rules of Tob" as a usage "confined to letters addressed to high-ranking kings in which a local ruler, who might elsewhere be called 'king', seeks to avoid offense by refraining from calling himself or another local ruler 'king'" (pp. 271–2) is conjecture with insufficient evidence.

[23] P. Dhorme, *Les livres de Samuel* (Paris, 1910), p. 349; A. Jirku, "Der 'Mann von Tob' (II Sam 10 6.8)", *ZAW* 62 (1950), p. 319; Koehler and Baumgartner, p. 42; P.R. Ackroyd, *The Second Book of Samuel* (Cambridge, 1977), p.97, mentions it as a possibility.

[24] It can be used interchangeably with the Akkadian term for "man, human being"; *amīlu.* Cf. *CAD* A1, p. 55.

[25] For edited collections of the Amarna text, cf. J.A. Knudtzon, *Die El-Amarna-Tafeln mit Einleitung und Erläuterungen* (Leipzig, 1915; Aalen, 1964); A.F. Rainey, *El*

letters was intended to identify the author as the person with the responsibility of oversight for the city. In the case of the Amarna texts, which were regularly written by these leaders to their own superior, either the pharaoh or one of his agents, the implication is that this title put them in the position of being responsible for all that went on in the city, or more accurately, the city-state.

With such an understanding of the usage of lú, the logogram for "man, human being" as used in the West Semitic world of the second millennium B.C., a comparison can be made with the usage of the Hebrew term *ʾdm* as it appears in Gen. ii-iv:

> (1) Both *ʾdm* and the lú sign have a similar semantic range in their usage in the written languages in which they occur.[26] They each carry meanings denoting "man", "human being", and "humanity" in general.
> (2) Both *ʾdm* and the lú sign are nouns which are linguistically marked as definite in their respective contexts. *ʾdm* is marked by the addition of the *h* article, and lú is marked by being placed in a bound construct relationship with the city name which follows it.
> (3) Both *ʾdm* and the lú sign, in their respective contexts, refer to a particular individual who has or is given responsibility for the care and maintenance of a particular geographical area, be that a city, a city-state, a region, or a garden.

These semantic, lingustic, and functional similarities suggest that, as lú may be regarded as a title, so also may *ʾdm* in those occurrences in the opening chapters of Genesis identified above. *ʾdm*, used as a title, is at home in the West Semitic world of the second millennium B.C.[27]

3. *ʾdm among the linguists*[28]

When we consider the question of the usage of *ʾdm*, some semantic distinctions may prove helpful.[29] A characteristic of some importance in proper name is reference. A name presumes something which is signified by that name. The relationship of the name to the thing

---

Amarna Tablets 359–379. Supplement to J.A. Knudtzon, Die El-Amarna-Tafeln (Kevelaer and Neukirchen-Vluyn, ²1978).

[26] In addition to Akkadian in its various dialects, lú is also used with a similar meaning in Sumerian and in Hittite.

[27] To some extent there is a universal aspect to the use of such a phrase as a means of denoting someone in charge. Cf. the use of "the Man" in American slang to denote civic authority; the Sumerian lugal as related to lú and gal, i.e. "great man"; or the title for El in Ugaritic, *ʾab ʾadm*, in which the generic *ʾdm* is used. However, what is argued here is its use as a distinctive title with a literary context.

[28] I thank Stanley Porter and David Tsumura for their suggestions on this section.

[29] The following observations draw heavily upon the work of John Lyons, *Semantics* (Cambridge, London, New York, and Melbourne, 1977).

which is signified is the reference. The thing which is signified is the referent. Thus, when the name ʾdm is used in the genealogies of Gen. i-v, it refers to a particular individual who is understood as created by God and as possessing the distinction of being the earliest member of the human race. The figure referred to as ʾdm is the referent in this case. The relationship by which the reader associates the name ʾdm to this individual is one of reference. An expression of reference that is definite is one in which the referent is a specific individual or class. Proper names, and personal pronouns include the sorts of reference which may be considered as definite. These categories can experience movement between them. Lyons writes:[30]

> Many place names and family names originated as definite descriptions or titles; and proper names can be regularly converted into descriptive lexemes and used as such in referring or predicative expressions.
> In many cases the use of a common noun preceded by the definite article will suffice without further description, even though the referent has not been previously mentioned, because the speaker can fairly assume, in the given situation or universe of discourse, that the hearer will know which of the potential referents satisfying the description he is referring to ... If an Englishman uses referentially the expression "the queen" and an American the expression "the president", in a context in which no queen or president has already been referred to, they will normally expect to be understood as referring to the queen of England and to the president of the United States respectively. Expressions of this latter kind come very close to acquiring, in the appropriate context, the status of uniquely referring titles (like "the Pope"); and uniquely referring titles have a tendency, as Strawson (1950) puts it, to grow capital letters and to be treated orthographically in written English as proper names. In general, titles constitute a class of expressions which "shades off into definite descriptions at one end and proper names at the other" (Searle, 1969: 81).

Of significance for our discussion is the association of definite descriptions, titles and names (whether family or personal). The personal name ʾdm is one which also is used as a generic description and title in the opening chapters of Genesis. The observation to be made here is the close semantic relationship of these categories of reference and the possibility for a single name to shift its referential use across these categories. Thus, a development in the use of ʾdm, beginning as a generic term, moving to a title, and eventually becoming a personal name, is linguistically feasible.

Along with reference, utterances may have sense. Sense is often

---

[30] Pp. 179, 181. The references in the quotation are to P.F. Strawson, "On referring", *Mind* 59 (1950), pp. 320–44; and to J.R. Searle, *Speech Acts* (London and New York, 1969).

understood as the descriptive meaning of a word or an expression. Thus vocabulary words in a language have sense, as do phrases and sentences constructed from them. This is different from the property of reference. Reference, because it always refers to a particular object or group of objects, is not found in individual vocabulary words. Such a vocabulary word or a lexeme possesses a sense which may be represented in the dictionary definition. On the other hand, by itself this lexeme does not point to a particular object. It may, however, describe a category of some things. This is not a referent because a particular thing is not envisaged here. Instead, it is a denotation which describes a relationship between the lexeme and the category of things intended. On the basis of this distinction, lexemes may have sense and denotation but they do not possess reference. Personal names have reference but normally are not understood as possessing sense. If personal names do not possess sense, they cannot denote any property or properties of which it is possible to describe the person so named. Therefore personal names do not possess denotation.

Application of these categories to the use of $^{\circ}dm$ in Gen. i-v provides an understanding of the shifts in the reference, sense, and denotation which occur there. As a description of humanity in general, $h^{\circ}dm$ in ch. i refers to all people who have existed and will ever exist. It has the sense of humanity in general. In ch. ii, $h^{\circ}dm$ as a title carries the sense of the male who is set in the Garden of Eden to take care of it. Here it is placed within a temporal context and therefore does not serve as a generic reference. Instead, it refers to that male who is responsible for the Garden of Eden. As a title such as "The Male" it may denote an individual member of that class of male members of the human race. The concept of such a class may also describe a sense to this usage. However, it is primarily as a referent that $^{\circ}dm$ with the article appears here. As a personal name, $^{\circ}dm$ in iv 25 and in the genealogy of ch. v reflects a movement from a referent which serves as a definite description (whether as a generic description or as a title) to a proper name – here a personal name. As such it has reference but no denotation or sense. This is true despite the etymology of $^{\circ}dm$ as a Hebrew term defined as "a human being".

An additional area of interest from the standpoint of semantics is that of vagueness and ambiguity. These terms have been defined from the prespective of linguistics[31] in such a way that vagueness is used of

---

[31] Cf. S. Ullmann, *Semantics. An Introduction to the Science of Meaning* (Oxford, 1972), pp. 116–40, 156–92; R.M Kempson, *Semantic Theory* (Cambridge, London, New York, New Rochelle, Melbourne, and Sydney, 1977), pp. 123–38; S. Porter and N. Gotteri, "Ambiguity, Vagueness and the Working Systemic Linguist", *Sheffield Working Papers in Language and Linguistics* 2 (1985), pp. 105–18.

a word when a single definition or meaning covers a variety of uses for the word, or more precisely, for the lexeme. Ambiguity, on the other hand, refers to a word which can be used with completely different meanings in various contexts. The meanings are sufficiently diverse to suggest more than one lexeme as being involved in the uses. To a degree the distinction between vagueness and ambiguity is something of a continuum on which the point of division between the two categories is somewhat arbitrary. However, the distinction remains legitimate and may be of use when considering the three different uses of *'dm*.

The generic use of *'dm* in Gen. i may be compared with its use as a title in ch. ii. Both of these are descriptions of humanity or of a particular human being. They share a similar semantic range and may be understood as two variants of the same concept. The relationship is one of vagueness. The relationship between the use of *'dm* as a title and its use as a personal name is one of designating a particular human figure. However, as personal names do not possess sense in the same way that titles may, there cannot be a relationship in meaning as there could between *'dm* in a generic sense and *'dm* as a title. Instead there is a distinction in meaning which is observable here so that the principle of ambiguity is present in the uses of *'dm* as a personal name and as a title. The same is true in comparing the uses of *'dm* as a generic term and as a personal name. It clear from the context of the appearances in these chapters that the personal name *'dm* is related to the other uses of *'dm* in more ways than merely as homophony. However, it is also clear from the use of these criteria that the relatedness of the uses of *'dm* in chs i and ii, i.e. in the narrative sections is closer than its use in chs iv and v, i.e. in the genealogies. (On the ambiguity in v 1–3 of uses of *'ādām* as a generic term and as a personal name, see above.)

4. *'dm among the theologians*

The theologians' emphasis falls into three areas: the relation of the two accounts of creation, the question of creation of *'dm* in the image of God, and the origin of the sin of ch. iii. There is not direct treatment of the different uses of *'dm*. Its appearance as a personal name in the genealogies is ignored as are the genealogies.

The discussion of G. von Rad focuses attention on the distinctive theological emphases of the P (i 1–ii 4a) and of the J (ii 4b–25) accounts of creation.[32] The P account places the generic *'dm* at the

---

[32] *Theologie des Alten Testaments* 1 (München, 1958), pp. 144–57.

apex of creation. With a chronological development of God's acts culminating in the creation of ᵓ*dm*. ᵓ*dm* is most closely related to God of all creation and is given particular responsibility over the rest of creation. On the other hand, the J account of creation is anthropocentric. It is concerned with the relationship of ᵓ*dm* to the garden, the animals, and the other sex. W. Eichrodt also contrasts the two accounts of creation, using as his starting point the distinction of creation in the image of God and creation with the breath of life.[33]

For H. Ringgren the distinction between the ᵓ*dm* of ch. i and the ᵓ*dm* of ch. ii is that between a weak and transitory creatury of dust, dependent upon God's spirit, and the likeness of God who has dominion over nature.[34] G. Fohrer emphasizes the distinctive aspect of the J account (ii 4b–25), where ᵓ*dm* is a male given responsibility to cultivate the garden and in need of a female partner.[35] In dealing with the P account, Fohrer focuses on the concept of ᵓ*dm* as created in the image and likeness of God. However, he draws a distinction between the reference in i 26–7, where he sees an emphasis on the transcendence of the deity and the separation of the deity from humanity; and the reference in v 3, where Fohrer finds a father-son relationship emphasized between the deity and ᵓ*dm* (pp. 307–8). This latter understanding is presumably based upon the genealogical context of ch. v. The work of Th. C. Vriezen distinguishes ᵓ*dm* as humanity in Gen. i and as "the father of man" in Gen. ii–iii.[36] The uses of ᵓ*dm* in Gen. ii ff. are not collective but intended as general descriptions. H.W. Wolff directs his attention to those points of agreement in the presentations of ᵓ*dm* in the J and P accounts.[37] C. Westermann finds the writer(s) of the opening chapters of Genesis to be concerned with what it means to be fully human.[38]

The tendency among these theologians to separate the narrative in ch. i from those in chs ii and iii is supported by the two different aspects of ᵓ*dm* proposed here. The idea of a generic ᵓ*dm* in ch. i lends support to those general concepts of ᵓ*dm* as the apex of creation and as created in the image of God. The concept of ᵓ*dm* as a title referring to one specific male figure in chs ii and iii reflects the importance of a single figure given specific duties and specific relationships. At the

---

[33] *Theologie des Alten Testaments* 2 (Leipzig, 1935), pp. 59–65; *Theology of the Old Testament* 2 (E. tr. by J.A. Baker; London, 1967), pp. 121–31.

[34] *Israelitische Religon* (Stuttgart, 1963), pp. 108–12.

[35] *Geschichte der israelitischen Religion* (Berlin, 1969), pp. 174–6. The concept of ᵓ*dm* as a male is not explicit in Fohrer's treatment, but implict in his discussion of the female partner.

[36] *An Outline of Old Testament Theology* (Oxford, ²1970), pp. 170, 406.

[37] *Anthropologie des Alten Testaments* (München, 1973), pp. 141–5

[38] *Theologie des Alten Testaments in Grundzügen* (Göttingen, 1978), pp. 81–5.

same time the identification of $^{\circ}dm$ in these chapters as a title, rather
than as a personal name, allows for the sort of generalizing of principle
found in the narrative. Such generalizing is useful for the theological
conclusions which are drawn from it.

The uses of $^{\circ}dm$ which have been proposed here add little to the
questions surrounding source criticism. Indeed, there is no need to
suppose a distinction in sources based upon the distinctive use of $^{\circ}dm$
in Gen. i and its use in chs ii–iii any more than there is need to argue
for an elimination of sources based upon the use of $^{\circ}dm$ in Gen. i as
distinct from its use in Gen. v 1a, 3–5. Such differences may be based
purely on literary distinctions without reference to sources.[39] However,
form-critical identifications may prove helpful in observing the
distinctions of the use of $^{\circ}dm$ and the value of that distinction.[40] Thus
the identification of Gen. i 1–ii 4a as a report implies a narrative which
is primarily didactic in character (Coats, pp. 10, 41–8). As a unit
intending to teach universal truths about origins it is fitting that the use
of the term $^{\circ}dm$ in this section should be universal with an identification
with all humanity. Gen. ii 4b–iii 24 appears in its present form as a tale,
possessing a simple plot with a limited number of characters (Coats, pp.
7–8, 49–60). Thus it is appropriate that the references to $^{\circ}dm$ in this
section be to a particular individual. However, as it intends to explain
or teach concerning the present status of humanity in relation to God
and the world, it is appropriate that the usage of $^{\circ}dm$ be more general
than a personal name, i.e. that it be potentially capable of application
to all humanity. A title, such as "The Man", suits these requirements.
Chs iv and v are composed of a mixture of story and list genres within
the framework of genealogies (Coats, pp. 60–73). Part of the intention
is to establish relationships with the narratives which precede and those
which follow. Therefore, it is not surprising to see a mixture of the uses
of $^{\circ}dm$ in these chapters, including, in the light of the nature of
genealogies, the introduction of $^{\circ}dm$ as a personal name.

In view of the great interest in the implications of $^{\circ}dm$ as created in
the "image and likeness of God" in Gen. i 26–7,[41] it may be of

---

[39] Cf. e.g. I.M. Kikawada and A. Quinn, *Before Abraham Was. The Unity of Genesis
1–11* (Nashville, 1985), pp. 54–69, despite attempts there to identify $^{\circ}dm$ in chs ii–iii
as a personal name.

[40] Cf. G.W. Coats, *Genesis with an Introduction to Narrative Literature* (Grand Rapids,
1983), pp. 3–73, and the literature cited there.

[41] Cf. e.g. J.J. Stamm, "Die Imago-Lehre von Karl Barth und die alttestament-
liche Wissenschaft", pp. 84–98, in *Antwort: Karl Barth zum siebzigsten Geburtstag*
(Zürich, 1956); D.J.A. Clines, " The Image of God in Man", *Tyndale Bulletin* 19
(1967), pp. 53–103; J.M. Miller, "In the 'Image' and 'Likeness' of God", *JBL* 91

significance to observe that the use of ʾdm in a generic sense is most important here. It is not merely one man or one couple who experience this but all humanity are envisioned as possessing this gift.[42] In addition, given the present form of the text, the reference to this passage in v 1b–2 suggests that it is something which was not lost in the events of chs ii–iv.

Various sorts of structural analyses of Gen. ii 4b–iii 24 have brought to light the changes in relationships which take place between the characters themselves and between the characters and their relationships with God, the land, and the Garden.[43] The titular use of ʾdm once again is significant because it allows for the identification of a particular character in the story which is analysed and yet also allows for the ready application of that character's experience to those who read or hear the story.

A significant dimension to the study of ʾdm that has appeared in publications of the last decade has to do with the feminist interpretation of the opening chapters of Genesis. Because of the theological significance of this approach it is appropriate to summarize some of the directions of this study and to suggest implications that may emerge from the interpretation of ʾdm which has been proposed here. One important contribution to feminist biblical interpretation has been the work of P. Trible.[44] As with many of the other theological

---

(1972), pp. 289–304; pp. O.H. Steck, *Der Schöpfungsbericht der Priesterschrift. Studien zur literarkritischen und überlieferungsgeschichtlichen Problematik von Genesis 1,1–2,4a* (Göttingen, ²1981), pp. 129–58; P.-E. Dion, "Image et ressemblance en araméen ancien (Tell Fakhariyah)", *Science & Esprit* 34 (1982), pp. 151–3; and the commentaries.

[42] Cf. the comment of Clines, p. 100.

[43] J.T. Walsh, "Genesis 2: 4b–3: 24: A Synchronic Approach", *JBL* 96 (1977), pp. 161–77; T.E. Boomershine, "The Structure of Narrative Rhetoric in Genesis 2–3", *Semeia* 18 (1980), pp. 113–29; R.C. Culley, "Action Sequences in Genesis 2–3", *Semeia* 18 (1980), pp. 25–33; D. Jobling, "The Myth Semantics of Genesis 2:4b–3:24", *Semeia* 18 (1980), pp. 41–9; D. Patte and J.F. Parker, "A Structural Exegesis of Genesis 2 and 3", *Semeia* 18 (1980) 55–75; H.C. White, "Direct and Third Person Discourse in the Narrative of the 'Fall' ", *Semeia* 18 (1980), pp. 91–106; A.J. Hauser, "Genesis 2–3: The Theme of Intimacy and Alienation", pp. 20–36 in D.J.A. Clines, D.M. Gunn, and A.J. Hauser (ed.), *Art and Meaning: Rhetoric in Biblical Literature* (Sheffield, 1982); I.M. Kikawada and A. Quinn, *Before Abraham Was*. Cf. also references listed under n. 8. To this list may be added recent interpretations which have focussed on various physchological aspects of the relations between God, woman, and man in (and out of) the Garden: A. Brenner, *The Israelite Woman. Social Role and Literary Type in Biblical Narrative* (Shieffield, 1985), pp. 123–9; D.E. Burns, "Dream Form in Genesis 2.4b–3.24: Asleep in the Garden", *JSOT* 37 (1987), pp. 3–14.

[44] *God and the Rhetoric of Sexuality* (Philadelphia, 1978). Cf. pp. 12–23, 72–143. Cf also, by the same author, "Depatriarchalizing in Biblical Interpretation", *JAAR* 41 (1971), pp. 30–48.

writers, a clear distinction in made between the use of ʾdm in ch. i and its use in chs ii and iii. In i 26–8, Trible finds ʾdm to refer to "two creatures, one male and one female". She translates the term as "humankind" and observes that both are given responsibilities for procreation and for dominion over the earth.[45] This accords well with a generic understanding of ʾdm for Gen. i. The term is inclusive in its reference to both male and female. However, the attribution of dominance over the earth may not have been applied to both male and female. The comments of P. Bird at this point are relevant as they reflect a generic understanding of ʾdm and its implication for this issue:

> There is no message of shared dominion here, no word about the distribution of roles, responsibility, and authority between the sexes, no word of sexual equality. What is described is a task for the species [kibšūhā] and the position of the species in relation to the other orders of creatures [rĕdû]. The social metaphors to which the key verbs point are male, derived from male experience and models, the dominant social models of patriarchal society. For P, as for J, the representative and determining image of the species was certainly male, as 5:1–3, 9:1, and the genealogies which structure the continuing account make clear.[46]

In chs ii and iii, Trible identifies ʾdm as an individual figure who is depicted in various ways. At the beginning of these narratives ʾdm is an "earth creature", closely associated with hʾdmh, the earth from which the creature is created. ʾdm, with the article, "is neither a particular person nor the typical person but rather the creature from the earth" (p. 80). This creature is not identified sexually, and receives senses and abilities only as they are mentioned in the narrative. Thus the creature evolves to the point where it is able to name the animals, but remains sexually undifferentiated. Only in ii 21–4, with the creation of woman, does this distinction appear. What is taken from ʾdm to create woman changes ʾdm into a male (pp. 97–8). Thus the creation of the two sexes is simultaneous, without one preceding the other. This male ʾdm, with all the acquired faculties of personhood, then remains unchanged throughout the remainder of the two chapters. The use of ʾdm in this final section of narrative is not unlike that proposed here, where the term forms a title or designation

---

[45] Cf. also F.R. McCurley, *Ancient Myths and Biblical Faith. Scriptural Transformations* (Philadelphia, 1983), p. 99.
[46] " 'Male and Female He Created Them': Gen 1: 27b in the Context of the Priestly Account of Creation", *HTR* 74 (1981), pp. 129–59 (esp. p. 151). Bird's analysis does not preclude a sexual distinction in the command concerning procreation (p. 150).

for the male. The distinction with what is proposed here concerns Trible's theory of an evolving earth creature without sexual differentiation that appears in ii 4b–20. B.S. Childs has raised three objections to this interpretation:

> (1) the description of the creation of woman in ch. ii has no hint of any division (split) in ʾdm nor of any simultaneous creation of sexuality;
> (2) contextually, ʾdm is not used differently before and after the formation of woman in chs ii and iii;
> (3) an oscillation between the generic term for man and the personal name Adam occurs in the two appearances of ʾdm in ii 20.[47]

The first two objections are important ones. The third argument of Childs ignores the likelihood of both occurrences in ii 20 being articular and titular. An additional objection may be made that Trible's perspective of an evolving (and dividing) earth creature does not agree with the way in which creatures are created in ch. ii. Throuhgout this narrative there is no mention of development or change in any of God's creation.

In addition to the above comments, Childs observes the relation of male and female in the opening chapters of Genesis as one which avoids a male centered ideology by insisting that male and female are created so as to constitute humanity only in their unity. On the other hand, there is a sexual differentiation in terms of function, so that "a man leaves his father and mother, and cleaves to his wife".[48] The unity of male and female is described by the generic use of ʾdm in Gen. i. The distinction in the function of the sexes may be reflected by the titular use of ʾdm in chs ii and iii, with its reference to "the Male". This is because the concern of such a title is primarily a functional one, a particular role or set of roles involving maintenance of the Garden and companionship with the female created by God.

---

[47] *Old Testament Theology in a Canonical Context* (London, 1985), p. 190.

[48] P. 192. Cf. also the philological and sociological analysis of this passage by C.L. Meyers, in "Gender Roles and Genesis 3:16 Revisited", in C.L. Meyers and M. O'Connor (ed.), *The Word of the Lord Shall Go Forth. Essays in Honor of David Noel Freedman in Celebration of His Sixtieth Birthday* (Winona Lake, 1983), pp. 337–54.

THE TOLEDOT OF ADAM

by

HOWARD N. WALLACE

Sydney

In his commentary on Genesis, G. von Rad records a statement by Franz Rosenzweig that:

> ... the sign R (for the redactor of the Hexateuch documents, so lowly esteemed in Protestant research) should be interpreted as Rabbenu, "our master", because basically we are dependent only on him, on his great work of compilation and his theology, and we receive the Hexateuch at all only from his hands.[1]

Von Rad sees the statement as appropriate from a Jewish perspective and then goes on to make a point about it from the view of Christian hermeneutics. His remarks are appropriate within certain constraints but it is unfortunate he does not pursue the literary-historical implications of Rosenzweig's remark. In this article I will focus on the work of the final redactor of the Pentateuch, responsible for combining the P source with the JE base. My interest will be in the literary techniques and devices used, the development of a theological viewpoint by means of the interlacing of sources and further theological issues raised as a result of the redactor's work.

As Rosenzweig notes, scholarly interest in the final redactor has not been extensive. Among those who follow the classic formulation of the Documentary Hypothesis, many have seen the final redaction as a priestly work or in the spirit of P. Many have conceded that some material assigned to P could come from a redactor's hand but such material is mostly confined to the later books of the Pentateuch. M. Noth is typical when he describes the work of the redactor combining JE with P as "by no means a dull or unperceptive editorial work". Nevertheless, it is still a "purely literary work" which contributes no new material or substantive viewpoint but which supplements P with

---

[1] *Das erste Buch Mose, Genesis* (5th edn, Göttingen, 1958) p. 32 = *Genesis: A Commentary*, trans. J.H. Marks (rev. edn, Philadelphia and London, 1972), p. 41.

elements of JE. When he considers whether something new was created in the process, he argues that the new contexts created by the juxtaposition of sources (e.g. in the juxtaposition of Gen. i 1–ii 4a with ii 4b–iii 24) must be considered but this new situation was likely unintentional.[2]

A second group of scholars has argued that P was not an independent source and that the collection or writing of the P material and the final redaction of the Pentateuch should be seen as one level of activity. F.M. Cross's view is typical here. He argues, in part, that in many places P material is dependent in one way or another on JE. For him this dependence argues against the existence of an independent P narrative and a later redactor of JE and P. One assumption he makes in this is that the work of an independent redactor would be largely of a "mechanical piecework" nature "simply juxtaposing blocks" of material. This is not consistent with the dependence of P on JE.[3] One can argue against Cross's basic thesis on P on a number of grounds[4] but for my purposes I want to note his assumption about the nature of a redactor's work. In this he is not far from the view of Noth and others.

In my opinion, the view and assumptions of these scholars on the nature and extent of the redactor's activity have been determined to too great an extent by source-critical criteria. In redaction analysis, source criticism and literary criticism need to go hand in hand. There is room for discussion of the redactor's work on a more detailed basis and that work can be seen as a little more creative and less mechanistic than has hitherto been conceded. I take as my point of departure for a study of the redaction of the Pentateuch the *tôlĕdōt* section on Adam (Gen. v 1–vi 8). Of course, the full scope of the redactor's work cannot be ascertained from this short section. This is merely the starting point for a much longer study. The redactor may well have operated in different ways in other passages depending on source materials available.

The *tôlĕdōt* of Adam (TA) provides a bridge between the stories of Eden, Cain and Abel and the genealogy of Cain (Gen. ii 4–iv 26) and the flood account and its immediate aftermath (vi 9–ix 29). It falls into two main sections. The first is a chronological genealogy (v

---

[2] *Überlieferungsgeschichte des Pentateuch* (Stuttgart, 1948), pp. 11–17, 267–71 = *A History of Pentateuchal Traditions*, trans. B.W. Anderson (Englewood Cliffs, 1972), pp. 11–16, 248–51.
[3] *Canaanite Myth and Hebrew Epic* (Cambridge, Mass., 1973), pp. 301–21.
[4] See e.g. J.A. Emerton, "The Priestly Writer in Genesis", *JTS*, NS 39 (1988), pp. 381–400.

1–32), largely attributed to P, covering the antediluvian patriarchs from Adam to Noah. The second consists of two brief narrative passages attributed to J, vi 1–4 (the marriage of gods to human women) and vi 5–8 (Yahweh's first statement on the destruction of all living creatures). This study of the redaction of the TA will look at the beginning of the section, verses 1b–3, the place of verse 29, and finally at the treatment of the J passages in vi 1–8.

I

We turn first to the beginning of the TA. Verses 1b–2 bear close similarity to the earlier P passage on the creation of ᵓādām in Gen. i 26–8 although differences can be seen. The initial verb forms are different, běṣalmô in i 27 is absent in v 1b,[5] and běṣelem is replaced by bidmût in the latter. In both i 26 and v 3 these words appear in conjunction although in reverse order. In the phrase bārāᵓ ᵓôtô in i 27, the verb is replaced by ᶜāśâ in v 1b, while the words of the blessing on humanity are omitted in v 2 and replaced by the naming formula. The writer of v 1b–2 has also added an independent touch to the citation in that the first and last clauses form an inclusio with parallelism. Thus while v 1b–2 are similar to i 27–8, they would appear to be an independent composition.

In addition, there are indications that verses 1b–2 and part of verse 3 (bidmûtô kěṣalmô wayyiqrāᵓ ᵓet-šěmô šēt, i.e. verse 3aβ–b) have been introduced secondarily into the Sethite genealogy of Gen. v. First, certain disjunctions are evident in the text related to v 1b–2 and 3. Verses 1b–2 form a unit in themselves with inclusio, while verse 3aβ–b does not correspond to the typical pattern of genealogical notices in Gen. v 1–28, 30–2 and xi 10b–26.[6] In verse 3aβ–b, the verb wayyôled, is not followed by an object which, in comparison with the rest of the genealogy, would be expected to be the son's name.[7] Secondly, there

---

[5] běṣalmô is also not reflected in the LXX of Gen. i 27. It could have been deleted through haplography.

[6] G. von Rad also sees v 2 as a secondary development of the original tôlědôt book heading (*Die Priesterschrift im Hexateuch* [Stuttgart and Berlin, 1934], pp. 39–40).

[7] Speiser and others have argued that the object is implied and the expression of it would have been stylistically undesirable (E.A. Speiser, *Genesis* [Garden City, New York, 1969], p. 40; A. Dillmann, *Die Genesis* [6th edn, Leipzig, 1892], p. 113 = *Genesis Critically and Exegetically Expounded*, trans. W.B. Stevenson [Edinburgh, 1897] 1, p. 223). In response one could note that the hiphil of *yld* is restricted to material assigned to P in the Pentateuch, and in all cases is followed by a direct object. *BHS* and H. Gunkel (*Genesis übersetzt und erklärt* [3rd edn, Göttingen, 1910], p. 135) suggest the restoration of *ben* which could have been lost through haplography.

is the shift in the use of ʾādām between a proper name and a generic term at the beginning of Gen. v. In the tôlĕdōt heading of v 1a, ʾādām is probably used as a proper name. In verses 1b–2, ʾādām is used in the generic sense, as in the creation story, as indicated by the pronominal suffixes and reference to "male and female". However, in contrast to Gen. i 27, ʾādām appears in v 1b–2 without the definite article.[8] Gen. v 3a, 4–5 reintroduce ʾādām as a proper name in an abrupt fashion with no real attempt to smooth the transition.[9]

These points suggest that not only are Gen. v 1b–2 of independent composition but they and verse 3aβ–b have been incorporated secondarily into the Sethite genealogy of Gen. v. The question remains, however, whether v 1b–2 and 3aβ–b are the work of the P writer or a later redactor. Reasons can be given in favour of the latter option. First, if Gen. v followed Gen. i 1–ii 3 in the P source before inclusion in the final Pentateuch, it is hard to see why the allusion to i 26–8 would be required so soon after the creation story. Secondly, we note that the names of Adam and Seth are introduced in v 2 and 3b by the full naming formula wayyiqrāʾ ʾet-šĕmām/šĕmô PN. A different naming formula is used in the P creation story (wayyiqrāʾ lĕ: Gen. i 5, 8, 10) while in only a few later P passages in Genesis (xvi 15, xxi 3, xxxv 10, 15) does the full formula used in v 2 and 3 occur. The full formula does occur, however, in J material preceding the TA, namely in iii 20, iv 17, 25–6. Gen. iv 25–6 are especially noteworthy. In contrast to the J genealogical material in iv 1, 2 and 17–24, where the mother of the son is said to (conceive and) bear PN, whose name is given directly, Gen. iv 25–6 report that the mother bore a son, or a son was born, and follow this with the full naming formula. The formula, therefore, provides a "catch phrase" between iv 25–6 and v 2–3. These verses are in fact the only ones in either J or P genealogies in Gen. iv and v where the naming formula is used with the exception of the naming of the city of "Enoch" in iv 17. In addition, iv 26b notes that at the time of Enosh, people began to call upon the name of Yahweh. The words šēm, "name", and qrʾ, "to call", occur again there.

The use of catchwords, the repetition of clauses most immediately present in J material, the shift in the use of ʾādām, and the disjunctions

---

[8] Although cf. Gen. i 26 with ʾādām. Gen. v 1b–2 could have been influenced by v 1a, 3–5. The LXX uses the generic term ὁ ἄνθρωπος in v 1a and then goes to the proper name Ἀδάμ thereafter. The definite article is used with the latter only in v 1b.

[9] J. Skinner, *A Critical and Exegetical Commentary on Genesis* (2nd edn, Edinburgh, 1930), p. 130, considers this situation sufficient to propose the work of a redactor in Gen. v 1b–2.

associated with Gen. v 1b–2, 3aβ–b suggest that these verses are the work of the redactor combining J and P material. If this conclusion is accepted then one final literary feature at the beginning of the TA should be noted. In the two genealogical entries, Gen. iv 25–6 and v 1–8, there is a repetition of the first three generations: Adam–Seth–Enosh. The origin of iv 25–6 has often been discussed[10] but, regardless of the tradition history of iv 17–26, the present position of verses 25–6 is clearly a choice of the final redactor whether by means of curtailment of a longer J Sethite genealogy or by manipulation of the J material in other ways. While the redactor apparently wanted to retain the notice in iv 26b of people beginning "to call on the name of Yahweh", he or she has also created a natural connection between iv 25–6 and v 1–8 through the repetition of the generations. Other repetitions of generations (e.g. Gen. x 22, 24–5 and xi 10b–17) or the names of sons (v 32 and vi 10; xi 26 and 27b) also occur across *tôlĕdōt* boundaries.

The work of the redactor at the beginning of the TA would appear, in the light of this discussion, to involve more than the mechanical juxtaposition of source material. By means of the devices noted, the redactor has provided distinct connections between the beginning of the TA in Gen. v and both the P and J sections preceding it. This ensures that Gen. v 1–vi 8 is read in the context of both the creation story (Gen. i 1–ii 3) and the *tôlĕdōt* of the heavens and the earth (Gen. ii 4–iv 26). It creates a different atmosphere in which the reader or listener interprets the various passages within the TA from those which would formerly have been present in the original sources. The P genealogy of Gen. v 3–28, 30–2 now becomes the sequence of generations which follows the events of Eden, and the reader or listener is expected to presume that the individuals of Gen. v constitute part of rebellious humanity and are under the power of the curses it bears from Gen. iii 16–19. But while human rebellion becomes the background for reading Gen. v, hope for the human condition is not absent. The sequence of generations from Adam to Enosh in iv 25–6 and v 1–8 stands at some distance from the events and lineage of iv

---

[10] The majority opinion regards these verses as a remnant of a J Sethite genealogy, initially separate from J's Cainite genealogy in iv 17–24. See e.g. von Rad. (n. 1), p. 91 = E. tr., p. 108; C. Westermann, *Genesis. I: Genesis 1–11* (Neukirchen-Vluyn, 1974) p. 458 = *Genesis 1–11: A Commentary*, trans. J.J. Scullion (London, 1984), p. 338. For an early discussion of opinions see Skinner (n. 9), pp. 90–1. For the idea of a single J genealogy behind Gen. iv 17–26 see J.M. Miller, "The Descendants of Cain: Notes on Genesis 4", *ZAW* 86 (1974), pp. 164–73. Most recently against this D.T. Bryan, "A Reevaluation of Gen 4 and 5 in Light of Recent Studies in Genealogical Fluidity", *ZAW* 99 (1987), pp. 180–8.

1–24 and includes the generation of people who begin "to call on the name of Yahweh" (iv 26b), that is to worship Yahweh, not in the sense of the full Yahwistic cult, but to begin worship in continuity with the later worship of Israel's ancestors.[11] Thus the genealogy in Gen. v develops against the background of the dual character of human nature and the divine human relationship evident in Gen. ii–iv.

The TA is also connected to Gen. i 1–ii 3. This connection lies most forcefully in the reiteration in v 1–3 of the three motifs: creation of humanity in the divine image; humanity as "male and female"; and the divine blessing. In Gen. v, the last two motifs find expression in the genealogy itself with the succession of long-lived generations. The first motif of the creation of humanity in the divine image would seem from Gen. v 3 to be envisaged by the redactor as something passed on from one generation to the next. The image of God in humanity has been neither negated nor abated by the rebellion in Gen. ii 4–iv 26.

We need to pause here to consider the nature of the image of God in humanity. In recent years, many scholars have tended towards a representative or functional interpretation of the motif.[12] Other views see humankind as a physical representation of the deity,[13] or created with a capacity for relationship with God.[14] Still others have opted for a combination of perspectives,[15] or argue we cannot be sure of what the brief references in Gen. i 26, v 2, 3, and ix 6 to the

---

[11] Gen. iv 26b does not indicate the origin of the name Yahweh for the J source (cf. iv 1), nor can it be the aetiology of the particular cult of Yahweh contrary, for example, to Gunkel (n. 7), p. 54, and Skinner (n. 9), p. 127. That comes gradually after the emergence of Israel's ancestors. The phrase *liqrā' bĕšēm* indicates the invocation of a deity (cf. Jer. x 25; Zeph. iii 9) but it does not just refer to the beginning of religion as a universal phenomenon; cf. Westermann [n. 10], pp. 460–1 = E. tr., p. 339). The fact that the deity whose name is invoked is Yahweh would suggest that both J and the later redactor would see some continuity between this early worship and the later worship of Yahweh, albeit not in terms of the full expression of the cult.

[12] This has been a widespread view since the early 1960s as noted by G.A. Jónsson, *The Image of God: Genesis 1:26–28 in a Century of Old Testament Research* (Stockholm, 1988), pp. 219–23. The proponents include von Rad (n. 1), pp. 44–7 = E. tr., pp. 55–9; H. Gross, "Die Gottenbenbildlichkeit des Menschen", in H. Gross and F. Mussner (ed.), *Lex tua veritas. Festschrift für Hubert Junker* (Trier, 1961), pp. 89–100; H. Wildberger, "Das Abbild Gottes Gen 1, 26–30", *TZ* 21 (1965), pp. 245–59, 481–501.

[13] Earlier proponents include Gunkel (n. 7), p. 112; P. Humbert, *Etudes sur le récit du paradis et de la chute dans la Genèse* (Neuchâtel, 1940), pp 153–75; and L. Köhler, "Die Grundstelle der Imago-Dei-Lehre, Genesis I, 26", *TZ* 4 (1948), pp. 16–22.

[14] Especially K. Barth, *The Doctrine of Creation: Church Dogmatics* III/1, trans. J.W. Edwards et al. (Edinburgh, 1958), pp. 183–206 = *Kirchliche Dogmatik* III/1 (Zürich, 1945), pp. 205–33; Westermann (n. 10), pp. 214–18 = E. tr., pp. 155–8.

[15] D.J.A. Clines, "The Image of God in Man", *Tyndale Bulletin* 19 (1968), pp. 53–103; T.N.D. Mettinger, "Abbild oder Urbild? »Imago Dei« in traditions-geschichtlicher Sicht", *ZAW* 86 (1974), pp. 403–24.

divine image indicate.[16] The philological discussion of the nouns *ṣelem* and *děmût*, and the prepositions *bě* and *kě* has been of limited value. If anything, the way the prepositions are used elsewhere and the possible meanings for the nouns, which are used synonymously here, lend weight to the physical-representation interpretation. Since the 1960s, and especially the work of J. Barr, emphasis has been given to the place of the texts within the P document. In Gen. i 26–8 the close association between the motif of humanity as the image of God and the command to dominate the animal world and all creation suggests a functional interpretation. Gen. v 1–3, which I would associate with the redactional level of the text, seem to connect the image of God more clearly with physical representation, since Seth is in Adam's likeness and image. Gen. ix 6, which could also be associated with the redactional level, is ambiguous with the prohibition against murder because human beings are in the divine image. At a redactional level, therefore, it would seem we must reckon with a coalescence of form and function in the understanding of the motif. This is not inconsistent with Egyptian evidence related to Pharaoh as divine image.[17] I would argue that the same conjunction of form and function could be be relevant in the case of the Tell Fekheriyeh inscription, where the image of the king Hadd-Yith ͨi is set up before Hadad and the inscription seeks in part the divine blessing on the king.[18] Some scholars have already argued such a view for the image of God in Genesis; e.g. W.H. Schmidt asks "How far can office and task, essential nature and consequence be separated from one another?"[19] This is especially true in the redacted level of the text.

If we return now to consider that level of text, the situation becomes even more complex when we note the interaction of J and P material in the *tôlědōt* sections. Gen. ii 4–iv 26 deals in part with the rejection by Yahweh of the human attempt to be like God by eating from the sacred tree (iii 5, 22–4). The redacted text makes it clear that there are limits to the ways human beings can be like God (or gods) and these will be jealously guarded by the deity. On the other hand the juxtaposition of Gen. iv 26b and v 1b–3, with their association across

---

[16] J. Barr, "The Image of God in Genesis - A Study in Terminology", *BJRL* 51 (1968), pp. 11–26; J.F.A. Sawyer, "The Meaning of *bṣlm* ͗*lhym* ('In the Image of God') in Genesis i–xi", FTS, NS 25 (1974), pp. 418–26.

[17] B. Ockinga, *Die Gottebenbildlichkeit im Alten Ägypten und im Alten Testament* (Wiesbaden, 1984).

[18] For the initial publication of this inscription see A. Abou Assaf, P. Bordreuil and A.R. Millard, *La Statue de Tell Fekherye et sa bilingue assyro-araméenne* (Paris, 1982).

[19] *Alttestamentlicher Glaube und seine Umwelt* (Neukirchen-Vluyn, 1968), p. 192 = *The Faith of the Old Testament*, trans. J. Sturdy (Oxford, 1983), p. 198.

the *tôlĕdōt* boundary of v 1a, suggests that the worship of Yahweh could be part of the total picture of the divine image in humanity.[20] This kind of interpretation of the image motif impinges on the relational interpretation of Barth and Westermann.

In summary, we may say that the redactional activity in Gen. v 1–3 has ensured that the P account of the development of humanity in the genealogy of Gen. v is now read in connection with both the creation story of i 1–ii 3 and the *tôlĕdōt* of the heavens and earth, ii 4–iv 26. The hope for humanity expressed at the end of the latter is maintained in the continuing presence of the divine image and blessing with humankind. These continue unabated in spite of human rebellion. Nevertheless, they have not remained untouched by the latter and the remainder of the TA is given over to further exploration of the interplay of the intent of God in creation, especially in humanity, and the rebellion of humanity. It remains to be seen how the image of God will be manifest and how it will be countered by a rebellious nature. The redactional context invites further deliberation on the nature of the image and its limitations.

II

The next clear evidence of the redactional hand in the TA comes in Gen. v 29. This verse is a clear intrusion of a J fragment into the P Sethite genealogy of v 3–28, 30–2. Besides the use of the name Yahweh, it has clear connections with other J passages, especially iii 16–19, vi 5–8 and viii 21–2. The verse also follows the genealogical style of iv 17–26, including the use of the naming formula. Only a few obvious literary remarks are required. The redactor has apparently isolated verse 29 from further genealogical material and has reshaped the main P genealogical line in v 1–32 to cater for the entry. The name of Lamech's first son has been replaced in v 28 by *ben* to make a smooth transition to the naming formula and etymology in verse 29.

The inclusion has a twofold effect. As in the case of v 1b–2, the reference in v 29 to a motif present in a previous section of Genesis, namely the curse on the ʾ*adāmâ*, brings the reading of the Sethite genealogy into the context of the *tôlĕdōt* section of Gen. ii 4–iv 26. The generations of the P genealogy are linked with those who suffer Yahweh's curse upon the ground. The lineage of Seth, which continues in the divine image, is not distinct in this matter. But in addition, v 29 also has the effect of focusing attention on the character

---

[20] Cf. Sawyer (n. 16), pp. 418–26.

in v 1–32 who will play the main role in the next *tôlĕdōt* section, Gen. vi 9–ix 29.[21] The Sethite genealogy, which dominates the TA, moves the development of creation and humanity forward. This development is in the light of the divine blessing but also in the shadow of human rebellion. The genealogy forms the beginning of the line which will come to focus in the traditional ancestors of Israel and in many ways already bespeaks their character.[22]

Gen. v 29 has not received much attention in relation to its context. Most interest has been shown in the verse as an etymology for the name of Noah.[23] But it plays a wider role when it records that Lamech named his son Noah (*nōaḥ*) saying: "This one will comfort us (*yĕnaḥămēnû*)[24] from our work and the pain of our hands, from the earth (*min-hā᾽ădāmâ*) which Yahweh has cursed."

At first sight, Lamech's statement carries a melancholic note of human struggle beneath the divine curse. But this melancholy is coupled with an expression of hope centred on the figure of Noah. He is the one anticipated as the comforter of those who struggle. The problem that has faced scholars for some time is how that comfort should be envisaged. It is in part a problem of translation. The phrase *min-hā᾽ădāmâ* is ambiguous in context. Does it relate to the verb *yĕnaḥămēnû* and hence to the source of the comfort Noah will bring or to the nominal phrase preceding it and hence to the source of the pain of their hands? It is also a matter of interpretation. Many scholars have argued that the comfort comes from the ground and relates to Noah's development of viticulture (Gen. ix 20–1).[25] They point out that the "us" for whom Lamech speaks is the generation which died in the flood. Therefore, the flood could not be their comfort. Some have even proposed a stratum of J which did not know the flood.[26] Passages extolling the joy and refreshment of wine (e.g. Ps. civ 15; Prov. xxxi 6–7; Judg. ix 13) are frequently cited in support of the

---

[21] Cf. A. Strus, *Nomen-Omen* (Rome, 1978), pp. 66, 158–62.

[22] Cf. B.S. Childs, *Introduction to the Old Testament as Scripture* (London, 1979), p. 153; S. Tengström, *Die Toledotformel und die literarische Struktur der priesterlichen Erweiterungsschicht im Pentateuch* (Lund, 1981), pp. 25, 44.

[23] Exceptions include the early articles of J. Martin, "A Famine Element in the Flood Story", *JBL* 45 (1926), pp. 129–33; E.G. Kraeling, "The Interpretation of the Name of Noah in Gen 5:29", *JBL* 48 (1929), pp. 138–43; and the recent article by N. Poulsson, "Time and Place in Genesis V", *OTS* 24 (1986), pp. 21–33.

[24] Many emend *yĕnaḥămēnu* to *yĕnîḥēnû* following LXX διαναπαύσει ἡμᾶς. Early Jewish writers also had difficulty with the etymology, cf. Gen. Rab. 25.2.

[25] E.g. K. Budde, *Die biblische Urgeschichte (Gen. 1–12, 5)* (Giessen, 1883), pp. 306–13; Gunkel (n. 7), pp. 54–5; von Rad (n. 1), p. 113 = E. tr., p. 132; Skinner (n. 9), p. 133; Westermann (n. 10), pp. 487–8 = E. tr. pp. 360.

[26] E.g. Gunkel, p. 55; Martin (n. 23), pp. 132–3.

argument for viticulture as human comfort. In opposition to this
view, others have upheld the view that the flood is envisaged in Gen.
v 29, and that the curse on the ground is mitigated in some way in viii
21 as the pious Noah stands at the beginning of a new epoch.[27]

The argument that the development of viticulture is in view in
Gen. v 29 cannot be strongly supported. First, the point made by
Budde and others that the generation of Lamech, on whose behalf the
statement of hope is uttered, would find no comfort in the flood in
which they all died can be applied equally to the situation in ix 20.
Lamech's generation finds no comfort in the post-diluvian development of viticulture either. Secondly, the reference in ix 20–1 to Noah
planting a vineyard and consuming its wine is certainly connected to
other J passages on the development of aspects of culture (e.g. Gen. iv
17–24). However, it is unlikely that the alleviation of the curse on the
ground is to be inferred from the passage. If it were, one would expect
a much clearer reference to it. The purpose of ix 20–1 in both the
J source and the final redacted form of the text seems to be simply as
a background to the blessing and cursing of Noah's sons, subsequent
to the transgression of Ham against his father. Thirdly, the place of
Gen. viii 20–2 in the sequence pertaining to the curse on the ground
must be considered. These verses record Yahweh's statement following
Noah's sacrifice after the flood. They do not record the abrogation of
the curse of Gen. iii 17–19 as, for example, R. Rendtorff has
suggested.[28] They do not mark the end of an age of curse and the
beginning of an age of blessing. Certainly there is an allusion to iii
17–19 in viii 21 with reference to the curse on the *ʾădāmâ baʿăbûr
hāʾādām*, although in iii 17 the root *ʾrr*, "to curse", is used while viii 21
uses the piel of *qll*. But it would seem most likely from the causal clause
following in viii 21, *kî yēṣer lēb hāʾādām raʿ minnĕʿurāyw* and the next
principal cause, *wĕlōʾ ʾōsīp ʿôd lĕhakkōt ʾet-kol-ḥay*, which is parallel in
construction to the first principal clause, that the flood is the curse
referred to here even though such a designation is not used elsewhere.
Both clauses recall expressions at the beginning of the flood.
Rendtorff's argument, that the piel of *qll* used in viii 21 has
a declarative meaning thereby making the allusion to the declaration
of the curse in iii 17–19 stronger, is not convincing.[29] Others argue
that the basic meaning of the piel of *qll* is "to treat with disdain" or "to

---

[27] S.R. Driver, *The Book of Genesis* (12th edn, London, 1926) pp. 77–8; Dillmann
(n. 7), pp. 115–16 = E. tr. 1, p. 228.
[28] "Genesis 8, 21 und die Urgeschichte des Yahwisten", *KD* 7 (1961), pp. 69–79.
[29] Ibid., pp. 73–4.

degrade shamefully".[30] We should note the parallel use of *ʾrr* and *qll* (piel) in Gen. xii 3, the only other place *qll* (piel) appears in J, and compare Gen. xxvii 19 where *qll* is replaced by *ʾrr* in the promise. It would seem, therefore, that the writer of viii 21 understood the flood as a curse upon the *ʾădāmâ* on account of human sin in the same vein as the curse of iii 16–19 was brought about by human disobedience. However, in Gen. viii, Yahweh vows never to repeat a curse like the flood. The earlier curse of thorns, thistles, hard labour and pain in childbirth (iii 16–19) is not necessarily terminated. Indeed, those things persist after the flood. The position of the adverb *ʿôd*, "again", in the first clause in viii 21 may even make this point.[31] Having declared that no further curse like the flood would come upon the ground on account of human beings, Yahweh goes on in verse 22 to set in place the seasons and times of year and day. The establishment of these patterns of nature, which are an intricate part of agricultural life, is not itself a reversal of the curse of iii 16–19. Hardships persist, given the regularity of seasons and times. The realities of Gen. iii 16–19 are neither avoided nor alleviated. Thus in regard to Gen. v 29, the divine response to the hope expressed in Lamech is to promise to add no further burden to the human lot in spite of the continued persistence of human sin. The development of viticulture in ix 20 is not an alleviation of the curse of Yahweh on the ground but something which fits within the continuing patterns of nature established at the end of the flood.

These arguments speak against seeing the fulfilment of Lamech's expressed hope in Gen. v 29 in the development of viticulture in Gen. ix 20–1. One is therefore inclined to fall back on to one's first instinct of some connection between v 29 and Noah's part in the flood. We may justifiably infer that the melancholic hope expressed by Lamech points forward to the beginning of the new era connected wth Noah's survival of the flood. However, when we consider the last argument above and some further details on v 29, we find that Lamech's words of hope express little beyond being a general pointer towards future events. The details of the statement are not fulfilled. This raises the question of the aim and result of the redactor's incorporation of Gen.

---

[30] W. Schottroff, *Der altisraelitische Fluchspruch* (Neukirchen-Vluyn, 1969), pp. 29–30. Cf also O.H. Steck, "Genesis 12:1–3 und die Urgeschichte des Jahwisten", in H.W. Wolff (ed.), *Probleme biblischer Theologie: Festschrift für G. von Rad* (Munich, 1971), pp. 525–54.

[31] See U. Cassuto, *A Commentary on the Book of Genesis: II. From Noah to Abraham*, trans. I. Abrahams from Hebrew, 1949 (Jerusalem, 1964), p. 120; G.J. Wenham, *Genesis 1–15* (Waco, 1987), p. 190.

v 29 where it now stands. The redactor's aim may simply have been to foreshadow the new situation to begin with Noah. The result of the redactor's work, however, may be more far reaching. A close examination of v 29 in context produces some interesting paradoxes and ironies.

First, as noted above, the hoped for relief from the curse upon the ground does not seem to be fulfilled. Rather, the generation of Lamech gains only death, not comfort. Secondly, the verbal connections between v 29 and vi 5–8, especially verse 6, strike a point of irony. Yahweh suffers pain like humanity. In a different way, it too is caused by human rebellion. The root ʿṣb occurs in both places. Human pain yearns for comfort but Yahweh's pain leads to destruction. In a strange twist, any hope for humanity to survive lies not so much with Noah as with the aggrieved Yahweh. Noah will certainly be seen as righteous and obedient, and he will play a crucial role, but ultimately it will be Yahweh who saves, for in his sight Noah finds favour (vi 6), and his remembrance of Noah (viii 1) leads to a new creation. It is with the sovereignty of Yahweh who curses the ground that human hope finally lies and it will not be manifest either in the form or by the means envisaged by Lamech. Thirdly, we find that while Lamech speaks of hope in v 29, in the preceding tôlĕdōt section another one called Lamech speaks of killing in a claim for exaggerated retribution (iv 23–4). The genealogy of Gen. iv provides its own picture of humanity juxtaposing cultural achievement with inner strife and alienation. It both contrasts and compares with the genealogy of v 1–32, which speaks highly of humanity in the divine image but reminds in verse 29 of the curse suffered. The relation of the two genealogies has always been of interest (see n. 10 above). The variation in the order of blocks of names, the repetition of the names Lamech and Enoch, and the similarity of several other names may point to oral variants behind the written forms of the genealogies. There is also the possibility of further conflation or assimilation in the written period.[32] At any rate, the juxtaposition and similarities of the genealogies invite further assimilation on the part of the reader or listener. One Lamech speaks of the hope of comfort while another speaks of revenge, and as iv 23–4 and v 29 are drawn together we again see the duplicity of human nature, a theme developed in other ways in the redacted text. One could well be led to ask whether, in some way, Lamech's statement in v 29 is not absorbed into the category of human thought classified as only evil by Yahweh in vi 5?

---

[32] Cf. Bryan (n. 10), p. 188.

After all, as we have noted, what is hoped for is not fulfilled in detail and the utterance serves only as a general pointer to the future. The actual structure of v 29 may support this, where at the beginning and end of Lamech's statement Noah, referred to by *zeh*, "this one", and Yahweh stand opposed to each other and are involved in opposite activities. Noah is to comfort (*yĕnaḥămēnû*) while Yahweh has cursed (*ʾērĕrāh*). Such opposition, of course, is not the hope of humanity. Lamech's expression of hope may simultaneously be seen as a statement of rebellion and deserve condemnation. The extent to which it is fulfilled and Noah participates in the dawn of a new epoch may itself be the greatest irony.

III

Finally, we turn to the conclusion of the TA. Most of the material in the two brief passages, vi 1–4 and 5–8, is generally accepted as coming from the J source. The language of verses 5–8, especially verses 6, 7aα, recalls the other J passages, iii 16–19, v 29 and viii 21–2, and brings Gen. vi 5–8 into the sequence relating to Yahweh's curse upon the ground. Moreover, the use of *lārōb* in vi 1 and *rabbâ* on vi 5, and the repetition of the phrase *ʿal-pĕnê hāʾădāmâ* in vi 1 and 7, draws a line between the record of the spread of humanity and the spread of wickedness. While these points are internal to the J source, they have been absorbed into the work of the redactor.

The activity of the redactor in vi 1–8 can be seen immediately in the relation between vi 1–4 and the genealogies of Gen. iv and v. The latter detail the increase of humanity which becomes the backdrop to the following episode, as Gen. vi 1 makes clear. In addition, reference to the birth of daughters in v 1–32 provides a brief link with vi 1 where the human daughters (*bĕnōt hāʾādām*) attract divine attention. The main activity of the redactor, however, can be seen in vi 7ab with the addition of the words *ʾăšer bārāʾtî*, and the catalogue of creatures to be wiped out by Yahweh. These have been attributed by many to the redactor writing in P style.[33] The redactional addition in vi 7 broadens the perspective of judgement in the J passage. It is no longer humankind alone that is involved in Yahweh's judgement but the whole creation. This brings the J passage into line with the

---

[33] See e.g. Skinner (n. 9), p. 151; Dillmann (n. 7), p. 125 = E.tr. 1, p. 244; Budde (n. 25), pp. 250–1; more recently Westermann (n. 10), pp. 546–7 = E. tr., pp. 406–7. Although the catalogues of creatures given by P (Gen. i 25, 26b, vi 19, vii 72, viii 17, 19) vary in expression and order, they stand in contrast to the usual J lists (cf. ii 20, vii 8, viii 20).

P statement in vi 11–12. The combination of vi 6 and 7 functions to recall again both the creation story and the *tôlĕdōt* of the heavens and the earth just as the earlier combination of material in Gen. v 1–3 did, while at the same time it prepares for the flood story about to unfold in the next *tôlĕdōt* section with its own interplay of J and P material. The cosmic element introduced by the redactor in vi 5–8 prepares for the priestly theme which will dominate the flood story.

A final observation should be made about the connection of the TA to the following *tôlĕdōt* of Noah, Gen. vi 9–ix 29. Again a catchword is employed across the boundary, this time in the word *rʾh*, "to see". Although the episodes vi 1–4, 5–8 and 9–13 vary in content, the divine action in each case is precipitated by divine observation. The divine beings "saw" (*wayyirʾû*) the human women (vi 2), Yahweh "saw" (*wayyarʾ*) that human wickedness was great (vi 5), and finally God "saw" (*wayyarʾ*) the earth which was corrupted (vi 12). In each case, Yahweh (or Elohim) speaks, decreeing either a limitation of age (vi 3) or in the latter cases general destruction (vi 7 and 13). In addition, between the J and P declarations of the flood in vi 5–8 and 9–13 and immediately surrounding the *tôlĕdōt* heading in verse 9 we find statements concerning Noah's favour with Yahweh and his righteousness. Thus a rough pattern is established in vi 5–13: Yahweh sees; Yahweh declares destruction; Noah finds favour; Noah is righteous, etc.; God sees corruption; God declares an end. The repetition of the birth of Noah's sons in vi 10 would tie the beginning of that *tôlĕdōt* section to the position in genealogical development reached at the end of the previous *tôlĕdōt* section (v 32). These elements again point to a redactional hand creating distinct links between J and P material and across *tôlĕdōt* heading boundaries.

By juxtaposing Gen. vi 1–8 with the surrounding P material the redactor has created new possibilities for interpretation. As noted above, Gen. vi 1 ties the development of the genealogy of v 1–32 to these J passages. There seems little justification to assume, as Westermann does, that the increase of humanity jeopardizes the divine-human relationship as in the Atrahasis epic.[34] At a basic level vi 1 allows for narrative flow.[35] It also picks up on the theme of the blessing of humanity and its multiplication. But it goes beyond these roles, for in tying the genealogy of v 1–32 to vi 1–4 with the additional

---

[34] Cf. Westermann, p. 500 = tr., p. 370.
[35] D.J.A. Clines, "The Significance of the 'Sons of God' Episode (Genesis 6:1–4) in the Context of the 'Primeval History' (Genesis 1–11)", *JSOT* 13 (1979), pp. 33–46, esp. pp. 38–40.

connection between vi 1 and vi 5 we again have the line of Seth, in whom the divine image persists, linked to statements about human limitations and sinfulness.

Gen. vi 1–4 has often been discussed independently in relation to the flood,[36] but the structure of the TA draws it into the broader picture of the run-up to the destruction to come. The identity of the *běnê-hāʾĕlōhîm* and the *běnōt-hāʾādām*, as well as the determination of the nature of the transgression, has received more than enough exegetical attention.[37] My own interpretation of the identities concurs with the most widely accepted and oldest view,[38] namely, that we have here intercourse between divine beings and mortal women. In regard to the nature of the transgression, no clear statement of any kind of moral rebellion on the part of human beings is made.[39] However, parallels between the actions of the *běnê-hāʾĕlōhîm* and the woman in Gen. iii 6, where each sees what is good and takes, suggests that the transgression lies with the *běnê-hāʾĕlōhîm*. In both cases Yahweh acts to prevent either human beings living for ever (iii 22) or having his breath "abide" (*yādôn*) within them for ever (vi 3). The action of Yahweh suggests the dilemma is one of mortality not morality. Gen. vi 3 does not indicate a second introduction of death.[40] On one level it is an aetiology for the supposed normal length of human life. On another, it functions to underline the mortality of humanity already signified by the introduction of death and in other ways in Gen. iii. Gen. vi 1–2 present a situation in which that mortality could be overcome, averted or changed, but in verse 3 Yahweh states otherwise, declaring that *ʾādām* is flesh and will live for 120 years.

---

[36] For earlier views see E.G. Kraeling, "The Significance and Origin of Gen 6, 1–4", *JNES* 6 (1947), pp. 193–208; von Rad (n. 1), p. 95 = E. tr., pp. 112–13. More recently note the discussion of R. Hendel, "Of Demigods and the Deluge: Toward an Interpretation of Genesis 6:1–4", *JBL* 106 (1987), pp. 13–26, and J. Van Seters, "The Primeval Histories of Greece and Israel Compared", *ZAW* 100 (1988), pp. 1–21, esp. pp. 5–9.

[37] See Westermann (n. 10), pp 501–3 = E. tr., pp. 371–2, for a summary of views.

[38] Cf. 1 Enoch vi 2ff; Jub. v 1; LXX and early Christian writers.

[39] The recent opinion of Wenham (n. 31), pp. 140–1 (cf. Cassuto [n. 31], p. 294), that the fault lies with the daughters, presumably by their consent to intercourse with the divine beings, is based on the use of the marriage formula in the passage. Such a view, however, is not supported in any other way by the text. The marriage formula seems to describe what happened, not assign fault.

[40] So B.S. Childs, *Myth and Reality in the Old Testament* (London, 1960), pp. 52–3, who interchanges verses 3 and 4 in his interpretation. But if we take the present arrangement of the text, the limitation of life seems to be the point not a second introduction of death. The limitation of life reinforces the notice of death in Gen. ii in a situation where death could be averted by the intermarriage.

The statements about ʾādām in vi 3 refer most immediately, of course, to ʾādāmʾ "humanity", in verse 1. Nevertheless, the question arises with verse 4 of the status of the offspring of the marriages, here equated with the "warriors from of old" and the nĕpîlîm. The present structure of the passage draws these hybrid beings into the scope of ʾādām, "humankind", who live within the limits of their flesh (bāśār). The warriors from of old are called ʾanšê haššēm, "men of renown", and are born in the same manner as the women of vi 1.

Furthermore, Gen. vi 1–4 is not simply an example of corporate human sin as Westermann would also have it.[41] It deals with mortality and Yahweh's action to maintain the divine-human distinction. It both parallels the stories of Eden and Babel and contrasts with them in that the direction of transgression is from divine to human. In the context of the TA with redaction of J and P material together, Gen. vi 1–4 takes on added significance. The production of offspring through the marriage of divine beings to human women stands in parallel to the procreation of Gen. v 1–32 but polarized to it. The allocation of only 120 years stands in sharp contrast to the ages enjoyed by the genealogy in Gen. v and makes its own clear judgement on the conditions of human existence. Also, in Gen. v the divine image is passed from generation to generation and the genealogy stands blessed. In vi 1–4 the potential for offspring reflecting the likeness of the gods in a new way emerges as a threat to creation, order and blessing. In the redactional context, the J theme of the breach of the divine-human boundary, whether by hybris (Gen. iii and xi 1–9) or by divine transgression (vi 1–4), is taken up into the overall theme of the corruption of creation emerging in P material (vi 9–12). As in other passages, Yahweh's sovereignty, which stands threatened in vi 1–4, inevitably brings the episode to a conclusion.[42]

The TA draws to a conclusion with Gen. vi 5–8. The inner-J contrast between human beings with only evil thoughts and Noah who finds favour in the divine eyes, which see only evil elsewhere, once again coincides with and reinforces the theme of the duality of the human nature. Within the context of the redaction, one may be

---

[41] (n. 10), p. 500 = E. tr., p. 370.

[42] On the role of the nĕpîlîm, see A.D. Kilmer, "The Mesopotamian Counterparts of the Biblical Nĕpîlîm, in E.W. Conrad and E.G. Newing (ed.), *Perspectives on Language and Text: Essays and Poems in Honor of Francis I. Andersen's Sixtieth Birthday, July 28, 1985* (Winona Lake, 1987), pp. 39–43. She argues that the Mesopotamian counterparts to the biblical nĕpîlîm suggest hybris activity on the part of these creatures.

invited to see in Noah, who finds divine favour, the continuity of humanity functioning appropriately in the divine image.

IV

In summary then, we can say that the redactor in the TA, has built upon themes introduced in the previous two sections of Genesis, the creation story and the *tôlĕdōt* of the heavens and the earth. At the beginning of the TA, there have been minor developments of the text, both at the end of Gen. ii 4–iv 26 and at the beginning of v 1–vi 8 to provide a connection across the transition, as well as the repetitions of both the statement on the creation of *ʾādām* in the divine image and the sequence of generations, Adam through Enosh. Later in the section, v 29 introduces the theme of the corruption of humanity and the curse of Gen. iii 16–19 into the chronological genealogy of Gen. v. At the end of the TA, once again literary connections span the *tôlĕdōt* boundary and the junction between J and P material. At the same time, minor redactional additions in vi 7 provide links with both the creation story and the *tôlĕdōt* of the heavens and the earth. The emphasis on judgement in the J passage, vi 5–8, is broadened in preparation for the *tôlĕdōt* of Noah to come.

The interplay of the J material with the P material in the TA develops a fuller perspective on the nature of humanity created in the divine image (Gen. i 26–7, v 1). It is a nature that is evil in its ways and yet remains in the divine image and under divine blessing. It is glimpsed in its fullness in the figure of Noah. The broader perspective on humanity and God noted by various scholars in the juxtaposition of Gen. i 1–ii 3 and ii 4–iv 26[43] is expanded deliberately by the redactor of the J and P sources in the pre-flood material. At last in this *tôlĕdōt* section, the final redactor becomes "our master" in a creative way.

---

[43] E.g. Noth (n. 2), p. 271 = E. tr., p. 251.

THE ISLES OF THE NATIONS:
GENESIS X AND BABYLONIAN GEOGRAPHY[1]

by

WAYNE HOROWITZ

Jerusalem/Almog

Gen. x preserves a list of eponymous descendants of Noah's three sons Shem, Ham, and Japheth interspersed with folkloristic material. The chapter is divided into three main sections. Following an introductory verse, Gen. x 2–5 names the descendants of Japheth, Gen. x 6–20 the descendants of Ham, and Gen. x 21–31 the descendants of Shem. The chapter then closes with a single verse summary:

> These are the families of the sons of Noah according to their descendants in their nations; and from them were the nations of the earth divided after the flood. (Gen. x 32)

The Japheth, Ham, and Shem sections close with comparable summaries:

> And from these were divided the "Isles of Nations" (*'iyyê haggôyīm*) in their lands, each according to his language, according to their families in their nations. (Gen. x 5)

> These are the sons of Ham according to their families, according to their languages, in their lands according to their nations. (Gen. x 20)

> These are the sons of Shem according to their families, according to their languages, in their lands according to their nations. (Gen. x 31)

Although the phrase *'iyyê haggôyīm*, "the Isles of the Nations", occurs in the summary of the entire Japheth List in the Masoretic Text of Gen. x 5, modern editors have emended the text on the basis of Gen. x 20, 31 so as to detach "the Isles of the Nations" from the Japheth summary:

---

[1] This article is a by-product of the author's research for a Ph.D. (1986) at the University of Birmingham (England) entitled *Mesopotamian Cosmic Geography*, which will appear in the future in book form. No up-to-date comprehensive study of Mesopotamian cosmographic traditions exists. In the meantime, the reader is directed to W.G. Lambert, "The Cosmology of Sumer and Babylon", in C. Blacker and M. Loewe (ed.), *Ancient Cosmologies* (London, 1975), pp. 42–65.

The sons of Javan are: Elishah and Tarshish, Kittim and "Rhodanim".

From these the coastal people spread. "These are the sons of Japheth" according to their lands, each with its own language, accordng to their clans within their nations.[2]

Here, "the Isles of the Nations" refers only to Javan and his line. Such emendations find support in identifications of Javan's sons with nations in the Mediterranean basin, while the remainder of Japheth's descendants have been identified with landlocked nations to the north and east of Israel.[3] Nonetheless, the structure of Gen. x, related passages in the Bible, and geographic materials from ancient cuneiform sources indicate that ancient Israelites may have considered all the descendants of Japheth to be maritime nations. This evidence may render emendations of Gen. x 5 unnecessary.

The Structure of Genesis x

The basic structural pattern of Gen. x is that of genealogical materials summarized by concluding lines. The concluding verse 32, "These are the families of the sons of Noah ...", summarizes the entire chapter referring backwards to all the descendants of Noah in all three branches of the family. Likewise, Gen. x 31 refers backwards to all the sons of Shem, and Gen. x 20 refers backwards to all the sons of Ham.[4] Thus, on the basis of structure alone, the term "the Isles of the Nations" in the Masoretic Text of Gen. x 5 should refer to all the sons of Japheth. However, such a hypothesis presents two main difficulties from a modern geographic perspective. First, as noted above, only Javan and his sons are Mediterranean nations. Secondly, some of the nations descending from Javan seem to be coastland peoples rather than islanders. Therefore, it is necessary to consider the meaning of "the Isles of the Nations", and to identify the nations descending from Japheth, before continuing onwards.

---

[2] C. Westermann, *Genesis 1–11* (Minneapolis and London, 1984), p. 496 = *Genesis 1–11* (Neukirchen-Vluyn, 1974), p. 663; cf. S.R. Driver, *The Book of Genesis* (12th edn, London, 1926), p. 117; P. Heinisch, *Das Buch Genesis* (Bonn, 1930), p. 189. Note, however, also E.A. Speiser who emends to "(These are the descendants of Japheth), and from them branched out the maritime nations, in their respective lands ..." (*Genesis* [Garden City, 1964], p. 64).

[3] For instance, Westermann, E. tr., p. 508 (= p. 679), argues:

... The first question is whether the $m^{\ni}lh$ refers to the "sons of Javan (A. Dillmann) or to all sons "sons of Japheth" (U. Cassuto). It can be solved easily by paying attention to the meaning of $^{\ni}yym$: countries (regions) that border on the sea, and so the coastal areas. This obviously holds for "the sons of Javan, and for Javan itself too, but not for the other "sons of Japheth". So "from these" can refer only to the sons of Javan".

For identifications of the nations of the Japheth list see pp. 38–40, and n. 7 below.

[4] Note also Gen. x 29, where the summary of the list of sons of Joktan begins *kol-$^{\ni}$elleh b^{e}nê yoqṭān* "All these are the sons of Joktan".

The Term "the Isles of the Nations"

Hebrew ᵓî is cognate with the Egyptian word *iw* which occurs in the context of Ramesses III (1195–1164) repulsing Mediterranean invaders.[5] In Gen. x the word occurs in a construct formation with the form "A of B" where the main term A (isles) is modified by B (nations). Consequentially, the term refers primarily to the "islands" where the nations live, rather than to the peoples living on the "islands". As such, "the Isles of the Nations" is a geographic term.

Elsewhere in the Bible ᵓî occurs many times with reference to lands in the Mediterranean basin, eastern areas by the Persian Gulf, and distant lands. In Ezek. xxvi 15–18, as in the Ramesses III inscriptions, the word occurs three times in the context of the Mediterranean Sea in a prophecy concerning the city of Tyre. In Jer. xxv 22 the term occurs in the context of the kings of Tyre and Sidon (see below).

In the books of Esther and Isaiah ᵓiyyê hayyām, "the Isles of the Sea", are identified with both the Mediterranean Sea and the Persian Gulf. In Esther x 1 the term includes all the islands of the Persian Empire:

> And King Ahasuerus laid a tax on the land (*hāᵓāreṣ*) and the "Isles of the Sea".

The islands include Achaemenid-controlled islands in the Persian Gulf, as well as Mediterranean islands under Persian hegemony.[6] In Isa. xi 11 "the Isles of the Sea" occurs after an ingathering of Jews from eastern areas along the Persian Gulf including Elam and Shinar (ancient Iran and Southern Iraq), as well as western Mediterranean lands including Egypt. Thus, "the Isles of the Nations" in Gen. x can include, at the very least, nations to the east of Israel by the Persian Gulf and Indian Ocean, as well as nations in the Mediterranean basin.

Other occurrences of ᵓî, however, indicate that these ᵓiyyîm need not necessarily be "islands" in the modern sense (i.e. land surrounded on all sides by water). In Jer. xxv 22 an "island" is located *bᵉᶜēber hayyām* "across the sea", rather than *bayyām* "in the sea":

> And all the kings of Tyre, all the kings of Sidon and the king of the "island" which is across the sea.

This "island" could perhaps be a continental area across the Mediterranean from Tyre and Sidon such as the distant Greek mainland, or a region along the southern coast of modern Turkey, since it is possible to sail across the sea to either location from both

[5] See *Encyclopaedia Biblica* (Hebrew) 1 (Jerusalem, 1964), col. 239.
[6] For Persian satrapies including the Persian Gulf and Cyprus see E.E. Herzfeld, *The Persian Empire* (Wiesbaden, 1968), pp. 283–4, 309.

cities. Similarly, in Isa. xxiii 2, 6 ʾî occurs in the context of overseas trade with Tarshish. In such contexts "island" can refer to any territory which is reached by sea travel, rather than an overland route. Thus, there is no reason to presuppose that all the nations descending from Japheth in Gen. x must be found on islands in the Mediterranean if "Isles of Nations" refers to the entire Japheth list.

The Descendants of Japheth[7]

Gen. x 2–4 preserves three generations of the line of Japheth. The first generation is represented by Japheth himself; the second generation consists of Japheth's sons Gomer, Magog, Madai, Javan, Tubal, Meshech, and Tiras in verse 2; and the third generation is represented by the sons of Gomer in verse 3 and sons of Javan in verse 4:

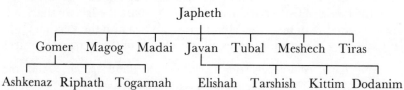

In this list, only Javan and his sons are Mediterranean peoples. Javan himself is to be identified with Greek ᾿Ιάϝωνες/ονες (Ionians). Ionian Greeks were those living on the Eurasian mainland in what is now Turkey, although Javan in Gen. x almost certainly includes all Greeks whether they lived in Ionia, the Greek islands, or the Greek mainland in Europe.

Javan's sons likewise live in the Mediterranean basin. Elishah is identified in Ezek. xxvii 7 as an island source for blue and purple dyes. Jonah sails for Tarshish from Jaffa on the Mediterranean coast of Israel in the book of Jonah. Both Ezek. xxvii 6 and Jer. ii 10 speak of isles of Kittim, which can now be identified with the site of Kition on Cyprus.[8] Finally, Dodanim (dōdānîm) of Gen. x 5 is replaced by Rodanim (rôdānîm) in 1 Chron. i 7 in a repeated version of the

---

[7] For studies of Gen. x 10 with identifications of the nations see F. Schmidtke, *Die Japhetiten der biblischen Völkertafel* (Breslau, 1926); Westermann, E. tr., pp. 495–530 = pp. 662–706; J. Skinner, *Genesis* (2nd edn, Edinburgh, 1930), pp. 187–233; U. Cassuto, *A Commentary on the Book of Genesis* II (Jerusalem, 1964), pp. 193–202; A.H. Sayce, *JBL* 44 (1925), pp. 193–202; E. Dhorme, *Syria* 32 (1951), pp. 28–49; W. Brandenstein, "Bemerkungen zur Völkertafel in der Genesis", in *Sprachgeschichte und Wortbedeutung, Festschrift Albert Debrunner* (Bern, 1954), pp. 57–83; D. Neiman in H.A. Hoffner (ed.), *Orient and Occident: Essays presented to Cyrus H. Gordon* (Kevelaer and Neukirchen-Vluyn, 1973), pp. 119–26. For "isles of nations" see also B. Oded, *ZAW* 98 (1986), p. 29. Note also Gen. xiv 9: "Tidal king of *gôyīm*". For further bibliography see Westermann, E. tr., pp. 495–6 = p. 662–3.

[8] See Skinner, p. 199; Cassuto, p. 193.

Japheth list, so Dodanim/Rodanim is to be identified with the island of Rhodes.

The remaining nations in the Japheth list are outside the Mediterranean area. Gomer and his sons Ashkenaz, Riphath and Togarmah have been identified with lands to the north of Israel. Gomer and Ashkenaz have been equated with the Scythians and Cimmerians (Akkadian *gimmirāja* and *ašguza*), two northern peoples who arrived in the Near East during the 8th and 9th centuries from the plains of Asia.[9] Madai is Media in Iran, and Tubal and Meshech are to be identified with Akkadian Tabali and Muški, two neighbouring lands in eastern Asia Minor to the north-west of Assyria which are often paired together in Assyrian royal inscriptions from the reign of Tiglath-pileser I (1114–1076) to the time of Sargon II (721–705).[10] Magog, Riphath and Tiras still cannot be positively identified.

Although the Japheth nations outside the line of Javan are not Mediterraean nations, there is ancient evidence indicating that many of them were believed to be coastal nations. In the Odyssey, Homer places the Cimmerians (Κιμμέριοι) on the shores of a mist-shrouded sea:

> And so she (the boat) came to the bounds of deep-flowing Oceanus. There is both the land and city of the Cimmerians always hidden in mist and cloud. (XI 13–15)

Similarly, the Bible itself seems to indicate that Togarmah, Tubal, and Meshech are maritime nations. In Ezek. xxvii 12–15 Togarmah, Tubal, and Meshech are listed as distant trading partners of Israel alongside Tarshish and Javan in the context of overseas trade, and Isa. lxvi 19 lists Tubal with Tarshish and Javan in the context of "distant isles" (*hāᵓiyyîm hārᵉḥôqîm*). Magog too may be associated with the term *ᵓî* in Ezek. xxxix 6:

> And I will send a fire on Magog and those that dwell on the "islands" and they shall know that I am the Lord.

Thus, it seems likely that the ancient Israelites considered Gomer (the Cimmerians), Togarmah, Tubal, Meshech, and perhaps even Magog to be maritime nations, although we know today that these nations

---

[9] For the *gimmirāja* and *ašguza* (*išguza*) in Neo-Assyrian sources see S. Parpola, *Neo-Assyrian Toponyms* (Kevelaer and Neukirchen-Vluyn, 1970), pp. 132–4, 178. Note also *Reallexikon der Assyriologie* 5 (Berlin and New York, 1976–80), pp. 594–5 ("Kimmerier").

[10] For *mušku* and *tabalu* see Parpola, pp. 252–3, 341–3. For *mušku* with *tabalu* see H. Winckler, *Die Keilschrifttexte Sargons* (Leipzig, 1889), p. 170, line 11; D. Lyon, *Keilschrifttexte Sargon's* (Leipzig, 1883), p. 3; line 15; A.G. Lie, *The Inscriptions of Sargon II, King of Assyria* (Paris, 1929), p. 4, line 9; p. 32, lines 199–200. For Meshech and Tabali in the Bible see Westermann, E. tr., p. 505 = p. 675.

were neither islands nor situated on sea-coasts. Such geographic misunderstandings, however, fit well with contemporary first millennium B.C. Mesopotamian geographic world-views.

The Japheth List and Babylonian Geography

Surviving Babylonian geographic materials demonstrate the first-millennium Babylonians believed that the most distant areas on earth from their homeland were located across the sea. This belief finds its clearest expression on a Babylonian world map from the 8th or 7th century. The text entitled "The Babylonian Map of the World"[11] depicts the Earth's Surface as two concentric circles with triangles radiating from the outer circle:

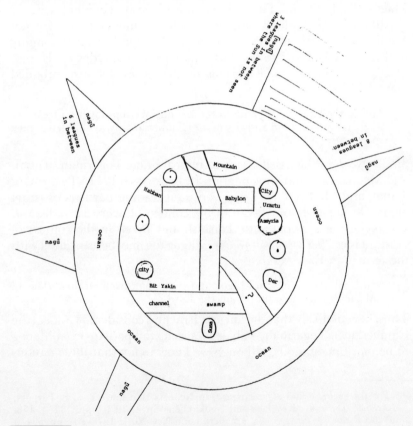

---

[11] An edition of "The Babylonian Map of the World" by this author is published in *Iraq* 50 (1988), pp. 147–65. The World Map is discussed in conjunction with Gen. x 10 by Brandenstein, p. 57, and G. Hölscher, *Drei Erdkarten. Ein Beitrag zur Erdkenntnis der hebräischen Altertums, Sitzungsberichte Heidelberger Akademie der Wissenschaften, Phil.-hist. Kl.* 34/3 (1944–8), p. 33.

The map, as preserved, divides the earth's surface into three zones. First is a central continent where Assyrian and Babylonia are situated. The second zone is a band between the two circles representing an ocean labelled *marratu* (Bitter Sea). The circles themselves represent the near and far shores of the *marratu*. The third zone lies beyond the outer circle and consists of triangles that are labeled *nagû* and uncharted space. The *nagû* may be islands in a cosmic sea that extends beyond the far shore of the *marratu*, regions belonging to a continent across the sea from Babylonia, or even appendages of the earth's surface that extend beyond the ends of the world. Thus these *nagû* can be compared to the *'iyyîm* of Jer. xxv 22 or Isa. xli 2, 6, which were either islands or distant continental lands.[12] Similarly, the general configuration of the map (central continent plus *nagû*) can be compared with the empire of Ahasuerus of Persia that consists of the land (*hā'āreṣ*) and "isles of the sea" in Esther x 1. In fact, the term *nagû* itself offers nearly indisputable proof that Gen. x and the Babylonian map are based on a shared geographic world-view.

The Term *nagû*

The geographic term *nagû* is common in Neo-Assyrian royal inscriptions, but rare in late-Babylonian royal inscriptions and literary texts. In Neo-Assyrian inscriptions, *nagû* is used with a political nuance to refer to administrative districts or provinces (see *CAD* N I, p. 121:1). In late-Babylonian royal inscriptions, however, the term *nagû* is used for distant unspecified areas. This sense of *nagû* parallels Hebrew *'î* and is appropriate for the World Map.

The term *nagû* occurs five times in late-Babylonian royal inscriptions, four times in the writings of Nebuchadnezzar II and once in the inscriptions of Nabonidus. In three of the Nebuchadnezzar inscriptions, *nagû* are located *ina qereb tâmti* "in the sea":

> All the lands, the entire inhabited world (*dadmu*) from the Upper Sea to the Lower Sea, distant lands, the people of vast territories, kings of far away mountains and remote *nagû* in the Upper and Lower Sea, whose

---

[12] In cuneiform sources, the land of Lydia and the Greek homeland are also placed across the sea even though both are located on the Eurasian mainland. In the inscriptions of Assurbanipal, the Lydian kingdom of Gyges is placed *nēberti tâmti*, "across the sea" (M. Streck, *Assurbanipal und die letzten assyrischen Könige bis zum Untergange Nineveh's* [Leipzig, 1916], II, p. 21, line 95, and p. 166, line 13) and the Akkadian portion of bilingual Xerxes inscriptions places Greeks *ina marrat* "in the ocean" and *ahullā marrat* "across the ocean" (see *CAD* M I, p. 285: *marratu* A b).

lead-rope Marduk, my lord, placed in my hand in order to pull his "yoke".[13]

Here the *nagû* must be islands in the Upper and Lower Seas beyond the shores of the inhabited world. In the other two inscriptions *nagû* are identified as distant places,[14] although it is unclear if the *nagû* are islands as both passages are broken.[15] In these royal inscriptions, the Babylonian *nagû* can be equated with Hebrew *ʾî* since both terms refer to distant territories that are associated with the sea. This equation between *nagû* and *ʾî* is confirmed by Tarqum Onkelos to Gen. x 5:

mʾylyn ʾytpršw ngwt ᶜmmyʾ bʾrᶜthwn gbr llyšnyh lzrᶜythwn bᶜmmyhwn.

Aramaic *ngwt* in the phrase *ngwt ᶜmmyʾ* is exactly equivalent to the Babylonian cognate *nagû*. Thus the descendants of Japheth living on "the Isles of the Nations" in Gen. x 5 need not be limited to the line of Javan along the Mediterranean west of Israel, since *nagû* can be found in all four compass point directions from Babylon on the World Map.

Conclusions

The Babylonian Map of the World demonstrates that the editor of the Japheth list was not alone in placing "islands" to the north, south, and east of the ancient Near East, as well as in the Mediterranean to the west. On the World Map, *nagû* extend south-east of Babylonia beyond Susa; to the north and east of Babylonia beyond Assyria and Urartu; and to the north and west of Babylonia past the region marked "mountain" and the circle labelled Habban. Similarly, the Japheth list of Gen. x 2–5 includes nations to the west of Israel (Javan and sons), north of Israel (Gomer and sons) and east of Israel (Madai = Media). Therefore, the Babylonian map supports an ancient identification of all Japheth descendants as "islanders", despite the fact that many of these nations do not live on islands according to modern criteria.

---

[13] S. Langdon, *Die neubabylonischen Königsinschriften, Vorderasiatische Bibliothek* 4 (Leipzig, 1912), p. 146: ii, lines 17–33; cf. p. 146: iii, lines 2–7; p. 206, line 17.

[14] W.G. Lambert and A.R. Millard, *Cuneiform Texts from Babylonian Tablets in the British Museum* 46: *Babylonian Literary Texts* (London, 1965), p. 45: v, lines 23–4; C.J. Gadd, *Anatolian Studies* 8(1958), p. 52, line 20.

[15] *CAD* N I, p. 123:2 lists "island" as a meaning of *nagû* citing a passage in the flood account of Gilgamesh XI where *nagû* emerge as the waters of the flood recede:

    I scanned the regions at the edge of the sea.
    At (each) 12 (var.) 14 a *nagû* appeared.

In this context, *nagû* are temporary islands surrounded by flood waters.

Although both Gen. x and the Babylonian Map of the World present false ethnographic and geographic models from a modern perspective, there is no reason to suspect that first-millennium B.C. Israelites and Babylonians would not have taken these models seriously. Therefore, it is plausible that ancient Israelites would have believed that the earth's surface consisted of a central continent, a cosmic sea, and maritime lands across the sea. Thus, the phrase "the Isles of the Nations" in Gen. x 5 may indicate that all the nations descending from Japheth were believed to live across the sea from ancient Israel's continental homeland.[16]

---

[16] That is not to say, however, that all ancient geographers would have accepted the false geographic models expressed in Gen. x and the Babylonian Map of the World. Such antique geographic notions were challenged as early as the 5th century B.C. by Herodotus:

> I laugh when I see so many men drawing maps of the earth, as none till now have drawn reasonably, for they draw Oceanus flowing in a circle around the earth as if drawn with a compass . . . (IV 36).

THE SITE OF SALEM, THE CITY OF MELCHIZEDEK (GENESIS XIV 18)[1]

by

J.A. EMERTON

Cambridge

Genesis xiv 18–20 tells of the meeting between Abram and Melchizedek, the king of Salem – and I shall use the familiar anglicized form Salem, even though Shalem would be a better representation of the Hebrew *šālēm*. Apart from this passage, there are two verses in the Old Testament that refer – either certainly or possibly – to a place called Salem. The certain reference (as will be argued below) is found in Ps. lxxvi 3, where the parallel Zion shows that Salem must be Jerusalem. With this verse may be compared Ps. cx, where someone in Zion (verse 2) is addressed as "a priest ... after the order of Melchizedek" (verse 4), and so the priest-king of Gen. xiv is linked with Jerusalem. The possible reference is in Gen. xxxiii 18, where the text of the *Revised Version* has "And Jacob came in peace (*šālēm*) to the city of Shechem", but the margin has "came to Shalem, a city of Shechem". The text follows the Targums (Onkelos, Pseudo-Jonathan, and Neofiti I), and the margin reflects the understanding of the verse in the LXX, Vulgate, and Peshiṭta, and in Jubilees xxx 1. Further, it has been maintained by some that, where the Massoretic Text of Jer. xli 5 refers to Shechem, Shiloh, and Samaria, the original reading has been preserved in the LXX (xlviii 5), which has Salem in place of Shiloh (which, it is argued, had long been in ruins). The valley of Salem in Judith iv 4 would also fit this site, whereas a reference to Jerusalem would be unsuitable in the context. Thus, whatever the original meaning of Gen. xxxiii 18 may have been (and it will be discussed later in the present article), it was believed at some time in the late period B.C. and the early centuries A.D. that there was a place called Salem near Shechem. Further, in the New Testament John iii 23 tells us of John the Baptist that he "also was baptizing in

---

[1] A list of publications cited in abbreviated form will be found at the end of the article. The dates of patristic writers are taken from *The Oxford Dictionary of the Christian Church*. I am indebted to Dr G.I. Davies and Dr H.G.M. Williamson for reading a draft of this article and making helpful suggestions.

Aenon near to Salim, because there was much water there", and the Greek word Σαλείμ probably represents the same Semitic original as the Old Testament Salem.

In an article of Gen. xiv published in 1971, I maintained that the Salem of which Melchizedek was king is to be identified with Jerusalem, and that a shortened form of the name is used as in Ps. lxxvi 3. Others, however, have contested this identification – and, indeed, alternative explanations have a long history. It is the purpose of the present article to reconsider the question of the identity of the Salem mentioned in Gen. xiv 18. It is also relevant to mention that Gen. xiv 17, immediately before the account of the meeting between Abram and Melchizedek, tells us that the king of Sodom went to meet Abram "at the vale of Shaveh (the same is the King's Vale)" ($^c\bar{e}meq$ $\check{s}\bar{a}w\bar{e}h\ h\hat{u}^{\circ}\ {}^c\bar{e}meq\ hammelek$). While verses 18–20 must be regarded as an interpolation (see my article of 1971, pp. 407–12), it is possible that the interpolator added them in a geographically appropriate place, and that they may thus be relevant to the identification of the site of Salem. On the other hand, we cannot exclude the possibility that the interpolator was not thinking of geographical questions when he made the insertion at this particular point in the narrative.

In seeking to identify Melchizedek's Salem, we must remember that there is nothing surprising in the possibility that the same name was shared by more than one place, as Jerome recognized long ago (*Heb. quaest.* on Gen. xxxiii 18, p. 42). It is unnecessary to discuss every theory that has been advanced. For example, the view that Salem was Mount Tabor is not found before the 10th century A.D., and it has been adequately refuted by Barnabé (pp. 19–21, 56–8).[2] I shall restrict the discussion to the principal suggestions that have been made. In 1903, Barnabé devoted a monograph to a discussion of the site of Melchizedek's Salem, but he has not said the last word on the subject, and the question is still a live one more than eighty years later.

---

[2] Hertzberg's argument for Mount Tabor lacks evidence before the 10th century A.D. It is impossible to attach weight to the argument that the reference in Deut. xxxiii 19 to *zibḥê ṣedeq*, which were offered on Mount Tabor, points to a connection with the second element in Melchizedek's name. At first sight, it is more plausible to argue that it is easier to think of a tradition being transferred from Tabor to Jerusalem than from Jerusalem to Tabor. But it is not difficult to think of local Christians wishing to claim an ancient holy site by locating it at the place where they themselves lived. Several centuries earlier, there were several places that were claimed to be Melchizedek's city, and so it is not a question of the transfer of a name only from Jerusalem. Moreover, if the claim of Tabor to be Salem had been known as early as the patristic sources mentioning other identifications we should have expected them to mention the fact.

I

Before discussing the identification of the Salem mentioned in Gen. xiv 18, it will be helpful to set out the evidence for the site in the early centuries A.D., and even before.

First, the view that Salem was Jerusalem is found in the Genesis Apocryphon XX 13 (and there is no reason to regard the words *hyʾ yrwšlm*, "that is, Jerusalem", as a later addition: see Fitzmyer), and in the versions mentioned above, and was held by Josephus (Jewish War, VI, § 438; Ant. I, §§ 180–1). It is also found in patristic writings, beginning with Theophilus of Antioch, *Ad Autolycum* II.31 (P.G. 92, col. 177B). Epiphanius of Salamis (*c.* A.D. 315–403) knew the identification with Jerusalem, though he was also aware of other opinions – see below (*Panarion*, 55. 2, p. 326).[3] The opinion of Jerome (*c.* 342–420) was not consistent. In some writings he accepts the identification of Salem with Jerusalem (*Heb. quaest.* on Gen. xiv 18–19 and xxxiii 18, pp. 19, 42; *Tractatus* on Ps. lxxv, pp. 49–50; Ep. XLVI. 3, *Paulae et Eustochiae ad Marcellam*, p. 331; Ep. CXXIX. 5, *Ad Dardanum*, p. 172; Ep. CVIII. 9, *Epitaphium Sanctae Paulae*, p. 314), but in Ep. LXIII. 2 and 7–8, *Ad Evangelum presbyterum – de Melchisedech*, pp. 20–1, he first lists writers who have identified Salem with Jerusalem (wrongly attributing the identification to Eusebius of Caesarea and Eusebius of Emesa), and then suggests a different view, which we shall consider below.

Second, whatever the intention of the writer of Gen. xxxiii 18 may have been, it was understood by some to refer to a place named Salem, and there seems to have been a site with that name in an appropriate part of Palestine in the early centuries A.D. Eusebius of Caesarea (*c.* 260–340) states in the entry for Συχέμ in his *Onomasticon* (p. 150) that it was also called Σαλήμ, and the entry for the latter name makes the same identification (p. 152) – and it should be noted that he appears to regard Salem as another name for Sychem, i.e. Shechem, not the name of a place near Shechem. (So too does the Madaba map of the 6th century,[4] probably in dependence on Eusebius.) The Greek of the latter entry in the *Onomasticon* is

---

[3] Cf. also *De mensuribus et ponderibus*, §§ 72 and 74. See P. de Lagarde, *Veteris Testamenti ab Origene recensiti fragmenta apud Syros servata quinque praemittitur Epiphani de mensuribus et ponderibus liber nunc primum integer et ipse syriacum* (Göttingen, 1880), p. 67; and *Symmicta II* (Göttingen, 1880), p. 205. This text adds to the sites named in *Panarion*, 55.2 (namely, Jerusalem and a place in the plain of Shechem) a third near Scythopolis.

[4] See R.T. O'Callaghan, "Madaba (Carte de)", *Supplément au Dictionnaire de la Bible* 5 (Paris, 1957), cols 627–704.

incomplete, but Jerome's Latin translation (p. 153) completes it, and
the Greek text is reproduced by Procopius of Gaza (c. 475–538) in his
comments on Gen. xiv 18 (P.G. 87/1, col. 333). He notes that there is
another Salem, also called Salumias (Σαλουμίας) near Scythopolis,
which we shall consider below. One of the traditions recorded by
Epiphanius (see above) places the Salem of Melchizedeck "in the
plain (πεδίῳ) of Shechem opposite (κατάντικρυ) what is now called
Neapolis", i.e. the modern Nablus. Epiphanius may thus identify
Salem, not with Shechem, but with a place near it (cf. Jubilees xxxl,
where Salem is said to be east of Shechem). Such a view is also
expressed by Eusebius of Emesa (died c. 359), who says that
Melchizedeck's Salem was neither Jerusalem nor Shechem, but was
"in the valley (κοιλάδι) in Shechem in the plain (πεδίόν) of the king"
(see Abel, *Revue Biblique*, N.S. 9 [1912], p. 294). The identification of
Salem with a site near Shechem was probably derived from the
Samaritans. Eusebius of Caesarea (*Praep. Evang.* IX. 17. 5–6, p. 503)
quotes an author whom Alexander Polyhistor describes as Eupolemus
(a Jewish writer of the 2nd century B.C.), but who is thought by some
to have been a Samaritan of the 2nd century B.C.[5] This writer associates
Melchizedek with "a city at the shrine of Argarizin" (ὑπὸ πόλεως ἱερόν
'Αργαρίζιν). The word Argarizin has been identified with Mount
Gerizim (*har gᵉrizzîm*), and its description as the "Mountain of the
Most High" (ὄρος ὑψίστου) probably includes an allusion to the
statement in Gen. xiv that Melchizedek was the priest of the Most
High God, El Elyon (*ʾēl ᶜelyôn*). Since the Samaritans regarded
Mount Gerizim, not Zion, as the sacred mountan, it was only to be
expected that they would believe Melchizedek's city to be nearby in
Samaritan territory. This belief is certainly found in later Samaritan
traditions, whose dates cannot always be determined with precision.
J. Macdonald, *The Theology of the Samaritans* (London, 1964), p. 44,
favours a date somewhere between the 3rd century B.C. (M. Gaster's
date) and the 9th century A.D. (T.H. Gaster) for the Asatir or
Chronicle I, which has been published by M. Gaster, *The Asatir*
(London, 1927). VII. 17 (p. 33* of the Aramaic text; English, p. 258)
recounts that Abraham and the kings of Sodom and Nahor went to
Great Salem (*šlm rbth*) where Abraham met Melchizedek (VII. 19),
and II. 6 (pp. 5*, 198) that "Jared begat Enoch, and he built a town

---

[5] Cf. C.R. Holladay, *Fragments from Hellenistic Jewish Authors* 1: *Historians* (Chico, 1983), 157; M. Goodman in E. Schürer (ed. G. Vermes, F. Miller, et al.), *A History of the Jewish People in the Age of Jesus Christ* III.1 (revised edn, Edinburgh, 1986), pp. 517–21.

called Great Salem" (cf. Gen. v 18–20, which says nothing about building a town). Neither passage says where Salem is, but the commentary of Meshalma (17th century, according to Macdonald, p. 48) identifies it with Shechem, and the Arabic text with Nablus (Gaster, p. 198). Macdonald (p. 44) refers to the difficulty of dating the various parts of Chronicle II, but says that the "earliest part of this work in biblical Hebrew may well antedate the early medieval period". He edited the text in *The Samaritan Chronicle No. II* (Berlin, 1969). There are references to *šlm rbth* (p. 48; English, p. 125) and *šlwm rbth* (pp. 49, 126) in Aramaic, and to *šlm hgdwlh* (pp. 77, 167) in Hebrew, and the last of these passages locates it near Mount Gerizim. The Tolidah or Chronicle III may go back in parts to the 12th century, but its contents extend as far as the 19th (Macdonald, *Theology*, p. 45). It too refers in Hebrew to Great Salem, which is said to be east of Mount Gerizim. See E.N. Adler and M. Séligsohn, *Revue des Études Juives* 44 (1902), pp. 206–7, 217, and 45 (1902), p. 91. It is to be noted that one of the above references spells the name as *šlwm*. That suggests that the fact that the Samaritan text of Gen. xxxiii 18 has *šlwm* does not necessarily imply that it was not regarded as a place name. The Samaritan Hebrew has *šlm* in Gen. xiv 18, and the Samaritan Targum has *šlm* in both passages, although some manuscripts have *šlwm* in xxxiii 18. See A. Tal, *The Samaritan Targum* (Hebrew) I (Tel-Aviv, 1980), p. 139. Abel (II, p. 442) associated this site with the modern Arab village Sālim five kilometres east of the site of ancient Shechem, and Alt (pp. 52–4) identified the ancient site of this Salem with Khirbet esh-Sheikh Naṣrallah near the village.

The use of the name Salem for this place could be pushed as far back as the early 13th century B.C. if it could be identified with a town named *šrm*, which is named in an Egyptian text from the eighth year of Ramesses II, and which may be found in J. Simons, *Handbook for the Study of Egyptian Topographical Lists of Western Asia* (Leiden, 1937), p. 149. The name is equated with Semitic *šlm*, but it is not clear where the town was situated. Abel (II, p. 26) notes that it may have been a town north-east of Taanach. M. Noth points out that neither it nor *mrm*, the name next to it on the list, can be located precisely; see his comments in *Zeitschrift des Deutschen Palästina-Vereins* 64 (1941), p. 59 = *Aufsätze zur biblischen Landes- und Altertumskunde* 2 (Neukirchen-Vluyn, 1971), p. 107. As Simons puts it in *Oudtestamentische Studiën* 2 (1943), p. 46, following Noth, "both these names are such as may be at home in any part of the Syro-Palestinian territory, not in Galilee or Samaria alone. Until the contrary is proved, it is only reasonable to suppose that the names in the upper part of the list with all the others belong to places in Syria." Gammie refers to the

Egyptian text in his argument against identifying Salem with Jerusalem, since šrm must have been "a town considerably north of Jerusalem", but he does not claim it as support for his own association of Salem with Shechem (p. 393). Kirkland goes further: he not only says that the identification of the place on the Egyptian list with Shechem has been proposed (by Landersdorfer, p. 204), but writes as if he favours the suggestion (p. 9).

Thirdly, it was noted above that Eusebius of Caesarea mentions a place called Salem or Salumias near Scythopolis (Beth-shean), which was also known to Epiphanius. The entry on Aἰνών in the *Onomasticon* (p. 40) says that the place near Salim that is mentioned in John iii 23 was eight Roman miles south of Scythopolis. The Madaba map also locates the Aenon near to Salim here. Although, as we have seen, Jerome was willing to identify Melchizedek's city with Jerusalem in most of his writings, he favoured a different identification in Ep. LXXIII. 7–8 (pp. 20–1), which was written in A.D. 398 (and therefore before Ep. CVIII. 9, which was written in 404, and in which he returned to the identification with Jerusalem). He also identified the site with the Salim near Aenon where John baptized. Why did Jerome believe that this was the place mentioned in Gen. xiv 18 and John iii 23? He says that "Hierusalem" is compounded of two words, one Greek and one Hebrew, but it is not clear whether he regards that as evidence or, if he does, how it can serve as an argument. It is, in any case, an etymological claim that cannot be taken seriously in the 20th century, however plausible it may have seemed in the 4th. His identification appears to be based on a local tradition, for he says that the ruins of Melchizedek's palace can be seen at the site, and that it bears the name of Salem *usque hodie*. He also claims that Jerusalem could not have been on Abram's route (*non devia Hierusalem*) when he travelled south from Dan. This was probably also the place that Egeria[6] (4th century A.D.) was told was Melchizedek's city and was formerly called Salem but now Sedima,[7] and was the place where

---

[6] Otherwise known as Etheria, Aetheria, etc. See J. Wilkinson, *Egeria's Travels* (London, 1971), pp. 235–6. The account of her travels was formerly thought to have been written by a pilgrim named Silvia. The text is published in A. Franceschini and R. Weber, *Itineraria et Alia Geographia*, Corpus Christianorum, Series Latina, 75 (Turnhout, 1965), pp. 27–90.

[7] Abel, *Revue Biblique*, N.S. 10 (1915), p 273, and *Géog.* II, p. 442, compares the way in which Arbela became Irbid. J. Ziegler, *Biblica* 12 (1931), p. 80, plausibly suggests a corruption of "Secima'" and gives evidence for the possibility of the mistake in Latin. The same suggestion was earlier made by Barnabé in his chapter on "L'opinion des Chrétiens de la Samarie au IVe siècle" (pp. 19 – 28)when discussing Egeria (whom he believed to be St Silvia of Aquitaine). I no longer have access to the book, which I read in the library of the École Biblique et Archéologique Française in Jerusalem, and I cannot give the page reference.

John baptized (§§ 13–15, pp. 55–6). In their journeys of 1851–2 and 1852, respectively, Van de Velde (pp. 354–6) and Robinson (pp. 315, 333) came across a weli called Sheikh Sālim near Tell el-Ridhghah (or Radhghah) at what would have been an appropriate place for this candidate for Salem. When, however, C.F. Tyrwhitt Drake went to the region just over twenty years later, "Inquiries of the Arabs and fellahin of the district resulted in not a man of them having heard of either of these places" – the other was Bir Salim (*PEFQS*, January 1875, p. 32). In any case, the chances of a weli preserving an ancient name are far from strong, as Robinson noted.

II

As far as I am aware, there are no candidates for identification with Melchizedek's Salem apart from the three places mentioned in the patristic texts listed above, and Hertzberg's minority plea for Mount Tabor, which I have already rejected. In modern discussions of Melchizedek's Salem I know of no claim for the Salim eight Roman miles south of Scythopolis, and it is unnecessary for the present purpose to discuss whether it is the place mentioned in John iii 23. Albright, indeed, has claimed that the place was not really called Salim at all, but Salumias (1924, pp. 193–4; 1956, p. 159); but we cannot be sure that, just because Eusebius of Caesarea records two names, only Salumias can have been the genuine one. Yet there seems no reason other than one of the three early Christian traditions to favour the site near Scythopolis, and I shall focus the discussion on the other two sites.

In 1971 I noted that Melchizedek and Zion appear to be linked in Ps. cx and I argued that Salem in Gen. xiv 18 is to be identified with Jerusalem as in Ps. lxxvi 3 (pp. 412–14). I was cautious about using Gen. xiv 17 as evidence, because verses 18–20 are an interpolation, and because the King's Vale looks like a gloss, but I noted that 2 Sam. xviii 18 also refers to the King's Vale and that Josephus (Ant. VII, § 243) places it near Jerusalem, and that this may offer some support for the identification of Salem with that city. Further, I expressed the opinion that Melchizedek's city was probably "a place of some importance, rather than one of the minor sites in Palestine with which some have identified it". I did not, however, follow those who use the element *ṣdq* in Melchizedek's name as an argument for believing his city to be Jerusalem. Although attention has been drawn to the second part of the name of Adonizedek (Josh. x 1, 3) who was king of Jerusalem, and other alleged evidence for connecting the root with Jerusalem has been advanced, "the element is quite common in North-West Semitic proper names" (p. 413), and scarcely supports a special connection with just one place. I shall, therefore, ignore this argument in the following discussion of the evidence.

The identification of Salem with Jerusalem, which probably remains the opinion of the majority of scholars, has been challenged since the appearance of my article (as, indeed, it was long before), and the old alternative view that it was Shechem or somewhere near it has been revived. J.T. Milik expressed support for the latter view in the *Journal of Jewish Studies* 27 (1972), p. 137, and referred back to what he had written in *Biblica* 42 (1961), p. 84, n. 2, but in neither article did he offer any arguments. Detailed arguments were, however, advanced by J.G. Gammie in 1971 in an article written without knowledge of the arguments in my article, which appeared in the same year, and by J.R. Kirkland in 1977. The discussion in the present article will be chiefly concerned with the arguments put forward by Gammie and Kirkland.

Both Gammie and Kirkland refer to earlier books and articles, and it is appropriate to take them into consideration. Two are by C. Mackay and R.H. Smith, and they were published in 1948–9 and 1962, respectively. It does not, however, seem necessary to devote much space to an examination of some of Mackay's weaker arguments. For example, he states on p. 121 that "The Greek version [of Gen. xiv 18] declines to understand Salem as Jerusalem", and maintains that "in the Septuagint view" Salem was a city of Shechem (Gen. xxxiii 18). In fact, the LXX simply transliterates the Hebrew place name in Gen. xiv 18, and there is no reason to have expected it to substitute an interpretation "Jerusalem" for a simple transliteration. In xxxiii 18 the translator rendered what he understood to be the meaning of the Hebrew text, and it is unjustified to claim that there was a LXX view that Salem was always and only a place near Shechem. Similarly, little can be made of Mackay's argument for his claim (p. 123) that Ezekiel's vision of the restored temple placed it at Shechem.[8] Ezekiel did not have a modern atlas and his visions of the future were probably determined by other influences than a precise knowledge of distances in his original homeland, and Ezek. xlvii 1–11 makes it plain that the new temple would be built to the west of the Dead Sea, that is, in Jerusalem. Further, it is questionable whether Ezekiel is deliberately "leaving no place for Melchizedek" in

---

[8] Cf. his article "Prolegomena to Ezekiel xl.–xlviii.", *Expository Times* 55 (1943–4), pp. 292–5.

his words on the origin of Jerusalem in xvi 5 (p. 124). Nor can any value for the interpretation of Gen. xiv 18 be attached to Mackay's use of Rev. xx 9 and other passages in the New Testament (pp. 123–4), to his interpretation of the Ugaritic tablets in a way that is now generally abandoned (p. 126), or to his attempt (p. 121) to connect Salem with Σααλείμ in the LXX of 1 Sam. ix 4, where the Hebrew šaᶜălîm is clearly different.

Gammie also refers to scholars of an earlier period who "have argued that the evidence for a prior relationship [of "the Melchizedek priesthood"] to Shechem was undeniable" (p. 387). That is certainly true of Jeremias (pp. 348, 350; E. tr., pp. 26, 29), and Landersdorfer. I have not had access to A. Schlatter, *Zur Topographie und Geschichte Palästinas* (Stuttgart, 1893), pp. 258 ff. Gammie is, however, wrong in attributing such a view about Shechem to I. Benzinger, "Zur Quellenscheidung in Gen 14", *Vom Alten Testament Karl Marti zum 70. Geburtstage gewidmet, BZAW* 41 (Giessen, 1925), pp. 21–7. Benzinger analyses the chapter into J and E strands, and it is clear from pp. 22–5 that he ascribes Gen. xiv 18–20 to J, which associates Melchizedek with Jerusalem and Abram with Hebron, whereas it is E that originally associated Abram with Shechem but apparently said nothing about Melchizedek. Nor does Nyberg ascribe priority to the relationship of Melchizedek's priesthood to Shechem on pp. 366–7, as Gammie claims. Nyberg says: "Offenbar war Sichem in vorisrael-itischer Zeit neben Jerusalem das große religiöse Zentrum, wo der Landesgott wohnte" (p. 367); and p. 357 helps to make his meaning clear. He thinks that both Jerusalem and Shechem were important for the deity, not that the latter had priority or a connection with Melchizedek. Moreover, Hertzberg (1928, p. 173) who, as Gammie notes, himself favours a connection of Salem with Mount Tabor, appears to say no more than that the connection with Gerizim was an ancient Samaritan tradition.

Kirkland rightly adds (pp. 8, 20) to the list of earlier scholars who identified Melchizedek's Salem with Shechem the names of Stanley (pp. 247–8), Erbt (pp. 73–4; cf. pp. 74–7 on Ps. cx), and Winckler (pp. 407–8, 441–2). He has, however, misunderstood Gammie when he says (p. 20, n. 32) "According to Gammie (393 n. 44), Edward Robinson, in 1841, was inclined to place Abram's Salem near Shechem". Gammie writes only of Robinson's identification of the modern village of Sālim with the Salem of Gen. xxxiii 18, and he has correctly reported what Robinson says in *Biblical Researches in Palestine, Mount Sinai and Arabia Petraea* III (London, 1841), p. 102. Robinson says nothing here about Melchizedek's Salem.

The views of the writers mentioned above are not identical, as has already been seen in the preceding paragraphs. Smith does not believe that *šālēm* in Gen. xiv 18 is a place-name at all, and he translates it "submissive" – a rendering that is improbable, as I maintained in 1971 (p. 413). Nevertheless, he believes that the meeting between Abram and Melchizedek took place at Shechem. Kirkland, on the other hand, claims, like Stanley, Jeremias, Winckler and Landersdorfer, that Salem was another name of Shechem – as Eusebius of Caesarea and the person responsible for the Madaba map appear to have believed. Gammie, however, "submits that the name Salem at the time of Abram and Melchizedek may have been applied to the entire valley or basin bounded on the north by Mount Ebal ... and *Jebel el-Kebîr* ... and on the south by Mount Gerizim ... and the scarp near Taanath-Shiloh" (p. 393). Because of that he writes, not of an identification of Salem with Shechem, but of an "association", and he understands Gen. xxxiii 18 to speak of "Salem, a city of Shechem" (p. 390), not "Salem, the city of Shechem". Yet the only evidence he offers for his speculation about the ancient use of Salem as the name of a valley, rather than a city, is the reference to "the valley of Salem" in Judith iv 4, and "the fact that to this day the land bounded by four above mentioned heights is quite naturally referred to as 'the basin of Salim'" (p. 393)–and he might have added a reference to Epiphanius's words "the plain of Shechem" and to Eusebius of Emesa. He does not consider the possibility that the reference is to a valley or basin near the town or village called Salem or Salim, and that the name remains that of the town or village. There is a district in England called the Vale of Evesham, but when people refer simply to Evesham they mean the town of that name, not the district as a whole. Further, there appears to be a discrepancy between his view that Salem was the name of a valley and his understanding of Gen. xxxiii 18 to say that it was a city. Gammie also believes that the Melchizedek priesthood later moved to Shiloh, thence to Nob, and finally to Jerusalem, but the arguments that he advances on pp. 393–5 are scarcely compelling. In any case, I shall confine myself to a consideration of arguments for locating Salem at or near Shechem, and I shall not discuss Gammie's theory about Shiloh. Finally, Mackay's view is not clear. Sometimes he writes as if Salem were to be identified with Shechem, but on p. 121 he takes Gen. xxxiii 18 to refer to a Salem "neighbour to Shechem and Samaria", and he also cites Jubilees xxx 1 where, as we have seen, Salem and Shechem are distinguished.

III

We shall begin a review of the arguments by considering those that have been advanced against the identification of Salem with Jerusalem. Of course, any positive arguments in favour of Shechem are, by implication, also arguments against Jerusalem, but it will be convenient to leave them until section IV of the present article.

First, it has been argued that the city of Jerusalem was known by the full form of its name from early times, and that the shorter form "Salem" was not used then. As Gammie puts it, "Salem was not used as a name for the Jerusalem of antiquity" (p. 389; cf. Kirkland, pp. 6–7). The Tell el-Amarna letters of the 14th century B.C. refer to the city as Urusalim, and there is also Egyptian evidence for the ancient date of the full form.

What, then, is to be made of Ps. lxxvi 3 and Ps. cx? It is difficult to accept Mackay's understanding of Ps. lxxvi 3, which he translates "In Shalem also is his covert, and his lair in Zion", and on which he comments "to identify Shalem with Zion there is as gratuitous as to identify Israel with Judah in the preceding verse, or a lion's covert with its lair" (p. 123). It is, indeed, true that words in so-called "synonymous" parallelism need not be identical in meaning, but the context does not favour a geographical distinction between Salem and Zion in the present passage. The words translated "his covert" (*sukkô*) and "his lair" (*mᵉᶜônātô*) by Mackay are probably figurative expressions for a sanctuary or temple (and the fact that a lion's covert and lair are different does not prevent them from being used figuratively to refer to the same thing). *sukkô* recalls *sukkōh* in Ps. xxvii 5, which is parallel to "his tent" and comes after a mention of the temple in verse 4; it also recalls *śukkô* (despite the different sibilant) in Lam. ii 6, where the context makes plain that the temple on Mount Zion is meant. *mᵉᶜônātô* recalls the use of the masculine form of the word for the temple in Ps. xxvi 8 and, presumably, 2 Chron. xxxvi 15. If the two words in Ps. lxxvi 3 do not refer to a sanctuary or temple, to what do they refer? It may be doubted whether the psalm is speaking of two sanctuaries, one in Jerusalem and one in Shechem. Ps. lxxvi was obviously written after David's capture of Jerusalem, and – unless the psalm is very early – the reference is more probably to Solomon's temple than to David's sanctuary. After David's establishment of Jerusalem as the cultic centre of the nation, it is unlikely that a psalm would allow equal status to Shechem as a holy place, and even less likely after the division of the kingdom. Further, the psalm speaks of what happened "there" (*šammâ*), and it is unlikely that the psalmist has in mind two different events in two different places. Even if the dubious theory that "there" should be emended[9] were to be accepted, it would still be difficult to suppose that the event of verses 4ff. took place in both Shechem and Jerusalem; and Ps. xlviii 5–7 refers to a similar event in or near Jerusalem. The use of the words "Judah" and "Israel" in Ps. lxxvi 2 does not tell against this interpretation of the psalm. "Israel" is probably used, not in the sense of North Israel as opposed to Judah, but in the broader sense of the land or people as a whole. The arguments brought against Mackay also tell against Horton's theory (pp. 49–50) that there may be a chiasmus in Ps. lxxvi 2–3, in which Judah corresponds to Zion and Israel to Salem. The identification of Salem with Zion in Ps. lxxvi 3 is thus securely established.

Mackay's way of dealing with Ps. cx is dependent on his unconvincing interpretation of Ps. lxxvi. After referring to Ps. cx, "wherein Zion is the royal seat of the Melchizedek priest", he says: "This raises the same question as Ps. lxxvi : if in Shalem is his 'place' (LXX), in Zion his seat, must sanctuary and throne be identical?" (p. 123). His reference to "place" in the LXX shows that in that part of the sentence he is still referring to Ps. lxxvi, but presumably the "throne" is meant to refer to the "royal seat" in Ps. cx. He appears to mean that the sanctuary in Salem is different from the site of Melchizedek's throne. He then mentions his theory that Ezekiel places the temple of the future in Shechem, and his further argument states explicitly that Shechem was the site of Melchizedek's sanctuary. It thus seems that he holds that Melchizedek's sanctuary was at Shechem, but that he reigned in Zion. If that is what he means, then it is indeed a strange argument. Gen. xiv 18 says that Melchizedek was "king of Salem", and the natural implication of those words is that he reigned in Salem. If, however, his "royal seat" was in Zion, then Salem should be identified with Zion – the very interpretation that Mackay is trying to avoid.

Gammie wisely does not try to explain away the meaning of Ps. lxxvi and Ps. cx. He asserts, rather, that "the use of Salem does not appear to be old" (p. 389). He has certainly shown that Jerusalem

---

[9] The suggestion is made by C.A. Briggs and E.G. Briggs, *A Critical and Exegetical Commentary on the Book of Psalms* II (Edinburgh, 1907), pp. 165, 168–9, that *šammâ* should be emended to *šîmâ* and attached to verse 3: "And His lair was (put) in Zion". Similarly, T.W. Davies, *The Psalms* II (Edinburgh and London, 1906), pp. 56–7, reads "He set it" (presumably *śāmāh*) and attaches it to verse 3. The emendation is made for the sake of metre to give verses 3 and 4 six words each (apart from "Selah"). Emendations solely for the sake of metre are, however, suspect, and there are other verses in this psalm that do not suit a theory of strict metrical regularity. Further, the presence of *šām* in Ps. xlviii 7 supports the M.T. in Ps. lxxvi 3.

was known by the full form of the name in ancient times and that that
form is attested before the composition of Ps. lxxvi. He has not,
however, shown that the abbreviated form "Salem" was impossible
when Gen. xiv 18 was written – whenever that may have been – or
that the usage in Ps. lxxvi 3 must be later than that verse. To show
that the full form was used in ancient times does not prove that an
abbreviated form could not have been used in Gen. xiv 18, or that the
shorter form was later than the account of Abram's meeting with
Melchizedek.

Kirkland seeks (p. 7) to counter the evidence of Ps. lxxvi 3 by
referring to the claim of R.H. Smith (p. 141) that it "was not
customary for the Canaanites or Hebrews to shorten a compound
name by dropping the first element of the compound". He says on p.
20, with reference to p. 413 of my article in 1971: "Emerton's
objection [to Smith's claim] . . . is baseless, since he cannot explain
the abbreviation of the specific place-name, 'Jerusalem'". He
strangely makes no mention of my appeal to the evidence that Pss
lxxvi and cx, "whenever they are dated, appear to imply an
identification of Salem with Jerusalem". He thus appears to rule out
something that is clearly found in Ps. lxxvi. Further, his surprising
statement that I "cannot explain the abbreviation" overlooks my
challenge to Smith's "general statement about compound names".
I referred to Y. Aharoni, *The Land of the Bible* (London, 1966), p. 97,
to which may now be added a reference to pp. 108–9 of the second
edition (1979). Aharoni cites a number of examples of the abbreviation
of place-names, to which some further examples may be added. Josh.
xiii 17 refers to Beth-baal-meon (cf. *bt b*ᶜ*lm*ᶜ*n* in lines 9 and 30 of the
Moabite Stone), but Num. xxxii 38; Ezek. xxv 9; 1 Chron. v 8 omit
"Beth", and Jer. xlviii 3 omits "baal". Similarly, Beth-rehob appears
in Judg. xviii 28; 2 Sam. x 6, but Rehob in Num. xiii 21. "Beth" was
not the only element that might be omitted. Abel-shittim in Num.
xxxiii 49 corresponds to Shittim in Num. xxv 1; Josh. ii 1, iii 1; Mic. vi
5. Kiriath-jearim is found in 1 Sam. vi 21, vii 1–2, etc., but Jaar in Ps.
cxxxii 6; another name for the same place was Kiriath-baal in Josh. xv
60, xviii 14, but Baalah in Josh. xv 9–10. It is also possible that
En-tappuah in Josh. xxii 7 is the same place as Tappuah in Josh. xii
17, xvi 8, xvii 8. There is nothing surprising about the abbreviation of
Jerusalem (perhaps meaning "foundation of Shalem") to Salem in
Ps. lxxvi 3, and the argument against its possibility in Gen. xiv 18 has
failed.

The second argument against the identification of Melchizedek's
city with Jerusalem is advanced by Gammie, who notes that in Gen.
xiv 18 Melchizedek "brought forth bread and wine", and comments:

"Wine did not play a prominent part in the liturgy and worship of
Jerusalem" (p. 390). It was used there, "but only in a minor and
subordinate way". In contrast, Judg. ix 27 tells how the people of
Shechem gathered and trod grapes and held a festival (*hillûlîm*), and
ate and drank in the temple of their god (p. 392). Thus, he believes,
the mention of wine in Gen. xiv 18 tells both against the identification
of Salem with Jerusalem and in favour of its identification with
Shechem. Gammie's argument is unconvincing. Melchizedek, who
brought out bread and wine, is said to have been a priest, but that
need not have any bearing on the prominence of the place of wine in
the Jerusalem cult performed either by Melchizedek or by Israelites
after the temple had been built. We are not told in Gen. xiv 18–20
that bread and wine were used in a cultic ceremony, and there is no
mention of a festival like the one in Judg. ix 27. Gen. xiv 18 may mean
no more than that Melchizedek welcomed Abram with appropriate
refreshment, just as the supplies brought by Ziba to David, when he
was fleeing from Absalom, included bread and wine to refresh
David's men (2 Sam. xvi 1–8).

The third argument, which is also put forward by Gammie, is that
"None of the personal names which emanate from Jerusalem indicate
that El ᶜElyon, the deity of Melchizedek, was worshipped there" (p.
389). Gammie's statement is true, but its value as evidence for the
identification of Salem is negligible. We know too little of the names of
people who lived in Jerusalem before David captured the city to be
able to say whether or not personal names were compounded with the
divine name El Elyon. Moreover, Elyon was certainly used as an
epithet of Yahweh in Israelite times, and yet the personal names do
not reflect the fact. Further, Gammie seems to have overlooked the
fact that, if his argument were valid against the identification of
Salem with Jerusalem, it would be no less valid against his own
attempt to connect it with Shechem – and that is not altered by his
argument, which is none too strong in any case, to associate El Elyon
with Shiloh.

Mackay, however, argues that there is a connection between El
Elyon and Shechem (p. 127), and it is convenient to consider his
argument here, although it belongs more strictly to the arguments
advanced for identifying Salem with Shechem, which will be
discussed later. Kirkland grants that Mackay's "argument may not
be compelling", but thinks it is "at least as good as the argument"
that El Elyon was worshipped in Jerusalem (p. 9), and so he appears
to attach some value to it. Mackay advances two arguments. The first
is based on the reference to Ἐλιοῦν καλούμενος Ὕψιστος by Philo of
Byblos as reported by Eusebius of Caesarea, *Praeparatio Evangelica*, I.

10. 14 (p. 46). The same passage refers to a female called βηρούθ, whom Mackay understands to have been Elioun's bride, and he relates her name to the Hebrew word for "covenant" that appears in the name of Baal-berith or El-berith, the god worshipped in Shechem (Judg. viii 37, ix 4, 46). This argument is worthless, for the Hebrew word for "covenant" (*b'rît*) has different vowels. Moreover, the passage cited by Eusebius says that she lived near Byblos (περὶ βύβλον), not Shechem. The second argument advanced by Mackay is that a temple to Zeus Hupsistos stood on Mount Gerizim, the ὄρος ὑψίστου, in Roman times, and that "the underworld bride of Adonis [whom he identifies with Elioun], Kore or Persephone, personification of the wheat, was still honoured at Shechem". The reference to Mount Gerizim is taken from *Praep. Evang.*, IX.17.5 (p. 451), but this is the passage derived from Eupolemus, which was noted above in section I, and which probably represents a Samaritan tradition of the 2nd century B.C. (incidentally, before Roman times). It is no surprise that the Samaritans claimed that Melchizedek's city was in their territory. Mackay's reference to Kore is supported by an appeal in a footnote to an article by A. Lods in H.W. Robinson (ed.), *Record and Revelation* (Oxford, 1938), p. 213. Lods says "Epiphanius informs us that in his day 'the daughter of Jephthah was honoured at Sichem in Palestine, by the name of Core, the equivalent of Proserpine'", and he refers to "*Panarion, Haer.* 55 and 78". The words apparently cited by Lods are an inaccurate reproduction of Epiphanius, 78.21.6 (p. 473), and the words "in Palestine" and "the equivalent of Proserpine" are not in the original; nor are they found in 55.1.10 (p. 325), the other reference to Jephthah's daughter. Mackay's identification of Elyon with Adonis leads him to infer that the goddess who was his bride was honoured at Shechem because of her identification with Jephthah's daughter. When ancient writers identified different mythical, legendary or biblical people with one another, it is of questionable legitimacy to use such identifications as evidence for further identifications that are not attested in the source. Epiphanius says nothing about Elyon being the husband of Jephthah's daughter (who was, in any case, unmarried) or of any association of him with Shechem.

The fourth argument, which is presented by Kirkland on p. 5, is directed not so much against the identification of Salem with Jerusalem as against the use of Josephus, the Targums, the Genesis Apocryphon, and "texts from the psalms" – presumably Pss lxxvi and cx. Kirkland argues: "Since a pre-Davidic tradition is generally admitted for the passage, how can one logically perform an exegesis of it by reference to texts which only saw their birth in the Davidic era or later?" Let us leave on one side the question whether it is really "generally admitted" that there was "a pre-Davidic tradition". It is difficult to see Kirkland's objection. The argument for an identification of Salem with Jerusalem is that, at least in later times – though Pss lxxvi and cx may not be much, if at all, later than Gen. xiv 18 – Jerusalem was called Salem. Of course, that does not prove that Salem in Gen. xiv 18 was Jerusalem, but it is early evidence that that is how it was understood, and that is part of the evidence available to us when we attempt to identify the place. Kirkland's argument is the more surprising because on pp. 8–9 and 21 he treats as evidence the books of Judith and Jubilees, texts cited by Eusebius of Caesarea, and the name of the modern village of Sālim, which are all later than Gen. xiv 18 and also than Pss lxxvi and cx.

The fifth argument, which Mackay puts forward on p. 124, concerns Gen. xiv 17 which, as we have seen, may be relevant to the location of Salem, even though verses 18–20 are an interpolation. The "case of Shechem . . . can also urge that the King's Vale ($^c\bar{e}meq$) must be a broad, open valley, not a ravine like the Kidron Valley, while the vale of Shaveh ('Plain') suggests the Shechem valley leading from the Plains of Salim and of Makhneh, which meet at right angles at its mouth". We may reject his further argument that Ezek. xvi 5 leaves "no place for Melchizedek" in Jerusalem, for the prophet is not attempting to give a sober and complete account of the traditions of the history of Jerusalem. Mackay's main argument is directed only against the theory that the King's Vale is the Kidron Valley, which is not the view held by everyone who identifies Salem with Jerusalem (see Schatz, p. 186). Moreover, the precise range of meanings of $š\bar{a}w\bar{e}h$ (which appears elsewhere in the Old Testament only in Gen. xiv 5) and $^c\bar{e}meq$ (from a root "to be deep") is uncertain.

Finally, for the sake of completeness, brief mention should be made of Jerome's opinion that Jerusalem was not on Abram's route. There was a road running from north to south along the mountain ridge – see Y. Aharoni, *The Land of the Bible* (2nd edn, London, 1979), pp. 44, 57 – and Judg. xix 11 shows that the road from Bethlehem to the hill country of Ephraim passed near Jerusalem.

The arguments against the identification of Salem with Jerusalem thus break down. It is still necessary, however, to assess the strength of the positive cases in favour of both Shechem and Jerusalem.

IV

In discussing the case for linking the Salem of Melchizedek with Shechem, it is important to bear in mind the three ways of interpreting the connection. First, Shechem and Salem may be understood as different names of the same city. That, as we have seen, was the view of Eusebius of Caesarea and the person who prepared the Madaba map. Second, Salem may have been a place near but distinct from Shechem, as in Jubilees xxx 1, Eusebius of Emesa, and probably Epiphanius, and this view can be related to the existence of the modern village of Sālim and its probable ancient site nearby. Third, there is Gammie's suggestion that Salem was originally the name of a valley; but we have seen that the theory lacks support and is also incompatible with Gammie's understanding of Gen. xxxiii 18. Only the first two views will be considered in the following discussion. As was noted above, the association by the Samaritans of Salem with the region of Mount Gerizim was only to be expected, for they would not have wished Abram to have had friendly dealings with a king of Jerusalem, the site of what was to become the rival temple in Judah. On the other hand, their claim should not be rejected solely on that ground, and the Jews similarly had a vested interest in claiming that Melchizedek's city was Jerusalem.

Before we consider the principal arguments, it will be convenient to dispose of several minor arguments, some of them eccentric. Winckler presents some strange examples of biblical interpretation. The fact that Gen. xiv 13 uses of Abram's "allies" the phrase $ba^c\check{a}l\hat{e}\ b^er\hat{\imath}t$ is said to contain a play on the Shechemite cult of Baal-berith (p. 407). This is far from self-evident. One can only describe as far-fetched his view that the altar that Gideon called $yhwh\ \check{s}al\hat{o}m$ in Judg. vi 24 was originally named Baal-shalem, in which "Yahweh" has been "natür-lich" substituted for "Baal" (p. 441). Similarly, when in Gen. xxxiv 21 Hamor and his son Shechem say of Jacob and his sons that "These men are peaceable ($\check{s}^el\bar{e}m\hat{\imath}m$) with us", Winckler thinks it means that they "will become Salemites with us" (p. 442); and when Gen. xxxvii 4 says that Joseph's brothers "could not speak peaceably ($l^e\check{s}al\hat{o}m$) to him", Winckler sees here a "motivwort des Sichemmythus" (p. 448). Such unconvincing interpretations of the text lead Winckler to believe that Salem in Gen. xiv 18 is Shechem, as in xxxiii 18 (pp. 408, 441). Erbt's way of arguing is no less eccentric. He mentions that Mamre, Eshcol and Aner (Gen. xiv 13) were not only three Amorite tribes, but tribes in the north of the country, and he argues from a comparison of 1 Chron. vi 55 with Josh. xxi 25 that Aner was the city in the north later known as Taanach. Melchizedek, he believes, was "the Amorite who dwelt in Hazazon-tamar" (Gen. xiv 7), the town that was the centre of the Shechem covenant. Only later was the scene moved to Judah (p. 73). Less far-fetched is Landersdorfer's argument (p. 206) that Melchizedek "brought out" bread and wine because Shechem's shrine lay outside, though near, the city. Although there was certainly a temple within Shechem, there may also have been a shrine outside, as some scholars have supposed. But there is nothing in Gen. xiv 18–20 to suggest that Melchizedek was on his way to a shrine when he came to meet Abram with bread and wine. None of the arguments considered in this paragraph has any force.

Two arguments concern Gen. xiv 17, where the king of Sodom meets Abram in the Vale of Shaveh, otherwise known as the King's Vale. First, Stanley (pp. 247–8) bases an argument on the mention of the King's Vale in 2 Sam. xviii 18, which says that Absalom had set up a pillar there in his lifetime. Against the statement of Josephus that this was two stadia from Jerusalem (Ant. VII, § 243), he maintains that the pillar was on the eastern side of the Jordan valley, "where the death of Absalom occurred, and where it could therefore be mentioned as a singular coincidence that he had erected his monument near the scene of his end". Yet, quite apart from the question whether a meeting between Abram and the king of Sodom east of the Jordan would offer support to the theory of a meeting with Melchizedek at Gerizim west of the Jordan, there is nothing in 2 Sam. xviii 18 to suggest that Absalom's pillar was near the place of his death. Secondly, Landersdorfer (pp. 205–6) notes that the meeting between Abram and the king of Sodom is said to have taken place after the former's return (ʾaḥărê šûbô) from the defeat of the eastern kings. Abram had not yet reached Hebron, from which he had set out, and he cannot be said to have returned to Jerusalem because, as far as is known, he had never had anything to do with it. But, argues Landersdorfer, he could have returned to Shechem, because Gen. xii 6 records that he had already been there. The argument is unconvincing. The passage is compatible with an identification of Jerusalem with Salem, from which Melchizedek came out to meet Abram. Abram was on his way back from the battle when the king of Sodom met him in the Vale of Shaveh: he had returned thus far on his way to Hebron. It is not necessarily implied that he had visited Jerusalem before, but only that he had returned thus far from his action in the north. In any case, if he came back by the same route by which he had travelled north, he must have been before at the same place in the Vale of Shaveh. Thus these two arguments based on Gen. xiv 17 break down, even apart from the question how far the verse can be said to determine the geography of the interpolation in verses 18–20.

A more important argument in favour of associating Melchizedek's Salem with Shechem, rather than with Jerusalem, concerns the relative importance of the two cities in the stories of the patriarchs. We have already seen that Landersdorfer points out (p. 206) that we are told nowhere else that Abram had anything to do with Jerusalem. Further (p. 208), Jerusalem plays no part at all in the patriarchal stories and, as far as we know, had no sanctuary until the time of

David (a dubious argument from silence). In contrast, Abram is said in Gen. xii 6–7 to have visited "the place of Shechem" (*mᵉqôm šᵉkem*), which Landersdorfer understands (p. 205) to have been a sanctuary outside the city, where Yahweh appeared to Abram, and he built an altar to Yahweh. Later, Jacob too built an altar there (Gen. xxxiii 20). There is other evidence for the importance of Shechem in early Israel (e.g. Deut. xi 29, xxviii 11; Josh. viii 33; 1 Kings xii; cf. Landersdorfer, p. 210). Shechem is thus more likely to have been the place of Melchizedek's city. Similarly, Gammie argues from Gen. xiv 18–20 and Melchizedek's blessing of Abram that "it is apparent that Abram was in direct contact with Melchizedek, and therefore, of course, with the domain in which Melchizedek governed"; and he notes that, according to Gen. xii 6, "Shechem is the first place in Canaan at which Abram stopped" (p. 392). He also notes that "Archaeological excavation has shown that Shechem was inhabited during the Middle Bronze Period (1900–1550 B.C.)", and that "nothing stands in the way of a probable contact between Abram and Melchizedek at Shechem some time during this period" (p. 393). Kirkland (p. 10) quotes Landersdorfer (p. 205), and endorses his arguments. He also challenges my claim in 1971 (p. 413) that the identification of Salem with Jerusalem is supported by "the inherent probability that Melchizedek's city was a place of some importance, rather than one of the minor sites with which some have identified it". He asks "what evidence is there that Jerusalem was more important than other second millennium cities?" (p. 7). While I regard the problem as one that primarily concerns a Hebrew document of the 1st millennium B.C., I must grant that the phrase "minor sites" was ill-chosen and inappropriate as far as Shechem is concerned, though it would apply to a smaller place such as the probable site of the ancient settlement corresponding to the modern village of Sālim or the site near Beth-shean.

What is to be said about the argument based on the fact that Jerusalem appears nowhere else in the patriarchal stories (unless it is thought to be the site of Mouth Moriah in Gen. xxii), whereas Shechem is mentioned several times and was important in early Israel? Gen. xiv is generally recognized to be different from the other narratives about Abram and the other patriarchs. The story of Abram's military success against the eastern kings has often been contrasted with the other stories (whatever may lie behind Gen. xlviii 22), and the chapter belongs to none of the major sources into which the Pentateuch has been analysed. Further, its incorporation into Genesis can scarcely be dated (except by very conservative scholars) before the Davidic monarchy (and some would date it several

centuries later), and the reference to Melchizedek in verses 18–20 is
an interpolation. Nor can the view of a number of scholars that these
verses were introduced precisely to serve the purposes of the Davidic
monarchy be dismissed as absurd. They may be rejected, but they
must be taken seriously. On such an hypothesis, the reason advanced
for preferring Shechem to Jerusalem as the site of Salem disappears.
The recognition of the unique character of Gen. xiv and the
hypothesis that verses 18–20 were intended to serve the purposes of
the Davidic monarchy do not prove that Salem was Jerusalem, not
Shechem, but they deprive of force the argument for the latter city
that is being discussed here.

    Another major argument is based on Gen. xxxiii 18. If this verse
refers to a city called Salem, which is either to be identified with
Shechem or was near it, then the patriarchal narrative itself knows of
a Salem that was not Jerusalem. The interpretation of this verse and
its implications is a matter of such importance that the whole of the
next section of this article will be devoted to it.

                                   V

    Before discussing the significance of Gen. xxxiii 18, it is necessary to
consider the translation of the words *wayyābōʾ yaʿăqōb šālēm ʿîr šᵉkem*).
The text of the *R.V.* has "And Jacob came in peace to the city of
Shechem", and that way of understanding the Hebrew is followed by
some other modern translations. The *R.S.V.* and *New English Bible*
have "safely" in place of "in peace", and the reference is probably
taken to be to Jacob's safe escape from Esau earlier in the chapter.
Nielsen offers a different explanation. He compares the use of the
same adjective (*šᵉlēmîm*) in Gen. xxxiv 21, where he renders it
"peace-minded", and suggests that it has the same meaning here. In
contrast to the violent events in the following chapter, "Jacob arrived
at Shechem without any bad intentions. A crime was committed by
the natives. *He* did not prepare any revenge. On the contrary, he
reproached his sons for their violent action" (p. 224). The former
interpretation seems to me to be more likely, but both views
understand *šālēm* to be an adjective, not a place-name. Gammie
objects to such an understanding of the word, and says that its use "in
such a manner is . . . without analogy. If the writer intended to convey
that Jacob arrived 'in good condition' or 'peace-minded,' the more
natural way to have expressed it would have been to use the term
adverbially, *bᵉšālôm* (cf. Gen. 26:19)" (p. 391). He notes that some
wish to emend the verse to obtain such a reading, but he objects that
"whenever the location (to which or from which the motion is

directed) is given, the adverb follows and generally does not precede
the location mentioned" – though he weakens the force of his own
argument by admitting that there are exceptions. When Gammie
writes "without analogy" he may be thinking of this particular
adjective, for the use of an adjective "expressing *state*, placed after the
verb" (G.K. § 118 *n*) is well attested in Hebrew, and Gammie's
objection cannot be sustained. Further, Gammie's comments on
word order are concerned with the use of a noun preceded by
a preposition, and it is not clear whether he would advance it against
the use of an adjective if he were brought to admit that the use of an
adjective in this verse is in order. Anyhow, it is worth noting that the
adjective precedes the location in Gen. xxxvii 35; Num. xvi 30, and
Job i 21. Kirkland (p. 8) offers no grammatical objection, but tells us
that Nyberg called the translation of the word as an adjective
"unallowable and little more than a falsification of the text". In fact,
the German words of Nyberg (p. 357) that are translated by Kirkland
refer to an emendation of the text, not to the translation of the
adjective as "in Frieden", but Nyberg does say that the Hebrew
cannot be translated other than as "Und Jakob kam nach Šālēm, der
Stadt Sichems", and regards the alternative rendering as a modern
watering down ("eine moderne Verwässerung") – although it is no
more modern that the Targums, and we have seen that it is in keeping
with Hebrew idiom. Kirkland also asks what the point of "safely"
would have been: "There does not seem to have been any danger
lurking which Jacob might be conceived as having escaped." He
appears to have overlooked the danger that Jacob had feared from
Esau, and he does not consider Nielsen's interpretation, even though
he refers to Nielsen three lines below. We may conclude that the way
of understanding the Hebrew grammar implied by the *R.V.* text is
possible, and that the objections that have been brought against it
have failed.

The *R.V.* margin understands the words differently: "And Jacob
came to Shalem, a city of Shechem", and we have seen that the
ancient versions other than the Targums take the verse to refer to
a place named Salem. Gammie and Kirkland accept this way of
understanding the text, and so does Nyberg except that he takes
"city" to be definite: "the city of Shechem". Nouns in the construct
state before a determinate noun, such as a proper noun, are usually
definite, but there are some exceptions (G.K. § 127 *e*). Either "a city"
or "the city" is possible. We must, however, ask whether both
possibilities are equally suitable in the context. If the noun is
indefinite, what does it mean? Does it mean a city belonging to
Shechem, or in the region of Shechem? The difficulty is, as Skinner

points out, that there is "no case of a village described as a 'city' of the neighbouring town" (p. 416). While what is unique is not necessarily impossible, such an understanding of Gen. xxxiii 18 seems unlikely. If, however, the word "city" is translated as a definite noun, then the construct relationship may express nearer definition (G.K. § 128 *k*), and Salem may be identified with Shechem. The alternative explanation that has been offered is that Shechem is here used as a personal name, as it is in Gen. xxxiv where Shechem is the father of Hamor and the city is never named. On this view, Gen. xxxiii 18 speaks of the city belonging to Shechem the father of Hamor (cf. "the city of David") and the verse is worded as it is to serve as part of the introduction to the story in the next chapter. It is true, as Nielsen points out (p. 223), that the LXX, which understands the verse to refer to a place called Salem, does not understand Shechem here to be a personal name (for it transcribes the name differently in ch. xxxiv), but that does not prove that the Hebrew was not intended to be understood thus. Incidentally, the view that the verse uses Shechem as a personal name is also compatible with the view that *šālēm* is here an adjective.

One way of understanding Gen. xxxiii 18 is thus that it says (or implies, if Shechem is here used as a personal name) that Salem was another name for the city of Shechem. The name would then have been transferred at some stage in its history to the village that still exists as Sālim (so Landersdorfer, p. 204; Kirkland, pp. 9, 20–1, n. 42), although there is a distance of five kilometres between the two sites.

There are, however, two difficulties. First, the existence of the village of Sālim is not the only evidence for a Salem near, but distinct from, Shechem. Jubilees xxx 1 distinguishes the sites, as does the tradition recorded by Eusebius of Emesa and Epiphanius some centuries later. Further, if the LXX of Jer. xlviii 5 (M.T. xli 5) is evidence for a Salem near Shechem, it is also evidence for a distinction between the two, because it mentions them as separate places. Landersdorfer cautiously mentions this verse in a footnote (p. 204, n. 5) to his presentation of the theory that the name of Salem was transferred from Shechem to another place. If, however, it has any value as evidence – and it is difficult to attach great value to a textual variant like this – it shows that there was a distinction between the two places in ancient times. The final destruction of Shechem did not take place until the late 2nd century B.C. (Wright, p. 368), and so it was probably still in existence when Jubilees was written, and very likely when the LXX version of Jeremiah was made. Why should Shechem's other name have been transferred to another place while Shechem itself was still standing?

The second difficulty is that Shechem is nowhere else called Salem. It is strange that those who argue that Jerusalem was not known as Salem in ancient times but had its full name fail to see that a similar problem arises for their identification of Salem with Shechem. Landersdorfer suggests (pp. 204–5) that Salem was an older name for Shechem. But, as Kirkland points out in arguing for an early date for Shechem in contrast to the lack of early attestation for the use of Salem for Jerusalem (p. 9; cf. p. 20, n. 41), Shechem is mentioned by name in an Egyptian execration text from the 19th or 20th century B.C. (cf. *ANET*, pp. 328–9). It is, of course, also mentioned in the Tell el-Amarna tablets from the 14th century B.C., where it appears as *ša-ak-mi*; see J.A. Knudtzon, *Die El-Amarna-Tafeln* (Leipzig, 1915), p. 1580. The problem is, in fact, far more serious for the champions of Shechem than it is for an identification of Salem with Jerusalem. Salem can be plausibly explained as a shortened form of Jerusalem as it is in the Psalter. It cannot be so related to Shechem. Shechem is mentioned a number of times in connection with the early history of Israel, as the champions of an identification of it with Salem stress, but nowhere outside Gen. xxxiii 18 is it called Salem, and we have seen that the evidence for it in that verse is at best ambiguous. The very fact of the importance of Shechem would lead us to expect an unambiguous identification of it with Salem somewhere in Genesis, if they were really two names for the same place. One might have expected, for example, the words *hw³ škm*, "that is, Shechem", after the mention of Salem in Gen. xiv 18. The lack of firm biblical evidence for the identification of Salem with Shechem is itself a reason for doubting it.

We turn now to the possibility that there was in ancient times a town called Salem near Shechem but distinct from it, probably at Khirbet esh-Sheikh Naṣrallah near the modern Sālim, as Alt believed. We have seen that is unlikely, though not perhaps impossible, that Gen. xxxiii 18 refers to it as "Salem [in the region of] the city of Shechem" (whether Shechem is a place-name or a personal name). Whether or not there is a reference to it there, the evidence of Jubilees xxx 1 of the tradition recorded by Eusebius of Emesa and Epiphanius attests its existence, and the reference to "the valley of Salem" in Judith iv 4 bears witness to a place called Salem in the region. When that evidence is combined with the existence of the village of Sālim, the case is further strengthened. While it would be unwise to attach much importance to Jer. xlviii 5 in the LXX, it may reflect knowledge of a Salem distinct from Shechem, and it is possible that the existence of this Salem influenced the LXX translation of Gen. xxxiii 18.

At first sight, the evidence of Eusebius of Caesarea and the Madaba map appears to tell against the existence of a Salem distinct from Shechem in their times, for they both record Salem as another name for Shechem. Yet it may be doubted whether Salem was really current as an alternative name for Shechem (then in ruins) in the time of Eusebius, unless it was a view that was itself derived from the LXX of Gen. xxxiii 18. Eusebius's entry on Salem in the *Onomasticon* begins with the words Σαλήμ, πόλις Σικίμων, ἥτις ἐστὶ Συχέμ, ὡς φησιν ἡ γραφή (p. 152). The mention of Scripture shows that Eusebius has in mind a passage in the Old Testament, and his first few words reproduce the LXX of Gen. xxxiii 18, apart from the difference of case ending: (εἰς) Σαλὴμ πόλιν Σικίμων. His words saying that Salem was an alternative name for Shechem are thus derived from the LXX. On the other hand, if there was a place nearby called Salem, it was not necessary for him to mention the fact, for he was concerned with identifying places mentioned in the Bible, and Gen. xxxiii 18 appeared to make Shechem the only candidate for identifying with Salem in the immediate region. Nor is the Madaba map to be regarded as independent evidence, for its reference to the Shechem that was also Salem reproduces verbatim what Eusebius says in his entry on Sychem (p. 150).

If there was a place named Salem near Shechem in ancient times, is it plausible to identify it with Melchizedek's city? As was noted above, I maintained in 1971 (p. 413) that is was inherently probable that "Melchizedek's city was of some importance". While Kirkland (pp. 7–8, 20, n. 31) agrees that it could not have been a small village, he suggests that it may have been a religious, rather than a political, centre. The mention of it in Genesis may be due to "Melchizedek's personal prestige" rather than to its importance as a city. We are, of course, in an area where one has to weigh probabilities rather than deal with certainties. But it still seems to me more likely that Gen. xiv 18–20 would have associated Abram with a king whose city was of some importance for the narrator. That would fit Shechem, though we have seen that there are serious objections to such a view. Would it also fit a Salem near Shechem? In 1903 Barnabé asked how Salem, the royal city of the priest of the Most High God, could have been no more than a town of the Shechemites at the time of his grandson Jacob (p. 55). His objection is related to a particular interpretation of Gen. xxxiii 18, but the question he raises about the significance of the Salem near Shechem has a wider validity.

Alt (p. 53) maintained that Salem's rise was related to the decline of Shechem, and Wächter builds on this suggestion (especially on pp. 63, 69–70). Further, he is able to report the results of a study of the site of Khirbet esh-Sheikh Naṣrallah in 1965 and 1967. No traces of a settlement in the Bronze Age were found, but some evidence for the

10th–9th and 6th centuries B.C. The settlement expanded in the 6th century A.D., and the beginnings of the village of Sālim are dated by him in late Byzantine times (pp. 65–9). He argues that, as long as the power of Shechem as a city remained unbroken, the whole plain east of it was controlled by this city-state, and it would have hindered the rise of any centre of settlement in the region. Shechem took a long time to recover from the destruction in the 12th century B.C. (probably by Abimelech), and there was a power-vacuum until the 10th century. Even after the city had been rebuilt, it was soon to be destroyed again in 918 B.C. by Shishak. Wächter suggests that the settlement on the site of Khirbet esh-Sheikh Naṣrallah began in Shechem's period of weakness either before its rebuilding in the early 4th century or after its destruction in 918. After that, Shechem was never strong enough to prevent the continuation of the settlement, although it may have tended to flourish most when Shechem was weak. He admits the hypothetical element in his historical reconstruction (p. 70), but it is plausible and well argued, and it is based on a correlation of archaeological evidence with other considerations. Kirkland's objection (pp. 20–1, n. 42) to Wächter's argument depends on his own identification of Salem with Shechem.

If Wächter's historical reconstruction is correct, the Salem near Shechem cannot be identified with Melchizedek's Salem. It is not just that the former does not seem to have existed in the Bronze Age, for we cannot be sure that Gen. xiv 18–20 is to be dated so early. It is rather that the site seems an unlikely setting for the story in the period of the Israelite monarchy or later. Why should a writer, whether in the period of the United Monarchy or later, have regarded so unimportant a place as the seat of Melchizedek? Melchizedek would have appeared more like a village priest than a king whose blessing would honour Abram and whose deity would be identified with Yahweh.

It is thus unlikely that Gen. xxxiii 18 can be regarded as good evidence that Salem was another name for Shechem, or even that the Hebrew text refers to a Salem nearby. It is more likely that šālēm is here an adjective. There is other evidence for the existence of a Salem five kilometres from Shechem, but it is unlikely to have been the Salem of Gen. xiv 18.

VI

We have seen that, although there were several places called Salem in ancient Palestine, only two are serious contenders for identification with Melchizedek's city: Jerusalem, and Shechem or a site near Shechem. We have also seen that the arguments brought against

Jerusalem are unconvincing, and that there are difficulties in the view
that Melchizedek's Salem was either Shechem or the Salem five
kilometres away. That leaves Jerusalem as the strongest candidate by
process of elimination. There are, however, positive arguments that
can be advanced in its favour.

The first argument, which is the least strong, is that the King's
Vale, which is mentioned in Gen. xiv 17, is said by Josephus to have
been near Jerusalem. The reasons for caution are that Josephus's
evidence is late, that "the King's Vale" may be a gloss in Gen. xiv 17,
and that verses 18–20 were inserted into the text and may not concern
precisely the same location as verse 17. This evidence is therefore far
from conclusive, and yet it is not negligible.

Secondly, Ps. lxxvi 3 testifies directly that Jerusalem was also
known as Salem, and Ps. cx implies that Jerusalem was believed to be
Melchizedek's city. While the possibility that these verses are based
on a misunderstanding or tendentious reinterpretation of the tradition
about Melchizedek cannot be disproved, at least they show how the
passage was understood at an early date. Salem was thus, in fact,
taken to be a shortened form of Jerusalem in accordance with
a practice of abbreviation that is attested for other place-names. The
onus of proof is on those who reject the testimony of these passages,
and it has been seen that a convincing case against the identification
of Jerusalem with Melchizedek's Salem has not been advanced.

Thirdly, in seeking to make sense of passages in the Old Testament
we must ask why they were written and what purpose they served.
Several scholars have suggested ways in which the passage about
Melchizedek would have served the needs of the Davidic monarchy,
and the interpretation that I offered in 1971 was along such lines.
Such an interpretation, it may be claimed, makes sense of the passage
and of its incorporation into the story in Gen. xiv. It does not of itself
prove that Melchizedek's Salem was Jerusalem, but it offers a plausible
setting for the understanding of Salem in Pss lxxvi and cx and for the
origin of the account of the meeting between Abram and Melchizedek.
If another theory is to be more convincing, it needs to suggest a better
setting.

The view that Melchizedek's Salem in Gen. xiv 18 was Jerusalem
remains the most probable interpretation of the available evidence.

List of publications cited in abbreviated form

ANET = J.B. Pritchard (ed.), *Ancient Near Eastern Texts Relating to the Old Testament*
    (Princeton, 1950).
F.M. Abel, *Géographie de la Palestine* II (3rd edn, Paris, 1967).
W.F. Albright, "Some Observations Favoring the Palestinian Origin of the Gospel of
    John", *Harvard Theological Review* 17 (1924), pp. 189–95.

—, "Recent discoveries in Palestine and the Gospel of St John", in W.D. Davies and D. Daube (ed.), *The Background of the New Testament and its Eschatology* (Cambridge, 1956), pp. 153–71.

A. Alt, "Das Institut im Jahre 1928", *Palästinajahrbuch* 25 (1929), pp. 5–59.

Le Père Barnabé, d'Alsace, O.F.M. (his surname is not recorded in the book, but it was Meistermann according to the catalogue of the Cambridge University Library), *Questions de topographie palestinienne: le lieu de la rencontre d'Abraham et de Melchisédech* (Jerusalem, 1903).

J.A. Emerton, "The riddle of Genesis xiv", *Vetus Testamentus* 21 (1971), pp. 403–39.

Epiphanius: K. Holl (ed.), *Epiphanius (Ancoratus und Panarion)* II: *Panarion Haer. 34–64*, Die griechischen christlichen Schriftsteller der ersten drei Jahrhunderte (Leipzig, 1922), and III: *Panarion Haer. 65–80* (1933).

W. Erbt, *Die Hebräer* (Leipzig, 1906).

Eusebius of Caesarea: E. Klostermann (ed.), *Eusebius Werke* III.1: *Das Onomastikon*, GCS (Leipzig, 1904).

K. Mras (ed.), *Eusebius Werke* VIII: *Die Praeparatio Evangelica*, 1. Teil: *Einleitung, die Bücher I bis X*, GCS (Berlin, 1954).

J.A. Fitzmyer, *The Genesis Apocryphon of Qumran Cave I* (2nd edn, Rome, 1971).

G.K. = *Gesenius' Hebrew Grammar as Edited and Enlarged by the Late E. Kautzsch* (2nd edn, Oxford, 1910 = the 28th German edn).

J.G. Gammie, "Loci of the Melchizedek Tradition of Genesis 14:18–20", *Journal of Biblical Literature* 90 (1971), pp. 385–96.

H.W. Hertzberg, "Die Melkiṣedeq-Traditionen", *Journal of the Palestine Oriental Society* 8 (1928), pp. 169–79; reprinted in Hertzberg, *Beiträge zur Traditionsgeschichte und Theologie des Alten Testaments* (Göttingen, 1962), pp. 36–44.

F.L. Horton, *The Melchizedek Tradition* (Cambridge, 1976).

A. Jeremias, *Das Alte Testament im Lichte des Alten Orients* (2nd edn, Leipzig, 1906). The part relevant to the present article appears in English translation in *The Old Testament in the Light of the Ancient East* 2 (London and New York, 1911).

Jerome: *Epistulae* in I. Hilberg (ed.), *Sancti Eusebii Hieronymi Epistulae*, I: *Epistulae I–LXX*, Corpus Scriptorum Ecclesiasticorum Latinorum, 54 (Vienna and Leipzig, 1910); II: *Epistulae LXXI-CXX*, CSEL 55 (1912); III: *Epistulae CXXI–CLIV*, CSEL 66 (1918).

Hebraicae quaestiones in libro Geneseos in P. Antin (ed.), *S. Hieronymi Presbyteri Opera*, I: *Opera exegetica*, Corpus Christianorum, Series Latina, 72 (Turnhout, 1959). *Tractatus* on Ps. 75 in G. Morin (ed.), *S. Hieronymi Presbyteri Opera*, II: *Opera homiletica*, CCSL 78 (1958).

J.R. Kirkland, "The incident at Salem: a re-examination of Genesis 14:18–20", *Studia Biblica et Theologica* 7/1 (1977), pp. 3–23.

S. Landersdorfer, "Das Priesterkönigtum von Salem", *Journal of the Society of Oriental Research* 9 (1925), pp. 203–16.

C. Mackay, "Salem", *Palestine Exploration Quarterly* (1948), pp. 121–30.

E. Nielsen, *Shechem: A Traditio-Historical Investigation* (2nd edn, Copenhagen, 1959).

H.S. Nyberg, "Studien zum Religionskampf im Alten Testament", *Archiv für Religionswissenschaft* 35 (1938), pp. 329–87.

E. Robinson, *Later Biblical Researches in Palestine and in the Adjacent Regions. A Journal of Travels in the Year 1852* (London and Berlin, 1856).

W. Schatz, *Genesis 14. Eine Untersuchung* (Bern and Frankfurt, 1972).

J. Skinner, *A Critical and Exegetical Commentary on Genesis* (2nd edn, Edinburgh, 1930).

R.H. Smith, "Abram and Melchizedek", *ZAW* 77 (1965), pp. 129–53.

A.P. Stanley, *Sinai and Palestine in Connection with their History* (2nd edn, London, 1856).

C.W.M. van de Velde, *Narrative of a Journey Through Syria and Palestine in 1851 and 1852* 2 (Edinburgh and London, 1854).

L. Wächter, "Salem bei Sichem", *Zeitschrift des Deutschen Palästina-Vereins* 84 (1968), pp. 63–72.

H. Winckler, *Altorientalische Forschungen*, III.1 (Leipzig, 1906).

G.E. Wright, "Shechem", in D.W. Thomas (ed.), *Archaeology and Old Testament Study* (Oxford, 1967), pp. 355–70.

SOME PROBLEMS IN GENESIS XIV[1]

by

J.A. EMERTON

Cambridge

In 1971 I published in *Vetus Testamentum* two articles on Gen. xiv. In the second I developed a theory about the composition of the chapter and suggested dates for the principal stages in the process. The purpose of the present article is to review the position in the light of arguments that have been advanced in support of opinions different from mine. I do not, however, intend to offer a comprehensive account of the relevant recent bibliography, for my aim is primarily to consider arguments rather than to describe all the theories that have been advanced.

Before beginning the discussion, I stress two points. The first is the familiar observation that we are dealing with what are at best probabilities, not certainties. We must weigh the arguments and seek to find the most likely conclusion. The second point is that I am discussing the literary history of the chapter, not the historicity of the events described in it.[2]

I

The theory of the composition of Gen. xiv that I put forward in 1971 saw the following elements in the story:

A.   Verses 1–9:   the campaign of the eastern kings

---

[1] A list of the principal publications relevant to this discussion of Gen. xiv will be found at the end of the article. I am grateful to Dr J. Day for making available to me a publication to which I did not have access. I am also grateful to Dr G.I. Davies and Dr H.G.M. Williamson for their comments on a draft of this article.

[2] See, for example, N.-E.A. Andreasen, "Genesis 14 in its Near Eastern Context", in C.D. Evans, W.W. Hallo and J.B. White (ed.), *Scripture in Context: Essays on the Comparative Method* (Pittsburgh, 1980), pp. 59–77.

B.	Verses *10–*11, 13a, *14–*16, 21, *22, 23:	Abram the noble hero and the king of Sodom
C.	Verses 18–20:	Abram and Melchizedek
D.	Verses 13b and 24:	Aner, Eshcol and Mamre
E.	Verse 12, parts of verses 14 and 16:	the references to Lot
F.	Glosses in verses 2 (Zoar), 3 (the Salt Sea), 7 (Kadesh), 8 (Zoar), 17 (the King's Vale)	

I suggested three main stages in the growth of the chapter. First came B, the story of Abram the noble hero. I expressed some uncertainty about the original beginning of the story (p. 434; cp. p. 437), which probably suffered some editorial change when this narrative was combined with what precedes, but verses 10–11 probably contain at least part of it. I did not mean that the story was in exactly the same words throughout as in the M.T., for there have been changes at the beginning, and also some additions, including the addition in verse 22 of a reference to El Elyon. Second came C, the account of Abram's meeting with Melchizedek. Like many other scholars, I recognized that these verses have been added to their present context, and I dated the addition in the time of David. I did not offer an opinion on the question whether they were composed for their present context or whether they once existed in a different context. Anyhow, B existed separately before C was added in the reign of David. Third, A, the story of the campaign of the eastern kings, was added later. I suggested that it was perhaps added in the same period when B and C were united, but I also allowed that A's addition might be later (pp. 436–7, 438). D, E and F represent various minor additions to the text, but they are not as important in my theory as the other parts. Finally, the chapter was added to the rest of Genesis in the Pentateuch.

At this point, it should be noted that Westermann favours a different allocation of verses to A and B: he ascribes verses 1–11 to A, and 12–17, 21–4 to B. It will be convenient in the following discussion not to distinguish between the two theories except where the difference is significant. The letters A and B will, therefore, be used in some places to refer either to Westermann's division or to mine.

II

We shall now consider some of the relevant publications that have appeared since my articles. The first, R. de Vaux's posthumous *Histoire ancienne d'Israël* (Paris, 1971), pp. 208–12 (E. tr., pp. 216–20), was written before the publication of my article (the preface is dated in June 1970). He argues that Gen. xiv contains a "mixture of early and more recent terms and of genuine and invented names", and that the mixture "can be explained by the fact that it is a late scholarly composition" (E. tr., p. 219 = p. 211). Another book that was written before the appearance of my second article is W. Schatz, *Genesis 14. Eine Untersuchung* (Bern and Frankfurt, 1972) – my first article is cited in the bibliography but not the second, and the reference was presumably added at a late stage, for the preface is dated in 1970. Schatz has worked out independently a theory similar in some ways to mine. He too finds the nucleus of the chapter in the story of Abram's victory and refusal to accept the booty as a gift from the king of Sodom. He also believes that the account of Abram's meeting with Melchizedek was added to the earlier story in the time of David. He differs from me in that he detects Deuteronomistic influence in the chapter and dates it as late as *c.* 550 B.C.

Gen. xiv is discussed in two important commentaries in German from the 1970s. W. Zimmerli, *1. Mose 12–25: Abraham* (Zürich, 1976), pp. 35–47, knows of Schatz's book (p. 35). He notes the clumsiness ("Unbeholfenheit") of the style in Gen. xiv, but does not accept a literary division of the chapter, apart from distinguishing verses 18–20 from their present context. Like de Vaux, he sees in the chapter a mixture of archaic and late expressions, of both authentic and invented names, and he thinks that the mixture is dependent on the example of analogous pseudo-historical Assyro-Babylonian texts (p. 42). Although Zimmerli does not suggest a date, his discussion of the greater part of the chapter implies that he regards it as late (e.g. the statement on p. 42 that the story presupposes the uniting of the traditions of Abraham with those of Lot, and the taking of elements of tradition from the J source and of language from P; or the statement on p. 39 that the reference in verse 7 to the Amorites of Hazazon-tamar is an archaizing naming from a late period). On the other hand, Zimmerli's discussion on pp. 43–7 of the Melchizedek episode in verses 18–20, which he regards as an insertion, notes characteristics that point to an early date. Thus, the kings of Israel and Judah once performed priestly acts (like Melchizedek), but such activity was unacceptable to later writers (2 Chron. xxvi 16ff.; cp. Ezek. xlvi), and Zimmerli notes possible links between the Davidic kingship and the earlier royal priesthood of the non-Israelite kings of Jerusalem who worshipped El Elyon. Zimmerli does not explain how the apparently early elements in verses 18–20 relate to the late narrative into which they have been inserted; nor does he account for the presence of both early and late elements in the rest of the chapter.

The fascicle of C. Westermann's commentary on Genesis that deals
with Gen. xiv was published in 1978, although the date of the
completed second volume in which it appears was 1981. It is
gratifying to me to see that he agrees with me in seeing in B (which for
him, as we have seen, is verses 12–17, 21–4) a story about Abram that
differs in character and origin from the story of the eastern kings in
A (verses 1–11). He also argues that B is a story from the period of the
judges, and that C (verses 18–20) was added in the time of David. He
goes beyond me in his discussion of verses 12–17, 21–4 because, as he
says, I did not note what transfer ("Übertragung") of a narrative of
the period of the judges to Abram involves. The transfer to Abram is
the second stage in the tradition, for the first stage did not name the
hero (p. 225 = E. tr., p. 191). In passing, I note that I wonder
whether this hypothesis of two stages is necessary. It seems to me
possible that a story characteristic of that period was told with
Abram's name in it from the beginning. Westermann regards verses
1–11 as late, and their combination with verses 12–24 as "'Schreib-
tischartig' aus der spätnachexilischer Zeit, anderen spätjüdischen
Schriften vergleichbar" (p. 227 = E. tr., p. 193).

In 1981, a modified solution to the problem was offered by J. Doré.
He accepts Westermann's theory that the story of Abram's defeat of
the enemy originated in the time of the judges, and that it was only
secondarily attached to the patriarch. But he criticizes Westermann
for failing to explain how and why it was attached to Abram's name.
That difficulty can be solved, he suggests, by finding "le 'principe' de
constitution de l'unité littéraire qui représente désormais pour nous
Gn 14" (p. 84) in the passage about Melchizedek. The defeat of the
enemy was ascribed to Abram when that story was combined with the
account of Abram's meeting with Melchizedek. The united composition was intended as an aetiology to meet the needs of the situation
that arose when David incorporated Jerusalem into his kingdom. The
story of the eastern kings in verses 1–11 was added in the period of the
Deuteronomist or later.

Further, Doré's theory differs from others in that he believes that
verses 17, 21–4 were not an original part of the story of Abram's defeat
of the enemy but were added at a similar time to the addition of verses
1–11, or even later. The words "who has delivered thine enemies into
thy hand", which are spoken by Melchizedek in verse 20, refer back
to verses 15–16, and verses 18–20 once came immediately after verse
16. Verses 17, 21–4 tell of the king of Sodom and Abram's refusal to
accept from him the gift of the booty. Doré knows but finds
unsatisfactory the view that the motive of the section is to show
Abram's magnanimity. It is, he claims, difficult to concentrate on the

question of material goods when Abram has just given a tenth to Melchizedek: that makes relative the redactor's interest in booty. Rather, the heart of the episode is Abram's oath in verse 22, which involves the identification with Yahweh of El Elyon, whom Melchizedek has just named in his blessing in verses 19–20. This passage is thus a later attempt to make Abram's own lips put first the name of Yahweh, the God of Israel. The verb *heᶜĕšartî* in verse 23 involves a play on words with *maᶜăśēr* in verse 20, and shows this section to be "un doublet" of verses 18–20. Finally, Doré claims to find confirmation of his theory in the attempt by E. Galbiati to detect a concentric structure in the chapter: the section about Melchizedek is in the middle of verses (12) 13–24, and verses 4–7 in the middle of verses 1–11, and verses (10) 11–12 are the suture between the first and second parts of the chapter. Similarly, in the first part of the chapter the two enumerations of the eastern kings in verses 1 and 9 and the two lists associated with the king of Sodom in verses 2 and 8 correspond in the second part of the chapter to the two references to Mamre, Eschol and Aner in verses 13–14 and 24 and the king of Sodom in verses 17 and 21. But why should this pattern (if it is intentional) be regarded as evidence for Dore's theory of the stages in the composition of the chapter, for it refers only to the final form, behind which, *ex hypothesi* – at least, as far as Doré is concerned – lie several stages of development.

A view of Gen. xiv that is both more conservative and more radical is put forward by J. Van Seters in *Abraham in History and Tradition* (New Haven, Conn., and London, 1975), in chapter 14, "Victory over the Kings of the East" (pp. 296–308), and on pp. 112–20. It is more conservative in that he defends the unity of most of Gen. xiv and is sceptical about theories of expansions or glosses (though he regards *ben-°ăḥî °abrām* in verse 12 as an addition), apart from verses 18–20, which he believes to be secondary. His view is, however, radical when it comes to the dating of the material. He argues that verses 1–11 belong to the genre of "a military campaign report" (p. 299), and the style in which it is written "does not come into vogue until the end of the Assyrian period but is very characteristic of the Neo-Babylonian period" (p. 120). Gen. xiv (minus the Melchizedek episode) reflects the "perspective" of "the late Persian empire", and in it "Elam really stands for Persia" (p. 305). Verses 18–20 are a legitimation of the syncretism of the worship of Yahweh with that of El Elyon, and this passage probably "belongs to the late Persian or early Hellenistic period when such syncretism became common throughout the Near East, and even the Jerusalem religious community was caught up in it" (p. 308).

Not all scholars have been convinced by theories that postulate two
or more stages in the composition of Gen. xiv, and G.J. Wenham goes
further than Van Seters (whom he never mentions) in his commentary
on Gen. i–xv, which was published in 1987. Although he recognizes
the presence of some explanatory glosses, he maintains that "the
chapter is a substantial unity" (p. 307). Unlike Van Seters, he
believes that the chapter "represents old tradition" (p. 307).

III

Before different views of the composition of Gen. xiv are discussed,
the reasons for distinguishing the main parts of the chapter must be
described. First, the reasons for regarding C (Abram and Melchizedek)
as an addition to B (Abram the noble hero and the king of Sodom)
will be considered, and then the reasons for distinguishing A (the
campaign of the eastern kings) from B.

The reasons for regarding C as an interpolation are widely
accepted, and were set out on pp. 407-8 my article. Verses 18–20
interrupt the connexion between verse 17 and its natural sequel in
verse 21, both of which are concerned with the king of Sodom.
Further, verses 21–3, in which Abram declines the offer of the spoil as
a gift, make no mention of the tenth that has been given to
Melchizedek in verse 20.

If verses 18–20 are an interpolation, it is necessary to give an
account of their relation to verse 22, where the words *yhwh* ʾ*ēl* ʾ*elyôn qōnēh*
šāmayim wāʾāreṣ appear to refer back to ʾ*ēl* ᶜ*elyôn qōnēh šāmayim wāʾāreṣ*
in verse 20. The LXX and Peshiṭta have no equivalent of *yhwh* in
verse 22, but the omission may be accidental and may have been
influenced by the proximity of the preposition ʾ*el* to the noun ʾ*ēl* in the
phrase ʾ*l yhwh* ʾ*l*. It is doubtful if it receives any support from the fact
that the Genesis Apocryphon also lacks anything corresponding to
yhwh in the relevant place (XXII 21). The Genesis Apocryphon is not
a translation, but a free telling afresh of the story in Genesis.
Moreover, the tetragrammaton never occurs in it. If an equivalent
had been sought, one might have expected the Aramaic word for
"Lord", but *mrh* is used later in the sentence (as in XXII 16) as the
counterpart of *qōnēh*. On the other hand, the Samaritan text has ʾ*lhym*,
which appears to be a variant of *yhwh*. Whether or not the reading
yhwh in Gen. xiv 22 is original – and the evidence against it is not
overwhelming – we have good reason to believe that verses 18–20 are
an interpolation. It is therefore likely that the reference to El Elyon in
verse 22 is an editorial assimilation to verse 20, which was made when
(or after) the two passages were combined. The alternative explana-

tion would be to suppose that the reference in verse 22 is original, and that the wording of verse 20 was influenced by it. In either case, the reasons for regarding verses 18–20 as an interpolation remain.

The distinction between A and B is not so widely accepted, but I discussed the reasons for it on pp. 429–32. It is based primarily on the difference in character between the two passages. A purports to offer an historical account of the activities of the eastern kings in Palestine and of their conflict with some local rulers; and Abram, who plays the leading part in B, is not yet mentioned. In contrast, the interest of B is centred on Abram, who is introduced in verse 13, on his heroic action, and on his meeting with the king of Sodom, whose offer of the booty as a gift is nobly declined. Westermann distinguishes between the story of the kings as a "Bericht" or "report", and the story of Abram as an "Erzählung" or "narrative". The story of Abram makes sense as a story on its own. This difference between the story of the kings and the story of Abram is not as compelling an argument as the case for regarding verses 18–20 as an interpolation, but I have regarded it as sufficient to justify setting out the hypothesis that one of the two stories once existed without the other.

Where should the dividing line be drawn between A and B? "It is", as I said in 1971, "difficult to be certain", and it "is probably wisest not to try to disentangle the beginning" of B (p. 434). I thought, however, that it was desirable to make some suggestion about the beginning. Later in B, verses 14, 16 and 21–3 imply that the king of Sodom has been defeated and his city plundered; and that presupposes something like what is recorded in verses 10–11. That is why I suggested that part of the beginning of B is preserved "probably in verses 10–11" (p. 437), but my words on p. 434 show that the opinion was presented tentatively, and that we do not now have the beginning of B as it was originally written. On the other hand, the narrative of A also needs an account of the result of the battle that is about to begin in verses 8–9 (though not necessarily an account of the plundering of Sodom). That is presumably why Westermann attaches verses 10–11 to verses 1–9. The contents of verses 10–11 thus suggest links both with what precedes and with what follows. If the hypothesis is accepted that A was added to B, then it is best to suppose that the editor was responsible for the suture in verses 10–11, and to leave open the question how far, if at all, the present form of these verses reproduces the wording of either A or B. It must suffice to say that the continuation of A and the beginning of B contained at least some of the information now found in verses 10–11, and that we no longer have the original beginning of B. This part of the hypothesis is not as tidy as could be wished, but tidiness cannot always be expected when there is reason to suspect editorial work by an ancient writer.

IV

If Wenham can successfully refute the arguments in favour of dividing of the chapter and also show that it must be a unity, then it will be unnecessary to discuss other theories further. We must therefore examine his arguments for the unity of Gen. xiv, and it will be convenient to discuss his case first for the unity of A and B, and then for the unity of A and B with C.

(1) *Wenham's Case for the Unity of A and B*

First, Wenham states on p. 307 what he sees as the case for distinguishing between verses 1–11 and 12ff. as a preliminary to answering it: "Abram is not mentioned before v 13 and . . . the style of the opening is much terser, more annalistic than later in the chapter". He maintains that the "brevity of the opening verses may be dictated by dramatic considerations as much as any other: the focus of interest is Abram's confrontation with the king of Sodom. The background details are therefore passed over more quickly." This is Wenham's strongest argument in defence of the unity of these two parts of the chapter, and it has some force as an interpretation of the chapter as it now stands. Yet it may be doubted whether it does justice to the differences in character between the two parts, between verses 1–11, which "give the impression of a document written by a learned student of annals", and verses 12ff., which portray "Abram as an heroic warrior" and describe "his dealings man to man with the king of Sodom", as I put it in 1971 (p. 431), although my division did not come between verses 11 and 12.

Secondly, Wenham maintains that the "story would . . . lose much of its punch were the introductory verses omitted. Abram's victory would no longer be the climactic third in a series of battles, and . . . triadic structures are beloved by Hebrew narrators" (p. 307). While the presence of triads in places in the Old Testament may be granted, they do not always appear, and it is precarious to use this as an argument for the unity of A and B. It would be perfectly intelligible, and acceptable from the literary point of view, to have a story in which Abram's victory counterbalanced an earlier defeat of the king of Sodom without an account of another battle.

Thirdly, Wenham attaches importance to the argument that "the phraseology of Abram's speech in vv 22–24 seems to use terminology drawn from vv 1–11 as well as 12–16" (p. 307). The terms he has in mind are the following: (1) the verb *lāqaḥ* in *wayyiqḥû* in verses 11 and 12, *qaḥ* in verse 21, and *ʾeqqaḥ* in verse 23; (2) the root *ḥlq* in *wayyēḥāleq* in verse 15, and *ḥēleq* and *ḥelqām* in verse 24 – and it "may be" that *wayyēḥāleq* "is a deliberate play on" *lqḥ*; (3) the root *ʾkl* in *ʾoklām* in verse 11, and *ᵓākᵉlû* in verse 24; (4) the verb *hālak* in *wayyēlᵉkû* in verse 12, and *hālᵉkû* in verse 24; (5) the noun *rᵉkūš* in verses 11, 12, 16, 21 (p. 305).

Even if the argument from terminology were strong, it would not tell against my theory of the hero story and its distinction from the story of the campaign of the eastern kings, for I suggested that verses 10–11 (at least, in their original form) belong to the hero story (pp. 434, 437), and none of Wenham's examples comes before verse 11. It also carries no weight against the view that verses 10–11 are an editorial suture. Nor does his argument have much force against those who make the division between verses 11 and 12. Arguments (2) and (4) concern only verses 12ff., except for the questionable suggestion (which Wenham put forward with words no stronger than "It may be") that there is a play on the roots *ḥlq* and *lqḥ*. Further, (2) involves the use of a verb and a noun in different senses, and *hālak* in (4) is a common verb, whose presence twice in a narrative is scarcely surprising. Similarly, *lāqaḥ* in (1) is common, as is the root *ᵓkl* in (3), and (3) involves two different parts of speech, a noun and a verb. These arguments are not impressive. Nor does (5) have much weight, for verses 1–11 were, *ex hypothesi*, added by someone who already knew verses 12ff., and it would not be surprising if the person who made the addition used in verse 11 a noun that had already been used in verses 12ff.

Wenham's arguments against the theory that verses 1–11 were added later to verses 12ff. are unconvincing, and have even less force against my suggestion that verses 10–11 belong, in part at least, to verses 12ff. or are an editorial suture. The central question at issue is whether the different character of section A, on the one hand, and section B, on the other, is sufficient to justify the theory of different origins. I believe it is, but Wenham does not. The reader must decide which view seems more probable.

(2) *Wenham's Case for the Unity of A and B with C*

Wenham admits that it is "strange" that the king of Sodom, who has appeared in verse 17, should say nothing until verse 21 (p. 306), but seems to hold that the strangeness is more than outweighed by other arguments. He also seeks to counter the argument that Abram could not have returned to the king of Sodom all the spoil (apart from what had been consumed by his allies) if he had given a tenth to Melchizedek. To "see a conflict" between verses 20 and 21 is, he believes, "oversubtle" (p. 317), and he maintains that victors had the right to keep spoil taken in battle. This does not, however, meet the difficulty that verse 24, which states the exceptions to what Abram is returning, fails to mention the gift to Melchizedek. Wenham has thus failed to solve satisfactorily the problems raised by verses 18–20.

It would be unfair to Wenham to ignore the arguments that he advances in support of his view that verses 18–20 are not a later addition but are an integral part of the narrative. There are, he maintains, "several remarks in Abram's speech to the king of Sodom that are inexplicable without the Melchizedek interruption" (pp. 306–7).

First, he sees here a contrast between Melchizedek and the king of Sodom. "The meanness of the king of Sodom stands in stark contrast to Melchizedek's warm generosity. Sodom brought nothing; whereas Melchizedek brought out bread and wine. Melchizedek blessed Abram. Sodom makes a short, almost rude demand of just six words . . . The word order (note how he mentions 'giving' before 'taking') reflects Sodom's ungracious self-centeredness" (p. 318; cp. pp. 305, 315). Abram, as the victor, had a right to the booty, but he was generous to the king of Sodom (see Wenham's note on verse 24 on p. 318).

The contrast drawn by Wenham may be overdone. It is not easy to judge whether the words of the king of Sodom would have been regarded as discourteous. In several passages in the Old Testament we find accounts of words that are so laconic that they might appear to us to be discourteous, but where that is obviously not the writer's intention. When Abraham offers his visitors refreshment, they accept with the words "Do as you have said" (Gen. xviii 5), but these words are not intended to be ungrateful or rude. When Jacob offers a present to Easu, the latter replies "I have enough, my brother; keep what you have for yourself" (Gen. xxxiii 9). When Araunah offers his threshing floor as a gift, David replies "No, but I will buy it of you for a price; I will not offer burnt offerings to Yahweh my God which cost me nothing" (2 Sam. xxiv 24). The king of Sodom is not accepting or declining a gift, but it may be doubted whether his laconic sentence is necessarily to be deemed discourteous. Nor can we be sure of his meanness. After all, he offers to let Abram keep the booty, and it is difficult to be certain whether the narrator would have regarded Abram as entitled to keep it in any case, notwithstanding the evidence adduced by Wenham that some people in the 2nd millennium recognized such a right.[3] Moreover, in this story Abram has come to the rescue after the defeat of the king of Sodom, and that suggests that

---

[3] Wenham refers on p. 318 to pp. 83–92 of Y. Muffs, "Abraham the Noble Warrior: Patriarchal Politics and Laws of War in Ancient Israel", *JJS* 33 (1982), pp. 81–107.

he was likely to return the booty to its original owner, whatever his own legal right may have been. If so, the offer of it to Abram by the king of Sodom is scarcely a sign of meanness. On the other hand, the generosity of Melchizedek who offered refreshment and a blessing (and received a tenth of the booty as a gift in return), though it is real, should not be exaggerated. Further, even if Wenham were right in claiming that there is a contrast between the two kings in the present text, it would not be strong evidence against the view that verses 18–20 are an interpolation. Unless he could find stronger arguments to counter the argument against the originality of verses 18–20, the contrast would be compatible with the view that these verses have been added.

Secondly, Wenham seeks to reinforce the first argument with the argument that verses 17–21 contain a chiasmus (p. 315):

Verse		
17	King of Sodom comes	A
18	Melchizedek King of Salem brings out bread and wine	B
19–20	Melchizedek speaks	B¹
21	King of Sodom replies	A¹

This is an unconvincing argument. All it amounts to is that Melchizedek is mentioned between the two references to the king of Sodom – something that is a reason for regarding verses 18–20 as an interpolation and can scarcely serve as evidence for the opposite conclusion. It is difficult to see anything else to justify the pattern ABB¹A¹. Indeed, "speaks" might be regarded as linking B¹ to "replies" in A¹. Incidentally, as we shall see in the next paragraph, Wenham also sees a chiasmus in verses 17–18 that links them together.

Thirdly, the alleged chiasmus in verses 17–18 involves the root $y\d{s}^\circ$: in verse 17 the king of Sodom comes out ($wayy\bar{e}\d{s}\bar{e}^\circ$), and in verse 18 the king of Sodom brings out ($h\^o\d{s}\^i^\circ$) bread and wine (pp. 307, 316). This recalls the argument used by H.S. Nyberg, which I considered in 1971. As I said then, "The fact that the verb [in verse 18] ... is from the same root as the verb at the beginning of verse 17 may be fortuitous" (and different themes of the verb are used), or the presence of the verb in verse 17 may have put it into the mind of the interpolator who added verse 18 (p. 412). Moreover, it is a strange form of chiasmus that consists only of a verb at the beginning of one verse and a verb near the middle of the next. Nor is the case made more convincing by the alleged "*taw-aleph* link" (pp. 307, 316), by which Wenham appears to mean the fact that verse 17 ends with $^\circ\bar{e}meq$ *hammelek* and verse 18 begins with $\^umalk\^i$-$\d{s}edeq$ *melek* $\check{s}\bar{a}l\bar{e}m$ (cp. p. 307) – especially since he seems to regard the former phrase as a gloss. Such arguments carry no weight.

Fourthly, the "mention of El-Elyon links" verse 22 with verse 18 (p. 318). This is certainly a link, but it is explicable as the result of editorial assimilation.

Fifthly, $he^c\check{e}\check{s}art\hat{i}$, "I have made rich", in verse 23 is said by Wenham (p. 318) to be "an almost identical root" with that found in "tithe", $ma^c\check{a}\check{s}\bar{e}r$, in verse 20, but he does not develop this argument. The word "almost" refers to the fact that one of the three consonants is different – they are both sibilants, it is true, but they are different sibilants – and the meanings are different. I mentioned in 1971 (pp. 409–10) E. Sellin's argument that the alleged play on words shows that verse 23 is dependent on verse 20, and I described the theory as "dubious". It is to Wenham's credit that he does not appeal to this questionable correspondence when he develops his argument for the unity of verses 18–20 with the surrounding verses.

Wenham's arguments, whether taken singly or together, do not succeed in proving that verses 18–20 are not an interpolation. On the other hand, he has not presented a convincing refutation of the arguments in favour of regarding them as an interpolation.

V

Unlike Wenham, Van Seters regards verses 18–20 as an addition, but he thinks that the rest of the chapter is a unity, including even those words that Wenham believes to be glosses. Van Seters discusses the relation between the story of the kings and the rest of the chapter on pp. 299–305, and here, as elsewhere in this chapter of his book, his words on p. 296 are relevant: "much of my own criticism will be directed at Emerton's study".

Van Seters analyses Gen. xiv into three main components (apart from verses 18–20): (1) verses 1–12; (2) verses 13–16; (3) verses 17, 21–3 (24) (p. 302). He opposes the view that (2) and (3) together constituted a hero story about Abram, which was once independent of (1), and which was derived from an oral tradition.

He attaches importance to his understanding of the literary form of the components of the chapter, and it is also relevant to his dating of Gen. xiv, which we shall consider later. Verses 1–11 are, he maintains, "a military campaign report", and he traces examples of it from Assyrian and Babylonian inscriptions in the first person singular to the late "Chronicle form, in which the events are regarded in a rather objective fashion using the third person and without reference to the deity" (p. 300). He finds "a still further development" in verses 1–11, in that the writer puts "the event in a larger context of affairs between the two regions involved" and writes "from a third party viewpoint of an uninvolved region". Van Seters lists the components that the royal inscriptions usually contain, and it seems likely that he finds the same ones in later developments of the form. They are (and I summarize for convenience but not, I hope, in a misleading way): (1) motivation, (2) preparations, (3) the campaign, (4) the results.

Although verse 12 continues the narrative, Van Seters recognizes a difference in it, for it mentions Lot, who "is not a political figure who might receive special attention in such a [military campaign] report" but "is a story figure connected with the Abraham tradition" (p. 301). The mention of Lot thus "creates an effective transition from mere report to story and becomes the vital connection between the two halves of the chapter". This apparent recognition of some difference between verses 1–11 and what follows does not, however, involve Van Seters in abandoning the unity of the chapter.

Verses 13–16 are thought by Van Seters to be the "core event" (p. 302) in Gen. xiv. These verses too are a "military campaign report" whose "motivation for the action by Abraham is the action of the earlier report", and which "certainly has no independence, and any effort to make it self-contained is forced to reconstruct a new setting for it. The fact that it follows the same type of literary convention of a reporting genre also speaks against any oral *Vorlage* and points to the same authorship as the preceding unit" (p. 301). The treatment "in this brief objective style scarcely justifies the characterization of the second part as a 'popular oral tradition'" – a reference to p. 437 of my article.

Verses 17, 21–3 (24 – Van Seters does not seem to be sure whether verse 24 is original; see pp. 297–8) contain a "dialogue" that concludes the "story", and is "a return to the story form". To judge by what he says on p. 301, it seems that he regards the "story" as beginning with verse 12 and including both verses 13–16 (in the form of a "report") and 17, 21–3/4 (in the form of a "dialogue"). The mention of the king of Sodom links this part of Gen. xiv with the report in verses 1–11. "Yet the story does not prepare us . . . for this confrontation between king and patriarch, so that it becomes hard to see it as a climax of the resolution of a situation of tension or need. At the most it is only a brief vignette that adds nothing of dramatic significance beyond the conclusion of" verse 16; and the ending in verse 23 or 24 "is very abrupt and most awkward for an actual story form" (p. 301).

Nor does Van Seters find the phrase "hero story" an appropriate description of the story. He refers to "vague statements about the remains of a 'hero story'", and says that the account of Abram's victory (sc. in verses 13–16) "does not have a scene of personal combat so typical of the *Heldensage*. It is in the same genre as the previous part" (p. 304). The "personal confrontation" begins only in verses 17, 21–4, "which is tied to both the previous campaign reports but in itself contains virtually no *dramatic* character ... It is only a pietistic vignette" (pp. 304–5). Van Seters therefore claims that "the description of the Abraham story as a hero story is very superficial and quite inadequate" (p. 305), and a footnote refers to pp. 431ff. of my article.

Van Seters has thus developed a powerful argument. Yet his theory is itself open to criticism. First, how strong is his case against the view that an oral tradition may underlie verses 12–17, 21–3 together with their original beginning? I should probably have made it plain in 1971 that what I had in mind was, not that the story as it stands necessarily reproduced an oral tradition word for word as it was transmitted orally, but that behind the written form as we have it there was an oral tradition. Nor did I claim that the characteristics of oral tradition are clearly visible in this part of Gen. xiv. If there was an independent story about Abram the hero, then it seemed to me inherently likely that it circulated orally, but that is not the same as saying that it displays the characteristics of oral tradition. Indeed, it is questionable whether such characteristics as Van Seters requires can be satisfactorily defined.[4] Nor is Van Seters's argument from form convincing. Verses 13–16 contain the four elements that Van Seters also finds in Mesopotamian royal inscriptions, but that does not prove literary dependence. When one reads the account of Abram's military action, each stage is natural and obvious. How else was the story to be told? Why should the fact that Van Seters describes the style as "brief" and "objective" be thought to justify him in denying that a "popular oral tradition" can lie behind this narrative? Are we really to suppose that an Israelite could not have told a story about Abram's victory in the third person until the idea of writing about battles in the third person had been invented in Mesopotamia? Has not Van Seters tried to prove from the form of the story more than the form can prove? Admittedly, "the proposals for a pre-literary stage are speculative", for there is a speculative element in any theory about this chapter (including the theory of Van Seters), but it is also speculative to deny the likelihood of a pre-literary stage.

Secondly, when Van Seters says that the "military campaign

---

[4] See Patricia G. Kirkpatrick, *The Old Testament and Folklore Studies* (Sheffield, 1988), and note her criticisms of Van Seters on pp. 55–9, 61–6.

report" in verses 13–16 "has no independence", and when he refers to "any attempt to make it self-contained", it is not clear whose theory he has in mind. Since the paragraph (p. 301) goes on to quote me, the reader might suppose that I have advanced the view that he opposes. But I have not suggested (nor has Schatz or Westermann) that verses 13–16 were ever a "self-contained" unit. They are part of the larger context of verses 12–17, 21–3 together with the original beginning of the story. Nor do I "reconstruct a new setting". It is legitimate to advance the hypothesis that there was once a different beginning of this section, if that seems the best way of solving one of the problems of the chapter. But a reconstruction would be much more than the postulating of a loss.

Thirdly, do verses (10–11), 12–17, 21–3 add up to a satisfactory story? Against Van Seters's claim that the story does not "prepare us in any way for the confrontation between king and patriarch", it may be asked what kind of a preparation was to be expected? We have had the raiders taking off prisoners and booty from Sodom, and we have had Abram's victory, and now we have the climax in Abram's noble declining of payment. It is strange that Van Seters, who argues for the unity of parts A and B of Gen. xiv, apparently fails to see how naturally this climax follows from verses 12–16. The story makes sense without the necessity of there being a "resolution of a situation of tension or need". Moreover, even on Van Seters's view of the chapter, it ends where it does in verse 24, and his judgement that the ending is "very abrupt and most awkward" applies to the story of the chapter as it now stands. If this ending is there in any case, is it legitimate to suppose that an ancient Israelite would have regarded it as an unsatisfactory close to a story? Abram has defeated the enemy, rescued the captives and the spoil, and shown himself magnanimous in refusing any recompense. Why should the story not end abruptly?

Attention must be paid to the beginning of this section of the chapter no less than to its end. Van Seters holds that verses 13ff. are by the same author as verses 1–11 because the king of Sodom appears in both, because both verses 1–11 and 13–16 are military campaign reports, and because the former verses supply the "motivation for the action by Abraham" in the latter. But no difficulty arises for the theory that verses 1–9 are a later addition and that they too referred to the king of Sodom and a battle; it is even conceivable that that is why they were added to the other story. The fact that Van Seters can label both verses 1–11 and 13–16 as military campaign reports does not prove common authorship, and I have questioned in an earlier paragraph the value for the analysis of the chapter of this labelling of verses 13–16: they are a natural way of describing a fight that need

owe nothing to Mesopotamian documents. On the other hand, there
are differences in character between verses 1–9 and what now follows
them (and we have seen that Van Seters appears to recognize at least
some difference), and I believe that they justify the hypothesis of
different authorship.

Fourthly, how much force is there in Van Seters's criticism of my
describing section B as a "hero story" and in his pointing out that
there is no "scene of personal combat so typical of the *Heldensage*"?
I stated explicitly on p. 431 that I used the expression "hero story" for
the sake of convenience, and that "the description should not be
understood to imply too precise a definition". This lack of precision
may be what Van Seters believes to be "vague", but my general
meaning should be clear. When Van Seters writes of a *Heldensage* and
a scene of personal combat, he is importing a particular kind of
precision that I never intended or gave any reason to expect, and I see
no reason why the story should have been thought likely to contain
such a scene. Van Seters also fails to discuss, or even mention, the
partial analogies in the Old Testament that I drew to what is
recorded in verses 17, 21–3 – and they are far from vague.

It may thus be claimed that section B is sufficiently different from
A to justify the hypothesis of a different origin, and that its contents
make sense as a story. While I do not claim that the passage exhibits
characteristics that show it to be based on an oral tradition, it is
reasonable to suggest such an origin, and the story may be described
as a "hero story" provided that the expression is not given too precise
a definition.

VI

Much less importance attaches to the question of possible minor
additions, and they will be discussed more briefly. Like most
commentators, I found glosses in verses 2, 3, 7, 8, 17 and regarded
them as attempts to explain archaic names. Van Seters suggests "that
explanatory phrases are used as a literary device in order to give an
archaic sense to the whole account", and states that "some of these
equivalents are clearly artificial" (p. 297). He takes as an example
Bela (a word that is glossed, rather than a gloss) in verse 2, which
"means 'devoured'", and from that proceeds (without further
argument) to express the opinion that it "is likely that all the
equivalents are purely artificial creations". He says, however, that
a decision about the character of the glosses depends on a decision
about "the form and literary character of the whole". Yet even if Van

Seters is right in supposing that Bela is a fictitious name, it does not follow that the gloss was not a genuine attempt to identify the place, or that all the place-names glossed are artificial.

The references to Aner, Eshcol and Mamre in verses 13 and 14 are of little more importance, although they may, if late, have a bearing on the dating of the passages. I argued in 1971 (p. 404) that they are secondary because "they play no part in the rest of the story". Van Seters recognizes a difficulty (p. 297), but says that there is also the difficulty of explaining how they got into the story if they are not original. I suggested a reason on p. 438.

Of greater importance are the references to Lot in verses 12, 14, 16. Admittedly, if they are not original, a different motive for Abram's intervention must be suggested, but that is not a fatal objection. I shall not discuss the question fully here, for my main analysis of the chapter could stand even if it were to be shown that the references to Lot were always part of the story of Abram the hero. I do not, however, find compelling the arguments that Van Seters directs against my suggestions on pp. 298–9. He thinks that the repetition in verse 12 of what has been said in verse 11 "may be used for deliberate effect to emphasize the capture of Lot". He does not, however, believe that the whole of the verse is original, for he argues that the words *ben-ʾăḥî ʾabrām* have been added. It seems to me that he underestimates the significance of the repetitiousness of verse 12, probably because he holds that "this is a rather difficult non-classical style of Hebrew throughout" – though this seems to me to be an exaggeration when applied to much of the chapter. He contrasts my use on p. 407 of "the criterion of awkward style as a clue to a foreign source in vv. 12 and 16" with my rejection on pp. 34–6 of "this criterion as evidence for a foreign source in vv. 1–2". But his contrast is not valid, for he uses the word "foreign" in two different senses. On pp. 34–6 I discussed theories of translation from a source in Accadian (a foreign language), but on p. 407 I regarded verse 12 and part of verse 16 as secondary (i.e. foreign to their context, but not in a foreign language). He rightly sees, however, that the "real crux of the matter" is the reference to Lot in verse 14. Verse 11 "only mentions that booty was taken, but vv. 22f. indicate that this could not have motivated Abraham since he shows disdain toward such goods", and Van Seters says that my view "involves the complete reconstruction of the story in which Abraham goes to the assistance of Sodom as a friendly act to rescue captives not previously mentioned", and he finds my "easy dismissal of this difficulty . . . unacceptable". While it is true that I postulate a different motivation, I do not offer a complete reconstruction of the story, and his criticism overlooks my suggestion that the story "told simply how captives had been taken from Sodom" (p. 407), which makes it plain that I hold that captives were "previously mentioned".

VII

Doré's article, which contains much that is convincing, argues for the more controversial view that verses 17, 21–4 were added after verses 1–11 and 18–20 were combined with the original story of the defeat of the intruders. His theory thus postulates a stage of redaction additional to those suggested by, for example, Schatz, Westermann and my article. The literary history of Gen. xiv is complicated, but the onus of proof must rest on anyone who postulates more complications than other scholars, and the arguments for Doré's analysis must be examined. It is, however, unnecessary to repeat here what was said above on p. 77 about his appeal to Galbiati's theory of concentric circles.

First, Doré believes that verses 18–20 were the "matrix" (p. 84) of the chapter, because they introduce Abram into the story. This argument presupposes the theory of Westermann that the account of the defeat of the intruders was a story from the period of the judges that did not originally mention Abram, but he criticizes Westermann for failing to explain how and why the exploit came to be ascribed to Abram (p. 93, n. 21; cp. p. 82). In his opinion, this happened when verses 18–20, which mention Abram and Melchizedek, were added to the story. If, however, it is thought unnecessary to postulate two stages in the story of the defeat of the intruders – one stage without Abram, and a later stage with him – then the argument loses its force. Why should not the story have been associated with Abram from the beginning (see also above, p. 76)?

Secondly, the reference to El Elyon in verse 22 is thought by Doré to be dependent on verse 20, and therefore later than it. This explanation of the relationship between the verses has the advantage of preserving the text of verse 22 unchanged, but it was seen above on p. 78 that the present text of verse 22 can be explained as the result of an editorial assimilation to verse 20.

Thirdly, Doré finds his theory confirmed by the assonance between *heᶜĕšartî* in verse 23 and *maᶜăśēr* in verse 20 (p. 90). This argument was considered above on p. 84 in a different context, and was rejected. However, even if there was a deliberate assonance, it would not tell us which verse came first.

The arguments in favour of Doré's theory are scarcely sufficient to justify his further complication of the analysis of this chapter. Against it stands the fact that verses 18–20 interrupt the connexion between verses 17 and 21, and it is easier to imagine an interpolation breaking the connexion than a later writer expanding the story in so awkward a way.

VIII

We turn now from the problem of the composition of the chapter to that of its dating. In 1971 I dated the insertion of section C in verses 18–20 into section B in verses (10–11) 12–17, 21–3 in the reign of David. That involved regarding section B as earlier than the insertion. My discussion (pp. 435–7) of section A in verses 1–9 was cautious: while I did not rule out a date for it in the Davidic period, I also allowed the possibility that it came from a later time. In contrast, even Schatz and Westermann, whose views of the earlier parts of Gen. xiv are similar to mine, regard section A (verses 1–11 for them) as much later. Schatz (p. 323) thinks of a Deuteronomistic edition c. 550 B.C., in which verses 1–11 were added, and Westermann of the late post-exilic period (p. 227; E. tr., p. 193). Similarly, de Vaux, who thinks of the chapter as a mixture of older and younger elements, draws attention to evidence for the late date of parts and believes that the present form of the text comes from a time after the Priestly Document (p. 211; E. tr., p. 219); and Zimmerli also seems to favour a late date, although he does not specify when it was. Van Seters, who believes the chapter to be a unity (apart from verses 18–20), dates it in the late Persian period. Most of his arguments are concerned with verses 1–11.

Since it is generally agreed that verses 18–20 are an addition, a discussion of their date will be postponed until the next section of this article, though it should be noted that, if an early date for this insertion into verses (10–11) 12–17, 21–3 seems probable, it will have implications for the date of the context into which they were inserted. There is no point in repeating here arguments that I put forward in 1971, unless it is required for a consideration of arguments advanced by others. I need not, for example, repeat what I wrote on p. 404 on the use in Gen. xiv of language that has been regarded as characteristic of the Priestly Document, for de Vaux (p. 211; E. tr., p. 219) adds nothing to the argument.

The first argument in favour of a date for section A after the time of David concerns the cities of the plain: Sodom, Gomorrah, Zoar, Admah and Zeboiim. It is pointed out by several scholars that Sodom and Gomorrah are usually mentioned together, and Admah and Zeboiim appear in Hosea xi 8, but Sodom and Gomorrah are not

mentioned alongside Admah and Zeboiim elsewhere except in Deut.
xxix 23, which is widely believed to be exilic. Gen. xiv 2 and 8 thus
imply the collocation of two groups of towns (plus Zoar) which is not
otherwise attested before the exile. This argument is scarcely decisive
against a pre-exilic date, but it has some force in a cumulative
argument.

Secondly, verse 7 mentions "the Amorites who lived in Hazazon-
tamar", and verse 13 "Mamre the Amorite". The latter verse is
probably secondary, but the former is part of section A. The location
of Amorites specifically in this region is unparalleled in the Old
Testament. It seems, however, to reflect the usage whereby "Amorite"
was used as a general term for people in Syria-Palestine. De Vaux
(p. 130; E. tr., p. 133) argues that this, in turn, reflects Assyrian usage
from the time of Tiglath-pileser I (1115–1070 B.C.), and a similar
point of view is expressed by Schatz and Van Seters. If this is correct,
then it is difficult to postulate its presence in an Israelite writing as
early as the time of David. A further argument, which is based by Van
Seters on the word "Amorite" will be considered below.

Thirdly, Gen. xiv 5 mentions "the Rephaim in Ashteroth-karnaim,
the Zuzim in Ham, the Emim in Shaveh-kiriathaim", and these
words are thought by some to be dependent on Deut. ii 10–11, which
says that the Emim, who once lived in what later became Moabite
territory, were Rephaim but that the Moabites call them Emim, and
on Deut. ii 20–1, which refers to the Zamzummim as an Ammonite
name for Rephaim. I argued on p. 405 that this evidence did not
prove dependence on Deuteronomy, for it has not been shown that
the names were invented by Deuteronomy without any basis in
tradition. Schatz sees here in Gen. xiv the work of the second
Deuteronomist c. 550 B.C. (p. 323; cp. his discussion of Gen. xiv 5–6
on pp. 101–5). Van Seters (pp. 117–18) finds here evidence of Gen.
xiv's dependence on Deuteronomy, though he does not believe that
this chapter in Genesis was written by a Deuteronomist. He claims to
detect several stages of development in the use of names of peoples,
and argues that the stage that appears in Gen. xiv is the latest. In his
opinion, Deuteronomy tended to identify the Amorites with the
mythical Anakim or Rephaim, who were thought to be giants, and
this cannot have happened before the 8th century B.C. In Deut. ii
the writer goes farther and says that the Rephaim in Transjordan
were called the Emim by the Moabites and Zamzummim by the
Ammonites. Gen. xiv 5 goes beyond that "by restricting these terms to
very specific regions as if they were distinct peoples corresponding to
the distinct political states of a later day" (p. 118). Although it is
impossible to be certain, because we do not have direct access to the

alleged Moabite and Ammonite usage, the force of Van Seter's argument must be recognized.

Fourthly, there is the question of the historical style used in section A of the chapter. We have seen that Van Seters argues that this reflects a relatively late Mesopotamian usage. If he is right, then section A cannot be a document from the time of David based on some older source, although the possibility of an older source should not be denied.[5] In any case, Van Seters presents an incomplete view of my position when he says that I suggested "a date in the time of the Davidic monarchy" (p. 119). It is true that I allowed that as a possibility. But I also allowed for the possibility of a later date, and I noted on pp. 405 and 435 similarities between Gen. xiv 1–9 and Israelite history writing, some of which is probably pre-Deuteronomic even though undoubtedly later than the reign of David. The argument against a Davidic date for this part of the chapter now seems stronger than it seemed to me in 1971, and I see the force of the case for a later date. We must be grateful to Van Seters for his study of ancient Near Eastern historiography.[6]

After considering the arguments listed above, I now think it unlikely that verses 1–9 (and their linking with what follows) can be dated as early as the time of David. Exactly when section A was written is difficult to determine. The first verse outside Gen. xiv that links Sodom and Gomorrah with Admah and Zeboiim (Deut. xxix 23) is probably exilic, but we cannot tell whether the story of the

---

[5] Van Seters dismisses on p. 119 my statement on p. 437 that the possibility that historical "records existed as early as the reign of David cannot be denied". His reasons are that the "only possible records . . . are some which came down from the Amarna period in which Jerusalem, but not the cities of the Jordan Valley, were subject to Egypt", and that "such a story is scarcely possible before the domination of Palestine and Transjordan by an Eastern power from the mid-eighth century onward". He adds on p. 300 that the "only possible form of a 'record' would have been a royal inscription boasting of the local king's conquests, which is not what we have". Further, "the manner of presentation" in Gen. xiv is based on that of the Deuteronomist "who . . . imitates the form of the Assyrian and Babylonian records" and uses "the third person as an objective account" (p. 120; cp. p. 300). While I no longer defend the possibility of a date in the Davidic period for section A of Gen. xiv, it seems to me that Van Seters goes too far in his confident assertion about what could and could not have been in existence, and I have questioned above the plausibility of the theory that an account of events in the third person would have been impossible until it had been borrowed from Mesopotamia. Moreover, my suggestion was not that section A reproduces the source as it stood, but that it borrowed some information from it; and Van Seters himself seems to recognize the possibility of a (later) source for some of the personal names (p. 120). My discussion of the question is presented with due caution on pp. 436–8, although I now see that one of the possibilities that I considered then must be questioned.

[6] See also his book *In Search of History* (New Haven, Conn., and London, 1983).

eastern kings is earlier or later than it. Nor does the use of the word
"Amorite" tell us more than that it is later – perhaps considerably
later – than the 11th century. The references in Gen. xiv 5 to the
Rephaim, the Zuzim, and the Emim have affinities with Deuteronomy
and perhaps point to a date near that of Deut. ii 10–11, though it
remains uncertain whether they are actually dependent on that
passage. The affinities with the narrative style of the books of Samuel
and Kings probably point to a time not before the late monarchy.
That suggests some time in the 7th century as the earliest likely date,
but leaves open the possibility of a later time in or after the exile.

Westermann advances three reasons for favouring a post-exilic
date for the composition of the chapter: (1) the elevation of Abram to
a figure of world history fits that period; (2) the uniting of such
different material as verses 1–11 and 12–24 fits that period alone; (3)
the antiquarian and scribal character of verses 1–11 and their lack of
historical perspective comes from the same age (p. 226; E. tr., p. 192).
Such arguments lack precision and are difficult to evaluate, and they
do not point to any particular time after the exile.

A date in the late Persian period for Gen. xiv 1–17, 21–4 is proposed
by Van Seters on pp. 305–6. He does not find "any programmatic or
legitimating function" in the story, whose "only point . . . according
to the closing discourse is to teach the virtues of courage, loyalty, and
piety by Abraham's example" – a view of its character that has
surprising affinities to my own opinion that section B can be called
a hero story. He advances four reasons for his dating.

First, he accepts the judgement of H. Gunkel[7] that the "form of the
story, in which one finds a mixture of quasi-historical reporting of
events with an admixture of heroic [sic] and legendary elements", was
"characteristic of Jewish popular stories in the Persian and Hellenistic
periods". (Gunkel compares Chronicles, Judith, the Testaments of
the XII Patriarchs, Jubilees, Esther and Daniel.) Van Seters comments:
"The perspective of these works is the confrontation of a world empire
by very few, the strong sense of individual piety, and the love of
a certain archaism by its efforts to reconstruct an elaborate past
historical setting." While, however, such writing flourished in the late
post-exilic period, it may be doubted whether Gen. xiv is incompatible
with an earlier date. The date may be so late, but it is not necessarily
so.

Secondly, Van Seters thinks that, since "virtually all the names of

---

[7] *Genesis* (3rd edn, Göttingen, 1910), pp. 289–90. Van Seters's reference on p. 305
to pp. 189–90 is either a misprint or a slip of the pen.

places and countries are intended to be the archaic counterparts of later entities it is clear that Elam must really stand for Persia"; and the "fact that Babylon is an ally [of Elam] probably points to a period long after the animosity between Persia and Babylon when all the three 'kingdoms' in league with Persia represented major satrapies of a later day. The perspective of the story is the late Persian empire". This statement about the nature of the names is, however, no more than an unproved assertion. It is not helped by the fact that it was well known by Jews that Persia had been an enemy of Babylon (e.g. Isa. xxi, and the book of Daniel).

Thirdly, Van Seters advances another argument about the word Amorite. It was accepted above that the term is used as a general term for people living in Syria-Palestine. Van Seters goes farther: "It appears that the term Amorite shifted in meaning in the Persian period from the indigenous population to the Arab peoples. So they could then be viewed as the nomadic and pastoral peoples of southern Judah including the region of Hebron" (p. 305). P. 36 quotes the Cyrus Cylinder's reference in 539 B.C. to "the kings of Amurru dwelling in tents", whom Van Seters reasonably understands to belong to tribes of North Arabia. He had earlier discussed the question in his article "The terms 'Amorite' and 'Hittite' in the Old Testament", *VT* 22 (1972), pp. 64–81. On p. 66 of the article he refers to the Persian evidence, and on pp. 71–2 and 76 he discusses Gen. xv 18–20 and Ezra ix 1, where he believes that the word "Amorite" is also used of Arabs. In Gen. xv 18–20 the traditional list of the seven peoples inhabiting the promised land is expanded by the addition of the Kenites, the Kenizzites and the Kadmonites, who were "nomadic peoples", and this is apparently thought by Van Seters to represent an association of the Amorites with Arabs. In Ezra ix 1, the reference is no longer to "the nations of the land" (*gôyê hā°āreṣ*) but to "the peoples of the lands" (*°ammê hā° ărāṣôt*), and the Amorites "are separated from the rest of the Palestinian inhabitants and placed after the Ammonites, Moabites, and Egyptians. This ordering only makes sense if Amorites are here understood as Arabs as in the Persian period texts" (p. 76).

The argument is open to question. Both Gen. xv 18–20 and Ezra ix 1 refer to people living in the land, whether they are nomadic or settled, and whether they come from elsewhere or not (the former passage states explicitly that they are in the land, and the latter is in the context of mixed marriages within the land). It is not obvious that the presence of people from these nations in the land has the slightest bearing on the meaning of the word "Amorite" or, indeed, of the other members of the traditional list of nations living in the land. Nor

is it obvious that the arrangement of people in the list in Ezra ix 1 has
any significance. A study of the other lists in the Old Testament
reveals considerable variety in order, and the place of the Amorites
after the Moabites, Ammonites and Egyptians in this verse may be
fortuitous (cp. Exod. iii 8, 17, xiii 5, xxiii 23, xxxiii 2, xxxiv 11; Deut.
vii 1, xx 17; Josh. iii 10, ix 1, xii 8, xxiv 11; Judg. iii 5; Neh. ix 8;
2 Chron. viii 7; and the shorter lists in Gen. xiii 7; Exod. xxiii 28). The
evidence is not strong enough to support Van Seters's claim.
Moreover, even if it could be shown that Gen. xiv reflects Persian
usage, the evidence of the Cyrus Cylinder could be turned against
Van Seters to show that the usage is as old as the middle of the 6th
century B.C., the beginning of the Persian period not the late Persian
period. Further, I doubt if "Amurru" in the Cyrus Cylinder means
more than "the West Land", which would include North Arabia but
would also include other parts of the west and their inhabitants,
whether or not they were Arabs.[8]

Fourthly, "the use of the term Hebrew to describe Abraham [in
Gen. xiv 13] is very similar to that of the Jonah story, which comes
from the same general period" (p. 305). Van Seters argues on p. 54
that "Hebrew" (ᶜibrî) is used here in an ethnic sense, like "Amorite".
After surveying the use of the word elsewhere in the Old Testament,
he concludes "Hebrew ... is always used in a context in which
Israelites are in contact with foreigners, and such stories are abundant
in the period of time before the monarchy and after the exile but rare
during the monarchies of Judah and Israel" (p. 55). It is unnecessary
to enter here into the vexed general question of the meaning or
meanings of ᶜibrî in the Bible, for it is enough to note that Van Seters
recognizes its use in both early and late times; while its use in Gen. xiv
13 is compatible with a late date, it does not demand it.

What, then, are we to say about the dates of sections A and B and

---

[8] Van Seters, *Abraham*, p. 46, refers to R.P. Dougherty, *Nabonidus and Belshazzar: A Study of the Neo-Babylonian Empire* (New Haven, Conn., and London, 1929), p. 109, apparently in support of his claim that "Amurru took on a new specialized use by the late Neo-Babylonian or early Persian period and referred to the region of North Arabia". Similarly, *VT* 22 (1972), p. 66, cites the same page to justify the statement that "in the Persian period 'Amorites' seems, instead [of referring to the settled population of Syria-Palestine], to refer to the Arab peoples of North Arabia". In fact, Dougherty says on p. 109 that in the Cyrus Cylinder "*Amurrû* is used in a general geographical sense denoting land extending as far west as Syria and Palestine. The text under consideration is the first to ascribe this descriptive term to a part of Arabia"; and on p. 150 he says of Arabia: "of the countries of the Westland it alone bordered on the real land of Babylonia". Dougherty clearly understands Amurru to refer to the west in general and to include part of Arabia, but not to be restricted in meaning to Arabia.

their uniting to form the present Gen. xiv (apart from minor additions and the more important section C, which will be considered below)? The earliest date for A is probably the 7th century, and the latest is the completion of the Pentateuch in the 5th, or perhaps the 4th, century B.C. It is not easy to date section B, but arguments for a late date have not been found convincing. Perhaps a discussion of section C will help to decide the matter.

IX

We turn now to the dating of section C, the account in verses 18–20 of Abram's meeting with Melchizedek. Schatz and Westermann accept a date for this passage in the time of David, in common with a number of earlier scholars, and in 1971 I accepted that date. I discussed various theories, and argued against a dating in the post-exilic period (pp. 414–19) or during the divided monarchy (pp. 419–20), and against H.H. Rowley's theory that the passage was intended to justify the position of Zadok in the reign of David. (pp. 420–1). Instead, I advanced arguments in favour of the view that the passage made best sense if it was dated in the time of David and intended to further his policy in several ways (pp. 421–6).

Van Seters, however, argues for a much later date. Indeed, he must, for he recognizes that verses 18–20 are an addition to the rest of Gen. xiv, which he dates in the late Persian period: the addition must, therefore, be later still. If verses 18–20 were dated much earlier, it would upset either his dating of the rest of the chapter or his defence of its unity.

Why does Van Seters believe that verses 18–20 were added in the late 4th century B.C. (p. 308)? He thinks that the passage presupposes a syncretistic identification of two deities who were originally distinct, namely, El and Elyon, and a further identification of El Elyon, the deity worshipped by Melchizedek, with Yahweh, the God of Israel. The passage is, he maintains, "concerned with the legitimation of this form of syncretism" (p. 307). The "process was begun by J and carried forward by P in their identifying forms of El with Yahweh, and it reached its culmination in Genesis 14" (p. 307). Further, Melchizedek's title, "priest of El Elyon", is not found until the Hasmoneans claimed in the 2nd century to be "high priests of God most high", a title which, according to Van Seters, they are unlikely to have invented or "simply borrowed" from Gen. xiv (p. 308). Admittedly, Jewish high priests before the Hasmoneans were not kings like Melchizedek, but royal claims for the priesthood were already at least implicit before their time.

Van Seters advances arguments against those who would date verses 18–20 in the time of David – in addition to his arguments about the rest of the chapter. First, he thinks that "early dating of these verses rests primarily upon a prior hypothesis about the nature of the Judean monarchy and the pre-Israelite form of religion in Jerusalem" (p. 306). This "prior hypothesis" is that the kingship of Judah was priestly (Ps. cx 4), and "derived this function from the previous 'Canaanite' form of the monarchy, whose 'founder' was Melchisedek" (p. 306); and that the god worshipped in Jerusalem before the Israelite capture of the city by David was El Elyon, whom David identified with Yahweh. But, Van Seters claims, there is no evidence for this theory, since "the dating and interpretation of Ps. 110 are very problematic" (p. 306), and to base the reconstruction on Gen. xiv 18–20 and then to use the reconstruction to to interpret the same passage is to argue in a circle. Second, "the early dating of vv. 18–20 must see in either Abraham or Melchisedek the figure of David" (p. 306). But neither of them is like David and, he says, "Emerton's suggestion . . . that David is to be seen in both Abraham and Melchisedek is too farfetched. He completely blurs the differences between David and Abraham, which are considerable" (p. 307) – and Van Seters proceeds to point out some differences.

How strong is Van Seters's case for a late dating of verses 18–20? It is open to objection no less than other theories of a late date, which I examined in 1971.

First, it is implausible to suggest that Melchizedek "represents the priesthood of the second temple" (p. 308). The Jerusalem priests based their claims on descent from an authentic priestly line. In Ezekiel it is descent from Zadok, but the Priestly parts of the Pentateuch and the books of Chronicles regard priestly rights as depending, more broadly, on descent from Aaron. It is unlikely that an appeal to a non-Israelite priest would have been thought appropriate, especially after the campaign of Ezra and Nehemiah against contamination with what was non-Jewish. This tells strongly against Van Seters's dating.

Secondly, there is the difficulty that Melchizedek was a king as well as a priest. In support of his assertion that "the royal claims of the priesthood" were "very clearly implicit" in the period before the Hasmoneans, Van Seters appeals (p. 308) to two pages in a book by de Vaux.[9] What, however, de Vaux is discussing is the view that the

---

[9] P. 308 cites de Vaux, *Ancient Israel: Its life and Institutions* (London, 1961), pp. 400–1 = *Les institutions de l'Ancien Testament* II (Paris, 1960), pp. 270–1.

post-exilic high priests inherited something of the position of the pre-exilic kings both in their status as head of the Jewish community and in their vestments. De Vaux says nothing to suggest that any post-exilic high priest before the Hasmoneans aspired to the kingship, and Van Seters adduces no evidence for that hypothesis. Against the unsubstantiated hypothesis of a priestly aspiration to kingship stands the tradition that the kingship belonged to the family of David, a tradition attested in post-exilic parts of the Hebrew Bible. The situation was entirely different in the 2nd century B.C., when a successful military leader, who happened to be of priestly descent, was offered the office of high priest, and then in the 1st century a later holder of the positions of high priest and secular leader exalted the latter office to the kingship. There is nothing to suggest that he was making explicit a much earlier implicit claim. Here too the evidence tells strongly against the late date for Gen. xiv 18–20 postulated by Van Seters.

Thirdly, it may be doubted whether the process of what Van Seters calls syncretism need, or should, be dated as late as he supposes. Are we really to think that Yahweh is unlikely to have been identified with El Elyon until the late Persian period? Van Seters dates the J writer, with whom he thinks the process of identifying Yahweh with El began, in the exilic period (pp. 310, etc.). It is not clear how Van Seters understands the place of P in the development in the direction of identifying Yahweh, not only with El, but also with El Elyon, for his reference to P's "consistent scheme" on p. 288 mentions only the stages: Elohim, then El Shaddai, and then Yahweh. Nor does p. 307 offer a date for the combination of El with Elyon, although p. 288 ascribes already to J "a syncretism between Yahweh and the various forms of El that were known to him", such as El Roi. Even if one were to accept Van Seters's controversial late date for J, it is not clear why he thinks that an identification of Yahweh with El Elyon must be as late as the late Persian period.

When did the identification of Yahweh with El begin? There are a number of proper names, most of which were borne by people who were presumably worshippers of Yahweh, that are compounded with ʾēl, such as Elijah. It is, of course, difficult to be sure whether ʾēl is here used as the proper name of a deity or whether it simply means "God", but perhaps the distinction is not to be drawn too sharply. There are also poetic texts in the Hebrew Bible where El and Elyon appear in parallel (Num. xxiv 16; Ps. lxxiii 11, cvii 11; Ps. lxxvii 10 speaks of El and verse 11 of Elyon), and that implies an identification, even though the combined expression El Elyon does not appear. Ps. lxxviii 35, where it does appear, may be late (though some date it before the exile), but it does not go beyond the other psalms in substance (and verses 7, 8, 19, 41 speak of El, and verses 17 and 56 of Elyon). Moreover, most of the relevant passages obviously use the words with reference to Yahweh. Ps. lxxxii speaks of "the assembly of El" in verse 1, and of Elyon in verse 6, and the absence of the tetragrammaton is probably due only to the fact that this is one of the Elohistic psalms in which the name Yahweh seems to have been changed to Elohim. There are also other psalms where either El or Elyon is used of Yahweh. (e.g. Ps. vii 18: *yhwh ʿelyôn*;[10] Ps. 11: *ʾēl ʾĕlōhîm* – originally *ʾēl yhwh*), and Elyon is also used of Yahweh in other books (e.g. Lam. iii 35, 38). The identification of Yahweh with El and Elyon is deeply embedded in the Hebrew Bible, especially in the Psalter, and it may be doubted whether it is necessary to date all the references in the post-exilic period. It may also be doubted whether the identification of Yahweh with El Elyon is to be regarded as unlikely until the late Persian period.

Fourthly, Van Seters fails to do justice to the view that the Davidic king had a priestly status in the pre-exilic period, and that Ps. cx 4 relates it to Melchizedek. It may be granted that, as he says, "the dating and interpretation of Psalm 110 are very problematic" (p. 306) in the sense that the text and translation of some verses raise problems, and that a variety of views has been expressed. But the evidence cannot be brushed aside so easily. The psalm is connected with Zion (verse 2), and Yahweh speaks to someone who is to rule and defeat kings and who is "a priest for ever after the order of Melchizedek". To whom are the words addressed? It was once fashionable to suppose that they are addressed to a Hasmonean ruler, but is is now widely recognized that so late a date is improbable. The natural interpretation is that the words are addressed to a pre-exilic Davidic king.

Further, the objections raised by Van Seters to my interpretation of the Melchizedek passage in Genesis depend on his presentation of my interpretation, not on what I myself wrote. I did not put forward the "farfetched" view that "David is to be seen in both Abraham and Melchisedek" (or, indeed, in either) or blur "the differences between David and Abraham". Rather, I regarded as "very plausible" the theory that David "adopted, in some form, the Jebusite cult", and that the story of Abram and Melchizedek implied that offence could not legitimately be taken by Israelites at the adoption. Further,

---

[10] The variant *ʾĕlōhîm yhwh* makes little difference to the argument.

"David, as king in Jerusalem, had inherited the priestly status of Melchizedek" (p. 421 – as Ps. cx implies). The story also helped to legitimate Jerusalem as the site of a holy place for Israelites, and the friendship between Abram and Melchizedek was intended to help to make David's occupying of the throne in a Jebusite city acceptable to both Israelites and Jebusites. The passage pointed to the military advantages of co-operation, for Abram had defeated the enemy from abroad. It is beside the point for Van Seters to say that David "did not fight foreign invaders from Mesopotamia or come to the aid of the Transjordanian peoples" and "did not defend anyone against an attack" (p. 307).

Nor is the reasoning in such an interpretation necessarily circular, though it is hypothetical in character as many interpretations of biblical passages must be. Verses 18–20 themselves tell us of a priestly king in Salem, who is foreign to Abram and yet blesses him in the name of the deity who is worshipped there. The exegete's task is to offer an interpretation of what is said in the text. We know from other evidence that there was syncretism in the early monarchy, that the words El and Elyon, which were used of foreign gods, were also used of Yahweh, and that Ps. xlviii 3 appears to identify Zion with Zaphon, the sacred mountain of Canaanite mythology. Further, Ps. cx 4 speaks of a ruler in Zion who is a priest after the order of Melchizedek, and who is probably to be identified with a Davidic king. To advance a theory on the basis of this evidence is not to reason in a circular way. It is to interpret what is said in Gen. xiv 18–20 in the light of other evidence.

Van Seters's attempt to date the Melchizedek passage in Gen. xiv 18–20 in the late 4th century B.C. is thus unconvincing. In particular, his judgement about the relevance of Melchizedek's status as priest and king to the needs of the period is improbable. A pre-exilic date seems more likely. In particular, I advanced a case in 1971 (pp. 421–6) for a dating in the reign of David which I need not repeat here, and Van Seters's arguments have not succeeded in refuting it. It is not claimed that a Davidic date has been proved conclusively, but that the passage makes good sense in that period, and that an alternative dating needs to offer at least as plausible an interpretation of the evidence. If verses 18–20 were added to section B in the time of David, then B must have existed at that time.

X

The present article has sought to defend the analysis of Gen. xiv that I presented in 1971, and the early dating of sections B and C, namely, that C was inserted into B, and that the most plausible period for the insertion was the reign of David. I have, however, modified my theory in that I now think it best to regard verses 10–11 as an editorial suture, and that I no longer think that a Davidic date is possible for section A: it is to be dated not earlier than the 7th century, and it may be later still.

List of principal publications relevant to this article

J. Doré, "La rencontre Abraham-Melchisédech et le problème de l'unité littéraire de Genèse 14", in M. Carrez, J. Doré and P. Grelot (ed.), *De la Tôrah au Messie. Mélanges Henri Cazelles* (Paris, 1981), pp. 75–95.

J.A. Emerton, "Some false clues in the study of Genesis xiv", *VT* 21 (1971), pp. 24–47.

J.A. Emerton, "The riddle of Genesis xiv", *VT* 21 (1971), pp. 403–39.

E. Galbiati, "L'episodio di Melchisedech nella struttura del cap. 14 della Genesi", *Scritti minori* 1 (Brescia, 1979), pp. 157–67, reprinted from *Miscellanea Carlo Figini* (Venegono Inferiore, 1964), pp. 3–10.

W. Schatz, *Genesis 14. Eine Untersuchung* (Bern and Frankfurt, 1972).

J. Van Seters, *Abraham in History and Tradition* (New Haven, Conn., and London, 1975).

R. de Vaux, *Histoire ancienne d'Israël* (Paris, 1971); E. tr., *The Early History of Israel* (London, 1978).

G.J. Wenham, *Genesis 1–15* (Waco, 1987).

C. Westermann, *Genesis 2: Genesis 12–36* (Neukirchen-Vluyn, 1981); E. tr., *Genesis 12–26. A Commentary* (Minneapolis, 1985; London, 1986).

W. Zimmerli, *1. Mose 12–25: Abraham* (Zürich, 1976).

ABRAHAM'S RIGHTEOUSNESS (GENESIS XV 6)

by

R.W.L. MOBERLY

Durham

Few individual texts from the OT have a more weighty history of
interpretation than the famous words of Gen. xv 6: "And he
[Abraham]¹ put his faith in Yahweh, and he [sc. Yahweh] reckoned it
to him as righteousness". Paul used Gen. xv 6 as a key text in his
argument for the nature of the Gospel (Gal. iii; Rom. iv) in a way that
was foundational for Christian theology. Other interpreters in the
Graeco-Roman world were also agreed about the importance of the
verse, although the Jewish tradition of reading it in close conjunction
with Gen. xxii meant that its significance could be developed in a way
somewhat different from that of Paul (e.g. James ii 14–26).² Later, the
centrality for Luther of the concepts of "righteousness" and of "faith"
ensured that Gen. xv 6, as interpreted by Paul and Luther, would
have an important role within Protestant theology.

It should be appreciated that these interpreters were in no way
arbitrary when they attributed great significance to Gen. xv 6, for the
verse is clearly remarkable on its own terms within its OT context.
First, the text uses two important theological terms, "have faith"
(heʾĕmīn) and "righteousness" (ṣᵉdāqâ), which only here in the OT
occur in conjunction with each other. Moreover, ṣᵉdāqâ is one of the
central concepts of the OT, which means that Gen. xv 6 necessarily
resonates within the wider context of the theology of the OT and its
interpretation must in one way or another take that wider context
into account. Secondly, the verse represents an interpretative

---

¹ For convenience, I will use the familiar form "Abraham" throughout the
article, even though within Gen. xv the form "Abram" is used.

² Another striking example is 1 Macc. ii 52, Ἀβρααμ οὐχὶ ἐν πειρασμῷ εὑρέθη
πιστός [i.e. Gen xxii 1, 12], καὶ ἐλογίσθη αὐτῷ εἰς δικαιοσύνην; [i.e. Gen. xv 6]. On
the understanding of Gen. xv 6 in Tannaitic literature and the NT, see e.g. F. Hahn,
"Genesis 15.6 im Neuen Testament", in H.W. Wolff (ed.), *Probleme biblischer
Theologie* (Munich, 1971), pp. 90–107; J.D.G. Dunn, *Romans 1–8* (Waco, Texas,
1988), pp. 200–1, 226–7.

comment about Abraham of a kind otherwise unparalleled in the
patriarchal narratives. Usually, editorial comments within the
Abraham stories relate to circumstances observable within the
normal context of life, noted from a temporal perspective ("at that
time", "to this day", Gen. xii 6, xiii 7, xxii 14), and do not purport to
give access to the mind and purposes of God. So far as the stories
contain explicit theological interpretation they present it within the
world of the story, most obviously within certain divine speeches (e.g.
Gen. xii 1–3, xviii 17–19). Only in Gen. xv 6 does the writer express
a theological judgement that to some extent stands outside the story,[3]
so far as he describes a divine attitude in the third person ("he [sc.
Yahweh] reckoned it to him as righteousness") rather than presenting
a statement by Yahweh in the first person as elsewhere. In terms of the
customary "I – thou" dialogue between Yahweh and Abraham one
might perhaps have expected the text to be something like "And
Yahweh said to him, 'You are righteous before me'" (*wayyōʾmer yhwh
ʾēlāyw ṣaddîq ʾattâ lᵉpānay*). It is the presentation of the theological
judgement in the third-person form that has enabled the verse to be
used as a theological principle independent (to some extent) of the
story in which it is set.[4] Thus both the content and the form of Gen. xv
6 mark it out as exceptional within the Abraham traditions.

I

At first sight, the interpretation of Gen. xv 6 does not appear to
present any obvious problems. Its context presents no difficulty: it is
a dialogue between Yahweh and Abraham.[5] Yahweh opens with

---

[3] The same is also true to a lesser degree with regard to Gen. xv 18a, "On that day
Yahweh made a covenant with Abram", which functions as an interpretation of the
accompanying narrative. However, it stands out less from its context, both because it
continues a third-person narrative, and because of the way it serves to introduce the
following speech. On xv 18a see below, p. 128.

[4] So, for example, von Rad comments that Gen. xv 6 is a "solemn statement"
which "almost has the quality of a general theological tenet": *Genesis* (3rd edn,
London, 1972), p. 185; cf. *Das erste Buch Mose. Genesis* (5th edn, Göttingen, 1958),
p. 156.

[5] It is commonly argued that the dialogue should be understood against the
traditio-historical background of human address and divine oracle in a cultic context
(so e.g. O. Kaiser, "Traditionsgeschichtliche Untersuchung von Gen. 15", *ZAW* 70
[1958], pp. 107–26; N. Lohfink, *Die Landverheissung als Eid* [Stuttgart, 1967], pp.
48–9; H.H. Schmid, "Gerechtigkeit und Glaube. Genesis 15, 1–6 und sein
biblisch-theologischer Kontext", *Ev Th* 40 [1980], pp. 398–9). But even if this is
correct (the main difficulty being that the precise sequence in Gen. xv 1–6, with the
divine assurance at the outset, is otherwise unparalleled), it lies sufficiently in the
background to be of only limited assistance in interpreting the passage as it stands in
its present narrative context.

words of assurance and promise (xv 1) to which Abraham responds with a question seeking further assurance (*vv.* 2–3).[6] Yahweh gives this in the form of a twofold promise, first that a child of Abraham's own body will be his heir and secondly that the descendants of Abraham will be as numerous as the stars (*vv.* 4–5). It is Abraham's response to this promise that is recounted in *v.* 6.

The Hebrew of Gen. xv 6 likewise presents relatively little difficulty, although two points of meaning, with regard to *wᵉheʾĕmīn*, and one ambiguity, as to the subject of *wayyaḥšᵉbehā*, need some comment.

The Hebrew phrase *heʾĕmīn bᵉ* means "to have faith in" in the sense of making a personal response of confident trust in someone,[7] and is usually distinct from *heʾĕmīn lᵉ* which tends to have the sense simply of "credit a report", "accept what someone is saying as true".[8] Of course, the sense of accepting something as true may also be present in *heʾĕmīn bᵉ*, as is the case in Gen. xv 6, but *heʾĕmīn lᵉ* does not necessarily carry the further implications of trusting self-commitment as does *heʾĕmīn bᵉ*.[9] The second point of meaning is that *wᵉheʾĕmīn* is, apparently, a perfect with *waw* consecutive, which makes the verb frequentative with the sense of repeated action.[10] The most natural meaning of this is that Abraham's faith in Yahweh was his constant response, and therefore the reference in Gen. xv 6 constitutes one particular example which represents and summarizes a regular occurrence.[11]

---

[6] For the theological importance of a faith in God which allows questioning of God, see R. Davidson, *The Courage to Doubt* (London, 1983), pp. 42ff.

[7] See e.g. Exod. xiv 31, xix 9; Num. xiv 11, xx 12; 1 Sam. xxvii 12; Jer. xii 6; Ps. cxix 66; 2 Chron. xx 20. Also, *heʾĕmīn bᵉ* can be used in parallelism to *bāṭaḥ* as in Mic. vii 5; Ps. lxxviii 22.

[8] Gen. xlv 26; 1 Kgs x 7//2 Chron. ix 6; Isa. liii 1; Jer. xl 14; Prov. xiv 15.

[9] Although there is a general idiomatic distinction between *heʾĕmīn* with *bᵉ* and with *lᵉ*, the distinction is not absolute. Sometimes *heʾĕmīn lᵉ* may imply a trusting personal response as a corollary of accepting someone's word as true; so Exod. iv 1, 8; Deut. ix 23; 2 Chron. xxxii 15. Note also the apparent parallelism between *bᵉ* and *lᵉ* in Ps. cvi 12, 24. For general discussion of the usage of *heʾĕmīn*, see A. Jepsen, "ʾāman", in G.J. Botterweck and H. Ringgren (ed.), *Theological Dictionary of the Old Testament* I (Grand Rapids, 1974), pp. 299–309 = *Theologisches Wörterbuch zum Alten Testament* I (Stuttgart, etc., 1973), cols 319–33.

[10] *GK* § 112 *ss* classifies Gen. xv 6 as a unusual use of the perfect with *waw* consecutive, and suggests it represents "constant continuance in a past state". The precise significance of the grammatical form is a matter of continuing debate; see e.g. K. Seybold, "*ḥāšab*", in Botterweck and Ringgren (ed.), *TDOT* V (1986), p. 242 = *TWAT* III (1982), col. 258.

[11] B. Vawter comments on Gen. xv 6 that *wᵉheʾĕmīn* should be rendered "he continued to believe" since the Hebrew form "suggests that a continuous rather than an incipient act is meant", and moreover in context "Abraham has already been presented as one totally abandoned to the designs of God" (*On Genesis* [London, 1977], p. 207). This point is lost in the LXX which renders *wᵉheʾĕmīn* not with the imperfect but with the aorist, καὶ ἐπίστευσεν, which is the form in which the verse is cited in Gal. iii 6; Rom. iv 3; James ii 23.

With regard to the subject of the second verb *wayyaḥš'beḥā*, it is usually assumed without discussion that the subject is Yahweh. It should be noted, however, that there has been a recurrent proposal among Jewish commentators (although even among Jewish commentators it has always been a minority option) to understand Abraham as the subject, i.e. "And he (Abraham) reckoned it to him (Yahweh) as righteousness". The most notable advocate of this position was Ramban.[12] Since this has also been proposed recently in two studies by L. Gaston and M. Oeming,[13] it is a possibility that must be taken seriously.[14]

This classic advocacy of this interpretation by Ramban involves a twofold argument, based on the wider context.[15] First, since there is no good reason for Abraham not to have believed Yahweh's word (Abraham being a prophet, and God being a faithful God who does not lie; Ramban also notes that a similar promise had been made previously, Gen. xiii 14–17, which Abraham had believed), it would be otiose for Yahweh specially to commend him on this occasion for doing so. Secondly, and more specifically, if Abraham could believe Yahweh in the hard matter of sacrificing his son (Gen. xxii), his faith in Yahweh's beneficial promise of descendants would seem a light matter by contrast and so hardly worthy of being singled out. Ramban therefore argued that the sense of the verse was that Abraham recognized Yahweh's promise as utterly sure, guaranteed in despite of either his merit or his sin, a word of irreversible *ṣ'dāqâ* as in Isa. xlv 23.

---

[12] Apart from standard editions of the *Mikraot Gedolot*, see esp. M. Zlotowitz (ed.), *Bereishis: Genesis/A New Translation with a Commentary Anthologized from Talmudic, Midrashic and Rabbinic Sources* 1(a) (New York, 1977, 1986), pp. 512–13; also B. Jacob, *Das Erste Buch der Tora: Genesis* (New York, n.d.; reprint from edn of Berlin, 1934), p. 394; J.D. Levenson, "Why Jews Are Not Interested in Biblical Theology", in J. Neusner, B.A. Levine and E.S. Frerichs (ed.), *Judaic Perspectives on Ancient Israel* (Philadelphia, 1987), p. 303.

[13] L. Gaston, "Abraham and the Righteousness of God", *Horizons in Biblical Theology* 2 (1980), pp. 39–68; M. Oeming, "Ist Genesis 15:6 ein Beleg für die Anrechnung des Glaubens zur Gerechtigkeit?", *ZAW* 95 (1983), pp. 182–97.

[14] As far as I am aware, Gaston's article has not been noted by OT scholars who have recently discussed Gen. xv 6. Oeming's proposal has been noted, but the tendency has been to pass over it without argument as self-evidently mistaken. Thus E. Blum comments that it "gibt in Kontext kaum einen Sinn" (*Die Komposition der Vätergeschichte* [Neukirchen-Vluyn, 1984], p. 369, n. 53), while M. Kockert dismisses it with a "(!)" (*Vätergott und Väterverheissungen* [Göttingen, 1988], p. 217, n. 260). G.J. Wenham, *Genesis 1–15* (Waco, Texas, 1988), p. 330, makes the valid point against Oeming that elsewhere in the Pentateuch *ṣ'dāqâ* always applies to human rather than divine activity. But since *ṣ'dāqâ* can be an attribute of God elsewhere in the OT, and is used in that way frequently, Wenham's point is of limited value.

[15] A full translation of Ramban's commentary on Gen. xv 6 is conveniently available in Gaston (n. 13), pp. 42–3. Curiously, Ramban's proposal is never mentioned by Oeming.

Ramban's argument has received little attention, not least because of the weight of interpretative tradition against him, and, in modern times, a reaction against a timeless and ahistorical use of the biblical text. The modern advocacy of the position is therefore based on grammatico-historical exegesis. Nonetheless, Ramban's basic sense of a difficulty in the text when read in the light of the wider story of Abraham is, I suggest, a sound insight, to which we will return in due course.

Gaston and Oeming put forward two major exegetical arguments. First, they argue that in the light of the Hebrew predilection for parallelism it is natural to take Abraham as the subject of "reckoned", so that the verse then portrays Abraham's two related responses to Yahweh. Secondly, they appeal to OT usage elsewhere, in which man, and not only God, can be the subject of ḥāšab (e.g. 2 Sam. xix 20), and ṣᵉdāqâ/ṣedeq can be an attribute or action of Yahweh, especially a gracious act of deliverance, a usage widespread in the OT (e.g. 1 Sam. xii 6–8; Mic. vi 4–5; Neh. ix 8) though especially common in the Psalms and Second Isaiah, whose language has many affinities to the Psalter (e.g. Ps. vii 17, xxii 30–1 [Heb. 31–2], xxxi 1 [Heb. 2]; Isa. xli 10, xlvi 13, li 6). They therefore understand "reckoning as righteousness" as Abraham's response of recognition and gratitude to Yahweh's gracious and salvific act of granting descendants to Abraham. Such a sense is certainly not inappropriate in context, and indeed it would fit the wider OT pattern of divine promise being met by human praise.[16] It was only at a later stage when the LXX made Abraham the recipient of righteousness, by rendering wayyaḥšᵉbehā with the passive καὶ ἐλογίσθη αὐτῷ, that the verse acquired the sense which it has had in most subsequent interpretation.

Gaston and Oeming have certainly shown that it is possible to construe the Hebrew in the way they propose. Nonetheless, there are good reasons why the consensus understanding, with Yahweh as subject of wayyaḥšᵉbehā, should be retained. First, there is the idiomatic usage of ḥāšab, which, when used with the technical sense of "reckoning", consistently denotes the situation of man before God, both when the verb is Niphal (Lev. vii 18b, xvii 4; Num. xviii 27, 30; Ps. cvi 31)[17] and when it is Qal (Ps. xxxii 2). Even 2 Sam. xix 20,

---

[16] See Gaston (n. 13), pp. 45–9. Interestingly, the widespread form-critical analysis of Gen. xv 1–6 (see n. 5) has not usually been brought to bear upon the exegesis and interpretation of xv 6, despite the fact that v. 6b does not, on its common interpretation, fit the form-critical pattern.

[17] Prov. xxvii 14 is an unusual usage, yet even here the language of blessing and curse presumably envisages the invoking of particular divine dispositions towards people.

where Shimei begs David "not to reckon his sin to him", is less of an
exception than may initially appear, partly because of the obvious
religious overtones of "reckoning sin" and partly because of the king's
position as God's vicegerent on earth. This regular idiomatic usage
creates a strong presumption that Gen. xv 6 also portrays God
reckoning something to man, i.e. Abraham, rather than vice versa.
Secondly, one must give weight to the only other passage in the OT in
which *ḥāšab* and *ṣᵉdāqâ* are combined, that is Ps. cvi 31. Here it is
unambiguous that it is Phinehas to whom righteousness is reckoned
by Yahweh, which again creates a strong presumption that Gen. xv
6 should be construed similarly with Abraham as recipient. It may be
concluded, therefore, that a traditional translation should be maintained and that Gen. xv 6 should be rendered, "And he (Abraham)
put his faith in Yahweh, and he (Yahweh) reckoned it to him
(Abraham) as righteousness".

II

If it is not difficult to determine what Gen. xv 6 says, it is quite
another matter when it comes to deciding what it means. This is
partly because the terms "faith", "reckon" and "righteousness" have
a range of meanings in the OT, and there has not always been
agreement as to their precise meaning in Gen. xv 6. The problem is
compounded by the fact that these terms resonate not only within the
OT but also within the two religions, Judaism and Christianity,
which relate themselves to the OT as scripture, with the result that
commentators have a certain tendency to attribute to the words of
Gen. xv 6 that meaning which is congenial to their own theological
understanding.

Thus, on the one hand, Protestant Christians (whose views have
formed the modern scholarly consensus) tend to find a meaning that
is consonant with Paul's interpretation in Gal. iii and Rom. iv.
"Reckon" and "righteousness" are given a less technical sense than
they have in Paul, but the general thrust is similar: the text is
concerned with faith and its approval by God: "it is stated
programmatically that belief alone has brought Abraham into
a proper relationship with God";[18] "A particular attitude to God is
declared correct";[19] "Abraham . . . is a man who responds in trust to

[18] Von Rad (n. 4), E. tr., p. 185 = p. 156.
[19] C. Westermann, *Genesis 12–36* (London, 1986), p. 223 = *Genesis 2: Genesis 12–36*
(Neukirchen-Vluyn, 1981), p. 264.

what God promises, and on this basis he is in a right relationship with, acceptable to, God",[20] "Yahweh 'reckoned it to him as righteousness', that is, certified him to be in a right relationship before God".[21]

On the other hand, many Jewish interpreters have tended to read the verse in a way that is consonant with their traditional belief in the "merit of the fathers" ($z^e k\hat{u}t$ $^\circ \bar{a}b\hat{o}t$), a belief which, among other things, includes the notion that many blessings have come to Israel because of their ancestors' obedience to God.[22] Biblical $\dot{s}^e d\bar{a}q\hat{a}$ is interpreted in terms of the rabbinic notion of $z^e k\hat{u}t$, and Gen. xv 6 is seen as a classic example of a life of obedience being rewarded by God (with blessing for Israel in view). Thus Gen. xv 6 is understood as referring to faithfulness and its reward by God. A.B. Ehrlich commented, "Das verbum hat seine gewöhnliche Bedeutung, und $\dot{s}dqh$ ist = Verdienst (cf. Neh. 2, 20 und sieh zu Deut. 24, 13). JHVH rechnete Abraham den Glauben an seine Verheissung, deren Erfüllung unter den obwaltenden Umstanden kaum wahrscheinlich erscheinen musste, als Verdienst an";[23] E.A. Speiser translated the verse, "He put his trust in Jahweh, who accounted it to his merit";[24] B. Jacob commented, "$\dot{s}^e d\bar{a}q\hat{a}$ ist dasselbe wie das neuhebräische $z^e k\hat{u}t$, der durch ein löbliches Verhalten erworbene Anspruch auf Anerkennung und Lohn ($lpny\,yy$', vor Gott)" ([n. 12], p. 394). The interpretation of Gen. xv 6 is thus a classic illustration of the fact that it is extremely difficult to determine the theological meaning of the OT apart from the appropriation of the material within historic and contemporary communities of faith.

III

The obvious way to attempt to understand Gen. xv 6 more clearly is to consider it in the light of its historical context of meaning as

---

[20] Davidson (n. 6), pp. 42–3.

[21] B.W. Anderson, "Abraham, the Friend of God", *Interpretation* 42 (1988), p. 361. For an older, thorough study of Gen. xv 6 from a Protestant perspective see H.W. Heidland, *Die Anrechnung des Glaubens zur Gerechtigkeit* (Stuttgart, 1936), or his shorter statement in the article "λογίζομαι" in G. Kittel (ed.), *Theologisches Wörterbuch zum Neuen Testament* 4 (Stuttgart, n.d.), pp. 287–95. = *Theological Dictionary of the New Testament* 4 (Grand Rapids, 1967), pp. 284–92.

[22] For recent discussion and bibliography, see E.P. Sanders, *Paul and Palestinian Judaism* (London, 1977), pp. 183ff.

[23] *Randglossen zur hebräischen Bibel* 1 (Leipzig, 1908; reprinted in Hildesheim, 1968), p. 59.

[24] *Genesis* (Garden City, New York, 1964), p. 110. Curiously, Speiser offers no comment whatever on his rendering of the text.

represented by the other writings of the OT. By general consensus,[25] the most significant modern study of Gen. xv 6 in this regard is G. von Rad's short article "Faith Reckoned as Righteousness".[26] His thesis is that Gen. xv 6 should be interpreted traditio-historically; that is, he argues that the theological sense of the verse is best understood when its terminology is viewed against the matrix of meaning from which it was derived, a matrix different from that within which it is now used. First, von Rad argues that the verb ḥāšab designates a formal "reckoning" pronounced by a priest on Yahweh's behalf within the cult as a response to a worshipper's offering (Lev. vii 18, xvii 4; Num. xviii 27). Secondly, he argues that the priest's judgement was communicated to the worshipper through a declaratory formula such as can be discerned in Lev. xix 7b or Ezek. xviii 9b (where a person is pronounced to be ṣaddîq). Thus both ḥāšab and ṣᵉdāqâ have a clear cultic meaning. Although ḥāšab and ṣᵉdāqâ are never actually combined in any of these texts, such a silence is not significant but is an accident of the differing functions of the texts in question.

Von Rad concludes that when Gen. xv 6 is read in the light of these cultic antecedents, "it is revealed as a polemical and indeed revolutionary declaration. The process of 'reckoning' is now transferred to the sphere of a free and wholly personal relationship between God and Abraham." Further, "The most astonishing difference . . . is that the cultic 'reckoning' depended on something done by the human worshipper, by way of sacrifice or specific obedience . . . Here, however, in a solemn statement concerning the divine purpose, it is laid down that is is *faith*[27] which sets men on a right footing with God . . . only faith *(nur der Glaube)*, which is the wholehearted acceptance of Yahweh's promise, brings man into a right relationship."[28] After making this grand assertion von Rad seems to have had second thoughts and backtracks somewhat. He allows that there may

---

[25] All subsequent discussions refer back to von Rad, for the most part accepting his case as established (so, e.g. W. Eichrodt, *Theology of the Old Testament* 2 [London, 1967], p. 279 = *Theologie des Alten Testaments* 2/3 [5th edn, Stuttgart and Göttingen, 1964], p. 192; J. Van Seters, *Abraham in History and Tradition* [New Haven, Connecticut, and London, 1975], pp. 257, 268–9; Schmid [n. 5], pp. 400, 408; Westermann [n. 19], E. tr., p. 223 = p. 264; D.G. Buttrick, "Genesis 15:1–18", *Interpretation* 42 [1988], p. 395), though sometimes there is disagreement (so e.g. Lohfink [n. 5], Seybold [n. 10], Gaston and Oeming [n. 13]).

[26] The essay is available in his *The Problem of the Hexateuch and Other Essays* (Edinburgh and London, 1966), pp. 125–30 = "Die Anrechnung des Glaubens zur Gerechtigkeit", *Gesammelte Studien zum Alten Testament* (Munich, 1958), pp. 130–5 = *ThLZ* 27 (1951), cols 129–32.

[27] The italics are provided by the translator, and are not in the German.

[28] E. tr., p. 129 = p. 133–4 = col. 132.

in fact be no deliberate polemic against cultic "reckoning", in which case "what is contrasted in *Gen.* xv. 6 with the cultic process of 'reckoning' (brought about through a multiplicity of particular acts) is actually the whole process of the relationship between Yahweh and mankind. Above all, this process is subjective and inward-looking, so that the accent is now upon the inward and personal attitude of the worshipper."[29]

These are indeed remarkable conclusions to be founded upon such unremarkable evidence, and it is astonishing that the article should have been so frequently referred to by later scholars without demur or criticism.[30] As a piece of theological argument it seems unduly indebted to von Rad's own Lutheran convictions (even though von Rad makes no reference to the history of interpretation). When he universalizes the significance of what is said of Abraham, portrays faith as something inward, and says that it is the sole requirement for a right relationship with God, it is clearly the Protestant understanding of faith in the light of Paul and Luther that is the determining factor in the argument. It is probably because von Rad himself realized that his conclusion outran his evidence that he expressed himself a little more moderately in his *Old Testament Theology* I:[31] "If it is there [i.e. Gen. xv 6] emphasised that faith was 'counted' as righteousness, this was certainly a striking and perhaps even revolutionary formulation for those contemporary with it . . . it represents the thesis that taking Jahweh's promise seriously, and responding to it as something perfectly concrete, was the true attitude in relationship to Jahweh." However, "we must not make the words absolute and exclusive, as if they ruled out any other possible way for men to exhibit righteousness, for they are of course bound up with Abraham's peculiar situation as the recipient of a promise with wide historical implications. Different situations might have demanded different expressions of faithfulness in relationship to Jahweh" (p. 379 = German, pp. 376–7).

Although von Rad himself appears to have recognized that his original conclusions may have been overstated, he nonetheless maintains a substantially similar position in the later work. The first step, therefore, will be to argue that, even if the premises about the cultic nature of the language of reckoning and righteousness are

---

[29] E. tr., p. 130 = p. 134 = col. 132.

[30] Such criticism as there has been has generally been directed to the question of the precise nature of the relationship of the language of Gen. xv 6 to the cult (see the discussions in n. 5). The sharpest criticism from a theological point of view has been that of Levenson ([n. 12], pp. 301–4), though see also Blum (n. 14), p. 369.

[31] (Edinburgh, 1962) = *Theologie des Alten Testaments* 1 (Munich, 1957).

correct (a matter to which we shall return), von Rad's conclusions, even in modified form, are unwarranted.

First, even if "reckoning as righteousness" normally had cultic associations, on what grounds could one know that its use within the non-cultic context of Gen. xv 1–6 should be understood as polemical? Within the context of Gen. xv there is no hint of an anti-cultic polemic. Indeed, Gen. xv 6 is followed by the description of a ritual which, although unique in the OT, has obvious affinities with the practices of the cult.[32] To read Gen. xv 6 in sharp contrast to the cultic uses of reckoning is to import concerns which are nowhere expressed in the text and may in fact be irrelevant to it.

Secondly, the problem of knowing whether to read Gen. xv 6 in the light of cultic concerns is exacerbated by the question of the dates of the respective texts. When von Rad wrote his original article (1951) the dating of pentateuchal sources had not yet become as problematic as it was soon to become. Yet even on the dating scheme that he accepted with reasonable confidence, it is odd that a text which von Rad ascribes to the Elohist (9th/8th century) should be seen as in some way dependent upon material ascribed to Ezekiel and the Priestly school (6th/5th century). Of course, because of the inherently conservative nature of cult, much of the content of P may be older than the literary context in which it now appears; but in any given case this needs to be argued and not just assumed, especially when the thesis depends upon it. In terms of the literary dates that von Rad accepted it would be just as reasonable to argue that an originally non-cultic understanding of righteousness (Gen. xv 6) was sub- sequently incorporated within the cult, rather than vice versa. (This problem is avoided by most recent scholars who tend both to be doubtful about the ascription of Gen. xv 1–6 to E and to bring the date of composition of Gen. xv down to the exile.)[33]

Thirdly, it is likely that von Rad did not give much thought to the two issues just raised because of his wider views about the history of Israel's religion. His whole discussion of Gen. xv 6 appears to be a sort of microcosm of his understanding of the origins of Israel's theological traditions within a world of wholly sacral/cultic practice and

---

[32] Von Rad discounted the significance of Gen. xv 7ff. on the grounds that it came from a source other than the Elohist to whom he ascribed xv 1–6 ([n. 26], E. tr., p. 130 = p. 134 = col. 132).

[33] See e.g. Westermann (n. 19), E. tr., pp. 209–10, 214–16 = pp. 247–9, 253–5, for bibliography and an overview of recent discussion; also R. Rendtorff, "Genesis 15 im Rahmen der theologischen Bearbeitung der Vätergeschichten", in R. Albertz et al. (ed.), *Werden und Wirken des Alten Testaments (Festschrift für C. Westermann)* (Göttingen and Neukirchen-Vluyn, 1980), pp. 74–81.

thought;[34] it was only subsequent to a fundamental shift from sacral to non-sacral in the early monarchical period ("The Solomonic Enlightenment") that traditions developed in the wider contexts of Israel's everyday life.[35] Although all the texts under discussion here were dated by von Rad later than the "Solomonic Enlightenment", he seems to have regarded the move of traditions from within to outside the cult as a basic and recurring feature of Israel's experience. But while there is much of value in this conception, it is highly debatable exactly how widespread such a process was (and, in particular, the central notion of a "Solomonic Enlightenment" has been heavily criticized as being unfounded);[36] its heuristic value for interpreting Gen. xv 6 is therefore doubtful.

Fourthly, there is one particular deficiency in von Rad's view of the sacral nature of Israel's premonarchical traditions that is of importance for Gen. xv 6. Within the early sacral traditions von Rad allows for no major distinction between the patriarchal and Mosaic traditions, but rather groups all the material together as belonging to a "patriarchal cultic world".[37] Here, "patriarchal" is not used specifically with reference to Abraham, Isaac, and Jacob, but rather as a general term to convey the early, pre-monarchical ethos as a whole; and the fact that he can thus classify all Israel's early traditions without distinction supports the contention that in von Rad's understanding no major distinction between patriarchal and Mosaic traditions is envisaged. Yet the OT itself clearly makes a distinction between the religion of the patriarchs and Yahwistic religion as mediated to Israel through Moses.[38] Despite the fact that all the patriarchal traditions as they now stand have been told from the perspective of Mosaic Yahwism, a perspective which has in varying degrees moulded the content of the traditions, there is clear evidence that the Yahwistic tradents of the patriarchal traditions were aware of the distinctiveness of the religion of the patriarchs (imbued as it is with attitudes and practices that are

---

[34] Von Rad asks rhetorically "Is it conceivable that the statement that faith is reckoned as righteousness arose wholly and solely from the reflections of a theologian?", and goes on to say that the pronouncement of xv 6 is "inconceivable... except on the basis of quite specific sacral traditions" ([n. 26], p. 125 = p. 130 = col. 129).

[35] See (n. 31), E. tr., pp. 33–4, 37–8, 263 = pp. 42–3, 45–6, 262, also his essay "The Beginnings of Historical Writing in Ancient Israel" in his *Problem of the Hexateuch* (n. 26), pp. 166–204 = "Der Anfang der Geschichtsschreibung im alten Israel", *Ges. St.*, pp. 148–88 = *Archiv für Kulturgeschichte* 32 (1944). pp. 1–42.

[36] See e.g. J.L. Crenshaw, *Old Testament Wisdom* (London, 1982), pp. 52–3, and n. 25.

[37] (n. 31), E. tr., pp. 37, 39, 396 = pp. 45–6, 47, 394.

[38] For the argument in the rest of this paragraph, see the fuller discussion in my forthcoming monograph *The Old Testament of the Old Testament*.

at variance with Israel's Torah), and on the whole imaginatively
retained this distinctiveness even when retelling the traditions within
the context of Israel. This distinctiveness is essentially that the context
within which the patriarchs are set precedes Israel, Sinai and the
Torah, a context in which the commandments given to Israel had not
yet been given and therefore did not necessarily apply. It is vital that
any interpretation of the patriarchal traditions takes this context
seriously.[39] Yet to compare Gen. xv 6 with Lev. vii 18, etc., and to
argue that the non-cultic context of the former may represent
a significant shift from the cultic context of the latter precisely fails to
allow for the possibility that the crucial consideration may be that
Gen. xv 6 is not anti-cultic or even simply non-cultic but rather
pre-cultic. It is not the case, of course, that the patriarchs are depicted
as without a cult of their own, but their cult is different from, and
antecedent to, Israel's cult, and it is the relationship between
Abraham's righteousness and that mediated through Israel's cult
that is the point at issue. A comparison on von Rad's terms is not to
the point.

IV

I propose that a fresh approach to the interpretation of Gen. xv 6 is
needed. In terms of method, I suggest that the discussion should begin
with the nearest parallel to Gen. xv 6 in the OT, the one other passage
in which "reckon" and "righteousness" occur in conjunction, that is
Ps. cvi 31. It is indeed customary for commentators to note the
parallel, but simply to note it without comment,[40] an omission which
is surprising given that the action of Phinehas which occasions the
"reckoning as righteousness" (Ps. cvi 30; cf. Num. xxv 6–13) is

---

[39] Of course, von Rad recognized both the distinctiveness of the patriarchal period
([n. 31], E. tr., p. 175 = pp. 176–7) and the appropriation and reinterpretation of
this material within a Yahwistic context (pp. 166–7). My point of disagreement is
with his apparent supposition that once the patriarchal material had been
appropriated within a Yahwistic context then the significance of the distinctive
salvation-historical context of the patriarchs (before Moses, Sinai and the Torah)
was forgotten. Von Rad says, "J and E seem to be completely unaware of it [the
patriarchal stage in cultic history], and even if memories of it did live on into their
time, the story-tellers attached no importance to them" ([n. 31], E. tr., p. 166 =
p. 170). It is against this that I argue in my OT of the OT (n. 38).

[40] So e.g. S.R. Driver, The Book of Genesis (12 edn, London, 1926), p. 176; J.
Skinner, Genesis (2nd edn, Edinburgh, 1930), p. 280; Wenham (n. 14), pp. 329–30.
Likewise, commentators on Ps. cvi usually do no more than simply note the parallel
with Gen. xv 6 without probing its possible significance; e.g. H. Gunkel, Die Psalmen
(Göttingen, 1926), p. 467; H.-J. Kraus, Psalmen 2 (Neukirchen Kreis Moers, 1960),
p. 731; A.A. Anderson, Psalms 2 (London, 1972), p. 745; L.C. Allen, Psalms 101–150
(Waco, Texas, 1983), p. 49.

strikingly different from the faith of Abraham as generally understood (Franz Delitzsch once observed that Ps. cvi 31 "bears the same relation to Gen. xv 6 that St. James does to St. Paul").[41] In most studies it appears that two assumptions are made. First, not unreasonably, it is assumed that because the same formula is used in both Ps. cvi 31 and Gen. xv 6 it has the same meaning in each passage. Secondly, more questionably, it is assumed that since the meaning of Gen. xv 6 is already known, Ps. cvi 31 is not needed to illuminate Gen. xv 6 but simply illustrates another use of the same already-known formula. So, for example, after he has noted that Abraham's faith is an attitude to God that is declared correct and noted the related use of *ṣᵉdāqâ* in Deut. xxiv 13, Westermann comments, "similarly Ps. 106:31:'that has been reckoned to him (Phinehas) as righteousness' (correct comportment in a critical situation); 'the attitude of a good, pious, loyal servant of God' (H. Gunkel)".[42]

In terms of method, I propose that this procedure should be reversed. Instead of starting with Gen. xv 6, whose meaning is controversial because of its history of interpretation, it would be better to start with Ps. cvi 31, which has little significant history of interpretation and whose meaning is therefore not controversial. If the meaning of the latter can be ascertained, then it may be able to serve as a control for deciding the meaning of the former. It is of course hardly possible to rule out the possibility that the phrase "reckon as righteousness" may be used in Ps. cvi 31 with a sense different from that which it has in Gen. xv 6. Nonetheless, the natural assumption is that where the same (and otherwise unparalleled) phrase is used the same meaning is intended, unless there are good reasons to suppose the contrary, and so similarity of meaning will be the heuristic assumption in this discussion.[43]

---

[41] *A New Commentary on Genesis* II (Edinburgh, 1889), p. 166 = *Neuer Commentar über die Genesis* (Leipzig, 1887), p. 276.

[42] (n. 19), E. tr., p. 223 = p. 265. Similarly Hahn ([n. 2], p. 92) notes the parallel between Gen. xv 6 and Ps. cvi 31, and assimilates the latter to the former; he comments that although Ps. cvi 31 does not use the term *heʾĕmīn* a reference back to Gen. xv 6 may nonetheless be intended, in which case Phinehas' action would be understood as an act of faith.

[43] Identity of meaning is a heuristic assumption which must be tested by its practical fruitfulness. If it could be shown that one usage significantly antedated the other, it would be possible to argue that the later passage might be reusing an old formula in a new way. Even if the two usages were contemporary with each other, that would not guarantee similarity of meaning. Nonetheless, despite the difficulty of dating Gen. xv 6, it will be argued that it probably dates from the same period as Ps. cvi 31 and that it also has a similar meaning. Since any argument as to the relationship between date and interpretation can easily become circular, it seems best to give attention primarily to linguistic and contextual evidence and to leave the question of dating until the end.

If we turn to study Ps. cvi 31, it should first be noted that the formulation of the crucial words "reckon as righteousness" is not in fact identical with that in Gen. xv 6:

Ps. cvi 30–1:   *wayyaᶜămōd pînhās wayᵉpallēl wattēᶜāṣar hammaggēpâ wattēḥāšeb lô liṣᵉdāqâ lᵉdōr wādōr ᶜad-ᶜôlām*

Gen. xv 6:   *wᵉheʾĕmīn bayhwh wayyaḥšᵉ behā lô ṣᵉdāqâ*

The two differences are that *ḥāšab* is Niphal in Ps. cvi 31, but Qal in Gen. xv 6, and that *ṣᵉdāqâ* in Ps. cvi 31 is preceded by *lᵉ*. It is unlikely, however, that either of these differences is significant. It has already been seen that *ḥāšab* can bear the same technical meaning of "reckon" in both Niphal and Qal (above, p. 107); while the *lᵉ* probably functions in Ps. cvi 31 simply to show that *ṣᵉdāqâ* is not the subject of the passive verb *wattēḥāšeb*, which is an impersonal form with God as the implied agent, but the outcome or result of the act of reckoning, as in Gen. xv 6.[44] Thus despite these small differences, the central formula "reckon as righteousness" is essentially the same in both texts.

There remains, however, one other difference between the two texts. This is the fact that Phinehas' righteousness is said to be "to all generations for ever". It is this that surely creates severe difficulties for the consensus view that *ṣᵉdāqâ* means "correct behaviour" in Gen. xv 6 and is no different in Ps. cvi 31. For what sense would it make to say that "correct comportment in a critical situation" or "the attitude of a good servant" lasts for ever? It may be that Ps. cvi 31 has a significance that has been generally overlooked, and the point of departure for a fresh study must be the fact that the psalmist envisages Phinehas' *ṣᵉdāqâ* as something enduring.

It should be noted that the rendering of Ps. cvi 31 is not in fact without ambiguity. The crucial syntactical question is whether the temporal phrase "to all generations for ever" qualifies the verb "reckoned" or the noun "righteousness". If the former, then the sense would be: "in every generation for ever this action of Phinehas is reckoned to be a righteous deed"; the one specific action is constantly recalled and extolled as a righteous action, presumably primarily by God but also, by natural implication, by Israel. If the latter, then the sense would be "this was reckoned to Phinehas as righteousness of a sort that endures to all generations for ever"; the one specific action had lasting effects, effects expressed by the term "righteousness". This latter sense would presumably include the former, since the

---

[44] The LXX rendering of *ṣᵉdāqâ* in Gen. xv 6 by εἰς δικαιοσύνην, which interprets *ṣᵉdāqâ* as though it were *liṣᵉdāqâ*, is a natural interpretative explication of no great significance.

enduring effects of the action would obviously cause it to be constantly recalled. Nonetheless it is markedly different, for it is the enduring quality of $ṣ^edāqâ$, rather than its constant recall, that would be the concern of the text.

It is the former interpretation that seems to have been preferred by scholars so far as they have addressed the issue.[45] It gives $ṣ^edāqâ$ its common meaning of a morally commendable action, and it makes obvious sense, for the story of the zeal of Phinehas (Num. xxv) was no doubt frequently retold in biblical as well as post-biblical times.[46] There are, however, two surely decisive considerations which favour the correctness of the second interpretation.[47] First, there is the form of the verb $wattēḥāšeb$, imperfect with waw consecutive, which naturally refers to a completed action (as e.g. $wattē^cāṣar$ in Ps. cvi 30b), not a continuous one, for which one would expect waw consecutive and perfect, i.e. $w^eneḥš^ebâ$. The verb form indicates a single reckoning, not a repeated one. Secondly, the psalmist is clearly alluding to the tradition recounted in Num. xxv where the central concern is that Phinehas' zealous action on Yahweh's behalf results in Yahweh giving to Phinehas a covenant of peace, which is specified as a "covenant of perpetual priesthood" ($b^erît k^ehunnat ^côlām$) for both "himself and his descendants after him" ($lô ûl^ezar^cô ᵓaḥărāyw$, Num. xxv 13). It is the empirical reality of the priesthood that the psalmist must have in mind when he says "to all generations for ever", a priesthood which, no doubt, was part of Israel contemporary with himself, and which validated its position by reference to Phinehas. This priesthood for Israel was understood as the lasting legacy of

---

[45] Some commentators and translators offer a rendering that simply preserves the ambiguity of the Hebrew (e.g. Gunkel [n. 40], Kraus [n. 40], A. Weiser, *The Psalms* [London, 1962], p. 678 = *Die Psalmen* [4th edn, Göttingen, 1955], p. 465. Also the *Revised Standard Version* and the *New English Bible*). Sometimes, however, an explication is offered. So, for example, Allen renders the verse, "It has been regarded by God as a virtuous act/throughout all generations forever" ([n. 40], p. 46). The *Jerusalem Bible* has "Hence his reputation for virtue/through successive generations for ever". This would appear also to be the implication of M. Dahood's rendering, "This was credited to his virtue/from generation to generation, forever" (*Psalms 101–150* [Garden City, New York, 1970], p. 65). Cf. P.J. Budd's comment that "in view of the tradition preserved by the psalmist in Ps. 106:28–31 it seems possible that Phinehas was one of those who acted decisively as 'judge,' and who thereby won for himself a lasting reputation as a righteous man" (*Numbers* [Waco, Texas, 1984], p. 281).

[46] For early Jewish use of the story and example of Phinehas, see M. Hengel, *Die Zeloten* (Leiden/Köln, 1961), pp. 154–81.

[47] This rendering seems to have been preferred by Gunkel, who commented that $ṣ^edāqâ$ in Ps. cvi 31 has the sense of "Verdienst", "Lohn", that is a reward constituted by the perpetual priesthood ([n. 40], p. 467).

Phinehas' action. Thus the meaning of Ps. cvi 31 is not that Phinehas' action was often recalled and cited as righteous, though no doubt that was the case, but that Phinehas' action had enduring effects for Israel because God reckoned it to Phinehas as $ṣ^edāqâ$.

If this construal of Ps. cvi 31 is correct, it raises the question precisely what $ṣ^edāqâ$ means in this context. But before we consider this, it will be worthwhile to return to Gen. xv 6 and see whether the proposed general sense of "reckon as righteousness" in Ps. cvi 31, that a specific action can be given enduring effects by God, would be applicable to Gen. xv 6. Admittedly, Gen. xv 6 does not use the language of "to all generations for ever", but it may be that "to all generations for ever" does not alter the meaning of "reckon as righteousness" but simply makes explicit, in the light of Num. xxv 13, the sort of implications that may also be present in Gen. xv 6. The likelihood of this is increased when one considers certain fundamental similarities between the stories of Phinehas and Abraham.

In order to set Gen. xv 6 in context and compare it with the story of Phinehas, two points must be made. The first is the fact that all the patriarchal stories, as they now stand, are told from the perspective of Israel. Although the stories contain much evidence of originating in a context which was not that of Israel with its Mosaic Yahwism, that original context is of real but restricted significance for the storytellers and editors who recount the stories from within the context of Israel and its faith. The stories have been appropriated by Yahwism and so have become Israel's stories. They are told from the point of view of Israel looking back to its origins and seeking to understand its contemporary position in the light of those origins. Although, therefore, the storytelling is imaginatively consistent in maintaining the world and perspective of the patriarchs as the primary focus, it is always legitimate to seek to discern whether the perspective of Israel may not also be present in the text.

Secondly, it is important to ask why the writer of Gen. xv 6 should have mentioned Abraham's faith and God's response to it at all, and why in this particular context – the basic issue that was seen by Ramban. For it is clear that a trusting and obedient attitude to Yahweh was Abraham's consistent response (cf. above, p. 105). It is highly doubtful that Abraham's believing response to the promise of Gen. xv 4–5 should be seen as a deeper or truer response than his response to the initial command to leave home, family and country (Gen. xii 1–4). Likewise, it is doubtful that his response to the promise of Gen. xv 4–5 should be seen as in any way different to his response to the promise of xiii 14–17. The promise of xiii 14–17 is in fact more amazing than that of xv 4–5, for it not only promises countless descendants in a similar way (the dust of the earth is hardly less than the stars of heaven) but also promises land at the same time. Although Abraham's response is not specified as such, it is hardly to be supposed that he was seen as disbelieving; rather, a trusting attitude is clearly presupposed by the writer. The promise of xiii 14–17 has received much less attention than that of xv 4–5, not least because it lacks the imaginative appeal of the scene envisaged in the latter. Nonetheless, it sharply poses the question why Abraham's faith and Yahweh's response should be specified at xv 6 rather than elsewhere.

The answer to this question must be sought by looking at the context of Gen. xv as a whole, and specifically the remarkable narrative of xv 7–21. Although the content of the double promise of both descendants and land (v. 18b) is not new within the Abraham story (cf. Gen. xii 1–3, 7, xiii 14–17), what is unprecedented is the strange and elaborate ritual that now accompanies it, and which the writer interprets as constituting a covenant (v. 18a) (see further below, p. 120). Whatever the precise significance of the ritual, it suggests a formal and symbolic commitment on Yahweh's part which furthers and enhances the promises already made.[48] Thus Gen. xv gives the impression of being the fullest and most formal portrayal of Yahweh's commitment to Israel (both people and land) in the whole Abraham cycle, a portrayal of unusual and imaginatively suggestive character.

It is this, I suggest, that accounts for the writer's inclusion of the statement in Gen. xv 6. The effect of xv 6 is to link Israel's existence as a people in the land (i.e. the concern of Gen. xv as a whole) to Abraham's trust in Yahweh. It was not only the promise of Yahweh that gave existence to Israel, primary and fundamental though that was, but also the faithful response of Abraham. It was because Abraham put his faith in Yahweh, and Yahweh reckoned this to him as $\d{s}^e d\bar{a}q\hat{a}$, that Yahweh entered into the ritual that constituted his covenant with Israel.

The perspective of the writer of Gen. xv 6 is therefore analogous to that of the psalmist in Ps. cvi 30–1. As the psalmist writes in the time of the priesthood of the house of Phinehas, and relates it back to the story of Phinehas' faithful zeal, so the Genesis writer works from the

---

[48] From a traditio-historical perspective it has been suggested that Gen. xv may represent the earliest form of the tradition of divine promise (so e.g. Lohfink [n. 5]), which would mean that the other promises in Gen. xii–xiv which now precede it in the literary tradition were once dependent on it. But whether or not this is so does not affect the central point of the argument that only in Gen. xv are the divine promises linked to a symbolic ritual.

perspective of Israel as Yahweh's people and relates this back to the stories of Abraham's faithfulness to Yahweh, and in particular the moving and mysterious story of Gen. xv. As Phinehas' faithfulness led to a perpetual covenant of priesthood, so Abraham's faithfulness led to a covenant (presumably perpetual)[49] of Yahweh's commitment to Israel as people and land. As Phinehas stands to the priesthood, so Abraham stands to Israel. As Ps. cvi 31 (with Num. xxv) shows how the priesthood owes its covenant status to Yahweh's response to Phinehas, so Gen. xv 6 shows how Israel owes its covenant status to Yahweh's response to Abraham.

If this general understanding of Ps. cvi 31 and Gen. xv 6 is along the right lines, it can be seen that our proposed interpretation of Gen. xv 6 is, broadly speaking, closer to the traditional Jewish interpretation, i.e. that the concern of the text is the faithfulness of Abraham and its value for Israel, than to the traditional Christian interpretation, i.e. that the concern of the text is the faith of Abraham in relation to Abraham's own standing before God. The latter interpretation is not, of course, thereby excluded, and may to some extent be included within the former, but the point is that the Jewish emphasis appears closer to the original concerns of the text. Nonetheless, however much the rabbinic conception of the "merit of the fathers" may represent a theological development that is sensitive to, and a legitimate extension of, the nuances of the biblical text, it remains an important task not to import too quickly into our interpretation the overtones of post-biblical interpretation, but rather still to seek to understand the meaning of the text in its biblical context.

---

[49] Admittedly, the term *b'rît* in Gen. xv 18a is not qualified by *ᶜôlām*, but such a sense may nonetheless have been considered by an ancient writer to be implicit in the text. On the one hand, there is the promissory form of the *b'rît*, analogous to the promissory covenants with Noah, Phinehas and David, all of which are specified as "perpetual" (*ᶜôlām*, Gen. ix 16; Num. xxv 13; 2 Sam. xxiii 5), and there is nothing in the text of Gen. xv to suggest that the covenant was contingent or temporary in nature. On the other hand, there is the covenant with Abraham in Gen. xvii, which is specified as "perpetual" (*v*. 7). As the text stands, this must be understood as a fuller unfolding of the the covenant of Gen. xv. Moreover, whatever the relationship between Gen. xv and xvii may have been traditio-historically, it is unlikely that P ever envisaged its Abrahamic covenant as depicting a covenant different from that in Gen. xv (also OT tradition elsewhere never implies that there was more than one covenant between Yahweh and Abraham; it understands the one covenant as "perpetual"; Ps. cv 8–11//1 Chron. xvi 15–18). If, therefore, the consistent understanding elsewhere in the OT is that the covenant between Yahweh and Abraham is "perpetual", it may well be that such a sense is implicit in Gen. xv 18a in its own right. In any case, it is likely that the text would have been understood in such a way from the exilic or early post-exilic period (which, as I shall argue below, may in fact have been the time when it was written).

V

What, then, is the precise meaning of the expression "to reckon as righteousness"? I suggest that the question may best be approached via von Rad's thesis about the cultic origins of such language. Although I have rejected the inferences von Rad drew from his thesis, it does not follow that his thesis in itself may not still be substantially correct and able to shed light upon Gen. xv 6 in a different way. There are two important insights in his thesis that I wish to affirm and extend; first, when *ḥāšab* is used with accusative and *lᵉ* of recipient (reckon something to somone), a usage akin to a double accusative (cf. GK §§ 117 *ii*, 119 *t*), it has a meaning distinct from that of other uses of *ḥāšab*; secondly, *ḥāšab* in this sense is consistently used as a religious term with reference to human standing before God.

The significance of the distinctive usage of *ḥāšab* has not always been sufficiently taken into account. For example, Gunkel argued that the meaning of Gen. xv 6 is that Abraham's trusting response to God's promise is appropriate behaviour that indicates that he is truly a pious, righteous man: "diese Tat des Glaubens wider. alle Wahrscheinlichkeit war in Gottes Augen ein deutlicher Beweis, dass Abraham gerecht sei: darum hat ihn Gott für seinen treuen und frommen Knecht gehalten".[50] However, if the writer had wished to say that God regarded Abraham as a righteous man (*ṣaddîq*), he would have used a different idiom. When *ḥāšab* is used to express an assessment of a person or thing as having a particular quality or character, the person under consideration is in the accusative, and the quality attributed to him is usually expressed by *lᵉ* (Gen. xxxviii 15; 1 Sam. i 13; Job xiii 24, xix 15, xxxiii 10, xli 27, 32 [Heb. 19, 24]; cf. Isa. xxix 17, xxxii 15; Lam. iv 2); although sometimes the quality attributed may be expressed without a preposition (Isa. liii 4; cf. Gen. xxxi 15). Thus, had the writer wished to say "and he considered him to be a righteous man" he would surely have written *wayyaḥšᵉbēhû lᵉṣaddîq* (or perhaps *wayyaḥšᵉbēhû ṣaddîq*). However, in Gen. xv 6 and Ps. cvi 31, and other related uses of *ḥāšab*, the person under consideration is referred to with *lᵉ*, and the thing reckoned to him is the accusative (or nominative, if the verb is passive). The idiom used in Gen. xv 6 indicates that the sense cannot be "consider someone to be something", but must rather be "reckon something to somone". It is important that this latter sense be recognized as distinct and not confused with the former.

It is also possible to extend von Rad's thesis about the idiom "to

---

[50] *Genesis* (3rd edn, Göttingen, 1910), p. 180.

reckon something to someone". Although von Rad was correct in pointing to the cultic uses of the phrase, it is unnecessary to suppose that it was always a cultic phrase. Apart from Gen. xv 6 there are at least three uses in clearly non-cultic contexts (2 Sam. xix 20; Ps. cvi 31; Prov. xxvii 14).[51] However, in every instance the context is religious, that is there is always reference in some way to human standing before God. The evidence suggests that although von Rad was right to argue that the idiom of "reckoning something to someone" was at home in the cult, and may well have originated there, it nonetheless became an idiom that could be used in religious language in a variety of contexts.

It may further be noted that the historical likelihood of "reckoning righteousness to someone" as a recognized religious idiom is increased by the fact that "reckoning iniquity ($^c\bar{a}w\bar{o}n$) to someone" also appears to have been a recognized idiom (2 Sam. xix 20; Ps. xxxii 2). The fact that $s^e d\bar{a}q\hat{a}$ and $^c\bar{a}w\bar{o}n$ are sometimes explicitly contrasted to each other (Ps. lxix 28, 29; 2 Sam. xxii 24, 25//Ps. xviii 23, 24 [Heb. 24, 25]; Isa. liii 11),[52] and that they are both used in a similar way with $h\bar{a}\check{s}ab$, suggests that the phrases $h\bar{a}\check{s}ab$ $s^e d\bar{a}q\hat{a}$ l^e and $h\bar{a}\check{s}ab$ $^c\bar{a}w\bar{o}n$ l^e should be seen as correlative expressions, representing two opposite pronouncements upon a person's position before Yahweh. It is against this general idiomatic background that the specific meaning of "reckon righteousness" in Gen. xv 6 and Ps. cvi 31 may now be explored.

VI

In the use of the idiom "to reckon righteousness/iniquity to someone" there appear to be four assumptions. First, there is a recognition of the inherent quality or value of what the addressee has done; an unacceptable sacrifice (Lev. vii 18), wrong conduct (2 Sam. xix 20), or right conduct (Ps. cvi 31; Gen. xv 6). Actions are subjected to a moral and religious assessment within the context of Yahwism.

Secondly, there is an assumption that actions have moral and religious consequences. As von Rad put it, "Israel was convinced that there was a definite and even clearly recognisable connexion between what a man does and what happens to him, such that the evil deed

---

[51] The cultic nature of Ps. xxxii 2 is a matter of debate because of the psalm's many affinities with Wisdom literature.

[52] When the root sdq is used in adjectival or verbal form, then it is usually contrasted with the root $r\check{s}^c$ (e.g. Ps. i; Ezek. xviii).

recoils banefully upon the agent, the good one beneficially." ". . . the presupposition . . . is the closest possible correspondence between action and fate: what is in question is a process which, in virtue of a power proper alike to all that is good and all that is evil, comes to a good or an evil end. Israel regarded this as a basic order of her whole existence, to which Jahweh had given effect and over whose functioning he himself kept watch."[53] In this context we may note the well-known point that ʿāwōn can signify both an evil act in itself and the result of that act, in such a way that it can sometimes be hard to distinguish between the different meanings;[54] the same difficulty in distinguishing between act and consequence is true also for ṣᵉdāqâ (e.g. Deut. vi 25, xxiv 13; Isa. lvi 1).

Thirdly, despite the close connection between action and consequence, there is little sense in the OT that the relationship is inflexible or inevitable. Rather, OT writers often emphasize that the outcome of actions is open to change, particularly with reference to the possibility of nullifying ʿāwōn, through either forgiveness (sālaḥ, e.g. Exod. xxxiv 9; Ps. cxxx 3–4) or expiation (kipper, e.g. Isa. xxvii 9; Prov. xvi 6).[55] Indeed, the two explicit uses of the phrase "reckon iniquity" (2 Sam. xix 20; Ps. xxxii 2) both depend on the possibility that actions designated as ʿāwōn should not be followed by their expected consequences.

Fourthly, when the phrase "reckon righteousness/iniquity" was used in the cult, it would have been spoken by the priest as an authoritative pronouncement on Yahweh's behalf, a "performative utterance" designed to enact what it says and looking to the future. However, in Gen. xv 6 and Ps. cvi 31, the reckoning is made directly by Yahweh himself and is set as something completed in the past. By giving this insight into the mind of Yahweh the writer lays emphasis both upon the validity of the judgement thus given and upon the certainty that what was reckoned was indeed enacted.

What, then, would be understood as the outcome of "reckoning righteousness"? In general terms, there is a consistent OT understanding that ṣᵉdāqâ leads to an enhanced quality of life for both individual and community. For example, the idealized descriptions of a righteous king consistently portray a life of blessing and peace for his subjects that will be the result of the king's righteousness (e.g. Ps. lxxii;

---

[53] (n. 31), E. tr., pp. 384, 265 = pp. 382, 264.

[54] Cf. von Rad (n. 32), E. tr., pp. 262ff., 385–6 = pp. 261ff., 382–4.

[55] Also important in this context is the common occurrence of divine "repentance", which I have discussed briefly in "Did the Serpent Get It Right"?, *JTS*, NS 39 (1988), pp. 10–12.

Isa. xi 1–9, xxxii 1–8, 15–20, esp. *v.* 17; Jer. xxiii 5–6, xxxiii 15–16). Or, in certain exemplary narratives, the *ṣaddîq* not only can expect life for himself, even at a time when divine judgement threatens, but can also cause life to be granted to others (Noah, Gen. vi 9, vii 1; Cf. Abraham's dialogue with Yahweh over Sodom, Gen. xviii 16–33).[56] One would therefore expect that the reckoning of righteousness to a person would lead to enhanced quality of life in some form or other.

More specifically, we may note with regard to *ṣᵉdāqâ* that, just as it may be difficult to distinguish between the righteous act and its consequence, so it can be difficult to distinguish between *ṣᵉdāqâ* as a human quality (correct behaviour) and as a divine quality (deliverance, vindication, blessing). Particularly significant is the statement in Deut. vi 25 that if Israel is careful to observe all that Yahweh has commanded them "it shall be righteousness for us" (*ûṣᵉdāqâ tihyeh-llānû*). In the wider context of Deuteronomy, the result of obedience is characteristically expressed in terms of blessing (xxviii 1–14), and so in general terms there is clearly a close connection between *ṣᵉdāqâ* and *bᵉrākâ*.[57] Moreover, the wording of vi 25 is noteworthy. The basic sense of the construction of noun with *lᵉ* and suffix is possessive, i.e. "we will have righteousness" (cf. Deut. v 7). The construction also appears to be analogous to that of "reckoning righteousness", for the related passage in Deut. xxiv 13, where it is said of the person who behaves generously in the matter of a loan and a pledge that "it shall be righteousness to you (*ûlᵉkā tihyeh ṣᵉdāqâ*) before Yahweh your God", shows that the phrase signifies some kind of divine approval of the action. The righteous action will be seen by Yahweh who will respond to it by ensuring that the person receives what is appropriate to, because it arises out of, that action – the person can be sure of divine blessing. The point, therefore, of Deut. vi 25 is not that Israel will be doing the right thing, i.e. will be righteous (*wᵉhāyînû ṣaddîqîm*), if they are obedient, which would be redundant in context; nor is it that they will be regarded as righteous by Yahweh (*wᵉneḥšabnû (lᵉ)ṣaddîqîm*); rather, their obedient behaviour will be approved by Yahweh in such a way that they will "have righteousness": their relationship with Yahweh will be enhanced and they can fully expect to receive the appropriate outcome of such an enhance-

---

[56] The question of the manner and extent to which the *ṣaddîq* could benefit others by his *ṣᵉdāqâ*, or the *rāšāᶜ* involve others in his *ᶜāwōn*, could become a difficult issue to determine (Ezek. xiv 12–20, xviii; Jer. xxxi 29–30).

[57] Cf. Ps. xxiv 5 where *bᵉrākâ* is used in parallelism with *ṣᵉdāqâ*, in the context of Yahweh's response to the worshipper who lives righteously (*v.* 4: the term *ṣaddîq* is not used, but the concept is present).

ment in the form of the bestowal of divine blessing. In this usage *ṣᵉdāqâ* as right human behaviour merges with *ṣᵉdāqâ* as divine blessing. I suggest that it is the same in Gen. xv 6 and Ps. cvi 31 also.

Finally, we should return to the striking statement about *ṣᵉdāqâ* in Ps. cvi 31 (and, as I have suggested, by implication in Gen. xv 6 also) that it represents something enduring. Although initially this may appear odd in the light of the discussion of *ṣᵉdāqâ* thus far, two points should be noted. First, there is the fact that ᶜāwōn, which we have argued can function as an opposite to *ṣᵉdāqâ*, is well known as representing a condition that can endure for a prolonged period of time. Three examples will suffice to illustrate the point. (i) There is the pronouncement in two of the central ethical and theological texts of the OT, the ten commandments and the divine self-revelation to Moses (Exod. xx 5, xxxiv 7), that ᶜāwōn may be visited by God upon several generations. (ii) There is the archetypal sin of Israel at Baal-peor (Num. xxv; cf. Num. xxxi 16; Deut. iv 3; Ps. cvi 28–31; Hos. ix 10), from whose ᶜāwōn, according to one tradition, Israel was still not cleansed when in the promised land (Josh. xxii 17). (iii) There is the divine pronouncement about the permanent exclusion of the house of Eli from the priesthood (1 Sam iii 11–14), where it is explicitly said that the iniquity of the house of Eli will never be expiated by sacrifice (ʾim-yitkappēr ᶜăwōn bêt-ᶜēlî bᵉzebaḥ ûbᵉminḥâ ᶜad-ᶜôlām). This last example may be particularly significant because of possible links between the house of Eli being excluded from priesthood "for ever" and the descendants of Phinehas being granted a priesthood "for ever" (Num. xxv 13; Ps. cvi 31). But whatever the historical processes and interrelationship underlying these texts,[58] the important point for our purpose is the theological conception of ᶜāwōn as depicting a lasting condition of human guilt and exclusion before God. Against this background it becomes easier to understand *ṣᵉdāqâ* as also depicting something lasting.

Secondly, it is likely that the conception of both Ps. cvi 31 and Gen. xv 6 of *ṣᵉdāqâ* as enduring is related to the bestowal of the covenants on Phinehas and Abraham respectively. So far as each covenant was understood as enduring, so the usage of *ṣᵉdāqâ* has been influenced by the theological conceptions associated with each covenant.

It is in the light of all these considerations that the meaning of "reckon as righteousness" in Ps. cvi 31 and Gen. xv 6 can be understood. The writers are using a recognized religious idiom with

---

[58] See e.g. F.M. Cross, *Canaanite Myth and Hebrew Epic* (Cambridge, Massachusetts, 1973), pp. 201–3.

regard to human obedience to God and what can be expected to flow from it, in the context of a wider understanding of the integral, though not inevitable, relationship between good or evil behaviour and its consequences for human life. The statement that Yahweh "reckoned righteousness" indicates both the divine recognition of the true quality of the behaviour of Abraham and Phinehas and the affirmative response which brought lasting blessing. It was a bold but appropriate idiom for the psalmist and the Genesis editor to use as they interpreted the traditions of Phinehas and Abraham respectively. In each case there was an outstanding example of human faithfulness to Yahweh, to which Yahweh had responded in a way that was of enduring benefit to Israel. The writers use this idiom of "reckoning righteousness" to show how Yahweh's bestowal of blessing on Israel, in the form of the two covenants, was integrally connected with, and grew out of, the human behaviour that occasioned it.

In theological terms this represents a profound understanding of the value of human behaviour in relation to God. The semantic point that it can be difficult to distinguish between $ṣ^edāqâ$ as behaviour of man and as action of God reflects the theological point that when man lives in full obedience to God there is a convergence between human and divine action. Not only is there the general point that righteous behaviour can enhance a relationship with God in a way that leads to blessing for the person(s) in question. There is the further and deeper point that in two archetypal and paradigmatic traditions, those of Abraham and Phinehas, the enhanced relationship with God led to a kind of overflow such that enduring blessing was bestowed on Israel also.

VII

In the light of this interpretation, is it possible to determine the context and date of the writer of Gen. xv 6? Although any proposal must necessarily be tentative, there are three converging indications which justify advancing a thesis.

First, there are the similarities between Gen. xv 6 and Gen. xxii 15–18. The striking theological conception of the value of Abraham's faithful response in Gen. xv 6 is in fact closely paralleled in Gen. xxii 15–18. In a study of the latter passage I concluded that: "A promise which previously was grounded solely in the will and purpose of Yahweh is transformed so that it is now grounded *both* in the will of Yahweh *and* in the obedience of Abraham. It is not that the divine promise has become contingent upon Abraham's obedience, but that

Abraham's obedience has been incorporated into the divine promise. Henceforth Israel owes its existence not just to Yahweh but also to Abraham."[59] Both passages display a similar concern to show how Israel's existence as a people is dependent upon both Yahweh and Abraham.

If the similarity of outlook justifies postulating a common hand at work, two further points may follow. (i) In my study of Gen. xxii 15–18 (pp. 308, 315–16, 322) I noted certain linguistic peculiarities with affinities to texts of the 7th and 6th centuries. Although these are hardly compelling, they nonetheless suggest some such date for Gen. xxii 15–18, and so for Gen. xv 6 also. (ii) In my study of Gen. xxii 15–18 I argued that the verses repesent a theological commentary on the otherwise already complete story of xxii 1–14, 19. I suggest that the same is true of Gen. xv 6. The text of Gen. xv could easily be read without *v.* 6, and indeed we have already noted how *v.* 6 does not conform either to the customary practice of theological interpretation in a divine speech or to the form-critical pattern of divine address and human response of lament or praise. The addition of *v.* 6 as a distinctive theological interpretation subsequent to the composition of the rest of the story is a not-unlikely explanation of this departure from normal practice.

Secondly, there is the likely date of Ps. cvi in the 6th century, either during or after the exile. Admittedly, the psalm is difficult to date. The most specific evidence it affords is the reference to exile in *vv.* 46–7. Although this may well be a reference to the Babylonian exile as something contemporary, it must be recognized that it need not be so. The exile might not be the Babylonian exile,[60] and the prayer to be gathered from the nations could belong to many different centuries. Nonetheless, the reference to exile together with the general theological tone of the psalm make a date in the mid 6th century as likely as any, and there is no good reason to reject the scholarly consensus which locates the psalm at about this period. If this is the correct date for the psalmist's use of "reckon as righteousness", the same may be the case for the Genesis editor also.

Thirdly, there is the fact that it was in the period of the exile that the figure of Abraham came into prominence in Israel's theological reflection (Ezek. xxxiii 24; Isa. xli 8, li 1–2).[61] It seems clear that part of Israel's response to the exile as it sought a hope for the future was to

---

[59] "The earliest commentary on the Akedah", *VT* 38 (1988), pp. 320–1.

[60] See the cautionary comments of Weiser (n. 45), E. tr., p. 680 = p. 467.

[61] This point is central to the thesis of Van Seters (n. 25), although he develops it differently from the way proposed here.

look to the traditions of Abraham and to seek in them a pattern for
their own self-understanding. The appeal of the prophet to "look to
the rock from which you were hewn . . . look to Abraham your father"
may have been precisely the concern that motivated the writer of
Gen. xv 6, xxii 15–18 as he sought to understand the implications of
the stories of Gen. xv and xxii (the only two stories in the Abraham
cycle in which active participation is restricted essentially to Yahweh
and Abraham, and in which the nature of the relationship between
Yahweh and Abraham is explored most deeply),[62] and to draw out
from them a theological basis for Israel's future.[63]

In the light of these factors I suggest that the likely context and date
for the writer of Gen. xv 6, xxii 15–18 is the period of the exile,
probably in the latter part, c. 550–540 B.C., roughly contemporary
with Second Isaiah.

The question whether this same writer made further contributions
to the interpretation of the Abraham stories lies beyond the scope of
the present article. However, it should be noted that within Gen. xv
there is one other part that could well be the work of the same writer,
that is xv 18a, bayyôm hahû᾽ kārat yhwh ᾽et-᾽abrām bᵉrît lē᾽mōr. V. 18a
shares five characteristics in common wth v. 6. First, it is a third-person
theological statement about Yahweh, rather than a first-person
statement by him. Secondly, it uses the term bᵉrît, which, like the
language of xv 6 but unlike most of the other vocabulary of Gen. xv,
resonates within a context of mature Hebrew theology. Thirdly, it
functions as does xv 6 to provide a specific interpretation of the
surrounding narrative and discourse. Fourthly, it specifies Abraham
as the object of Yahweh's dealings, but just as in xv 6 a concern for
Israel is in view. Fifthly, it can easily be removed from the text
without disturbing the flow of the story, as long as there was some
speech introduction, such as wayyō᾽mer yhwh, in its place. It would be
consistent with my thesis if xv 18a came from the same hand as xv 6.

---

[62] The restriction of focus to Yahweh and Abraham is also the case in Gen. xvii.
However, in Gen. xvii dialogue predominates to such an extent that there is little
narrative context or development, with the consequence that the relationship
between Yahweh and Abraham is not explored in the same sort of way as in the
stories of Gen. xv, xxii.
[63] It may be the case that the kind of interpretation of Gen. xv, xxii for which
I have argued with regard to xv 6, xxii 15–18 should be seen as part of a wider
tendency, beginning perhaps in the exile, to revere Israel's past as normative for the
present and future and to consider its texts as sources of appropriate guidance. For an
account of such a process with regard to prophecy, see J. Barton, *Oracles of God*
(London, 1986), esp. ch. 3. The phenomenon of inner-biblical exegesis is discussed
extensively by M. Fishbane, *Biblical Interpretation in Ancient Israel* (Oxford, 1985), who
does not, however, refer to either Gen. xv 6 or xxii 15–18.

My study, therefore, to some extent supports the current growing scholarly consensus that also dates Gen. xv 6 to the time of the exile. This was indeed a period when theological interpretation of the Abraham traditions came to the fore, and this has become incorporated into the traditions as we know them. However, I disagree with the consensus so far as it dates Gen. xv as a whole to the exile, for I see Gen. xv 6 (and xv 18a), like xxii 15–18, as a distinct theological commentary on an already-existing and authoritative tradition. For the composition of the story of Gen. xv as a whole, it is to a time prior to the exile to which we must look.

VIII

Finally, although I cannot at present offer any thorough re-examination of the NT use of Gen. xv 6 in the light of my discussion, one or two pointers for possible lines of argument may be noted.

First, the tradition of interpretation represented in James ii 14–26, whereby Gen. xv 6 is understood in conjunction with Gen. xxii, stands in continuity with the editorial interpretation of Abraham in the OT itself. Moreover, the point that Abraham's faith cannot be understood apart from his whole life of obedient response to God is entirely in keeping with the concerns of the OT text. It is notable, however, that despite his continuity with mainstream Jewish interpretation James makes no use of the rabbinic conception of $z^e k\hat{u}t$ $^{\circ}\bar{a}b\hat{o}t$, perhaps simply because it was not appropriate to his ethical exhortations.

Secondly, although Paul's use of Gen. xv 6 is strikingly different from that of James, it too is genuinely sensitive to the OT text. (i) Paul takes with utmost seriousness the overall context of the Abraham stories within a period of salvation-history prior to, and distinct from, that of Moses and Israel. He argues that if faith and righteousness were possible in this pre-Sinai, pre-Torah context, then that, among other things, relativizes the claim that obedience to Torah is a *sine qua non* of faith and righteousness. (ii) In Gal. iii Paul uses Gen. xv 6 as part of an argument that God's promises made to Abraham apply to Gentiles as much as to Jews. That is, Paul is concerned with the implications of God's dealings with Abraham for those who come after in a way analogous to what we have argued for Gen. xv 6 in its own right – though with the crucial difference that Gen. xv is concerned solely for Israel, while Paul argues that when it is read in the light of Gen. xii 3 then its scope may legitimately be extended to include Gentiles also.

The use of Gen. xv 6 thus remains a classic case-study for the wider question of the use of the Hebrew Bible as scripture by both Jew and

Christian.[64] I have argued that the rabbinic tradition of $z^ekût$ $^{\circ}\bar{a}b\hat{o}t$ probably stands closer to the concerns of the Genesis writer than does the usage of either James or Paul, and yet both James and Paul were themselves developing genuine implications of the Genesis text in its wider context. Different interpreters developed different implications because of their own differing theological contexts, and this will necessarily continue to be the case with contemporary interpreters, both Jewish and Christian. Nonetheless, while it would be idle to seek unanimity as to *the* meaning of the text, it remains the case both that some interpretations are better than others and that misunderstanding of alternative interpretations should be avoided.[65]

---

[64] For a recent study which seeks to overcome the impasse between Jewish and Christian approaches to Gen. xv 6, though touching only briefly on the hermeneutical issues at stake, see R.W. Klein, "Call, Covenant, and Community", *Currents in Theology and Mission* 15 (1988), pp. 120–7. Fuller attention to these hermeneutical issues is given by Gaston (n. 13).

[65] I am grateful to Dr A. Gelston for his comments on a draft of this article.

THE HAGAR TRADITIONS IN GENESIS XVI AND XXI

by

T.D. ALEXANDER

Belfast

I

Recent years have witnessed significant developments regarding the source analysis of the Pentateuch. Various aspects of the Documentary Hypothesis, as expounded during the last century by K.H. Graf, A. Kuenen and J. Wellhausen, have been challenged by modern writers. These include the nature of the Elohistic source (E). There is now a strong trend towards viewing it no longer as a continuous document parallel to the Yahwistic source (J), but rather as material that merely supplemented this source.[1] It is in the light of this development that the present article is offered. Our study will focus on two episodes in Genesis which have traditionally been regarded as J and E accounts of the same incident. This material concerns the departure of Hagar from the household of Abraham as recorded in chs xvi and xxi.

Initially, on account of the divine epithet Yahweh, ch. xvi was assigned to the J source. In contrast, because it employed the name Elohim, xxi 8–21 was ascribed to E. Subsequently, it was noted that both accounts contained certain common features. On this basis it was suggested that they were variant accounts of the same incident. This view gained general acceptance and has been adopted by many of the leading scholars of the past hundred years.[2]

---

[1] E.g. R.N. Whybray, "The Joseph story and Pentateuchal criticism", *VT* 28 (1968), pp. 552–8; B.D. Redford, *A Study of the Biblical Story of Joseph (Genesis 37–50)*, *SVT* 20 (Leiden, 1970); G.W. Coats, *From Canaan to Egypt* (Washington, 1976); C. Westermann, *Genesis 12–36* (Neukirchen, 1981).

[2] E.g. A. Dillmann, *Die Genesis* (6th edn, Leipzig, 1892), p. 284; H. Gunkel, *Genesis* (2nd edn, Göttingen, 1910), p. 159; J. Skinner, *A Critical and Exegetical Commentary on Genesis* (2nd edn, Edinburgh, 1930), p. 285; E.A. Speiser, *Genesis* (Garden City, 1964), p. 156; M. Noth, *Überlieferungsgeschichte des Pentateuch* (Stuttgart, 1948), p. 22; G. von Rad, *Das erste Buch Mose. Genesis* (5th edn, Göttingen, 1958), pp. 165–6; W. Zimmerli, *1 Mose 12–25: Abraham* (Zürich, 1976), p. 101.

In recent discussions of these passages there has been little attempt to demonstrate that they are parallel records of the same event. One exception, however, is R.C. Culley. Examining the similarities which exist between xvi 6–14 and xxi 14–19, he concludes:

> . . . for the two Hagar stories, the outline of the action common to both is very short and rather general.
> (a) Hagar flees or is driven out to the wilderness from Abram (Abraham) with Sarai (Sarah) as instigator.
> (b) Messenger intervenes with promise about son.[3]

The parallels between chs xvi and xxi are clearly limited.

Before accepting that xvi 1–16 and xxi 1–21 were originally parallel accounts of the same incident, there are at least eight significant differences for which some explanation must be found.

(a) The stories have different points of departure. In ch. xvi Sarah is barren, with no child of her own. In ch. xxi she has given birth to a son, who, at the time of Hagar's departure, has just been weaned.

(b) The cause of the contention between Sarah and Hagar varies between the accounts. In the first Hagar becomes proud, because, unlike Sarah, she has become pregnant with Abraham's child (xvi 4). This displeases Sarah, who then asks Abraham to intervene. In the second account, Sarah becomes jealous when she sees the two children together (xxi 9–10). She fears that the son of Hagar will be Abraham's heir rather than her own son who is much younger. Thus Hagar is no longer directly responsible for Sarah's antagonism.[4]

(c) Abraham's involvement differs markedly in the two episodes. In the former, he willingly consents to all that his wife suggests. Initially, he agrees to Sarah's plan concerning the birth of a son by Hagar (xvi 2). When the plan goes astray, and Sarah looks to Abraham for help, he concedes to her without delay (xvi 6). In the later episode, Abraham plays a different role. No reference is made to him prior to Sarah's request that he should cast out Hagar and her son. Moreover Abraham is reluctant to please Sarah, and it is only when God intervenes that he gives in to her demand (xxi 11–14).

(d) Hagar is portrayed differently in the two accounts. In ch. xvi she becomes proud when she achieves that which her mistress could not. She, not Sarah, carries Abraham's child. Ch. xxi reveals her in a different light. No longer is she arrogant. This change in character is

---

[3] *Studies in the Structure of Hebrew Narrative* (Philadelphia and Missoula, 1976), p. 45.
[4] Cf. J. Van Seters, *Abraham in History and Tradition* (New Haven, Conn., and London, 1975), pp. 199–200.

quite understandable. Now that Sarah herself has given Abraham a son, the reason for Hagar's earlier pride is removed.[5]

(e) Hagar's departure from the household of Abraham is recorded differently in the two episodes. In the earlier incident Hagar runs away after being treated harshly (xvi 6). It is of her own volition that she flees. In ch. xxi Sarah demands that Hagar be expelled (xxi 10). Abraham actually sends her away (xxi 14).

(f) The function of the well varies between the two episodes. In the first, the well provides the setting for the encounter with the angel of the Lord (xvi 7). In the second pericope Hagar and her son are unable to find water. Only after the theophany does the well miraculously appear (xxi 19).

(g) The chapters also vary in the importance they place upon names. Ch. xvi provides us with etymologies for the names Ishmael and Beer-lahai-roi, names associated with the events recorded in the story. In contrast ch. xxi mentions neither of these names. The well remains unnamed, and the narrator uses the expression "son of Hagar" when referring to Ishmael.

(h) The outcomes of the two episodes are also different. In ch. xvi Hagar is commanded by the angel of Yahweh to return and submit to her mistress (xvi 9). This she does. In contrast, ch. xxi records how Hagar and her son go and dwell in the wilderness of Paran, where the boy grows up and eventually marries an Egyptian (xxi 20–1).

To explain this particular difference it is argued that an earlier version of ch. xvi was modified by a redactor in order for both accounts to be included in the Abraham narrative. Yet, if an earlier version was altered, it is evident that the redactor introduced into the revised account a significant modification regarding God's attitude towards Hagar. Whereas in ch. xxi, which presumably reflects the original form of the tradition, God commands Abraham to expel Hagar from his household, in ch. xvi he instructs Hagar to return to Abraham's household. Unless the redactor placed exceptionally little value upon the original content of his source material, it is surely unlikely that he would have dared reverse completely the divine attitude towards Hagar's presence in the household of Abraham.

From the above discussion it is apparent that these two accounts

---

[5] It is frequently stated that this change in Hagar's character supports the view that the two passages are doublets. For example, Speiser comments, "So complete a dichotomy would be inconceivable in the work of the same author, or in a fixed written tradition" (p. 156). Yet as the narratives stand, this "dichotomy" is explicable. If, on the other hand, these accounts are doublets arising from a common tradition, then one would expect them to portray their characters in a similar fashion.

involving Hagar are quite dissimilar. Although one cannot discount completely the suggestion that they may have originated from a common tradition, it is surely more probable that they refer to two separate incidents. The differences noted above far outweigh any similarities that exist. The widely held opinion that chs xvi and xxi preserve parallel records of the same original event must be rejected.

II

If chs xvi and xxi are not duplicate records of the same incident, ought they still to be assigned to the sources J and E? What criteria indicate that they are from J and E respectively?

There is widespread agreement that ch. xvi should be divided into the following sources:[6] J verses 1b, 2, 4–14; P verses 1a, 3, 15–16. The reasons for this analysis are as follows (Skinner, p. 285): (a) The use of Yahweh in verses 2, 5, 7, 9, 10, 11, 13 is typical of J. (b) *špḥh* in verses 1, 2, 5, 6, 8 is a J word. (c) The expressions *nʾ* and *hnh-nʾ* in verse 2 are typical of J. (d) Verses 3 and 16 contain chronological material which is a feature of P. (e) In verse 15 the child is named by the father (a mark of P), whereas in verse 11 it is the mother who is told to name the child (a mark of J). (f) Verse 3 contains the P expression "land of Canaan". J. Skinner also notes "the stiff and formal precision of the style" used in the P passages. The nature of P's style is developed further by S. McEvenue:[7]

> We must note first the meticulous repetition: . . . Secondly, the story is told externally, without any suspense or psychological suggestiveness. Thirdly, we must note the circular structure of the unit, a stylistic technique best named "palistrophe", which is common in biblical literature but especially common in the priestly document . . . .
> A. (Sarai) has (no) child for Abram (1a)
>   B. Indication of the year (3ab)
>   C. HAGAR HAS A SON FOR ABRAM (15a)
>   B. Indication of the year (16a)
> A. (Hagar) has a child for Abram (16b).

Thus in verses 1a, 3, 15–16 we have a plausible reconstruction of the original P narrative concerning the birth of Ishmael.

---

[6] Cf. Gunkel, p. 184; S.R. Driver, *The Book of Genesis* (12th edn, London, 1926), p. 180; Skinner, p. 285; Speiser, p. 116; G. Fohrer, *Einleitung in das Alte Testament* (2nd edn, Heidelberg, 1979), p. 160; Zimmerli, p. 60; B. Vawter, *On Genesis: A New Reading* (Garden City, 1977), pp. 213–15; Westermann, p. 281.
[7] "A Comparison of Narrative Styles in the Hagar Stories", *Semeia* 3 (1975), pp. 65–6. But note the criticisms of G.W. Coats, "Critical Comments. On Narrative Criticism", *Semeia* 3 (1975), pp. 139–40.

The above source analysis, however, has been seriously questioned by J. Van Seters: "There is no basis to suppose there was a separate P version of the story that was combined by a redactor" (p. 194). To reach this conclusion, Van Seters adopts an alternative approach for analysing the sources used in this passage; he argues that the form of the story is the best criterion for source analysis.[8] Noting that the narrative in ch. xvi resembles closely that of xii 10–20 (both are "anecdotal folktales"), Van Seters attributes to them the following structure (p. 168): (a) a situation of need, problem, or crisis; (b) a plan to deal with the problem (wise or foolish); (c) the execution of the plan with some complication; (d) an unexpected outside intervention; (e) fortunate or unfortunate consequences. On the basis of this structure he concludes:

> Once the form of the story is recognized as a folktale, this has important implications for literary criticism. For instance, v. 1a is regularly ascribed to P but this half-verse is vital to the basic form of the story; it sets the situation of need. Similarly, the whole of v. 3 is also given to P. But in v. 2 Sarah states her plan and in v. 3 she carries it through, the same pattern that occurs in 12:10–20. There is no good reason to exclude the whole of v. 3 from the story [p. 193].

Van Seters, however, does attribute the chronological statement in verse 3 to P.

There is much to commend the approach of Van Seters regarding the initial verses of ch. xvi. Additional arguments against assigning verses 1a and 3 to P may be offered.

The case for attributing verse 1a to P is weak.
Dillmann summarizes it thus:

> If we cannot ascribe the whole verse to A [i.e., P], at least the first part is his, seeing that he has yet to mention Sarai's barrenness, whereas C [i.e., J] has already done so in ch. xi. 30.[9]

Yet, can one exclude so easily the possibility that the author of J may have wished to remind the reader of a fact already alluded to much earlier? The argument of H. Holzinger[10] and H. Gunkel (p. 264) for assigning verse 1a to P is dismissed by R. Rendtorff:

> Nach Holzinger und Gunkel ist in v. 1a der "pedantische Zusatz" ʾšt ʾbrm "Abrams Frau" ein Zeichen für P. Ein Blick in die Konkordanz lehrt, daß dieser "pedantische Zusatz" sich auch in Gen 12.17, also in

---

[8] p. 193. He comments, "It is precisely *form* that gives the best control over literary criticism".

[9] *Genesis* 2 (Edinburgh, 1897), p. 68 = *Die Genesis* (n. 2), p. 253.

[10] *Genesis* (Leipzig and Tübingen, 1898), p. 124.

einem geradezu klassischen "J"-Stück, und in 20.18, also in einem in
aller Regel "E" zugerechneten Stück, findet. Diesen Konkordanzbefund
könnte man also eher als sicheres Indiz *gegen* eine Zugehörigkeit dieses
Versteils zu P werten.[11]

Furthermore, if verse 1a is ascribed to P, it becomes necessary to
supply a new introduction to the J material. It is extremely unlikely
that the original J narrative commenced with the expression *wlh šphh
mṣryt wšmh hgr* (cf. Van Seters, p. 193, n. 2). McEvenue seeks to
circumvent this problem by suggesting that the Pentateuchal editor
tended to retain the P reading where it paralleled J or E. Thus he
attributes the whole of verse 1 to P.[12] Westermann, on the other hand,
considers verse 1a as common to both J and P (p. 281). Clearly, apart
from the assumption that P must have contained a parallel record of
Sarah's barrenness, there is no reason to assign verse 1 to P.

Three reasons are suggested for attributing verse 3 to P. First, there
is the chronological notice that Abraham had dwelt ten years in the
land of Canaan. Secondly, the term "land of Canaan" is reckoned to
be a P expression. Thirdly, verse 3 is regarded as out of sequence in the
order of events.

> Vers 3 ist nach 2a (J) überflüssig, kommt nach 2b zu spät und trennt in
> J den Zusammenhang zwischen 2 und 4: auf Saras Wort *bōʾ-nāʾ* 2 heißt
> es in 4 *wayyābōʾ* dazwischen würde 3 nur stören [Gunkel, p. 264].

Skinner regards verse 3 as the P parallel of the J material in verses 2b
and 4a (p. 286).

Unfortunately, difficulties arise with each of these three arguments.
The expression "land of Canaan" also occurs in passages which are
not generally attributed to P. These include Gen. xxxv 6, xlii 5, 7, 13,
29, 32, all of which are assigned to E, and Gen. xliv 8 which is J.[13] It is
therefore impossible to maintain that the phrase "land of Canaan" is
unique to P.

We have already noted above that on the basis of form Van Seters
does not view verse 3 as superfluous or out of sequence. On the
contrary, it describes the execution of Sarah's plan. Repetition by
itself cannot constitute a criterion for source analysis. It is a feature of

---

[11] *Das überlieferungsgeschichtliche Problem des Pentateuch* (Berlin and New York, 1977),
p. 124.
[12] McEvenue, p. 67. To separate verse 1 into two parts ruins its literary structure.
At present it forms a chiasmus which conveys here the idea of contrast: "Sarai
Abram's wife bore him no children; *but* she had an Egyptian maid-servant named
Hagar".
[13] S.R. Driver, *Introduction to the Literature of the Old Testament* (9th edn, Edinburgh,
1913), pp. 16–17.

Hebrew prose which likes to follow plans, promises or commands with an almost exact repetition of their fulfilment. As Van Seters rightly observes,

> Repetition within a story or other prose narrative passage can have a large variety of reasons depending upon an author's style, intention, or source material. Only in the case of awkward repetition that breaks the continuity of thought and action would source division be indicated [p. 156].

Most scholars accept that chronological notices are a mark of P. However, even if one accepts this in principle, there are grounds for believing that the present chronological notice may not be the work of P. Rendtorff observes that the chronological notice in xvi 3 differs significantly in form from other notices found throughout Genesis (pp. 131–6; see in particular p. 134). This suggests that it may not come from P. Van Seters allows for the possibility that the chronological statement in verse 3 may belong to the earliest collector (J) of these stories. In this case P would be dependent upon his source for constructing his chronological framework (p. 194, n. 3).

In the light of the preceding observations the arguments in favour of attributing verse 3 to P are not persuasive. On the other hand the present structure of the narrative suggests that the initial verses of ch. xvi form a unified account. When the opening six verses are separated into literary units or paragraphs the following structure is obtained:[14]

1.	Introduction	v. 1
2.	Sarah speaks to Abraham	v. 2a
3.	Abraham responds	v. 2b
4.	Sarah acts, and Hagar reacts	vv. 3–4
5.	Sarah speaks to Abraham	v. 5
6.	Abraham responds	v. 6a
7.	Sarah acts, and Hagar reacts	v. 6b

If we exclude the first paragraph, which functions as an introduction, it is obvious that paragraphs 5, 6, 7 parallel paragraphs 2, 3, 4. If verse 3 is excluded from the narrative, this literary structure is destroyed.[15] When the form and structure of these verses is taken into consideration it seems unnecessary to challenge their present unity.[16]

---

[14] Following the approach of F.I. Andersen, *The Sentence in Biblical Hebrew* (The Hague and Paris, 1974), p. 64.

[15] The description of Hagar in verses 1 and 3 also forms an interesting pattern. In verse 1 we discover the order maidservant, Egyptian, Hagar; in verse 3 this is reversed to give Hagar, Egyptian, maidservant. A simiar type of pattern occurs in xiv 13 and xiv 24, where the names Mamre, Eshcol and Aner are reversed.

[16] Cf. E. König, *Die Genesis* (Gütersloh, 1925), pp. 71–2.

A new scene occurs in verses 7–14, in which Hagar and the angel of Yahweh are the main participants. The section consists of four paragraphs (verses 7–8, 9, 10, 11–14), each of which commences with the same explicit noun subject, "the angel of Yahweh". Moreover, three of the paragraphs begin with the phrase "the angel of Yahweh said to her". This, however, creates difficulties for those scholars who regard such repetitions with suspicion.[17] As a result many commentators regard verses 9–10 as a redactional addition, provided to establish a logical link between this chapter and the supposed parallel passage in ch. xxi.[18] Alternatively, one could possibly view as redactional verse 10 (Van Seters, p. 194) or verses 11–12.[19]

These attempts, however, to remove the threefold repetition of "the angel of Yahweh said to her" may be unnecessary. First, elsewhere throughout the Abraham cycle similar repetitions occur.[20] Secondly, if a redactor adopted such a supposedly clumsy style, it is surely also possible that an original author might have done likewise. Thirdly, in spite of suggestions to the contrary, it is difficult to remove any one of the angel's speeches without creating further problems for the remaining text.

Concerning verse 9, Van Seters argues that it need not be a later redactional insertion: "V. 9 fits very well in the context, and without it the question posed in v. 8 would be rather meaningless" (p. 194). The angel's command that Hagar is to return to Sarah (verse 9) ties in neatly with Hagar's statement that she is fleeing from her mistress (verse 8). Furthermore, verse 9 follows on better from verse 8 than either verse 10 or verse 11.

McEvenue argues that the presence of the root ʿnh in verse 9, "destroys the logical link between the same root in 11a and 6a (sic)" (p. 67). Yet the opposite appears to be the case. We might translate verse 6b as, "Sarai humiliated her", and verse 9b as, "Humble yourself before her". Through the root ʿnh the author skilfully unites

---

[17] Skinner (p. 285) comments, "The redactional addition in 9f. betrays its origin by the threefold repetition of wayyōʾmer lāh malʾak yhwh, a fault of style which is in striking contrast to the exquisite artistic form of the original narrative, though otherwise the language shows no decided departure from Yahwistic usage."

[18] E.g. J. Wellhausen, Die Composition des Hexateuchs und der Historischen Bücher des Alten Testaments (Berlin, 1889), pp. 19–20; Gunkel, p. 184; O. Procksch, Die Genesis (Leipzig, 1924), pp. 114–15; L. Ruppert, Das Buch Genesis I (Düsseldorf, 1976), p. 176.

[19] R.W. Neff, "The Annunciation of the Birth Narrative of Ishmael", BR 15 (1972), pp. 51–62.

[20] E.g. xv 2, 3, xvii 3, 9, 15, xxi 6, 7; cf. C.J. Labuschagne, "The pattern of the divine speech formulas in the Pentateuch. The key to its literary structure", VT 32 (1982), pp. 268–9.

the theme of "humiliation and flight" with that of "submission and return".

Finally, if it is accepted that xvi 1–16 and xxi 1–21 are not doublets, then it can no longer be maintained that verse 9 was added in order to bring about the necessary return of Hagar to the household of Abraham. A new rationale for the insertion of verse 9 must be found. Thus there are substantial grounds for maintaining that verse 9 was part of the original story.

Could verse 10 be redactional? Van Seters argues that the logical order of the verse ought to be, first, details about the birth of a son, and then the promise of numerous descendants (p. 194). As the text now stands, the reference to numerous descendants precedes the announcement of the birth of a son. Yet this particular order occurs elsewhere in the Abraham cycle. In ch. xvii Abraham is informed in verse 2 that he will have numerous descendants, but it is not until verse 16 that the specific promise of a son is introduced. Also, it is apparent that the announcement in verse 10 is not primarily concerned with informing Hagar that she is pregnant, a fact already known to her.

As far as verses 11–12 are concerned, R.W. Neff suggests two reasons for viewing them as later additions. First, he notes that the birth announcement is unnecessary because Hagar is already aware that she is pregnant (p. 54). Yet verses 11–12 reveal the name, destiny and character of the child. Obviously without the divine revelation Hagar could not have known these facts. Second, Neff believes that the redactor introduced this announcement in order to maintain the original ending of the J account which told of the birth of Ishmael and his living in the wilderness (pp. 59–60). Yet need this be so? Whereas in verse 9 Hagar is commanded to return and submit to her mistress, in verses 11–12 she has the comfort of knowing that her son will submit to no one. As with verses 9 and 10, there seems to be no substantial reason for regarding verses 11–12 as redactional. This conclusion is supported by the language "which shows no decided departure from Yahwistic usage" (Skinner, p. 285).

Having concluded that the content of verses 9–12 is relevant and necessary to the present account, we must assume that the triple repetition of "the angel of Yahweh said to her" is a feature of the author's style. Possibly it serves to emphasize who was speaking. The reader is left in no doubt that the angel of Yahweh spoke these words to Hagar. Alternatively, the narrator may have wished to break up the angel's speech in order to highlight the various elements constituting it (cf. xvii 3, 9, 15). It may even be that the repetition of "the angel of Yahweh said to her" provides an opportunity for the significance of the preceding words to register with the reader or hearer. Perhaps one, or all, of these ideas determined the author's style in the present context.

Verses 13–14 are generally assigned to J. Hagar's reaction to the theophany is finally revealed through the inclusion of certain aetiological material. These details bring the second scene to a conclusion.

The remaining two verses of the chapter are attributed to P because of (a) the chronological material (verse 16), and (b) the naming of the child by the father (verse 15). Of these two criteria, the latter cannot be applied with complete certainty. It is usually maintained that in J the mother names the child, whereas in P this function is performed by the father. Yet in iv 26 and xxxviii 3, both J passages, Seth and Judah respectively name their children. U. Cassuto also notes that of the four occasions in P where a father names his child, two are attributed to P on the basis of this criterion alone.[21] For these reasons the naming of the child by the father hardly repesents an adequate criterion for source analysis.

Our investigation of the criteria used to separate J and P material in ch. xvi reveals weaknesses regarding the generally accepted source analysis. Reservations must be expressed about the validity of most of the arguments offered in support of assigning the account to two separate sources. If sources were employed, they cannot be detected as easily as is often supposed. In its present form xvi 1–16 appears to be a carefully constructed narrative. On the basis of the divine name Yahweh the entire narrative, apart possibly from the chronological notices in verses 3 and 16, may be assigned to J.

III

Before examining the source analysis of the Hagar incident in ch. xxi, it is necessary to determine the precise extent of the account. Clearly, verses 8–21 comprise the bulk of the narrative. Yet the initial seven verses of the chapter provide an indispensable introduction to what follows. In xxi 1–7 the birth of Isaac to Sarah is recorded. Ultimately, it is this event which leads to the expulsion of Hagar. Although Sarah has now given birth to a son, she is fearful that Hagar's son, Abraham's firstborn, will actually be his main heir. Thus verses 1–7 provide the background against which the following narrative develops. Moreover, there is no clear break between the

---

[21] *The Documentary Hypothesis* (Jerusalem, 1961), pp. 65–6.

initial verses of the chapter and the account of the expulsion of Hagar. Verse 8 can hardly be regarded as a fitting introduction to a new narrative. The phrase "and the child grew and was weaned" assumes that the identity of the child is already known from the preceding verses. Also, since many scholars assign verses 6 and 7 to the same source as verses 8–21, there is good reason to maintain the unity of verses 6–21. Yet to argue that the narrative once commenced in verse 6 is no better. Verse 6 itself requires prior knowledge of the name Isaac, otherwise the play on the root ṣḥq becomes meaningless. This aside, it is unlikely that a Hebrew author would have commenced his narrative with verse 6. The next possible introduction to the narrative must be verse 2, since verses 2, 3, 5 cannot be separated. They constitute a fixed form used to describe the birth and naming of a child. Verse 2, however, follows on well from verse 1, and, as Andersen notes, the word order in verse 1 is episode initial (p. 41). As verses 1–7 stand at present they provide an essential and unified introduction to verses 8–21. Attempts to reconstruct an alternative introduction for xxi 8–21 are fraught with difficulties.

As it proves exceptionally awkward to separate verses 8–21 from the preceding verses, we shall treat xxi 1–21 as a unified narrative. However, whereas verses 8–21 are usually attributed to E, most scholars assign verses 1–7 between the three sources J, E and P. For convenience, therefore, we shall examine the source analysis of verses 1–7 and verses 8–21 separately.

The following table permits us to see the ways in which various scholars have analysed verses 1–7 into sources:[22]

	J	E	P
Driver	1a, 2a	6, 7	1b, 2b–5
Gunkel	1a, 2a, 7, 6b	6a	1b, 2b–5
Procksch	1b, 2a, 7, 6b	1a, 6a	2b–5
König	1a, (1b?), 2a	6, 7	2b–5
Skinner	1a, 2a, 7, 6b	6a	1b, 2b–5
Speiser	1a, 2a	6, 7	1b, 2b–5
Fohrer	1a, 2a, 7	1b, 6	2b–5
Zimmerli	1a, 7	6	1b, 2–5
Westermann	1–2, 6–7	—	(1–2), 3–5

Van Seters, who departs from the traditional labels J, E and P, assigns verses 2, 6–7 to his pre-Yahwistic first stage, verse 1 to his Yahwist, and verses 3–5 to the Priestly writer.

---

[22] Driver, pp. 209–10; Gunkel, pp. 226–7; Procksch, pp. 137–8, 309, 526; König, pp. 539–40; Skinner, pp. 320–1; Speiser, pp. 153–7; Fohrer, pp. 160, 167, 195; Zimmerli, pp. 99–100; Westermann, p. 405.

It is apparent that the source analysis of verses 1–7 presents difficulties. Verses 2b–5 are almost unanimously given to P, and there is general agreement that verses 1a and 2a are from J, and verse 6a from E. However, regarding verses 1b, 6b, 7 there is no consensus as to which of the sources these verses should be assigned.

Verse 1 presents an initial problem. J. Astruc and J.G. Eichhorn were satisfied to assign the whole verse to J on account of the presence of the divine name Yahweh in both halves of the verse. Other scholars, however, on the basis that the second half of the verse needlessly repeats the first part, divided the verse, ascribing the first part to J and the rest to P (e.g. Dillmann, p. IX; Skinner, p. 320). As a result it became necessary to explain the unexpected presence of Yahweh in verse 1b. Dillmann puts it down to the redactor R (p. 284). Skinner suggests that it is due to a scribal error (p. 320).

Yet the evidence for attributing verse 1 to two sources is weak. We have already noted Van Seter's comment on the use of repetition as a criterion for source analysis: "Only in the case of awkward repetition that breaks the continuity of thought and action would source division be indicated" (p. 156). But can one regard the repetition of verse 1 as "awkward"? Surely the repetition stresses the actual fulfilment of the earlier promises.[23] Apart from "Yahweh", the only other term in verse 1 thought to be indicative of a particular source is the verb *pqd*, a J term. Yet *pqd* occurs in Genesis in two passages assigned to E (xl 4, 1 24–5). As a result this verb can hardly be used to support the claim that verse 1a is J. The one remaining criterion for the analysis of verse 1 is the divine name Yahweh.

Verse 2a is usually considered to be J and verse 2b P. The first part of the verse is credited to J because of the supposed J expression *bn lzqnyw*, an expression found in Genesis only here and in xxi 7. Although some scholars regard verse 7 as J, others treat it as E. For those who assign verse 7 to E, the phrase *bn lzqnyw* is not taken to be indicative of J.[24] Furthermore, verse 7 is usually ascribed to J solely on the basis of *bn lzqnyw* (Skinner, p. 320). Clearly, this expression cannot be employed with any confidence for analysing verses 2 and 7. The

---

[23] Andersen (p. 130; cf. p. 42) notes that the verse forms a rare kind of chiasmus: Subject/perfect verb – imperfect verb/subject. Normally the first verb is in the imperfect tense and the second in the perfect. The reversal of the tenses in the present context occurs because the first clause is, according to Andersen, "episode initial" (p. 80). This chiastic structure offers an alternative explanation for the repetition which occurs in the verse. Westermann (p. 406) also concludes that the parallelism is deliberate.

[24] Cf. Driver, p. 210; König, p. 67; Speiser, p. 153.

criteria usually cited for ascribing the second half of verse 2 to P are the use of the divine name Elohim and the term lmw^cd. Yet lmw^cd is not unique to P, occurring as it does in xviii 14, a J passage. This leaves one single criterion for the analysis of verse 2, the divine name Elohim. Further evidence, however, for the source analysis of verse 2 will be introduced as we consider verse 3.

Verse 3 has been assigned almost unanimously to P on the basis of the father naming his son. This criterion has already been encountered in xvi 15, and in our discussion of that verse we noted that it is not necessarily indicative of P.

A comparison of xxi 2–3 and xvi 15 proves instructive.

xvi 15	*xxi 2–3*
	And she conceived,
And Hagar bore Abram	and Sarah bore Abraham
a son;	a son in his old age at the
	time of which God had spoken
	to him.
and Abram called the	Abraham called the name of
name of his son,	his son who was born to him,
whom Hagar bore, Ishmael.	whom Sarah bore him, Isaac.

First, although xxi 2–3 offers a fuller account, both passages follow a set form for describing the birth and naming of a child. Secondly, xxi 2aβ is an integral part of this form.[25] Whereas verses 1–2aα emphasize Sarah's conception, verses 2aβ–3 are concerned with the subsequent birth and naming of Isaac. Thirdly, within this set form the birth of the son is recorded twice. This repetition is due to the fixed form of the expression rather than different sources. Since xxi 2aβ–3 contains a set formula for expressing the birth and naming of a child there seems to be no reason to assign this material to two separate sources. Also, the natural link formed by placing $lzqnyw$ and lmw^cd in apposition supports the original unity of verse 2 (cf. Andersen, pp. 36, 60).

Verses 4 and 5 are credited to P; verse 4 on account of the presence of Elohim and the reference to circumcision; verse 5 because of the chronological notice concerning the age of Abraham. Verse 4 obviously alludes to the events of ch. xvii and the divine command that Abraham should circumcise every male who is eight days old (cf. xvii 10–14). The chronological notice of verse 5 resembles closely xvi 16. We have already observed the close parallels that exist between xxi 2–3 and xvi 15. This suggests that xxi 2–3, 5 follows a set formula used

---

[25] The inclusion of the explicit noun subject, Sarah, after "and she conceived" marks the start of a new paragraph in the Hebrew; cf. Andersen, p. 64.

to describe not only the birth and naming of a son but also when the birth occurred. If this is so, then verse 4 interrupts this form. Certainly, the mention of Isaac's circumcision before the chronological notice of his date of birth seems strange. Yet in spite of this no commentator has suggested that verse 4 is a later addition.

Although most scholars attribute the first part of verse 6 to E, there is a division of opinion whether the rest of the verse should be ascribed to E or J. Those who divide the verse between the two sources argue that the second half of verse 6 repeats the first (Skinner, p. 320). Yet, as in verse 2, the two halves are closely connected by being placed in apposition. The use of apposition here, according to Andersen, shows the casual relationship which exists between the two halves of the verse: "God made laughter for me; (therefore) everyone who hears it will laugh for me" (p. 58). There seems to be no compelling reason for assigning verse 6 to two different sources.

Lack of decisive criteria creates difficulties for the source analysis of verse 7. The verse has been generally assigned to either J and E. In favour of J is the expression *bn lzqnyw*. However, we have already noted in considering xxi 2 that this phrase is not necessarily indicative of the J source.

From the preceding discussion three conclusions may be drawn. First, if we exclude the divine names and chronological notices, the criteria cited in favour of the source analysis of this section prove inadequate. Secondly, verses 1–7 may have been influenced in their content and style by earlier sections of the Abraham cycle, in particular xvi 15–xviii 15. Thus Westermann comments,

> Man kann dann die Verse 1–2 nur als communis bezeichnen, was aus der Absicht des Redaktors, die Erzählungen Gn 17 und 18 zusammenfassend abzuschliessen, voll begründet ist. Dasselbe gilt für v. 6–7, wo auch sichere Quellenscheidung nicht möglich ist (pp. 406–7).

Finally, the present unity of verses 1–7 must surely weigh heavily against any unnecessary division of the text into sources.

Whereas verses 1–7 are assigned to various sources, verses 8–21 are usually ascribed to E. Skinner bases his analysis on the following criteria (p. 321): (a) The use of the divine name Elohim in verses 12, 17, 19, 20 is typical of E. (b) *ʾmh* in verses 10, 12, 13, is an E word. (c) The expression *śym lgwy* in verses 13, 18 is an E phrase. J employs *ᶜśh lgwy* (cf. xxi 2) and P *ntn lgwy* (cf. xvii 10). (d) The rare expressions *ḥmt* (verses 14, 15, 19), *mṭḥwy qśt* (verse 16), and *rbh qśt* (verse 20) are from E. (e) The revelation of God by night (verses 12–13) is typical of E. (f) The voice from heaven (verse 17) is an E characteristic. It is generally held that these criteria support the view that xxi 8–21 is E's version of the J account in ch. xvi. Yet from our earlier investigation of these incidents we concluded that there is little evidence to support the view that the narratives in chs xvi and xxi are doublets. Such a conclusion, however, does not rule out the possibility that the two accounts come from different sources.

Doubts must be raised about the validity of some of the various criteria offered in favour of assigning verses 8–21 to E. The expressions *ḥmt* (verses 14, 15, 19), *mṭḥwy qšt* (verse 16) and *rbh qšt* (verse 20) occur only here in the whole of the Old Testament. This hardly qualifies them as suitable criteria for source analysis. Similarly *śym lgwy* (verses 13, 18) occurs elsewhere in the Pentateuch only in Gen. xlvi 3, a passage usually attributed to E. On the basis of these two passages it is surely impossible to state with any certainty that *śym lgwy* is a typical E expression. A similar construction, *śym lḥq* occurs in xlvii 26, a J section.

The term *'mh* is taken to be the E equivalent of the J word *špḥh* (cf. xvi 1, 2, 5, 6, 8). However, the inadequacy of these terms for distinguishing sources has been demonstrated by A. Jepsen.[26]

Regarding the "voice from heaven" it is not at all apparent that this must be an E expression. In xxii 11, 15 the angel of Yahweh calls to Abraham from heaven. Although these verses are often, but not always, assigned to E, this analysis is not without its difficulties. The presence of the divine name Yahweh weighs heavily against assigning these verses to E. If this is accepted, this criterion can no longer be exclusively an E characteristic.

Another feature taken to be characteristic of E is the revelation by night (verses 12–13). This particular criterion has been examined in detail by M. Lichtenstein who considers various incidents of "dream-theophanies" in Genesis, in particular xv 1ff. and xxviii 12ff. He concludes, "No consistent distinction can be drawn between J and E with respect to the use of dream-theophanies as the medium of revelation."[27] The criterion of God appearing in a dream has also been rejected in several recent studies on the Joseph Story in Gen. xxxvii–l (Redford, pp. 68–71; Coats, p. 62).

The age of Ishmael in ch. xxi presents a problem for some scholars. From the chronological notices in xvi 16, xvii 24–5, xxi 5 it is

---

[26] "*Amaʰ* und *Schiphchaʰ*", *VT* 8 (1958), pp. 293–7; cf. M.H. Segal, *The Pentateuch* (Jerusalem, 1967), p. 15; Van Seters, p. 202.

[27] "Dream-Theophany and the E Document", *JANESCU* 1/2 (1968–9), p. 48. Later he concludes, "Both the evolutionary theories of biblical revelation media, as well as the validity of their implications for source divisions in the text of the Pentateuch, must be seriously questioned" (p. 54). Cf. Redford, pp. 69–71, 252, n. 1.

apparent that Ishmael must be some sixteen years old at the time of
the events recorded in xxi 1–21. Yet it is maintained that in ch. xxi
Ishmael is portrayed as a young child.[28] From these observations it is
argued that the accounts in chs xvi and xxi were not originally part of
the same document. Therefore they must be derived from two
separate sources. This difficulty regarding the age of Ishmael,
however, arises only when one includes the chronological notices in
xvi 16, xvii 24–5, xxi 5. Yet, since these are all assigned to P, and are
therefore redactional, there no longer remains any reason why the
two accounts could not have originally formed part of the same
document.

From the above discussion it is apparent that, if we exclude the
divine names, the main criteria cited in favour of assigning xxi 8–21 to
E cannot be relied upon with any certainty.

In considering the source analysis of xxi 8–21 Van Seters makes
two interesting observations. First, on the basis of A. Olrik's epic laws,
he concludes that "21:8–21 must be a literary composition drawing
its material from chap. 16, but written for its own distinctive purpose
and concern" (p. 200). Even if one rejects Van Seters's use of Olrik's
epic laws,[29] xxi 8–21 does rely heavily upon the reader being aware of
ch. xvi. This becomes even more apparent when xxi 1–7 is included.
In their present form verses 1–21 make complete sense only in the
light of chs xvi and xvii. Verses 1–7 speak of the fulfilment of promises
made in ch. xvii. The birth and naming formula in xxi 2, 3, 5 is similar
to that of xvi 15–16. Verses 9–10 presuppose the events of ch. xvi;
otherwise, one would hardly expect the son of a slave to inherit before
Sarah's son. Abraham's reluctance to expel Hagar and Ishmael
reflects the fact that Hagar was divinely commanded to return to
Abraham's house in xvi 9. The promises concerning Ishmael in xxi
13, 18 resemble those made in xvi 10 and xvii 20. The narrative in xxi
1–21 clearly presupposes a familiarity with the content of chs xvi and
xvii.

Secondly, Van Seters notes that the two main themes of ch. xxi

---

[28] Cf. Dillmann, p. 286; Skinner, pp. 322–3. Support for this view is derived from
the LXX and Syriac translations of verse 14, "And he (Abraham) placed the child on
her shoulder". However, Speiser (pp. 154–5) notes that the text is obscure here and
the word order of the LXX and Syriac may not represent the most original reading.
He translates verse 14 as follows: "Early next morning Abraham got some bread and
a skin of water to give to Hagar. He placed them on her back and sent her away with
the child."

[29] Cf. S.M. Warner, "Primitive saga men", *VT* 29 (1979), pp. 325–35; R.N.
Whybray, *The Making of the Pentateuch: A Methodological Study* (Sheffield, 1987), pp.
133–219.

concern descendants and inheritance. Yet "these themes are easily recognized as the central concern of the Yahwist" (p. 200). As a result he concludes: "The thematic concerns of 21:8–21 would strongly suggest that the author is, in fact, J" (p. 202). Certainly, in J the themes of descendants and inheritance are prominent. Yet a consideration of ch. xvii shows that they are also present there, and, since both themes are widespread throughout the Abraham cycle, it is unlikely that they can be limited to one source. However, ch. xxi resolves an important issue involving inheritance which arises out of events occurring earlier in the cycle. Ishmael is older that Isaac, and would have a claim to Abraham's inheritance. By expelling both Hagar and Ishmael it becomes apparent that Isaac will be the sole heir. Thus ch. xxi resolves the tension created by the birth of Ishmael in ch. xvi. This suggests that the narratives were originally composed together as part of a family history.[30]

IV

We may now draw three conclusions regarding the Hagar traditions in chs xvi and xxi. First, the narratives are sufficiently different to indicate that they are not variant accounts of the same event. Secondly, the narrative in ch. xxi presupposes that the reader is already familiar with the events recorded in ch. xvi. Thirdly, almost all the criteria cited in favour of assigning these narratives to J and E prove unconvincing. But for the use of the different divine names Yahweh and Elohim, there would be no compelling reason to assign chs xvi and xxi to different sources.

This naturally raises the question: how decisive is the criterion of divine names in this instance? Westermann, for example, questions its usefulness in xxi 1–7: "Es hat den Anschein, als gebrauche der Redaktor in 21,1–7 die beiden Gottesbezeichnungen bewußt ohne Unterschied" (p. 408). However, as regards xvi 1–16 and xxi 8–21 he still considers it a helpful indicator of sources. If these accounts were originally composed by a single author, it is difficult to see why he should have employed the name Yahweh in ch. xvi and the name Elohim in ch. xxi. Consequently Westermann rejects the suggestion of Van Seters that ch. xxi is from J. Yet if we approach this issue from another angle, there is perhaps evidence to suggest that the earliest form of ch. xvi did not use the divine epithet Yahweh. Recently, G.J.

---

[30] Cf. G.W. Coats, *Genesis with an Introduction to Narrative Literature* (Grand Rapids, 1983), pp. 127–8.

Wenham has argued that the presence of the divine name Yahweh in Genesis may be due to the work of a Yahwistic editor who used this designation to replace an older name.

> The evidence for supposing that the editor sometimes introduced Yahweh instead of El or Elohim is quite clear. For example, Hagar is told to name her son "Ishmael, because the LORD has given heed to your affliction . . . So she called the name of the LORD who spoke to her, 'You are El Roi'" (16:11, 13).[31]

On the basis of the etymologies in xvi 11, 13 Wenham suggests that the name Yahweh was not part of the original text. Westermann is also of the opinion that the name Yahweh in verses 11 and 13 is not original (pp. 246–7). If, however, an older divine epithet has been altered in favour of Yahweh in verses 11 and 13, is it not also possible that the same change occurred elsewhere in the chapter? Might not the expression "angel of Yahweh" (xvi 7, 9, 10, 11) have originally read "angel of Elohim"? Clearly such a transformation would be impossible to demonstrate. Yet in the light of our earlier discussion, it certainly deserves thoughtful consideration. If Wenham's theory were accepted, there would no longer remain any need to assign chs xvi and xxi to J and E respectively.

At the outset we noted that some writers now question the existence of an independent E document, paralleling J in content. Our examination of the Hagar narratives points in the same general direction. Certainly, there are insufficient grounds for believing that chs xvi and xxi preserve duplicate accounts of the same event. Moreover, the generally accepted criteria for assigning these chapters to J and E are inadequate. On the other hand, there are strong grounds for suggesting that both accounts come from a single source. Although these observations relate specifically to only two chapters of Genesis, they lend support to demands for a revision of the Documentary Hypothesis.

---

[31] "The Religion of the Patriarchs", in A.R. Millard and D.J. Wiseman (ed.), *Essays on the Patriarchal Narratives* (Leicester, 1980), p. 181.

THE ELOHISTIC DEPICTION OF AARON: A STUDY IN THE LEVITE—ZADOKITE CONTROVERSY

by

MARSHA WHITE

Cambridge, Massachusetts

The purpose of this study[1] is to examine one stage in the history of the Aaron tradition. A survey of biblical literature with reference to Aaron indicates that the tradition emerged rather late. There is no reference to Aaron in the ancient poetry, and even the Yahwist lacks mention of Moses' "brother".[2] The first coverage of Aaron occurs in the two Elohistic narratives of Exod. xxxii and Num. xii,[3] where it is appended to the received tradition.[4] Because the Elohist's portrayal of Aaron is so negative and because he regards Aaron as a priest, it is

---

[1] Read in part at the New England Section of the Society of Biblical Literature in Cambridge, Massachusetts, on 25 March 1988.

[2] J. Wellhausen, *Prolegomena to the History of Israel* (Edinburgh, 1885), p. 142, n. 2 = *Prolegomena zur Geschichte des Israels* (2nd edn, Berlin, 1883), p. 147, n. 1.

[3] If the Aaron passages in Exod. xxxii and Num. xii are Elohistic and all other non-Priestly Aaron passages in the Tetrateuch belong to the redactor of J and E, there are two coherent pictures of Aaron. The Elohist assaults and lampoons Aaron, whereas the JE redactor exalts him as Moses' partner. In R^{JE} Aaron goes to Pharaoh with Moses (Exod. v 1, 4, 20, ix 27, x 3, 8, 16), supports Moses' hands in battle (Exod. xvii 10, 12), joins Moses for two meals before God (Exod. xviii 12, xxiv 1, 9), ascends the mountain with Moses (Exod. xix 24), and stands in for Moses in legal matters (Exod. xxiv 14). According to R^{JE}, Aaron is Moses' companion and assistant. In Exod. xxxii and Num. xii, however, Aaron is a rival priest who must be reprimanded for leading the people astray and for assuming parity with Moses.

[4] The originality of Aaron in the traditions lying behind these passages is a matter of debate. I follow Wellhausen's analysis of the priesthood (*Prolegomena*, ch.4) and K. Möhlenbrink's dictum "dass Aaron in den Mosegeschichten sekundär ist" ("Die levitischen Überlieferungen des Alten Testaments", *ZAW* 52 [1923], p. 219). M. Noth accepts Aaron's secondary status (*A History of Pentateuchal Traditions*, tr. B.W. Anderson [Englewood Cliffs, New Jersey, 1972], pp. 178–9 = *Überlieferungsgeschichte des Pentateuch* [Stuttgart, 1948], pp. 195–6) and develops it with respect to both Exod. xxxii (*Exodus: A Commentary* [London and Philadelphia, 1962], pp. 244–5 = *Das zweite Buch Mose, Exodus* [Göttingen, 1959], pp. 200–1), and Num. xii (*Numbers: A Commentary* [London, 1968], pp. 92–3 = *Das vierte Buch Mose, Numeri* [Göttingen, 1966], pp. 82–3). With reference to the Aaron additions in Exod. xxxii Noth says, "Unfortunately we can no longer ascertain the time or circumstances of the addition of these passages. They must derive from circles in which the (priestly) sons of Aaron

most reasonable to assume that the Elohistic depiction of Aaron
constitutes a polemic against a priestly group. Scholarship has long
recognized such a priestly polemic, generally regarding Exod. xxxii as
an attack on an Aaronid priesthood at Bethel. This opinion was
advanced initially by R.H. Kennett,[5] and further developed by T.J.
Meek,[6] O. Eissfeldt,[7] F.S. North,[8] M. Aberbach and L. Smolar,[9] and
F.M. Cross.[10]

However, the favorable and even paradigmatic place that Bethel
holds in other Elohistic literature (e.g. Gen. xxxv 1–10, 13–15)
seriously questions the notion of an Elohistic polemic against Bethel.
It is unlikely that a source, which shares the tendentious quality of all
sources in advancing certain positions, would both honor and
demean the same place. A more likely candidate for a source
harboring a grudge against Bethel is the Deuteronomistic Historian
or someone influenced by him, and a source analysis made with
reference to other Elohistic and Deuteronomistic passages will
distinguish between the two strata in Exod. xxxii. Once the
Deuteronomistic counter-attack against Bethel is removed from
Exod. xxxii, one is left with a Northern polemic against the Zadokite
(Aaronid) priests of Jerusalem, which accords with the Elohistic
advocacy of the Levitical position in Num. xii. The priestly controversy in which the Elohist was engaged was therefore between the
Zadokites of Jerusalem and the Levites of the North.[11] The non-

---

were accused of participating in illegitimate cults and must in any case have come
into being before Aaron had become the ancestor of the sole legitimate priesthood of
Yahweh (thus P)" (*Exodus*, p. 245 = p. 201). The purpose of this study is to specify the
time and circumstances of the Aaron additions to Exod. xxxii and Num. xii.

[5] "The Origin of the Aaronite Priesthood", *JTS* 6 (1905), pp. 161–86.

[6] "Aaronites and Zadokites", *AJSLL* 45 (1929), pp. 149–66.

[7] "Lade und Stierbild", *ZAW* 58 (1940–1), pp. 190–215.

[8] "Aaron's Rise in Prestige", *ZAW* 66 (1954), pp. 191–9.

[9] "Aaron, Jeroboam, and the Golden Calves", *JBL* 86 (1967), pp. 129–40.

[10] *Canaanite Myth and Hebrew Epic: Essays in the History of the Religion of Israel*
(Cambridge, Mass., 1973), pp. 198–9.

[11] For a different opinion of the origins of priestly rivalry, see Cross, *CMHE*, ch.8.
Cross proposes that the wilderness conflict stories, David's appointment of two royal
priests, and Jeroboam's establishment of two state shrines can all be explained by an
ancient conflict between "Aaronid" and "Mushite" priestly houses, involving
"Aaronid" bull iconography and "Mushite" cherubim iconography. I am grateful to
Professor Cross for the idea that priestly rivalry lies behind the wilderness conflict
stories, but we disagree regarding the origins and nature of that conflict. I see
a Levitical (Mosaic) priesthood originating early in the tribal League, and
continuing to serve tribal interests well into the monarchy. The royal Zadokite
(Aaronid) priesthood was instituted alongside the tribal priesthood by David and
established more securely by Solomon, which initiated the conflict. The royal
priesthood eventually overcame the tribal priesthood during Josiah's reform, forcing
the Levites into a subservient role, but the disenfranchised tribal priests continued to
voice their displeasure in Malachi and Trito-Isaiah (see P.D. Hanson, *The Dawn of
Apocalyptic: The Historical and Sociological Roots of Jewish Apocalyptic Eschatology*
[Philadelphia, 1979]).

Levitical Zadokites[12] had usurped the priesthood in the nation's capital, and one of Jeroboam's ambitions was to re-establish the Levitical priesthood in Israel.[13] The Elohistic source is therefore best regarded as a state program, comparable with and opposed to the Yahwistic state program. The Elohist was Jeroboam's court writer,[14] whose purpose was to advocate Northern interests, including the primacy of Bethel and the sole legitimacy of the Levitical priesthood.

1. *Exod. xxxii 1–6*

Most commentators have assigned this passage to the Elohist.[15] The polemic against Aaron is unmistakable, and the Yahwist would hardly oppose Zadok's wilderness ancestor. In addition to the polemic against Aaron, there is also a polemic against Jeroboam's Bethel cult: the molten calf and the cultic proclamation of *v.* 4 are virtually identical with the two golden calves and the proclamation in 1 Kgs xii 28. Indeed, the duality of Jeroboam's calves accounts for the odd plurals in Exod. xxxii 4b, 8b.[16] Also, the altar and feast made by

---

[12] Zadok's membership in the clan of Aaron is authentic (cf. 1 Chr. xii 27–8) and is the origin of the association between Zadok and Aaron (compare the "sons of Aaron" in P with the "sons of Zadok" in Ezekiel), but it is doubtful that the Aaronid clan was originally Levitical (cf. Num. xxvi 58a, an early Levitical genealogy lacking the Aaronids, according to Möhlenbrink [n. 4], p. 196). Instead, the later genealogical fiction of an attachment to the Kohathites (Exod. vi 14–27, etc.) supported the Zadokite bid for legitimacy, since priests had always been Levites.

[13] The statement by the Deuteronomist in 1 Kgs xii 31 that Jeroboam "made priests from among all the people who were not of the sons of Levi" is almost certainy a polemical falsification (see Cross, *CMHE*, p. 199). Rather, Jeroboam sought to "archaize even more radically than the astute David had done" (p. 74), which would include the re-establishment of the tribal Levitical priesthood. The Deuteronomist's accusation represents an attempt to cover the tracks of the non-Levitical Zadokites by blaming their rivals with their own weakness.

[14] A. Jenks has proposed that the Elohist articulates the viewpoint of a "north-Israelite prophetic-levitical circle during the eleventh and tenth centuries" (*The Elohist and North Israelite Traditions* [Missoula, 1977], p. 104). According to Jenks, the process of formulation began during Samuel's lifetime and was completed under the reign of Jeroboam I. His interpretation of the affinities between Exod. xxxii and 1 Kgs xii prompts him to postulate that the Elohist waged a polemic against Jeroboam's Bethel cult, and can therefore be located in circles opposed to that cult. Although his argument for E as a 10th-century collection is convincing, a fresh examination of Exod. xxxii should demonstrate that the Elohist does not attack Jeroboam's Bethel, but rather represents Jeroboam's Bethel.

[15] According to J. Hahn, *Das "Goldene Kalb": Die Jahwe-Verehrung bei Stierbildern in der Geschichte Israels* (Frankfurt, 1981), pp. 141–2, nineteen out of forty-eight critics assign *vv.* 1–6 to E, from numerous other possibilities that receive significantly less attention.

[16] The proclamation can be read either in the singular or in the plural; as B.S. Childs states, "The issue is exegetical rather than grammatical" (*Exodus: A Commentary* [London, 1968], p. 556). Although the grammar allows for either, ancient exegesis favoured the plural (Cf. B. Sanhedrin 63a).

Aaron without divine sanction in *v*. 5 correspond to the Bethel altar
and feast established independently by Jeroboam in 1 Kgs xii 32a, 33.
The majority opinion considers that Exod. xxxii reflects a polemic
against a bull cult served by an Aaronid priesthood at Bethel, existing
before Jeroboam and reinstated by him. However, there is no
evidence outside Exod. xxxii for an Aaronid priesthood at Bethel at
any time,[17] and there is no evidence for a bull cult at Bethel prior to
Jeroboam. The assertion that the Deuteronomist's polemic against
Bethel in 1 Kgs xii follows an Elohistic polemic against Bethel in
Exod. xxxii is based on the assumption that the Deuteronomistic
Historian did not interfere with the Priestly Tetrateuch. But Josiah's
historian, who was in league with the Zadokite priests,[18] would have
had access to the JE Epic which was probably kept in the Temple
archives. He may not have altered the Epic at any other point, but the
close parallels between Exod. xxxii 4–5 and 1 Kgs xii 28, 32–3 suggest
that he did have a hand in shaping Exod. xxxii.[19] In fact, the calf, the
cultic shout, and the feast are tangential to the Exodus narrative. All
that is important to the Elohistic polemic against Aaron is that he led
the people into apostasy through the fabrication of an image.
However, the bull iconography, the rebuilt altar, the Yahwistic cultic
shout, and the altered feast date are all essential elements of
Jeroboam's Bethel cult. It would appear that the Deuteronomistic
Historian has re-written the Elohistic polemic against Aaron (i.e. the
Zadokites of Jerusalem) in order to direct it back against Bethel.

A source analysis of the ancestral narratives in Genesis confirms this
suspicion. As the Yahwist focuses on Abraham and locates him
primarily at Hebron, so does the Elohist focus on Jacob and locate
him primarily at Bethel. All passages linking Jacob to Bethel can be
identified as Elohistic through the use of "Elohim" and the absence of
Priestly language. The Elohist relocates Jacob from Shechem to
Bethel, has "Elohim" command him to build an altar there, changes
his name from Jacob to Israel there, and has Jacob name the place

---

[17] The only other passage connecting Aaron with Bethel is Judg. xx 27b–28a.
These verses are an obvious interpolation, since they interrupt the narrative to
provide information from a later time. If Bethel had been Aaronid, we would expect
it to appear in the list of Levitical cities given to the "sons of Aaron" (Josh. xxi
13–19), but it does not.

[18] Cf. 1 Sam. ii 27–36 and iii 10–14. These Deuteronomistic compositions foretell
the triumph of the Zadokites over the Levites at the time of Josiah in an oracle to Eli
and a vision to Samuel.

[19] Cf. Jacques Vermeylen, "L'affaire du veau d'or (Ex 32–34): Une clé pour la
'question deutéronomiste'?", ZAW 97 (1985), pp. 1–23. Vermeylen views Exod.
xxxii-xxxiv as the product of successive Deuteronomistic redactions.

"Bethel" (Gen. xxv 1–10, 13–15). A narrative source's attachment to a particular place could hardly be more telling. It is for this reason that the notion of an Elohistic polemic against Bethel is to be rejected. The Elohist does not attack Bethel; he advocates it.

And yet the polemic against Aaron in *vv.* 1–6 identifies the passage as Elohistic. Therefore, the two polemics must be separated: the diatribe against Aaron is Elohistic, whereas the diatribe against Bethel is Deuteronomistic. Distinguishing the two literary strata is not easy, since they have been skillfully blended by the Deuteronomist. However, one is aided in this task by reference to Gen. xxxv 1–4(E). In this passage God commands Jacob to move to Bethel and build an altar there, whereupon Jacob directs his household to put away their foreign gods. "So they gave to Jacob all the foreign gods which they had, and the rings which were in their ears (*w^{e}et-hann^{e}zāmîm $^{\circ}$ăšer b$^{e\circ}$oznêhem*); and Jacob hid them under the oak which was near Shechem." When this passage is compared to Exod. xxxii 1–6, one sees the Elohist contrasting Jacob (Israel) and Aaron (the Zadokites).[20] Whereas Jacob faithfully obeys God's command to build an altar, in preparation for which he puts away the people's foreign gods and earrings,[21] Aaron builds an altar on his own initiative and converts the people's earrings into a foreign god. Because Exod. xxxii 1–6 and Gen. xxxv 1–4 are mirror images of each other, the unadulterated Elohistic account of Jacob can be used for the purpose of separating out the Elohistic stratum in Exod. xxxii 1–6. Accordingly, the operative factors in the Jacob story are Jacob, his household, Bethel, the altar, the foreign gods, and the earrings. Although the location at Horeb is assumed in Exod. xxxii, all the other factors have explicit counterparts in the Aaron account. Thus, the Elohistic elements in

---

[20] J.D. Safren, "Balaam and Abraham", *VT* 38 (1988), p. 106, citing Y. Zakovitz, "Reflection Story – Another Dimension of the Evalutation of Characters in Biblical Narrative", *Tarbiz* 54/2 (1985), pp. 165–76, defines a "reflection story" as "one in which can be discerned the outlines of another narrative, but in inverse form, as one's reflection in the mirror. The 'reflected' character and his actions are perceived as the antithesis of the original figure and his actions. The reader, appreciating the affinity between the original and its reflection, gains new insights in evaluating the characters – both the original and the invert – and their actions". Just as Safren sees in the Tale of Balaam's Ass a "reflection story" of the Akedah, I would describe the Elohistic stratum of Exod. xxxii 1–6 as a "reflection story" of Gen. xxxv 1–4. The purpose was to use obedient Jacob as a foil for apostate Aaron.

[21] The plural of *nezem – n^{e}zāmîn/nizmê* – occurs only in Gen. xxxv 4; Exod. xxxii 2–3; Judg. viii 24–6; and Isa iii 21. The virtual identity of the wording in Gen. xxxv 4 – *hann^{e}zāmîm $^{\circ}$ăšer b$^{e\circ}$oznêhem*, with Exod. xxxii 3 – *nizmê hazzāhāb $^{\circ}$ăšer b$^{e\circ}$oznêhem*, clinches the connection between the two passages. Judg. viii 24b explains the significance of gold earrings as a foreign intrusion.

Exod. xxxii 1–6 include Aaron, the people, the altar, the molten image, and the earrings.

These can be distinguished from the Deuteronomistic elements, which correspond to 1 Kgs xii 28–33: the image as a calf, the cultic proclamation, the feast, and the altar. It is apparent that the altar figures in both strata, functioning as a "hinge" that fastens together the Elohistic and Deuteronomistic strata. In its final form, however, it is Deuteronomistic. This source analysis of *vv.* 1–6 therefore assigns *vv.* 1–4a to the Elohist, and *vv.* 4b–6 to the Deuteronomist.

2. *The Elohistic Redaction of Exod. xxxii*

Although the exact form and function of the original narrative are uncertain, one can assume that the Elohist received a story of the people's apostasy through the making of an image. Because the Zadokite priests of Jerusalem were not Levitical and because Jeroboam re-established the Levitical along with other traditional Israelite institutions, conflict raged between these rival priestly groups. Whereas the Zadokite priesthood represented the prerogatives of the Jerusalem monarchy to institute Canaanizing innovations, Jeroboam's Levitical priesthood represented the Northern re-assertion of traditional practices.

As Jenks has demonstrated (n. 14), the Elohist is best dated to the late 10th-century, under Jeroboam. Contrary to Jenks, an examination of the ancestral narratives has located E at Bethel, the more influential of Jeroboam's two cult centers. The E source therefore articulates the Northern version of national origins as a foundation document for the new Israelite state, in opposition to the Yahwistic advocacy of Judean interests. The author, a supporter of Jeroboam's Bethel and his new state, most probably was one of the newly re-appointed Levitical priests.

The Elohistic redaction of the golden calf tradition supports such an identitiy. The Elohist took a tradition of the people's apostasy and converted it into Aaron's apostasy. He retold the original story to condemn Aaron for leading the people into a violation of the covenant prohibition against images. When it is rememberced that Aaron represents the Zadokites of Jerusalem, one sees a story of apostsy that condemns the Zadokites for leading the people astray.[22]

---

[22] At the Elohistic stage of the Aaron tradition, Aaron is neither a Levite nor the brother of Moses. Those connections are made later by Zadokites wishing to legitimize their claims to the priesthood; they do not appear in the text until the redaction of J and E.

In *vv.* 21–4 the Elohist shifts his attack to lampoon the Zadokites. Having condemned Aaron as apostate, he then protrays him as cowardly and dishonest, blaming the people for his sin and claiming that the image manufactured itself.[23] By so questioning the Jerusalem priests' authority and integrity, the Elohistic attack on Zadokite incompetence is complete.

The real focus of the Elohistic redaction, though, comes in *vv.* 25–9. Here the Elohist takes an ancient etiology of Levitical consecration to the priesthood (cf. Dt. xxxiii 9) and converts it into an apology for exclusive priestly rights.[24] The etiology explains the original ordination of the Levites. In the context of Aaron's apostasy, however, it contrasts Zadodite infidelity with Levitical faithfulness. That contrast is the basis for an implied statement that only Levites are fit for the priesthood: it was the Levites who rallied to Moses when he summoned those faithful to the Lord (*v.* 26), and it was the Levites who carried out the divinely ordained purge of brothers, friends, and neighbours (*vv.* 27–8). For this adherence to Moses and God despite the consequences to family and friends, the Levites receive the blessing of the priesthood (*v.* 29). Having dispatched the Zadokite infidelity and incompetence in *vv.* 1–6 and *vv.* 21–4, the Elohist's final statement is therefore an assertion of exclusively Levitical priestly prerogatives. The Zadokites were not Levites, and only Levites were ordained to the priesthood by God and by Moses.

3. *The Deuteronomistic Redaction of Exod. xxxii*

The Deuteronomistic Historian or someone influenced by him had access to the JE Epic, which contained the Elohistic redaction of the golden calf tradition. The Elohist had introduced Aaron and made him responsible for the image, in order to condemn the Zadokites for apostasy. The Deuteronomist could have left the Epic untouched,

---

[23] S.E. Loewenstamm, following U. Cassuto, argued that there is no contradiction between *v.* 4 and *v.* 24, because "in ancient Canaan there obtained the belief that cultic objects were produced by themselves and not by human workmanship" ("The Making and Destruction of the Golden Calf", *Bib* 48 [1967], p. 488). L.G. Perdue challenged Loewenstamm's use of the Ugaritic parallel, asserting that "the statement attributed to Aaron in *v.* 24 is best explained as a satire with Aaron as the object of ridicule" ("The Making and Destruction of the Golden Calf – A Reply", *Bib* 54 [1973], p. 239).

[24] Cf. S. Lehming, "Versuch zu Ex. xxxii", *VT* 10 (1960), p. 43. Lehming is correct that the finished piece functions as an apology, but a comparison with the related Levitical etiology in Dt. xxxiii 9 yields the judgement that an etiology existed before the Elohistic apology.

but he was a friend of the Jerusalem priesthood. It is apparent that
he was unable to expunge Aaron, presumably because the story was
too well-known and established, despite its anti-Judean polemic.
Although the Deuteronomist was unable to substract from the
tradition, he was able to add to it, which he did in *vv.* 4b–6, 8b, and
30–4.

The placement of *vv.* 4b–6 in the midst of Aaron's apostasy reverses
the polemic against the Zadokites, and directs it back against Bethel.
The Deuteronomist could not directly counter the Elohistic assertion
of exclusively Levitical rights to the priesthood; everyone knew that
priests should be Levites. However, the Deuteronomic tradition gave
him the basis for a different sort of exclusivity, namely, the command
to "seek the Lord at the place which the Lord your God shall choose
from all your tribes, to establish his name there for his dwelling" (Dt.
xii 5). Deuteronomistic editing had established "the place" as
Jerusalem, although the original reference is less sure.[25] The command
to worship only at Jerusalem provided the Deuteronomist with the
ammunition necessary for his polemic aganst Bethel (cf. 1 Kgs xii
26–33; 2 Kgs xxiii 15–18). By introducing Jeroboam's bull, his
Yahwistic cultic shout, and his irregular feast into Exod. xxxii, the
Deuteronomist succeeded in loosening the polemic against the
Zadokites and re-directing it against the Northern cult, specifically
the cult at Bethel. The altar made by Aaron on his own initiative in
the Elohistic stratum then becomes the Bethel altar illegitimately
rebuilt by Jeroboam, which violates Dt. xii 1–14.

Even though the transformation of the Elohistic polemic against
the Zadokites into one directed against the Nortern cult has the
unfortunate effect of turning Aaron into the prototype of Jeroboam,[26]
the Deuteronomist dispels the impression of Aaron's culpability by
re-asserting the people's responsibility in *vv.* 30–4. Because he was
unable to subtract from the tradition, the Deuteronomist left intact

---

[25] Cf. G.E. Wright, "The Book of Deuteronomy", *The Interpreter's Bible* 2 (New
York and Nashville, 1953), pp. 311–31. Wright believed that the original reference
was to Shechem, but Cross prefers Shiloh (personal communication).

[26] For an analysis of the similarities between Aaron and Jeroboam, see M.
Aberbach and L. Smolar. They conclude "that Jeroboam deliberately patterned his
religious changes upon a well-known cult which was traced back to Aaron" (p. 134).
The alternative solution "would be to assume that most [sic] of our account of
Aaron's golden calf was tendentiously narrated by the Zadokite priesthood of
Jerusalem with a view to discrediting the northern kingdom and its bull cult" (p.
140). This study seeks to develop the alternative hypothesis, with the modification that
most of the account is attributable to the Elohist. The Deuteronomist was able to
reverse the polemic by including a few short verses in the Elohistic section and by
adding a new conclusion in *vv.* 30–4.

the original punishment of the people in *v.* 20 and the Elohistic punishment of Aaron in *vv.* 25–9. However, he added the deferred punishment of the people for their "great sin" (*ḥăṭāʾâ gᵉdōlâ*) in *vv.* 30–4, which is not fulfilled until the rejection of Israel for their "great sin" (*ḥăṭāʾâ gᵉdōlâ*) of following Jeroboam (2 Kgs xvii 20–3).

4. *Num. xii*

Numerous key words and phrases identify the final composition of Num. xii as Elohistic.[27] A traditio-historical analysis, however, distinguishes two levels of tradition: Miriam's criticism of Moses on account of the Cushite woman, which is punished by her leprosy (*vv.* 1, 10–15), and Aaron's and Miriam's questioning of Moses' sole authority in mediating the divine word, which is answered by a heavenly rebuff (*vv.* 2–9).[28] Because Miriam is placed before Aaron in *v.* 1 whereas subsequently the order is reversed, and because the punishment of leprosy is hers alone, the earlier tradition most likely presented only Miriam in opposition to Moses.[29] Appended to the earlier tradition is the theme of Aaron and Miriam doubting Moses' privileged position.[30] Since Aaron is introduced at this stage, the stress lies on his opposition to Moses' authority. It is important to note that the passage nowhere states nor assumes that Moses, Aaron, and Miriam are brothers and sisters,[31] but simply poses them as contending leaders.

On the basis of the foregoing analysis of Exod. xxxii and the unambiguous identification of Num. xii as Elohistic, the development of the tradition can be clarified further. The story that the Elohist received was that of Miriam's opposition to Moses. Because it posed two wilderness figures as rivals, the Elohist was able to use it as the vehicle for another attack on the Zadokite priesthood. He introduced Aaron as illegitimately advancing his own (i.e. the Zadokite) position as mediator for God (*v.* 2), in order to present an apology for exclusively Mosaic (i.e. Levitical) mediation, rendered authoritative by the divine speech (*vv.* 6–8). Whereas prophets receive indirect communication through visions and dreams (and it is not stated or implied that Aaron is even a prophet), only Moses communicates

---

[27] E.g. *ʾōhel moʿēd, hāʾîš mōšeh, ʿal ʾōdôt, marʾâ*, and *ḥālôm*. See BDB.
[28] Noth, *Numbers*, p. 92 = p. 82.
[29] Ibid., p. 92 = pp. 82–3.
[30] Ibid., p. 93 = p. 83; *Pentateuchal Traditions, pp.* 127, 180 = pp. 140, 197.
[31] Noth, *Numbers* p. 94 = pp. 83–4.

directly with God. In God's "house" only Moses is "faithful"; i.e. in the priesthood only the Levites are established and secure.[32] Only the Levitical priests are the legitimate mediators of God's words; only they have the prerequisite authority. The Zadokites are usurpers; they assumed a priestly role apart from God's will.

As in Exod. xxxii, the Elohistic couples his attack on the Zadokites and defense of the Levites with a parody of Aaron. After assuming equal status in *v.* 2, Aaron is forced to humble himself before Moses in *v.* 11. The particle of entreaty *bî* is used only by one "craving permission to address a superior" (BDB). Others who employ *bî ʾădōnî* in entreaty are Judah before Joseph in Pharaoh's court (Gen. xliv 18), Gideon before the angel of Yahweh (Judg. vi 13), Hannah before Eli (1 Sam. i 26), and the harlot before Solomon (1 Kgs iii 17, 26). Aaron's colleagues are Judah, Gideon, Hannah, and the harlot.[33] The Elohist thus blends Aaron into the account of Miriam's punishment in order to illustrate the judgement pronounced in *vv.* 6–8. Only Moses is able to approach God; if Aaron wishes to intercede for Miriam, he must entreat the sole mediator to do so. The Elohist therefore states and illustrates that only Levites may mediate God's will and word.

Conclusion

The starting point for this study was Möhlenbrink's dictum that Aaron is secondary in the tradition, as developed by Noth's separation of Aaron from the pre-existing narratives in both Exod. xxxii and Num. xii. In addition, the consensus regarding Exod. xxxii as primarily Elohistic and Num. xii as entirely Elohistic, comprising the only E accounts of Aaron, was accepted. Finally, A. Jenks's assignment of the E source to the late 10th-century under Jeroboam I of Israel was followed.

Additionally, E's attachment to Bethel and the tendentiousness of the Elohistic polemic in Exod. xxxii and Num. xii against a non-Levitical priesthood has been noted. Therefore, the conclusion is reached that the Elohist was a Levitical priest who served as Jeroboam's historian. He composed an account of national origins

---

[32] The Deuteronomist counters this divine judgement with an opposing divine judgement in 1 Sam. ii 35, which promises an enduring "house" to the "faithful" priest, Zadok. For the identity of the "faithful priest" as Zadok, see P.K. McCarter, *I Samuel* (Garden City, 1980), p. 87.

[33] I am not implying that the Elohist referred to these stories in his humbling of Aaron, only that the literature – whether early or late – amply illustrates the nature of a relationship in which the use of *bî* is appropriate.

that focuses on Bethel and upholds the sole rights of the Levites to Israel's priesthood. The target of his polemic in both Exod. xxxii and Num. xii is the non-Levitical Zadokite priesthood, which had usurped the traditionally Levitical priesthood in Jerusalem. In Exod. xxxii the Elohist transformed a story of the people's apostasy into Aaron's apostasy in order to condemn the Zadokites for infidelity and incompetence and to present an apology for an exclusively Levitical priesthood. In Num. xii he modified a story of Miriam questioning Moses by the addition of Aaron challenging Moses' authority, which again provided the pretext for an assertion of solely Levitical priestly rights.

In sum, Jeroboam did not appoint non-Levites as priests; he restored the Levitical priesthood. And the Elohist did not attack Bethel; he advocated it. The Elohistic polemic was directed against the non-Levitical usurping Zadokites, whose establishment in Jerusalem had shifted Israel's practices and beliefs away from its early foundations.

THE WILDERNESS ITINERARIES AND RECENT ARCHAEOLOGICAL RESEARCH

by

G.I. DAVIES

Cambridge

The constant flow, one might say flood, of news about archaeological discoveries in Palestine and neighbouring areas leads, quite properly, to new suggestions about the course of biblical history or the interpretation of difficult texts, and also to fresh consideration of earlier theories. Such "new light" is particularly to be expected from excavations and surveys in the land where ancient Israel lived for most of its history and where most of the Old Testament was written. A recent example of great importance is the publication of I. Finkelstein's detailed study of *The Archaeology of the Israelite Settlement* (Jerusalem, 1988). But archaeological research in more outlying areas, such as the Sinai peninsula and the extreme south of Palestine, may also be illuminating, and in the past decade details have been published of two major projects which, it is claimed, have important contributions to make to the geographical aspects of the Exodus and wilderness traditions. It is the purpose of this article to assess the validity of these new proposals and also to lay down some more general guidelines for the evaluation of future reconstructions based on archaeological discoveries which, it may be hoped, will be made in these and other areas.

The episode of the crossing of the "sea" (Ex. xiv 1–xv 21) is given a location in some passages by means of the term *yam sûp*, which has been variously interpreted by scholars, but in two itinerary texts (Ex. xiv 2, 9; Num. xxxiii 7) the place is identified by no less than three place-names: *pî haḥîrōt*, *migdōl* and *baʿal ṣᵉpōn*. Following the lead of the Egyptologist H. Brugsch and O. Eissfeldt, who was able to make use of Ugaritic evidence, an apparently growing number of scholars sees in this an indication that one strand at least of the Pentateuchal narrative placed the "sea"-crossing at Lake Bardawil (Lake Sirbonis of the classical authors), a lagoon on the Mediterranean coast east of Port Said which is separated from the sea by a narrow spit of land through which the sea has been known to break from time to time.[1] This feature might, it is thought, provide a clue to the catastrophe which befell the Egyptians and allowed the Israelites to escape, just as in later periods of antiquity disasters were known to have occurred at this point (Diodorus Siculus i 30, xvi 46; Strabo, *Geog.* xvi 2:26–34; Polybius v 80). It is particularly the names *migdōl* and *baᶜal ṣᵉpōn* which have seemed to point to the northern coastal route. The former can be equated with a *migdōl* mentioned by Jeremiah and Ezekiel, which appears from Ezek. xxix 10, xxx 6 to mark the northernmost extremity of Egypt just as *sᵉwēnēh* denotes its southern limit. This place can be more exactly located with the help of the *Itinerarium Antonini* (3rd century A.D.), which mentions a place MAGDOLVM twelve Roman miles from Pelusium,[2] and the identification with Tell el-Ḥēr was favoured by Eissfeldt ([n. 1], p. 55) and Cazelles, the latter with some hesitation, as neither the topography nor early archaeological exploration of the site seemed to fit the requirments perfectly ([n. 1], p. 347; cf. p. 344). Baal Zaphon was shown by Eissfeldt (pp. 1–39) to be the Semitic antecedent of Zeus Casios, so that it is possible in principle that the Mount Casios on the Bardawil spit which is first mentioned by Herodotus (ii 6, 158, iii 5) in the mid-5th century B.C. had previously been known by, for example, Phoenician sailors as *baᶜal ṣᵉpōn*. Opinions have differed over its precise location, ever since the early exploration by J. Clédat at the beginning of the century. Eissfeldt followed Clédat's original view that Mount Casios was at Maḥammadiye at the western end of the spit, where a small temple was found on a hill 13 m. high, with two inscriptions from Hellenistic or Roman times bearing the name

---

[1] H. Brugsch, *L'Exode et les monuments égyptiens* (Leipzig, 1875); O. Eissfeldt, *Baal Zaphon, Zeus Kasios und der Durchzug des Israeliten durchs Meer* (Halle, 1932), pp. 48–65. On Brugsch see H. Engel, *Die Vorfahren Israels in Ägypten. Forschungsgeschichtlicher Überblick über die Darstellungen seit Richard Lepsius (1849)* (Frankfurt, 1979), pp. 25–7, who mentions a little-known forerunner of Brugsch in this respect. They are followed by M. Noth in J. Fueck (ed.), *Festschrift für O. Eissfeldt* (Halle, 1947), pp. 184–5; H. Cazelles, *RB* 62 (1955), pp. 321–64; Y. Aharoni, *The Land of the Bible* (London, 1966), p. 179; M. Dothan, *Proceedings of the Fifth World Congress of Jewish Studies, 1969* (Jerusalem, n.d.), pp. 223–4; G. Fohrer, *Geschichte der israelitischen Religion* (Berlin, 1969), p. 59; S. Herrmann, *Israels Aufenthalt in Ägypten* (Stuttgart, 1970), pp. 87–91; S. Norin, *Er Spaltete das Meer* (Lund, 1977), pp. 32–3; M.A. Klopfenstein, in B. Rothenberg and H. Weyer, *Sinai: Pharaonen, Bergleute, Pilger und Soldaten* (Berne, 1979), p. 21; H. Donner, *Geschichte des Volkes Israel und seiner Nachbarn in Grundzügen* (Göttingen, 1987), p. 94. There is an aerial photograph of the spit in Rothenberg and Weyer, pl. 1.
[2] O. Cuntz, *Itineraria Romana* I (Leipzig, 1929), p. 23.

"Casios" in the vicinity.[3] Cazelles, on the other hand, after reviewing all the literary evidence, concluded that Clédat's later view, which placed Mount Casios at Ras Qasrun, a hill over 100 m. in height near the middle of the spit where it juts out furthest into the sea, was correct (pp. 332–5), and it is difficult to argue with his deductions from the ancient geographical writers.

Difficulties for the theory that locates the sea-crossing on the Mediterranean coast have been pointed out by various writers.[4] But it is only in the past fifteen years that a thorough archaeological survey of the region in question, based on up-to-date knowledge of pottery chronology, has been made by E. Oren of Ben Gurion University at Beersheba, in the context of his Northern Sinai Expedition. Although its results have not been fully published, the preliminary reports allow an account of his findings to be given and they are of considerable interest for the evaluation of the "northern" interpretation of the Exodus route.[5] The survey, which began in 1972, recorded over 1000 sites along the coast between the Suez Canal and the Gaza Strip, showing that in the Early Bronze Age (Egyptian Old Kingdom), the Late Bronze Age (Egyptian New Kingdom) and from the Persian to the Early Islamic periods the area was heavily populated. As far as the Late Bronze Age is concerned, the survey brought to light a number of fortified sites which must have formed part of the Egyptian military road, "the Ways of Horus", which has long been known from contemporary reliefs and texts, and showed that the fortification of this route began in the early 18th Dynasty, probably in the reign of Tuthmosis III. But, to quote Oren,

> The sites from the period of the New Kingdom were recorded, as indicated, in areas to the south of Lake Bardawil. On the other hand sites from this period were not found on the coastal strip or on the spit north of the lake, including the area of Mount Casios. (*Qadmoniot Sinai* [n. 5], p. 114 – my translation; cf. Rothenberg and Weyer [n. 1], p. 190.)

In fact, it is only much later, in the Persian period, that evidence of

---

[3] Pp. 40–1, with detailed references to the archaeological reports; so also Donner (n. 1), pp. 94–5.

[4] E.g. J. Simons, *The Geographical and Topographical Texts of the Old Testament* (Leiden, 1959), pp. 234–41, 248–50; C. de Wit, *The Date and Route of the Exodus* (London, 1960), pp. 18–20; G.I. Davies, *The Way of the Wilderness* (Cambridge, 1979), pp. 80–2.

[5] The fullest account is in Z. Meshel and I. Finkelstein (ed.), *Qadmoniot Sinai* (Sinai in Antiquity) (Tel Aviv, 1980), pp. 101–58 (Heb.). See also E. Oren, *IEJ* 23 (1973), pp. 198–205; *BASOR* 256 (1984), pp. 7–10; and in Rothenberg and Weyer (n. 1), pp. 181–92.

occupation in the vicinity of Ras Qasrun begins to appear:

> The Northern Sinai Expedition investigated over forty sites in this
> region, most of them small camping-places and a few of them permanent
> settlements with remains of buildings whose date was fixed in the
> Roman-Byzantine period. At the earliest sites, from the Persian period,
> were found fragments of Greek wine amphorae, Attic black-figured
> vessels, arrowheads of Irano-Scythian type and also some Athenian
> coins from the fifth century B.C. At two sites (M26–27) many
> fragments were collected of a type of storage jar which is characteristic of
> sites in southern Palestine from the end of the Iron Age and the
> beginning of the Persian period. In a trial excavation carried out on the
> northern edge of Mount Casios (M36) it became clear that the earliest
> remains upon the *kurkhar* surfaces were not earlier than the Persian
> period. The complete lack of archaeological finds from the period prior
> to the Persian conquest, let alone from the point of time associated with
> the Exodus from Egypt, in fact completely excludes the possibility of
> locating the journey along the road on the spit. Furthermore, the
> identification of biblical Baal-zephon with Mount Casios – one of the
> starting points for the theory of a journey along the spit – does not stand
> up to critical examination in the face of the new finds in the excavations
> at the site of Mount Casios, since the place was dedicated to the worship
> of Zeus only from the Persian period onwards.[6]

Oren also notes that recent geological investigations by D. Niv of
the Institute of Geology in Jerusalem suggest that the spit is
a "relatively recent" phenomenon resulting from tectonic activity,
which may explain why no earlier archaeological evidence is found on
it.[7] Of course, one cannot be sure what "relatively recent" may mean
in geological terms, and the absence of archaeological remains does
not necessarily imply that the spit emerged only in the first
millennium B.C. Even so, there is some textual evidence that still in
late antiquity the region was not yet geologically stable. Among the
passages cited by Eissfeldt and others to show that Lake Bardawil was
a place where a spectacular catastrophe might take place is one from
the geographer Strabo, who wrote under Augustus:

> Similar events also occur around the Mount Casios near Egypt, when
> the land suffers a single sharp convulsion (σπασμῷ τινι ὀξεῖ καὶ ἁπλῷ) and
> moves at the same time in both directions, so that the part of it which is
> raised up holds back the sea while that which has subsided lets it in, and
> when it (i.e. the land) shifts again the place once more resumes its

---

[6] p. 122 (my translation). In a footnote (p. 157, n. 61) Oren discounts claims that
evidence of earlier occupation had been found there. See also below, p. 166.

[7] He refers to D. Niv, *Preliminary Report on Geological Observations on the Coastal Plain
of Northern Sinai*, Development Office, Institute of Geology, Jerusalem, September
1967. See also D. Niv, *Teva vaAretz* 11/4 (1969), pp. 179–84. I have not been able to
see either of these reports.

previous position, sometimes with some alteration, sometimes not. (xvi 2:26 – my translation. Cf. i 3.17)

While problems for travellers may also have been caused by storms at sea, it seems clear that Strabo knew of seismic disturbances in the area, which may have been the continuation of movements of the earth which had brought the spit into being only a few hundred years earlier.

It may be, therefore, that there was no Lake Bardawil at the time of the Exodus, and the archaeological evidence certainly gives no support to the idea that there was a Baal-zephon there in the 13th or 12th century B.C.[8] It is not even certain that Ras Qasrun was ever known as Baal-zephon, since the first attestation of the name Casios there is so late (Herodotus) and so close to the beginning of occupation that no antecedent Semitic name need be presupposed. According to Oren, his results exclude the "northern" route of the Exodus from consideration, and as far as a historical reconstruction of the route actually taken by some "proto-Israelites" is concerned he seems to be correct. But it is important to distinguish such a reconstruction, and the assumptions on which it is based, from a view which holds that the itinerary represents an attempt by later generations to fix the route by which their ancestors had once travelled from Egypt to Canaan by way of Mount Sinai. If such a view is taken it might still be possible (if the other difficulties could be overcome) to hold to a "northern" interpretation of the route, provided that the origin of the itinerary-material were placed late enough for there to be a place called Baal-zephon at Ras Qasrun, i.e. in the 5th or at the earliest in the 6th century B.C. This is not inconceivable, although some features of Num xxxiii 1–49 suggest that a pre-exilic date is more likely.[9] Alternatively, the attempt might be made to defend a "northern" interpretation of the route without reference to Ras Qasrun, as M. Bietak has done,[10] and in a recent article Oren seems to incline in this direction, on the basis of the name Migdol, to which we must turn in a moment.

First, it is necessary to consider a possible objection to Oren's and my own line of reasoning. If there is no possibility of a Baal-zephon at

---

[8] The proposal of Cazelles, that *ḥtyn* in Papyrus Anastasi I, 27.4, might be an early attestation of the name Casios (*RB* 62 [1955], pp. 335–6), should therefore probably be discarded.

[9] Cf. M. Noth, *PJB* 36 (1940), p. 28; G.I. Davies, *Tyndale Bulletin* 25 (1974), pp. 50–1, 79–80.

[10] *Tell el-Dab^c a II* (Vienna, 1975), pp. 135–7, 217–20; *Proceedings of the British Academy* 65 (1979), p. 280. Cf. Donner (n. 1), pp. 94–6.

Ras Qasrun at the time of the Exodus, should we not go back to
Eissfeldt's view that Mount Casios and Baal-zephon were located not
there, but at Maḥammadiye? It has already been seen, however, that
the ancient geographical texts give no support to this proposal, and
the inscriptional evidence is inconclusive, as there was clearly
a temple of Zeus Casios even further to the west at Pelusium.
Moreover, the results of Oren's survey are no more favourable to the
existence of an early settlement at Maḥammadiye than they are to
one at Ras Qasrun: the evidence points to an origin in the Hellenistic
period (*Qadmoniot Sinai* [n. 5], p. 124).

As for the equation of biblical Migdol with Tell el-Ḥēr, Cazelles's
hesitation has proved to have been well-placed, as the recent survey of
Oren has confirmed the earlier indications that its occupation began
too late, in the 5th century B.C. (cf. *BASOR* 256 [1984], p. 34).
Nearby there is a site (T.21) described at length by Oren, which was
occupied from perhaps the late 7th century until *c*. 525 B.C., and the
nature of the remains as well as its location strongly support its
identification with the Migdol referred to by Jeremiah and Ezekiel.[11]
But, as Oren clearly sees, this does not necessarily resolve the problem
of the Migdol in the wilderness itinerary, and he himself suggests as
a working hypothesis that the latter may be located at one of the New
Kingdom (i.e. Late Bronze Age) sites recorded by his expedition in
the neighbourhood of Tell el-Ḥēr.[12] Such a hypothesis of course rests
on two assumptions, one recognized by Oren, the other not. It
presumes first of all that the itinerary reflects New Kingdom
conditions, i.e. those of the time of the Exodus itself, rather than those
of some later period; but it also presumes, as Oren is aware, that
identifications for the places named in the itinerary are indeed to be
sought "on the border of the eastern Delta, at the Egyptian terminus
of the military highway – 'Ways of Horus' or biblical 'Way of the
Land of the Philistines'". But what basis is there for this latter
assumption, now that the location of Baal-zephon at Ras Qasrun has
to be given up? It is, as indicated above, perhaps still a possibility, but
it may be doubted whether it is the most likely possibility and, as Oren
recognizes (*BASOR* 256 [1984], p. 31), the Egyptian occurrences of
the name Migdol may relate to several different places.

In this case, therefore, the new archaeological evidence has
undermined a central pillar of the theory which traces the route

---

[11] *BASOR* 256 (1984), pp. 7–44; see also *Qadmoniot* 10 (1977), pp. 71–6 (Heb.).
[12] *BASOR* 256 (1984), p. 35: for further information on these sites see *Qadmoniot
Sinai*, pp. 109–11.

described in the biblical itinerary along the Mediterranean coast, without as yet having been able to re-establish this theory on firmer foundations. Some clarification may be hoped for from the much fuller knowledge which is now available about ancient waterways in the eastern Delta and the Suez isthmus.[13] The overall context of the itinerary still seems to point to a southerly route, but renewed archaeological exploration of the central and southern parts of the Suez isthmus is needed to determine the full range of possibilities for identification of the early stages of the route described.

The second archaeological project whose results (and their implications for the wilderness itinerary) will be examined here is the work which has been carried out by E. Anati, a prehistorian, since 1978 in the far south of modern Israel, between Kadesh-barnea and Eilat. This centres on a mountain formerly known as Jebel Ideid (or ʿUdeid)[14] but renamed on more recent Israeli maps as Har Karkom ("Saffron Mountain"), Israel grid reference 125966. By 1983 Anati had recorded over 200 "sites" in the vicinity of this mountain, at which rock drawings, ruins or both had been found.[15] A large number of these sites witness to "occupation", according to Anati and his co-workers, in the Early Bronze Age and the period which has been variously referred to as Middle Bronze I, the Intermediate Early Bronze-Middle Bronze Period and, especially in recent years, Early Bronze IV. In this respect Anati's work adds to the results of the surveys of Nelson Glueck and Beno Rothenerg, which pointed to intensive occupation in Early Bronze IV in the Negev mountains and the central Sinai peninsula:[16] Glueck in fact recorded several sites from EB IV/MB I within a few miles of Har Karkom.[17] On the other hand, none of Anati's sites (except for an isolated rock-drawing) is thought by him to belong to the Middle or Late Bronze Ages or the Iron Age or the Persian period. This long gap (c. 2000–332 B.C.) was followed by periods in which once again a human presence is

---

[13] See W.H. Shea, *BASOR* 226 (1977), pp. 31–8; Bietak, *PBA* 65 (1979), pp. 271–83; also Oren, *BASOR* 256 (1984), pp. 9–10 (bibliography).

[14] E. Anati, *PEQ* 83 (1956), pp. 5–13; cf. T.L. Thompson, *The Settlement of Sinai and the Negew in the Bronze Age* (Wiesbaden, 1975), pp. 116–17.

[15] I am dependent in what follows on Anati's book *Har Karkom: Montagna Sacra nel Deserto dell'Esodo* (Milan, 1984). A more recent account of his work, *La montagna di Dio – Har Karkom. Ricerche archeologiche sulla strada dell'Esodo* (Milan, 1986), which is briefly reviewed in *ZAW* 99 (1987), p. 282, has not been available to me.

[16] See Glueck's popular account, *Rivers in the Desert* (rev. edn, New York, 1968), which was based on a series of reports in *BASOR*; Rothenberg and Weyer (n. 1), pp. 121–2; and the summary and analysis in Thompson (n. 14), pp. 14–24.

[17] *BASOR* 179 (1965) 13–15; cf. Thompson, pp. 116–17.

archaeologically attested in the area, in line with a more general southward enlargement of the settled occupation of Palestine (Nabataean, Roman, Byzantine, early Arab).[18]

It is the remains from the Early Bronze Age (including EB IV) which have suggested to Anati that Har Karkom may be the site of Mount Sinai. The "Bronze Age Complex", as he calls it, comprises structures both on the mountain itself and in the valley on its west side. On the mountain the remains are described as "chiefly religious and funerary structures", including groups of funerary mounds (*tumuli*), stone circles and orthostats. Three sites, one near the summit and the other two in the valley, had the form of a round courtyard with an altar-like platform on one side, accompanied by standing stones, and a small room, perhaps once roofed, on the other. A cultic interpretation of these structures seems probable. In the valley below ten "encampments" were discovered, including a central one comprising at least 52 dwelling units. Both the construction of some of these units and the pottery found in them seem to imply that they were used over a long period. Different types of house-plan suggest the possibility that three groups with divergent forms of social organization congregated in this inhospitable area around what looks very like a sacred site. Anati states (p. 214) that it was certain discoveries made in 1983, particularly at his site 52, which convinced him that Har Karkom was Mount Sinai. Site 52 is located at the foot of the mountain on the western terrace of the wadi, and near its centre are two rows of orthostats, each comprising six stones, most of them still standing in their original position. Nearby was an open space with a small rock in it, shaped like a human being, in front of which were the remains of hearths, and on the opposite side of it from the orthostats were the remains of a structure 4 m. × 1 m. with a platform upon it (cf. pp. 53–4). The similarity to what is described in Ex. xxiv 4 is certainly striking:

wayyiben mizbēaḥ taḥat hāhār ûštêm ᶜeśreh maṣṣēbâ lišnēm ᶜāśār šibṭê yiśrāᵓēl

The possibility of an identification of Har Karkom with Mount Sinai is already broached at the end of Part 1 of the book, which describes the archaeological finds (see pp. 87–99). The argument is more fully developed in Part 2, especially in chs 4–8. Two chapters deal with the wilderness itinerary, first the Egypt-Sinai section (ch. 4) and then the Sinai-Kadesh section (ch. 7). It is claimed that the

---

[18] See the summary in Anati, pp. 25–36, especially the chart on p. 35, and the detailed listing of the sites on pp. 37–85.

former describes a route via the Lake Sirbonis spit which at first aimed towards Kadesh-barnea, but then turned south and subsequently east to arrive at Har Karkom. From there the route is traced on to Wadi Arabah, which was followed first northwards towards the Dead Sea, according to Anati, and then, after the episode of the spies, southwards to Ezion-Geber near Aqaba and Eilat. From here a north-westerly route leads to Kadesh-barnea. Another chapter (ch. 5) argues that according to Exodus Mount Sinai was adjacent to the territories of both Midian and Amalek and that Har Karkom is precisely on the border between them. The correspondences between the archaeological remains at Har Karkom and the Sinai narrative are examined in ch. 6, and it is argued that "No other mountain among all those proposed for an identification with Sinai and, so far as is known, among all those which we know in the whole area of Sinai and the Negev, corresponds to all these characteristics" (p. 183). Finally, in ch. 8, the chronological problem of relating third-millennium remains to the Exodus narrative is discussed: among the "solutions" proposed are the possible survival of the EB IV culture in marginal areas well into the second millennium, the possibility that (although the Bible omits all mention of it) the Israelites spent several centuries in Transjordan before entering Canaan, and a date for the conquest of Canaan *c.* 1550 B.C.

It is impossible in a short article to discuss every detail of this theory, and we will confine ourselves to its principal weaknesses. It is open to objections that are geographical, historical and literary-critical.

(a) *geographical objections*. We have already seen that there is no basis for the view that the wilderness itinerary refers to the Lake Bardawil spit unless the text is supposed to have originated at a very late date, and I have referred to the difficulties which exist for any version of the "northern route" theory (above, p. 163). Anati quotes a report of M. Dothan which stated that Early Bronze Age pottery was found at Ras Qasrun,[19] but this conflicts with the findings of Oren, which have been outlined above. According to Oren, only one EB IV site was found in the area, and that was on the south side of the lake, not on the spit (*Qadmoniot Sinai*, p. 108). The continuation of the route is reconstructed on the doubtful basis that *midbar šûr* and *midbar ʾēṭām* (Ex. xv 22; Num. xxxiii 8) were names for the whole of northern Sinai

---

[19] P. 146. The reference is to *Hadashot Arkeologiyot* 24 (1967), pp. 39–41 (the date is wrongly given by Anati as "1957"), where Dothan mentions "a few sherds" from the Early Bronze Age at Ras Burun. See above, n. 6.

and that the Israelites were at first heading for Kadesh-barnea. *yam sûp* in Num. xxxiii 10–11 is effectively left out of account in the reconstruction of the route. The journey from Har Karkom to Kadesh-barnea by way of Wadi Arabah is most improbable. It is assumed that the Israelites were aiming for Hazazon-Tamar (Gen. xiv 7), located at Ein Husb, because of the Amorites there: Anati translates *derek har hā*ᵃ*môrî* in Deut. i 19 as "by the mountain road of the Amorites" rather than "by the road to the mountain (or hill-country) of the Amorites", which is clearly the correct rendering (cf. i 20, 44). He also relies on the identification of the Wilderness of Paran with one of the wadies that lead into Wadi Arabah from the west, but although this reflects modern Israeli nomenclature it is without foundation in biblical and other texts.[20] The route reconstructed is without any logic or foundation, and cannot be claimed to lend any support whatever to the proposed location of Sinai. The suggestion that the inclusion of some names which probably refer to water sources in this section of the itinerary favours a location of them in Wadi Arabah (p. 190) is refuted by the fact that such names are also attested in the modern Bedouin names in the Sinai peninsula.[21] Moreover, a location of Sinai at Har Karkom cannot be reconciled with the data of Deut. i 2, which places Horeb at a distance of eleven days' journey from Kadesh-barnea. The basis for the elucidation of this verse must be the standard ancient rate of travel of c. 30 km./day, not the 8–15 km./day assumed by Anati (p. 136) on the basis of the distance between wells in the area south of Kadesh-Barnea.[22] Since Har Karkom is less than 100 km. from Kadesh-barnea, whichever of the alternative sites for the latter is preferred, it cannot be the site of Horeb.[23] The claim that Har Karkom is at the point where Amalekite and Midianite territories met is very questionable geographically and of doubtful relevance to the identification of Sinai.

(b) *historical objections*. Anati is well aware of the chronological difficulties involved in his proposal, since according to the normal dating of his pottery finds the Har Karkom sites would have gone out of use some eight hundred years, at least, before the generally accepted date of the Exodus in the 13th century B.C. The question is whether he has been able to overcome them. It may be acknowledged as in principle possible that, in outlying areas especially, a culture

---

[20] Cf. B. Rothenberg and Y. Aharoni, *God's Wilderness* (London, 1961), pp. 167–9.
[21] C. Bailey, *PEQ* 116 (1984), pp. 42–57, esp. p. 55
[22] Cf. G.I. Davies, *PEQ* 111 (1979), pp. 87–101.
[23] On the possible sites of Kadesh-barnea, see C.H.J. de Geus, *OTS* 20 (1977), pp. 56–66.

which had been superseded in the main centres of population continued to exist for a time. Such overlaps seem indeed to be attested at certain points of cultural change in the early history of Palestine, for example at the beginning and end of the Early Bronze Age.[24] But a continuation of the older culture is unlikely to have lasted more than a century or two, and it needs to be remembered that, in the absence of clear second millennium finds, it remains no more than a hypothesis in this case. Anati's other proposals are also highly unlikely. On the one hand, a date for the Exodus prior to the 13th century can be maintained only by ignoring the key geographical and historical indications in Ex. i–xiii, and a date prior to the establishment of the Hyksos capital at Avaris in the Delta is absolutely out of the question. On the other hand, the theory that the Israelites spent centuries in Transjordan before entering Canaan is entirely without foundation, and goes against all the indications of the biblical sources, including the genealogies which Anati regards as particularly reliable and ancient documents (p. 197). More generally, the reconstruction is vitiated by its failure to present or refer to any systematic investigation of the literary sources. The conclusion must be that the chronological difficulties for the identification of Har Karkom with Mount Sinai have not been overcome.

(c) *literary-critical objections.* Anati's estimate of the literary integrity of the biblical traditions is not entirely consistent. At one point he says: "The epic of the Exodus and the revelation at Mount Sinai constitutes, in the biblical narratives, a monumental literary work which has been handed down almost intact for about three thousand years, after being transmitted orally for several centuries" (p. 119). In particular, he holds that the itinerary "is probably composed of elements which found their matrix at the very beginning of the oral tradition" (p. 197). Nevertheless, he also recognizes that various factors may have operated to transform the original account of the events into an idealized, abbreviated, story (pp. 197–9), and he is prepared to allow elsewhere that the itinerary may reflect only the topographical knowledge of the compilers (pp. 87–8, 139–40). The problem is that these different viewpoints are not deployed systematically or precisely, but appealed to as they fit in with the treatment accorded to various parts of the tradition. Thus the geographical details of Exodus and Numbers are treated as a consistent, unified

---

[24] Cf. K.M. Kenyon, *Archaeology in the Holy Land* (4th edn, London, 1979), p. 79; P. Gerstenblith, *The Levant at the Beginning of the Middle Bronze Age* (Winona Lake, 1983), p. 107, n. 3.

system which can be used as it stands to map the route through the
desert, while the narrative sequence in Joshua-Judges can be
stretched to cover almost a thousand years, and the hypothesis of
a "missing book of the Bible" can be readily entertained. For our
present purpose it is the failure to take account of the complex origin
and relatively late date of the itinerary-material which is the most
serious weakness of the presentation. Those who have studied the
texts with an eye both to the development of the biblical literature
and to the geographical realities of the Sinai peninsula have generally
come to the view that the Pentateuch contains more than one account
of the wilderness route.[25] This is particularly clear with regard to the
relationship of the "spies" story to the visit to Kadesh and the
direction of the journey from Kadesh. According to the Priestly
source Kadesh was reached (Num. xx 1) only after the mission of the
spies and the resultant forty years of wanderings, and from there the
route led more or less directly to "the plains of Moab" (Num. xxii 1).
In Deuteronomy, however, the spies were sent out from Kadesh
(Deut. i 19–25; cf. Num. xiii 26) and the wanderings followed the
departure from there, which took a southerly direction (Deut.
i 34–40, ii 1–3). Anati entirely ignores the tradition of the sending of
the spies from Kadesh, and it is arguable that the complexities of his
handling of the post-Sinai section of the itinerary in Num. xxxiii are
due not only to his location for Mount Sinai being wrong but to his
lack of awareness of the way in which these two traditions about the
central part of the wilderness journey have affected the corresponding
section of the itinerary.

According to the traditional view (which the present writer holds
to be still the most likely) that the writers of the Old Testament
located Mount Sinai in the south of the peninsula, certain problems
arise in the interpretation of Num. xxxiii 1–49. There is first the
distribution of names over the section of route from the Wilderness of
Sinai to Kadesh. For the first part of this, as far as Ezion-Geber,
nineteen intermediate stations are given. But for the second part,
from Ezion-Geber to Kadesh, which covers only a slightly shorter
distance if Sinai is located in the south of the peninsula, no
intermediate stations are given. Secondly, some names which occur
before Ezion-Geber seem to refer to places further north than it. This

---

[25] This is set out with particular clarity by M. Haran, *Ages and Institutions in the Bible*
(Tel Aviv, 1972), 37–76 (Heb.) (cf. *Tarbiz* 40 [1970–1], pp. 113–43, and *IDBS*
[Nashville, 1976], pp. 307–10), although the present writer would not agree with all
aspects of Haran's presentation.

is most clearly the case with Bene-jaakan, which 1 Chr. i 42 associates with Seir, which in the Chronicler's time at least was the name of the hill country which rises to the west of Wadi Arabah.[26] But it is also tempting to associate Hashmonah with Heshmon (Josh. xv 27), one of the cities belonging to the tribe of Judah in the Negeb. These geographical improbabilities can be removed if one adopts a theory about the order of the stages in Num. xxxiii 1–49 which was apparently first proposed by G.H.A. Ewald in the mid-19th century, and has enjoyed considerable popularity since then.[27] The suggestion is that originally the section of the itinerary relating to Kadesh and Mount Hor (verses 36b–41a) stood between the first and second halves of verse 30, so that the order of the stations in this section would be: Hashmonah – Kadesh – Mount Hor – Moseroth – Bene-jaakan – Hor haggidgad – Jotbathah – Abronah – Ezion-Geber – Zalmonah – Punon, etc. A further reason put forward in support of this rearrangement of the text concerns the traditions of Aaron's death, which are variously located at Moserah/-oth (Deut. x 6) and Mount Hor (Num. xx 27–8, xxxiii 38). While it would be uncritical to demand that these traditions be harmonized with each other, it is perhaps more likely that the Priestly Work, to which the location at Mount Hor is probably due, associated the story with a place adjacent to the traditional burial-place of Aaron at Moserah/-oth than that it transferred it to a quite different area. Finally, it is striking that the route which emerges if the order is changed as suggested is not some unparalleled alternative for the Israelites' journey through the wilderness, but a more detailed account of the route described in outline in Deut. i–ii: from Sinai/Horeb through the desert to Kadesh, without touching the coast (cf. Deut. i 19); then south-east towards the Red Sea (i.e. the Gulf of Aqaba) and Ezion-Geber (Deut. ii 1), northwards up Wadi Arabah (Deut. ii 3, 8) and through the territory of the Moabites (Deut. ii 29)

Such a theory ought, if it is to be accepted, to be able not only to explain certain peculiarities in the text as it has been transmitted, but

---

[26] On this location of Seir cf. J.R. Bartlett, *JTS* N.S. 20 (1969), pp. 1–12, and R. de Vaux, *Histoire ancienne d'Israël* (1) (Paris, 1971), pp. 516–17, who maintain that the term was so used from an early date (against N. Glueck, *HUCA* 11 [1936], pp. 141–57, who thought that this was so only in the post-exilic period).

[27] G.H.A. Ewald, *Geschichte des Volkes Israel* (3rd edn, Göttingen, 1864–8) 2, pp. 283–5, especially p. 285, n. 2. Cf. M.J. Lagrange, *RB* 9 (1900), pp. 273–4; B. Baentsch, *Exodus-Numeri* (Göttingen, 1903), pp. 674, 680; F.-M. Abel, *Géographie de la Palestine* 2 (Paris, 1933, 1938), pp. 213–14; Simons (n. 4), pp. 254–5; W. Rudolph, *BHS*, ad loc. (with query). It was rejected as unnecessary by A. Dillmann, *Die Bücher Numeri, Deuteronomium und Josua* (2nd edn, Leipzig, 1886), p. 206, and H. Holzinger, *Numeri* (Tübingen and Leipzig, 1903), p. 163.

also to account for the alleged disruption of the original order which has produced the present form of the text. A plausible account can in fact be given, one which makes use of the divergences between the Deuteronomic description of the wilderness route and the Priestly description of it as outlined above. It is possible to see the present form of Num. xxxiii 1–49 as being due to the redaction of a text which originally reflected the Deuteronomic view, to make it agree with the Priestly account. It is this latter version which is reflected in the dating of Aaron's death in the fortieth year of the Exodus era (Num. xxxiii 38), for it is hardly likely that the Israelites spent thirty-eight years travelling from Kadesh to Mount Hor in any version of the story. The change in order suggested may therefore have been made at the same time as the Priestly material about Aaron's death (and other material derived from P) was introduced into Num. xxxiii 1–49.

Clearly, an approach to the wilderness journeys which takes no account of these literary complexities cannot hope to make geographical sense of them, nor is it in a position to say whether the itinerary favours one identification of Mount Sinai or another.

On all three counts, therefore, Anati's treatment of the problem is seriously deficient. In the face of the difficulties outlined, the correspondences between Har Karkom and the Sinai tradition must be regarded as coincidences. They are not so very remarkable. Given the importance of standing stones in West Semitic religion and the associations of the number "twelve", it is to be expected that sets of twelve standing stones would appear at cultic sites in various places, and Anati himself mentions two more, one at Har Karkom itself and the other in Nahal ʿUvda near Wadi Arabah (pp. 38, 90). One may also recall the stones set up west of the Jordan according to Josh. iv 20–3. Further away, J. Koenig appealed to the presence of twelve stones below Halaʾ l-Bedr in Arabia to support his theory that it was Mount Sinai.[28] It should also be noted that the "human-shaped stone" in Site 52 is not mentioned in Exodus and is unlikely to have been a part of early Yahwistic worship, and that the stone dwelling-units at Har Karkom, which were used over a period of several centuries, do not fit the Exodus story at all well, according to which the Israelites lived in tents, not houses (cf. Ex. xviii 7, xxxiii 8, 10). It is only by careful selection that the archaeological data can be made to fit the biblical narrative.

---

[28] *Le site de al-Jaw dans l'ancien pays de Madian* (Paris, 1971), pp. 112–23; cf. *RHR* 167 (1965), pp. 135–6.

Har Karkom is therefore not Mount Sinai. Once this is recognized, it is possible for Anati's important discoveries to be placed in their proper context. He has made a significant addition to the evidence of EB IV civilization in the far south of Palestine collected by Glueck and Rothenberg, and it seems likely that he has identified a major religious centre whose origins go back to the early third millennium, which is already known to be a period when contacts existed between southern Palestine (Arad) and the Sinai peninsula. These connections deserve study in their own right, so that they can make their proper contribution to the history of Semitic society and religion in the Levant.

In conclusion, some principles of more general relevance to the study of the itineraries may be identified:[29]

(i) due recognition must be given to the fact that the itinerary material is not all from the same source, and to the effect of different conceptions of the wilderness route upon it;

(ii) the integrity of Num. xxxiii 1–49 and its literary priority to the corresponding itinerary-notes in the main narrative may be assumed;[30]

(iii) a distinction should be made between those texts (if any) which relate to the period of the Exodus itself and those which merely reflect later views of the wilderness route;

(iv) specific identifications should be based, as far as possible, on texts and archaeological and other extra-biblical evidence which are known to be contemporary with each other.

Attention to these principles should set the correlation of the itineraries and archaeological evidence on a firmer footing, and prevent the multiplication of untenable theories.

---

[29] See further Davies (n. 4), ch. 6.
[30] Cf. Davies, *VT* 33 (1983), pp. 1–13.

THE BIBLICAL DIETARY LAWS
AND THE CONCEPT OF HOLINESS[1]

by

EDWIN FIRMAGE

Jerusalem

When Mary Douglas's interpretation of the biblical dietary law was published, it appeared to many, and when I read it years later I too felt, that at last we had received a convincing explanation of the criteria distinguishing clean and unclean animals. Prior to the appearance of her seminal studies in *Purity and Danger* (London, 1966) and *Implicit Meanings* (London, 1975) these criteria had remained without any systematic interpretation. Indeed, although any number of reasons had been suggested for the exclusion of the unclean species named in Lev. xi, almost everyone agreed in principle that no single reason could be operative, that the real reasons were no longer understood when the law in its present form was written, and that the present criteria are secondary (see appendix 1). If it has done nothing more than to shake our confidence in these assumptions, Douglas's work merits recognition.

While one should not deny in principle that the present dietary law may be the product of a long evolution, one should also not begin by assuming that it is. In order to decide that issue, we must discover whether in fact the present criteria can be explained as indicating a coherent purpose behind the definitions of animal purity. Only having done that is it admissible to speculate about the prehistory of the present law. The text before us must be the starting point for any discussion of the issue. This would be true even if we were to suppose, for example, with scholarship prior to Douglas, that the animal tabus of Lev. xi are in fact not the creation of the priests, and that they were motivated by reasons that have nothing to do with the present

---

[1] I wish to thank those who have offered criticisms of various drafts of this article: Professors M. Weinfeld, Jacob Milgrom, David Wright and Shalom Paul, and fellow student Roy Gane.

criteria, or conceivably even with problems of interest to the priests.
In that case, we should still have to ask why the priests chose to
formulate these tabus by means of the present criteria. That is,
whatever the original motivation was, are the priests perhaps
reinterpreting old tabus according to a system of their own? There is
an instructive example in our own system of table manners that will
illustrate what I mean. Most people today probably assume that the
practice of eating with one's own utensils is a product of rational
considerations of hygiene. But in fact it is not.[2] Nevertheless, when,
toward the end of the 18th century, concern for hygiene began to take
on increasing importance, people also began to suppose that that was
in fact what had motivated the use of utensils all along. For us today of
course, hygiene is what justifies their use. It is conceivable, then, that
Israel's dietary code underwent such reinterpretation over the years.
It may be that the priests in particular reinterpreted old tabus, and
justified them in the terms which we now have in Lev. xi. What is
more, if there were dietary tabus before the present law came into
being, then it cannot be taken for granted that all these popular tabus
were taken over by the priests, and we should then have to ask what
guidelines the priests used in selecting those animals which the
present law regards as unclean. In sum, whatever version of the
prehistory of the dietary law we accept, there remain a number of
important questions whose answers must largely come from the
present text, the organizing principles of which are precisely those
neglected crieria, for which modern scholarship has had no use. With
Mary Douglas, these found an interpreter who was alert to their
significance. She has drawn our attention to the fact that such codes of
behavior are inseparable from the larger social system of their
creators, whose values they embody. It is now with Mary Douglas
that any further discussion of the dietary law must begin. Before
turning to my own analysis of the animal categories, I should like,
then, to highlight some weaknesses in Mary Douglas's approach, as
the issues raised will enable us to ask more probing questions of our
text.

Douglas believed that she had discovered in the biblical criteria of
selection an essential unity of motivation: animals were expected to
have those essential physical features proper to their respective
habitats. Douglas identified the means of locomotion as the most
crucial of these features. Thus, cattle were expected to go on four

---

[2] Cf. Norbert Elias, *A History of Manners* (New York, 1976).

(cloven) hooves, birds primarily to fly (rather than to walk), and fish to have fins. Rodents were prohibited because of their indeterminate movement, indicated, Douglas supposed, by the verb šāraṣ. The biblical classification "rejects creatures which are anomalous, whether in living between two spheres, or having defining features of another sphere, or lacking defining features" (*Implicit Meanings*, p. 266). Although no criteria are given for the birds, Douglas tentatively suggested[3] that, if the exact identity of the birds were known, they would perhaps prove to be diving and swimming birds, and therefore "anomalous" in regard to their means of locomotion.

Has Douglas done justice to the criteria? Let us start with the birds. Granted that the identification of many of the twenty bird species listed in Lev. xi is uncertain, it can scarcely be maintained that all the birds are of the diving or swimming type. Indeed, apart from what we can say by way of identifying certain of the unclean birds, Douglas's statement is unlikely from the start. Although some Israelites would have been familiar with bird life around the Sea of Galilee, most had only limited access to the coast during most of Israel's history. The Israelites were at home in the central highlands, and it is probable that most of the birds known to them, whether clean or unclean, would have been landlubbers as well. Far more importantly, however, birds that dive and swim still fly, and it is their wings, which are their principal means of locomotion. There is nothing about their wings that is at all anomalous. In contrast, it is the precisely the unclean animals' missing hoof or cleft in the hoof, and the marine creature's lack of proper fins, which make it "anomalous". That some birds also swim or dive is no more remarkable than that they walk in addition to flying. Unlike fish, which can only swim, and land animals, which can only walk on the ground, all birds can locomote in at least two ways, and if in two, why should three be remarkable? In other words, if diving and swimming birds appear to straddle two environmental categories, land and sea, all birds may just as well be said to straddle air and land, and all would, according to this logic, be unclean. Thus, neither in regard to their means of locomotion, nor in their moving between two environmental spheres can the unclean birds be said to be anomalous.

Next, it is not the case that šĕrāṣîm are automatically excluded because they swarm. Lev. xi 10, for example, makes it clear that the prohibited aquatic species are only a sub-set of "everything that

---

[3] *Purity and Danger*, p. 57; cf. her more probable explanation in *Implicit Meanings*, p. 270.

swarms in the water" (*mikkōl šereṣ hammayim*). Indeed, according to the priestly account of creation everything in the water swarms (Gen. i 20). It is no less clear that the category of air-borne swarmers includes the clean species of locusts (v. 21: *ʾakʾet-zeh tōʾkĕlû mikkōl šereṣ hāʿôp*). Finally, man himself is at one point commanded to swarm upon the earth (Gen. ix 7–P). It is therefore unlikely that, in the case of rodents, swarming is itself the reason for their exclusion. What is more, the verb *šāraṣ* does not denote indeterminate motion. In a number of cases, the subject is inanimate (Gen. i 21; Ex. vii 28; Ps. cv 30), and in others it is perhaps not movement, but fertility that is indicated (Gen. viii 17, ix 7). (In these last two instances, swarming movement indicative of fertility is conceivable, but impossible to prove.) The means of locomotion is therefore again of no importance in the determination of the criteria of selection. Even with the fish, where the requirement that they have fins would agree with Douglas's interpretation, a second criterion is given – scales – which has nothing to do with motion in the water.

We come then to the land animals. While hooves might be said to have something to do with movement on land, that is not true of the other specified criterion for land animals – that they be ruminants. What is more, Douglas fails to explain why cloven hooves and not simple hooves are required, as the cleft really has nothing to do with the way the animal moves on land. Why, for example, should a horse's hoof be considered less proper to locomotion on land than a gazelle's?

Without any doubt, therefore, the means of locomotion is not the unifying principle behind the perception of uncleanness. This need not force us altogether to abandon Douglas's more general thesis, that "holiness requires that individuals shall conform to the class to which they belong ... that different classes of things shall not be confused" (*Purity and Danger*, p. 53). However, we must seek another defining feature, if one in fact exists.

There are more fundamental shortcomings in Douglas's explanation. She mistakenly asserts[4] that contact with the living animal disqualifies one from entering the temple. The fact is that the prohibited animals, while alive, were not abhorred, nor did they communicate impurity. Only their being eaten, and (secondarily) contact with their carcasses are of interest to the priestly legislators (see appendix 6). In fact, the issues of carcass contamination and dietary prohibition arise from quite different concerns. But, if the criterion is

---

[4] *Purity and Danger*, p. 55; *Implicit Meanings*, esp. p. 266.

simply conformance with class characteristics, why is only the dead animal, and especially its use as food, of concern? There is every reason to suppose (and Douglas does) that if she were right, any contact would be prohibited. The failure of her theory to show a strong inherent relationship between the fact that Lev. xi is primarily a dietary law and the motivation behind the criteria of selection is one of its greatest weaknesses.

A related and no less basic question is why the biblical dietary law is given as a set of prohibitions in the first place. One important feature of the biblical system of impurity into which the dietary law has been incorporated is that one is not in general prohibited from contracting impurity. Only failure to purify oneself as required, and the potential threat which that failure poses to the sanctuary (cf. Lev. xv 31), are subject to penalty. The singularity of the core of the dietary law (vv. 1–23) is thus apparent, for, in contrast to the rest of the impurity system, it forbids one to become impure by eating any of the forbidden species. Why this singularity?

Another desideratum lacking in Douglas's theory is an explanation of the use of largely morphological characteristics as the basis for the system of selection. That these anatomical features should be used is not to be taken for granted. The manifold (non-biblical) rationales suggested by ancient and modern interpretations alike (see appendix 1) are evidence of the fact that superficial morphological features are by no means the only possible bases for making such a selection. Dietary codes in other cultures often justify the prohibition of unclean animals on non-morphological grounds (cf. e.g. *Laws of Manu* v. 2–56). Indeed, according to the hygienic explanation (see appendix 1) merely superficial characteristics would convey the least significant information. In Douglas's terms, what constitutes anomaly or variation from the norm need not be defined by morphology, so why is it?

Finally, why should those features in which the prohibited animals supposedly distinguish themselves from their class type necessarily make them unclean? Why does anomaly *ipso facto* make these things unclean and inedible? Douglas herself highlights this problem: "Anomalous creatures are unfit for altar and table. *This is a peculiarity of the Mosaic code* [italics mine]. In other societies anomaly is not always so treated. Indeed, in some, the anomalous creature is treated as the source of blessing and is especially fit for the altar, or as a noble beast ... " The attempt might be made to supply this omission in Douglas's treatment by arguing, for example, that before the creation of the criteria at least some of the excluded species, such as the pig, were already popularly regarded with some repugnance. This possibility must not be rejected out of hand, as Douglas pointedly rejects it in the case of the pig. But, even if it could be demonstrated in a few cases, it clearly does not apply in many more. What is particularly repugnant about the camel, the hare or the hyrax, about crustaceans, or, indeed, about predatory animals? Our own predispositions are unsure guides in this matter. But Mary Douglas denies in principle that the prohibited animals were held in disfavor before the creation of the criteria by which they were judged anomalous. Douglas maintains that since there is an analogy between the animal and the human spheres,[5] and since the human specimens (the Israelites) are under injunction to be holy or perfect, so their animals must be correspondingly free from defect. Anomaly, that is, variation from the general type, is therefore defined as a defect (p. 269). But the problem is how one is to determine significant anomaly. Which anomalies signify defect, and which do not? We still lack an explanation why precisely those morphological variations singled out by the dietary law were perceived as defects.

In summary, then, we have grounds to question not only the validity of Douglas's original criterion (proper means of locomotion), but also the value of the general statement of her thesis that the notion of impurity underlying the biblical dietary laws is based on the anomaly of the prohibited animals relative to their respective classifications (e.g. as cattle, fish or fowl).

With Douglas's explanation thus eliminated, we must go back to the drawing board. By way of background, I would stress first of all the way in which the dietary law differs from the rest of the priestly system of impurity (cf. Lev. xii–xv; Num. xix, etc.). In this system, purity and impurity are meaningful only with respect to the sanctuary. In Israel, as in the rest of the ancient Near East, impurity was perhaps originally thought to be an independent demonic agent. But in the priestly system of the Bible it has altogether lost its demonic aspect. It no longer poses a threat to the individual, but only to the sanctuary. Thus, the temple ritual associated with severe impurity, the ḥaṭṭāʾt, is designed not to purge the individual of a potentially dangerous demonic agent, but rather to cleanse the sanctuary from the contamination consequent on an individual's sin or severe impurity.[6] Hence, non-Israelites living in Israel (gērîm) too must

---

[5] See her discussion in *Implicit Meanings*, pp. 267–9.

[6] On points discussed here see the following articles by J. Milgrom: "The Function of the *Ḥaṭṭāʾt*-Offering", *Tarbiz* 40 (1970), pp. 1–8; "Israel's Sanctuary: The Priestly 'Picture of Dorian Gray'", *RB* 83 (1976), pp. 391–9; "Sacrifices and Offerings–OT", "Atonement in the OT", *IDBS*; "The Graduated *Ḥaṭṭāʾt* of Leviticus 5:1–13", *JAOS* 103 (1983), pp. 249–54.

observe the laws of personal purity and the prohibitive commandments, the violation of either of which would pollute the sanctuary
(Lev. xvi 29, xvii 8, 12–13, 15, xviii 26, xx 2, xxiv 16; Num. xv 26,
29–30, xix 10). In this system, purity is negatively defined simply as
the absence of impurity; it does not confer upon a person or thing
"holy" status or special power. It is a necessary condition of holiness,
but may also characterize the profane world as well. Thus, any person
or thing may be pure. However, purity, impurity and holiness, do not
inhere in people or in things, the one exception being the sanctuary,
and it must be specially anointed in order to become holy. (Cf. further
n.8.)

As just described, the priestly system of impurity, while it severely
restricts almost universally held notions of physical impurity, nevertheless reveals its indebtedness to them.[7] They are part of Israel's
prehistoric pagan legacy, and not surprisingly are reflected in
historical texts (cf. e.g. 2 Sam. xi 4 [menstruant]; 2 Kgs v, vii 3ff.
["leper"]; 1 Sam. xx 26 [nocturnal emission]; 1 Sam. xxi 5 [sexual
intercourse]). In contrast, with the possible exception of the pig, there
is no evidence prior to the appearance of the present dietary law that
the Israelites regarded any of the animals prohibited by Lev. xi as
unclean. Therefore, while Israel's dietary tabus often overlap with
those of contemporary cultures, one cannot assume that its aversion
to these animals originated from the same long-standing, popular
source.

In contrast to the rest of the system of impurity as just described,
the dietary law posits the existence of non-human sources of
"impurity" – animals – which are moreover inherently "unclean", All
the impurities listed in Lev. xii–xv and Num. xix, however, arise from
man alone, and all are regarded as temporary, and subject to
purification.

Also unique to the dietary law is the rationale underlying this new
category of uncleanness. In restricting his diet to the flesh of "clean"
animals, the Israelite not only avoids impurity – thus remaining pure
in the negative sense defined above – but also positively undertakes,
as we shall see, a sort of *imitatio dei*. Whereas, for example, the ordinary
Israelite is not prohibited from becoming impure by contact with the
sources of impurity described in Lev. xii-xv or Num. xix, he is
positively forbidden to eat the flesh of "unclean" animals, and by
observing this prohibition maintains a kind of "purity" that is
positively valued. To abstain is a virtue, whereas the avoidance of

---

[7] Cf. e.g. J. Doeller, *Die Reinheits- und Speisegesetze des ATs in religionsgeschichtlicher
Beleuchtung* (Münster, 1917). At this point well-known further literature is omitted.

secondary contamination from any of the personal impurities of chs xii–xv or Num. xix is neither required, nor indeed necessarily desirable. Sex, for example, though it conveys impurity, is not discouraged. Neither is entry into the house of the deceased. Put simply, it is not a sin to contract impurity or to be impure. (Only priests are positively forbidden to contract impurity [Lev. xxi 1–4, 11–12], but it is clear that this prohibition does not apply to all communicable impurities.) Being impure is a sin only when the Israelite fails to purify himself at the proper time (Lev. v 2–3; cf. xv 31, xvii 15–16).

To repeat, then, unlike the rest of the code of impurities, the dietary law places a value on behaviour, and so belongs in the category of moral imperatives. I suggest, therefore, that the dietary law originates not in age-old notions of miasma, but in a self-conscious attempt on the part of the priests to put a singular tenet of Israelite theology into practice – that Israel is to be holy, not simply pure (in the technical meaning of "free from impurity").[8] Thus, unlike the laws of personal impurity which applied even to non-Israelites, the dietary law was to be kept by the Israelites alone. Its violation seems to have been taken as an offense comparable to certain sexual acts, punishable by God (cf. Lev. xx 17–25),[9] which are explicitly labelled as offenses against Israel's calling to be a holy people. If so, we must ask why the priests believed that the use of certain kinds of animals as food was inconsistent with that calling.

---

[8] One measure of the "holiness" of a thing in technical usage is the degree to which it is capable of infecting other things with holiness. In the priestly system (excluding Ezekiel) such power is had only by consecrated objects inside the sanctuary designated as "most holy" (e.g. Ex. xxix 37 [the altar]; Lev. vi 11 [the minḥâ, once consecrated]). The priests, though they regularly come in contact with most holy objects, cannot make the things they touch holy. Priests are consecrated to be "holy" (a grade of holiness below "most holy"), and this enables them to officiate in the sanctuary, but they lack the power had by "most holy" objects to communicate their holiness to other people or to things. By the same token, though the priest is under stricter rules of personal purity, it is not an act of desecration for a person to make a priest impure, whereas desecration of sancta proper is punishable by kārēt, extirpation. In neither P nor H is Israel at present holy in this strict sense. In H, however, it is to become holy. This ideology is implicit in ch. xi also. It is explicit, of course, in the H addition (vv. 41–5). But it is present, I would argue, in the body of ch. xi as well, in that the observance of the dietary law is so inextricably linked with Israel's identity as a nation under special obligations of holiness. Thus, while Lev. xi 1–23 lack the code-words that scholars immediately associate with H, its underlying purpose, as I hope to show, is fundamentally in keeping with the character of H's ideology. I am not saying that ch. xi belongs to the historical source we call H, but only that they share a common point of view.

[9] The general principle is that sins against God, such as the pollution of the sanctuary, are punishable by God, and by God alone. See Milgrom, *Studies in Levitical Terminology* (Berkeley, 1970), pp. 5ff.

At the outset, it must be recognized that from long before the Israelite priesthood came on the scene, a handful of domestic species had provided the bulk of the ordinary man's diet, as well as virtually all the animals sacrificed to local deities (see appendix 2). If written or unwritten dietary codes existed in pre-Israelite Palestine, then in at least one essential respect they would certainly have resembled Israel's: domestic cattle would have been regarded as clean, if for no other reason than that from time immemorial people had eaten them and offered them to their gods. We can document this fact in Ugarit, where the make-up of the cult as concerns animal sacrifice is substantially the same as in Israel.[10] That domestic cattle were clean was therefore a given in the considerations that eventually gave rise to the biblical dietary law. The first and most important criteria of this law (Lev. xi 3) were perforce derived from these few domestic species because they constituted *de facto* the category of clean food.

Why should Israel's priesthood have transformed this socio-economic preference for domestic cattle into such a key element of its religious constitution? Clearly, a religious consideration is at work. That consideration has transformed a limited dietary preference into an all encompassing classification scheme of singular signifance that is without parallel in the ancient Near East. The driving force behind this novel consideration was surely the notion that Israel had been called to be a holy people. It was the priest's special concern to see to it that the conditions for holiness were observed, first of all in the sanctuary, but also among the people at large. He was to teach the people what consistuted ritual uncleanness, and how it was to be eliminated. The priests took the notion of Israel's calling a step further, however, when they created the dietary law. As we have seen, it goes beyond the more limited notion of personal purity, in that it distinguishes not any person who is pure from one who is not, but Israelites as against other nations. When, therefore, the priests realized that the Israelite diet too should come under the requirements of the injunction of holiness, they had in the sacrificial animals ready made models of cleanness by which they could judge the "purity" of items in the Israelite diet. Now, as we have seen, these same commonly sacrificed species also provided the bulk of the ordinary man's diet of meat. However, while man's diet included those animals regularly given to the deity, man nevertheless enjoyed a greater

---

[10] In fact, at Ugarit animals other than domestic cattle were on rare occasions sacrificed. There is a solitary Ugaritic text (*UT* 62 [= *CTA* 6.I]. 18ff.) which mentions among the victims the wild goat (y^cl), the ass (*ḥmr*), and the buffalo (*rum*). Nevertheless, the usual sacrificial victims are precisely those found in the Bible.

variety of meats than the deity. The question for the priest was, then: which of these other meats were consistent with the paradigm of "proper" meats defined by the sacrifical species? The handful of species fit for God's altar-table,[11] universally accepted as such from the beginning, provided the required definition of cleanness for the rest of the animal world. The priests drew an analogy between the Israelite diet and that of YHWH, whose staples (the sacrificial species) became the measure of fitness for all other animals in the ordinary Israelite's diet.

When it came to applying this standard of comparison, only those animals which superficially resembled the sacrificial model were allowed. But the sole issue at stake was the animal's fitness for the Israelite diet. As I suggested above, if Mary Douglas were right, not only the prohibited animal's carcass, but even the live specimen would be abhorred. Yet this was plainly not the case. On the contrary, a number of the unclean animals such as the equids and the camel played important roles in daily life, and others, such as the lion or the eagle, were far more often objects of admiration than symbols of uncleanness. Unclean animals as such were not abhorrent to the average Israelite or to the priests. The question was simply whether they were acceptable as food.

The criteria for the selection of clean quadrupeds are therefore a précis of the paradigm constituted by the cattle, sheep and goats. They are those features which the priests judged to be both comprehensive and easily applicable. And, in fact, of the superficial features apparent (as they had to be) even to the most inexperienced

---

[11] For this idea of sacrifice as divine food, cf. the use of the ancient term *šulḥan yhwh* (Ezek. xl 16; Mal. i 7, 12), and the related designation of sacrifice as *leḥem ᵓĕlōhîm* (Lev. xxi 6, 8, 17, 21, 22, xxii 25; Ezek. xl 7). In addition to the explicit designation of the altar as God's table, we have the complex of temple services, which provided for the deity's basic needs. Thus, in addition to meat, his offerings also included cereal or bread (the *minḥâ*) mixed with oil (Lev. ii 1, 4, xxiii 13; Num. xv 1–12; cf. also Judg. ix 9, 13) and wine (the *nesek*; cf. also 1 Sam. i 24, x 3; Hos. ix 4). All the basic components of the Palestinian diet – meat, bread, oil and wine – are present. In addition to the private offerings, twice a day, without fail, the deity is provided with another basic meal, the *tāmîd*. Special loaves of bread (the *leḥem pānîm*, Ex. xxv 30; Lev. xxiv 5–9; 1 Sam. xxi 5–7) were also set out on the table inside the tent. These offerings are a "pleasing aroma" to YHWH (Ex. xxix 18; Lev. i 9, 13, 17, ii 2, 9, iii 5, vi 8, 14, xxiii 13, 18, etc.). He is provided with other amenities such as light (the *měnôrâ*, Ex. xxv 31ff.; Lev. xxiv 2–4), and a luxurious apartment befitting his majesty. All this is not to say that in historical times the priests or even the people took this anthropomorphic service literally. Nonetheless, Israel inherited and adapted what is patently a service designed to meet the needs of an anthropomorphic deity, and it is this primitive conception that predetermined the identification of the altar as the table of God. Cf. further M. Haran, "The Complex of Ritual Acts Inside the Tabernacle", *Scripta Hierosolymitana* 8 (1961), pp. 272–302.

observer, these are logical choices, among the only ones which are constant across species boundaries.[12]

The criteria, then, were from the beginning an essential element of the law, and the ultimate basis for determining an animal's cleanness. But the priests needed no criteria to tell them that bears, lions, dogs, rodents, and countless other animals were different from the domestic livestock which they offered to God. The differences from the temple paradigm were self-evident. Before specific criteria were over mentioned it was therefore obvious that these land animals were "unclean". The problem was that as a legal principle it was not enough simply to prohibit all animals that did not "look like" domestic livestock. Inevitably, there would have to be guidelines for deciding difficult cases and guaranteeing consistency of application. Some sort of criteria were necessary if the prohibition were to be practicable. Our criteria are therefore those features which the priests believed could be most simply and unambiguously applied by the layman, to whom the law is addressed (Lev. xi 1). The present criteria themselves are therefore not exactly the *raison d'être* of most of the dietary prohibitions. They are, however, indicative of the more general and fundamental criterion of dissimilarity with the temple paradigm. It is this which is the mainspring of the dietary law.[13]

According to Lev. xi 3 all clean land animals satisfy two criteria.

---

[12] The rabbis observed one other feature that could have served as a criterion: the presence of horns in the adult (B. Ḥul. 59b). They made a distinction not present in our biblical text between clean animals that are sacrificeable and those that are not, based on the nature of the animal's horns, in order to ensure that the fat of species suitable for sacrifice goes on the altar, as required by law. The law allowed one to eat the fat of species unsuitable for sacrifice.

[13] After arriving at this conclusion, I discovered that I had been partially anticipated by Sir James Frazer (*Folklore In The Old Testament* 3 [London, 1919], pp. 160–1):

> . . . the aversion of pastoral tribes to the eating of game is derived from a belief that cows are directly injured whenever their milk comes into contact with the flesh of wild animals in the stomachs of the tribesmen, and that the consequent danger to the cattle can only be averted, either by abstaining from game altogether, or at all events by leaving a sufficient interval between the consumption of game and the consumption of milk to allow of the stomach being completely cleared of the one food before it receives the other. The remarkable exceptions which some of these tribes make to the general rule, by permitting the consumption of wild animals that bear a more or less distant resemblance to cattle, suggests a comparison with the ancient Hebrew distinction of clean and unclean animals. Can it be that the distinction in question originated in the rudimentary zoology of a pastoral people, who divided the whole animal kingdom into creatures which resembled, and creatures which differed from, their own domestic cattle, and on the basis of that fundamental classification laid down a law of capital importance, that the first of these classes might be eaten and that the second might not?

What relation, if any, the separation of milk and meat has to the dietary law of Lev. xi will be the subject of a forthcoming article by the present writer.

First, they have cloven hooves, and second they are ruminants. The four outlawed species singled out for special mention at the beginning of Lev. xi (*vv.* 4–8) are there because they are anomalous in having one but not both required characteristics, but they are not the only ones excluded by these criteria. Mary Douglas failed to recognize that these two criteria alone suffice to exclude all land animals which are not cloven-hooved, including domestic species such as dogs, horses, carnivores and rodents – all mentioned later in the text (*vv.* 26–30).[14] In fact, the four species of *vv.* 4–7 are the only ones in Israel's immediate environment which meet one but not both criteria.[15] Within this tiny group the pig has a special place, for it alone in the entire animal world known to Israel has cloven hooves but does not chew the cud. Of all prohibited quadrupeds only the pig is excluded on the basis of the criterion of ruminance. With this one exception, all unclean animals could have been excluded simply by the requirement that they have cloven hooves. No new criteria are given for rodents and predatory animals, etc. (*vv.* 27, 29), because they are automatically excluded by the requirement of cloven hooves. Note the repetition of the criteria of *v.* 3 by way of reminder before the explicit prohibition of horses, predators, etc. (*vv.* 26ff.; cf. appendix 6).

If all land animals are judged solely on the basis of the criteria of *v.* 3, then the usual treatment of the four exceptional cases (*vv.* 4–7) needs re-assessment. Too much attention has been focused on these four alone. When, for example, W.F. Albright maintains that the unclean species are unhealthy, his entire attention is devoted to just these four. But in order to prove his thesis, he would have to show that the countless other unclean animals, which are not named because they lack both required characteristics, are also unhealthy, and that is manifestly not the case. The same oversight plagues those who try to identify the unclean species with animals prominent in pagan cults. Once again, they must show such connections not only in the case of

---

[14] See appendix 6 for a discussion of the text.

[15] I owe this observation to my teacher, Jacob Milgrom. Those other animals also fail to meet these requirements, but were either wholly unknown or found only outside Israel: the hippopotamus and the llama. The hippopotamus may have been known (Job xl 15–23). In fact, hippopotamus bones have been found in the Iron Age strata (XII–XI) at Tell Qasîle; cf. Georg Hass, "On the Occurrence of Hippopotamus in the Iron Age of the Coastal Area of Israel (Tell Qasîleh)", *BASOR* 132 (1953), pp. 30–4; Simon Davis, "The Large Animal Bones", in A. Mazar (ed.), *Excavations at Tell Qasîle, Qedem* 20 (Jerusalem, 1985), p. 248. The strata in question are Philistine. According to Davis, one of the bones, a metacarpus, bears cut marks, which suggests that the animal was slaughtered for meat. Hippopotamus bones are also reported to have been found at Aphek and Dan. The hippopotamus therefore survived in Israel's marshy areas, but would not necessarily have been known to the early Israelites.

the pig, the camel, etc., but also in the case of every unnamed species. To repeat, then, in *vv.* 4–7 only those four animals are named which have one but not both necessary characteristics. Countless other animals have neither, and are consequently unnamed.

When it comes to fish, our model seems to shipwreck on the fact that there was no temple paradigm as in the previous case, for fish were not allowed on the altar, and there was therefore no reason that any fish should have been declared unclean. In principle, all marine life would have been licit, for tere was no potentially restrictive temple model that would have obliged the priests to exclude certain species as unclean.[16] Why, then, are certain forms of marine life prohibited, and criteria given? The answer, I think, is that certain species were excluded because in lacking fins and scales they were thought to resemble land species that were prohibited by the criteria of *v.* 3. Eels, and some other scaleless fish, for instance, were probably compared with snakes (see appendix 3). These few species in turn became a model which negatively defined what clean fish should look like. In this case, therefore, the criteria are secondary. In fact, it is possible that the inclusion of fish in the dietary law was altogether a later development.[17] Be that as it may, such marine life as is judged unclean by the present law was thus initially not considered off-limits because it failed to measure up to an idealized image of the fish (Douglas), but because it superficially resembled prohibited land animals.

This conclusion is consistent with the fact that the treatment accorded the fish shows no awareness of the existence of exceptional cases such as are noted in *vv.* 4–7. Just as before, two criteria are given (fins and scales), yet creatures which satisfy only one criterion are not mentioned. There are nevertheless many such exceptions. Sharks, catfish and sturgeons, for example, have fins, but no scales. Why, then, is nothing said of these exceptions? Perhaps, because they were

---

[16] It might be objected that the absence of a food category from the temple paradigm would, on the contrary, have forced the priests to regard that category as unclean. But this was clearly not the case, or else all fish would have been declared unclean. There are any number of other common food items that are not included among the altar offerings, such as fruit, nuts, herbs and vegetables. Further, items such as yeast and honey, which are specifically prohibited from being offered on the altar (Lev. ii 11), are also allowed in the ordinary diet. We may conclude that the dietary law excludes only a minimum of animals – those for which there was a temple paradigm, and which did not resemble that paradigm.

[17] It is noteworthy that in the résumé of dietary tabus found in Lev. xx 25 only the fish are missing. In the light of what has been said, the reason may be that this résumé reflects an earlier version of the dietary law, in which fish had not yet been included. I hasten to add, however, that I do not view the absence of fish in Lev. xx as necessarily leading to this conclusion.

far less likely to confront most Israelites, whose diet included relatively little fish. It is also doubtful whether most people would have recognized the names of the fish even if they had been given. The Israelites' lack of first-hand familiarity with fish is reflected in the fact that in the entire Bible not a single species name is preserved. Such fish as was available inland seems largely to have been marketed by non-Israelites (Job xl 30; Neh. xiii 16), and in such forms as would make morphological analysis very difficult.[18] Such exceptions may, therefore, actually have gone unnoticed by the priests themselves. The fact that special cases such as the catfish are not taken up further strengthens our supposition that the criteria for the fish are secondary, for if the criteria had been arrived at by an exhaustive investigation of the fish world, such as was carried out for land animals, then these exceptional cases could hardly have escaped notice.

We come next to the birds. At this point no theory can avoid being speculative, for no criteria are given. I offer the following educated guesses. It is widely held that the twenty unclean species and their sub-species (designated by *lĕmînēhû/-āh/-ô*) are excluded because they are predatory or carrion birds. This explanation is found already in the Letter of Aristeas (146). The Mishnah too gives it as the rationale: "a bird that seizes food in its claws is unclean; one which has an extra talon,[19] a claw, and the skin of whose stomach can be pealed[20] is clean" (M. Ḥul. III 6). If we assume that diet was the basis of the selection, the first question that comes to mind is why a behavioral characteristic such as diet should be chosen, when the criteria in the previous cases suggest that the priests were simply judging superficial appearance. Perhaps, when it came to birds, those self-evident differences from the temple paradigm which enabled the priests even without specific criteria to say that certain animals were unclean (cf. above p. 18) may no longer have been morphological but behavioral. Among the most obvious characteristics of the dove and

---

[18] Fish were usually dried, salted or pickled; on pickling in post-biblical times; cf. G. Dalman, *Arbeit und Sitte in Palästina* 6 (Gütersloh, 1939), pp. 81, 343; S. Kraus, *Talmudische Archäologie* I (Leipzig, 1910), p. 111. However preserved, fish were usually skinned or scraped beforehand (cf. Salonen [see p. 200], pp. 258ff.), thus limiting what the priests could discover about their morphology. This raises the question how the law was to be applied, for whereas the layman might be expected to do his own hunting, he would, if living at any distance from the sea, be at the mercy of the fish merchants. How could the *kašrût* of fish be guaranteed? What, if any, practical measures were taken along this line we cannot say, as we lack detailed information about even the simplest aspects of the actual marketing of food in urban centers of this period.

[19] Characteristic of birds which walk on the ground and eat grain (J. Feliks, *Encyclopaedia Judaica* [Jerusalem, 1971], col. 31).

[20] Perhaps a reflection of the heavier musculature in grain-eating birds?

the pigeon are the very features that made them domesticable in the first place. "All birds which man has succeeded in domesticating have certain common traits. The first is gregariousness . . . All domesticated birds are also either vegetarians – graminivorous like gamebirds and pigeons or herbivorous like geese – or omnivorous like ducks."[21] There could be no doubt about the basic difference between the diet of the pigeon/dove paradigm on the one hand, and that of vultures, owls, eagles and the like on the other. Everyone could be expected to know that much about common species. But, of course, for many other species the nature of their diet would have been known only to experts. If there was to be any consistency in the selection of birds based on as potentially complex a characteristic as diet, then the selection would have to be centrally decided. In that case, the inclusion of the criteria with the list would if anything only have created confusion. Hence, criteria were omitted in the dietary law. Where criteria could be given, as in the other animal species, it of course greatly simplified matters, since a complete list of all prohibited animals would in general be far too large for most people to recall. Given the relatively small number of unclean bird species, the priests judged a list of these alone to be the most practicable and unambiguous guide. We cannot know exactly how many unclean birds are covered by our list, but we can be sure that it comprises all prohibited species. Since one has only the list to go on, it must be assumed to be complete (see appendix 4). Over against this small number, say the rabbis, "there are innumerable species of clean birds" (B. Ḥul. 63b). So long as people knew the handful of prohibitied bird families there would be little ambiguity.

Strangely, to our way of thinking, flying insects are dealt with as a sub-set of the birds, because they too have wings. Lev. xi classifies them as ꜥôp, of the swarming variety (šereṣ hāꜥôp). As winged creatures, they presumably came under the paradigm of the pigeon and the dove. Yet the criteria specified in the biblical text have nothing to do with the one suggested for the preceding list of birds (i.e. diet). In the case of insects, however, their much more obvious physical dissimilarity with the paradigm would automatically have excluded them to begin with. They were as self-evidently different from the paradigmatic birds, as lions, horses and rats were from the cattle paradigm. Thus, in principle, all flying insects would be excluded from the diet, because they do not resemble the birds under whose paradigm they fall. (Crawling insects without wings would of course be excluded, with all other land šĕrāṣîm, on the basis of the domestic cattle paradigm.)

---

[21] Jean Dorst, *The Life of Birds* (New York, 1974), p. 669.

Therefore, in fact, the text states that "all swarming winged creatures which go on all fours shall be an abomination to you" (v. 21). But the law makes an immediate concession: "But these you may eat from among all the winged swarmers which go on all fours – those with joints above the lower legs (or feet) which they use for leaping across the ground" (v. 22). These four-legged winged insects are allowed by way of concession (ʾak).

That the priests were concerned that the concession might be abused is evident in the fact that, uniquely in Lev. xi, the licit species are specified by name (v. 23). The reason for the concession can only be guessed at. Perhaps it was in consideration of the poor, who could use them as food (Milgrom). The fundamental question which faces us here is whether the criterion given in the text represents the rationale for the concession or simply a mnemonic aid which has nothing whatever to do with any rationale. Let us suppose for the moment that it was the former. In that case, it would seem to have been precisely the fact that locusts can move by jumping that the priests used to justify their concession. Could the rationale be Mary Douglas's notion of means of locomotion? In the light of all that has been said that seems unlikely. In any case, so far as the šereṣ hāʿôp were brought under the aegis of the birds, they would be expected to fly not to jump. (Douglas errs in classifying them with creatures that move on land, for whom "leaping" would indeed be more appropriate than flying.) The means or manner of locomotion looks to me like a dead end. I hazard the guess that the criterion for the locusts, like those for the fish, is secondary. It does not explain the concession, but only aids in the identification of those locust species which on other grounds have been declared acceptable. What those grounds were we shall probably never know.[22]

---

[22] I have not thought it worth-while to enter into the difficult problem of the identity of the four locust species. On this issue see the article ʾarbeh, Encyclopaedia Biblica (Hebrew) 1 (Jerusalem, 1964), cols 520–6, and L. Koehler, "Die Bezeichnungen d. Heuschrecke im Alten Testament", ZDPV 49 (1926), pp. 328–33. The use of locusts as food was (and is) widespead. Cf. F.S. Bodenheimer, Insects as Human Food (The Hague, 1950), pp. 40ff., 160–5, 202ff., 210ff. While the locust is often a staple of the poor, its use as food is generally not simply a matter of class. In Lev. xi, therefore, we probably have to do with something more than a concession to the poor. One consideration may have been its long-standing popularity as a source of cheaply acquired protein during those seasons when it would appear in swarms. Few, if any, insects are as cost-effective a source of nourishment. Since locusts would be an important food source precisely while they were devouring a community's crops, to eat them in turn would be the only alternative to starvation. On the locust and the problem of insects in the diet in general, see further Marvin Harris, The Sacred Cow and the Abominable Pig (New York, 1985), pp. 154–74. Whether Harris's use of optimal foraging theory also explains Israel's insect tabu is to my mind doubtful, but the problem is too complex for resolution here.

I shall now summarize my observations concerning the criteria of the dietary law and draw some conclusions. I have suggested that in the two principal categories, land animals and birds, the priests already had a general notion of what animals would be unclean, because their dissimilarity to the sacrificial paradigm was obvious. In order to make this elemental observation practicable the priests drew up criteria which the layman could be expected to apply without difficulty. The criteria for fish were added some time later, as a result of a secondary analogy with the land animals. In the case of the birds, the priests opted to publish a brief but complete list of the prohibited species, without criteria, in order to avoid confusion. Flying insects, classified under the birds, were prohibited *en masse*, because of their obvious dissimilarity with the paradigm of flying creatures (ʿôp). An exception was made for locusts, for unknown reasons, and criteria were given in order to aid in the identification of the clean species.

In the three cases where criteria are given, they are morphological, and there is probably a reason for this bias. It was one of the priest's responsibilities to make sure that animal offerings were unblemished. The likelihood is that just as it was physical features, in this case accidental blemishes (cf. Lev. xxii 22), which disqualified a sacrificial animal from the altar, so it was also physical features, in this case necessarily regular ones, since the comparison was between species, which disqualified certain animals from the ordinary diet. Thus, a single methodology underlies the selection both of proper sacrificial victims (for God) and of animals for the table (for man). Another of the priest's jobs was to examine those suffering from skin diseases for signs of "leprosy". The criteria for leprosy given in Lev. xiii are again of the most superficial kind. This is not diagnosis as we know it. Whatever is not immediately apparent to the eye is of no concern to the priest. In his role as inspector, therefore, whether it concerns the leper, the animal brought to the altar, or the selection of animals for the ordinary diet, the priest bases his judgement on visual examination, nothing more. The priest's involvement in the dietary law is thus of a piece with the rest of his activity.

Of the criteria, the most singular is certainly that of chewing the cud. The reader will recall, however, that the pig is the only animal excluded by this requirement that could not just as well have been outlawed solely because it did not have cloven hooves. Its status is undeniably unique, and it is therefore not unreasonable to suggest that when the criteria were first developed, the only basis of selection was whether the animal had cloven hooves or not. The fact that a second criterion was extrapolated from the sacrificial species solely in order to exclude the pig, would indicate that, alone among the

prohibited animals of Lev. xi, the pig was already an unfavored
species, for reasons that likely had nothing to do with the motivation
of our present dietary law.[23] This is the only demonstrable instance in
the dietary law where the priests would seem to have accepted an
ancient tabu.

It has been shown that, with the possible exception of the pig, the
selection of unclean animals of Lev. xi can be systematically
explained without reference to pre-existing tabus. It has also been
demonstrated how this explanation improves in basic ways on that of
Mary Douglas. It explains, for instance, the most elemental fact
about Lev. xi – that it is a dietary law and not a general tabu. The
reason, we have seen, is that, from the start, the purpose was to draw
an analogy between two diets, God's and man's. It explains why as
a rule morphological characteristics are preferred. It explains why
plants did not come in for consideration, since without a sacrificial
paradigm – and plants as such are not offered on the altar – the priests

---

[23] The most commonly accepted reason is that the pig is an unhealthy, dirty
animal. When in 1859 Trichinosis was linked to pork, this connection became
a standard explanation for the prohibition. But this theory ignores several facts. First,
cattle, sheep and goats also transmit diseases, such as Brucellosis (Undulant Fever)
and Anthrax, of which the latter is marked by the same visible symptoms (boils) in
both men and animals. We may therefore fairly expect it too to have been noticed. M.
Harris even identifies the plague of boils inflicted on Pharaoh with this disease
(*Cannibals and Kings* [New York, 1977], p. 200). Second, Trichinosis itself is less
common in the Near East than in Europe and America. As for dirty habits, the pig is
by no means unique. Chickens and goats, for example, will also eat dung. In any
event, it is clear that had most people felt so disgusted by these habits as this theory
suggests, then the pig would never have been domesticated or maintained.

Harris has suggested that the reasons for the abomination of the pig may have been
ecological. Unlike other domesticated animals, the pig cannot be used for haulage,
riding or milk production. It is therefore useful only as a source of meat. In its natural
forest habitat, the pig eats roots, tubers, fruits and nuts, and converts these into
animal protein far more efficiently than cattle do grass. Since these were marginal
foods for sedentary Near Eastern communities, the pig was a cheap source of protein.
But once the forest cover disappeared, pigs had to be raised on grain, and thus
competed for man's own food resources. They were a luxury that few communities
could afford. According to Harris, the pig was probably "the first domesticated
animal to become too expensive to serve as a source of meat". Its designation as
unclean in Lev. xi was Israel's means of ensuring that farmers did not yield to the
temptation to raise pigs for short-term benefits at the expense of the long-term good of
the community (pp. 195–8). While I do not accept Harris's thoroughgoing analysis of
the dietary law in ecological terms, this explanation of the pig's peculiar status
vis-à-vis other domesticated animals deserves consideration. It hinges, of course, on
the problem of the diet of domesticated pigs in the ancient Near East. If, in fact, pigs
were raised on marginal foods, refuse or even feces – the dirty habit that led
Maimonides to condemn the pig as unhealty – then it is doubtful that they
constituted a sufficient threat to merit pariah status. It also depends on the extent of
deforestation and the relationship between Israelite communities and forested areas.
I hope to deal with these issues in a future article.

were not obliged to make any separation between clean and unclean. The paradigm constituted by the sacrificial animals compelled the priests to draw distinctions, but left many possible edible items uncovered, since it was itself limited by a lack of variety. If, as in the case of the fish, an animal did not come under one of the categories, it was not initially considered. At some point marine life was included, but only by way of secondary analogy. All the same, I have argued that the biblical dietary law excludes only a minimum of animals.[24]

I shall conclude with two more general reflections. Mary Douglas's explanation of the dietary law was based on a comprehensive and appealing concept of boundary definition, which she set forth as follows:

> At the level of general taxonomy of living beings *the purity in question is the purity of the categories*... The *sanctity of cognitive boundaries* is made known by valuing the integrity of the physical forms. The perfect physical specimens point to the perfectly bounded temple, altar and sanctuary. And these in turn point to the hard-won and hard-to-defend territorial *boundaries* of the promised land... Edmund Leach has pointed out how over and over again they were concerned with the threat to Israel's holy calling from marriages with outsiders. Foreign husbands and foreign wives led to false gods and political defections. So sex is not omitted from the meanings in the common meal. (*Implicit Meanings*, pp. 269ff.)

While it is true that the dietary law served to separate Israel from her neighbors, and that the idea of separation is intimately involved in Israel's selection as a "holy" people, the concern for boundaries does not explain the method which the priests used to arrive at their definitions of clean and unclean. This, as we have seen, is not a reflex

---

[24] Contra J. Milgrom, "The Biblical Diet Laws as an Ethical System", *Interpretation* 17 (1963), pp. 288–301. In Milgrom's view, the purpose of the dietary law was to limit the number of animal species available for consumption, and hence to teach respect for life. Since, however, game such as deer, and most fish and fowl may be eaten in unlimited quantity, this proposal seems quite unlikely. Moreover, the law itself places no restriction on the use of domestic cattle as food. There were to be sure practical limitations on their use, but these must be considered apart from the law as such. Milgrom argues this thesis in a more systematic way in the collection of articles published in E.B. Firmage, John W. Welch and Bernard Weiss, *Religion and Law: Biblical, Jewish and Islamic Perspectives* (Winona Lake, 1990). A second objection to Milgrom's thesis is that if the priests had wanted to teach respect for life by limiting the consumption of meat, it would have been more appropriate to designate the protected species as holy rather than as unclean, just as in India the cow is protected by its status as a holy animal. By designating those animals that are protected from being eaten as unclean (*ṭāmēʾ*) or abominable (*šeqeṣ*), the Israelite priests would have contradicted their own first principle, that such animal life is holy, i.e. reserved for God.

of cosmological or socio-political categories. But, although the particular sociological grounding in which Douglas seeks to anchor her taxonomy must be denied, I am not presenting an ordered system of thought that lacks a social context. The explanation offered in this article is in fact solidly grounded in the thought and activity of its creators. I have stressed the unity and consistency of purpose shared by the dietary law and priestly activity as a whole. This is however, a much more limited context. The dietary law became an Israelite institution, but the priests alone are responsible for its creation.

How, then, does the dietary law fit into the larger whole of priestly theology? Commentators have long recognized that, according to P at least, the antediluvians were vegetarians. God gave man as food every plant which bears seed, and all kinds of fruit, and in this respect man's food was like that of the beasts, who were also at this point, one supposes, vegetarian (Gen. i 29, 30; cf. Isa. xi 7). At least as far as the priestly writer was concerned, this remained the state of affairs until God instituted his covenant with Noah, who is told that he may now eat meat. He may now eat anything as freely as he has previously eaten greens (*kol-remeś ʾăšer hûʾ-ḥay lākem yihyeh leʾoklâ kĕyereq ʿēśeb nātattî lākem ʾet-kōl*, Gen. ix 3). God himself had nevertheless from the beginning been accustomed to animal sacrifices (cf. Gen. iv 4, viii 20ff. [J]).[25] It is therefore clear that in P's view there is nothing inherently reprehensible about eating meat, nor any inherent virtue in vegetarianism. The change in human diet instituted by God with Noah has nevertheless been taken as a concession to man's weakness (see appendix 5). But nothing in the text supports such an assertion. Noah's descendants may be inferior to the antediluvians, but if so it is not because they eat meat, nor should their diet be seen as a sign of decadence. In fact, since it could well be argued that by being allowed to eat meat man was thought to have been granted access to what had previously been God's exclusive reserve, the contrary is if anything closer to the truth: man took a step up when he began to eat meat. The text makes it clear that accompanying this radical change in man's diet was a no less fundamental alteration of the animals' relationship to man. From that point on, they would fear him (v. 2). The two changes go hand in hand. Whereas in antediluvian times man, like the animals, had eaten plants, and had apparently enjoyed a fellowship with animals, without fear or aggression on either side, after the Flood this primitive fellowship was lost for ever. There is

---

[25] Although these latter texts belong to J, I see no reason for supposing that P's view was fundamentally different. On this problem see appendix 5.

indeed something awe-inspiring in the act of eating animal flesh, for in doing so man takes life – a right that God jeaously guards. Man's diet therefore comes to resemble God's at the same time that he is given a measure of divine power in the right to take animal life with impunity. The only limitation that God places on this power is that man must reserve the blood – the life source – for God, who is the source of all life (cf. Lev. xvii).

The Israelites at last take still another step up, when God gives them the dietary law of Lev. xi. They continue to eat meat, but no longer indiscriminately as their neighbors do. They must now be concerned that the animals they raise for food and those that they hunt be like those that God "eats" (in the form of sacrifices). The Israelites are also to observe other laws which befit their holy calling. Other nations remain bound only by the "Noachite laws", but correspondingly enjoy a smaller measure of the divine presence. In conclusion, therefore, I would say that, in the priestly view, the dietary law represented the culmination of a progression in holiness, by which God had brought a people by steps to enjoy unprecedented proximity to himself.

APPENDIX 1

Scholars have felt little compunction in ignoring the significance of the biblical criteria altogether, as if their irrelevance were axiomatic. See especially Noth, below. The following is a representative sample of scholarly option.

Maimonides enunciated two of the leading "explanations" in his *Guide of the Perplexed* (3.48). Certain of the prohibited animals such as the pig are unhealthy and loathsome. Other aspects of what came to be Jewish dietary law, but which do not figure in Lev. xi, such as the boiling of the kid in its mother's milk, Maimonides suggests, may have had pagan religious associations. As for the criteria, "they are merely signs"; their existence or its lack has nothing to do with the reason for an animal's being clean or unclean. The hygienic rationale was also advanced in the case of unclean fish, on the grounds that they frequent the unhealthy shallows (Ramban on Lev. xi 9). In our own time, W.F. Albright has championed the hygienic explanation of the pig and the fish on similar, if more correct, grounds (*Yahweh and the Gods of Canaan* [New York, 1968], pp. 177ff.). Of the criteria he says, "... these rules can scarcely have been drawn up on the basis of any knowledge of the aetiology underlying the prohibition of certain mammals, fish and other animals. It is rather a kind of mnemonic device to make abstention from certain kinds of flesh easier for the young or unsophisticated person" (p. 178).

M. Noth opts exclusively for the religious motivation: "Es ist jedoch nicht anzunehmen, dass in diesen Äusserlichkeiten der eigentliche Grund der Unterscheidung gegeben ist; sie dienten vielmehr nur einer leidlich einfachen und übersichtlichen Klassifizierung. Der eigentliche Grund ist auf kultischem Gebiet zu suchen; denn es handelt sich durchweg um die Begriffe 'kultisch rein' und 'kultisch unrein'. Der Ausgangspunkt der Unterscheidung war gewiss die 'Unrein'–Erklärung bestimmter Tiere; was danach nicht 'unrein' war, konnte als 'rein' gelten. 'Unrein' aber war, was sich mit dem legitimen Kult Israels nicht vertrug und was auch ausserhalb des kultischen Bereichs im engeren Sinne für die durch ihren Gottesdienst an ihren Gott gebundenen Israeliten verpönt war und daher nicht gegessen werden durfte. Dieser Gesichtspunkt betraf vor allem diejenigen Tiere, die in bestimmten Fremdkulten der Umwelt als 'heilige' Tiere und als Opfertiere eine Rolle spielten oder für abgöttische Praktiken (Mantik, Zauber) von Bedeutung waren oder aber mit widergöttlichen Mächten (Chaos) in besonderer Verbindung zu stehen schienen. Das Essen solcher Tiere würde für die Israeliten, auch wenn sie dabei keine Kult- oder Zauberhandlungen o. dgl. vornahmen, eine Beziehung zu illegitimen Kulten, Praktiken und Mächten bedeutet haben ... Wahrscheinlich war dieser Ausgangspunkt der Unterscheidung der späteren Zeit nicht mehr allgemein bewusst; und so hielt man sich einfach an bestimmte herkömmliche Klassifizierungen 'reiner' und 'unreiner' Tiere, weil es einmal so üblich und so geboten war" (*Das dritte Buch Mose* [Göttingen, 1962], p. 77).

Finally, we may quote Karl Elliger: "... vielmehr dürfte es sich bei den einzelnen Tieren um sehr verschiedene und vielleicht auch nicht immer religionsgeschichtliche Hintergründe handeln ... Zur Zeit des P sind die historischen Wurzeln bereits abgestorben oder im Absterben begriffen; die Bräuche sind weithin Tradition geworden und werden theologisch interpretiert: Klassifizierung der Tiere nach Rein und Unrein und die damit zusammenhängenden Vorschriften ... gründen zuletzt einfach in Jahwes vor langen Zeiten erklärten Willen ... Die Sitte, diese und andere Tiere nicht zu essen, dürfte z. T. im Zeiten des Animismus und Totemismus zurückgehen, z. T. mögen sie bestimmten Gottheiten heilige Tiere gewesen sein ... Unrein blieben sie auch nach dem Untergang jener Anschauung, insofern ihr Genuss verboten blieb" (*Leviticus* [Tübingen, 1966], p. 150). There are many assertions here but little hard evidence to back them up.

For an account of all the major schools of thought (excepting Mary

Douglas's) see Walter Kornfeld, "Die Unreinen Tiere im Alten Testament", Josef Kisser et al. (ed.), *Wissenschaft im Dienste des Glaubens: Fests. f. Abt Dr. Hermann Peichl O.S.B.* (Vienna, 1969) = *Kairos* 7 (1965), pp. 134–47. This article is a thorough, comparative examination of the status of Israel's unclean animals in the rest of the ancient Near East. Although Kornfeld rightly, I think, insists that a satisfactory explanation must cover all the animals, his own proposal – that the unclean animals constitute a threat to life – still leaves the biblical criteria aside. What is more, it ignores the fact that the unclean animals listed in our text are but a fraction of the total number of unclean species, as I shall have occasion to observe further on. It is impossible to regard all these as a threat to life.

APPENDIX 2

The fact that certain species were overwhelmingly favored for sacrifice is more important for our purposes than the reasons for it. Nevertheless, I suggest that these species were favored, because the community depended on their fertility. It was therefore to ensure divine blessing on the entire herd or flock that choice members of them were offered. (The same principle would apply to cereals: it was upon wheat and other domesticated grains, and not upon the abundance of wild flowers, berries, fruits or the like, that concentrated human society depended, and it was accordingly these domestic grains that became part of the cult.) Traces of this connection between domestic dependence and prominence in the cult are recognizable in the Israelite institution of the First-born (Ex. xiii 1–2, 11–16, xxxiv 19–20). Only first-born animals belonging to unclean (sc. economically less important) domestic species (e.g. horses, donkeys and the like) could be redeemed, since no unclean animal was allowed upon the altar. (The law of the first-born mentions only the donkey [Ex. xiii 13, xxxiv 20], probably because it was the one species of large animals unsuitable for sacrifice that Israelites would commonly have. But the generalization in terms of clean and unclean is, I think, a reasonable extrapolation. Compare the law for special dedications [Lev. xxvii 26ff.].) The distinction made between offerable and non-offerable animals thus does no more than reformulate in cultic terms what was economic reality. However individually valuable large animals such as the horse and the donkey were, it was not only or perhaps even primarily this value which militated against their being sacrificed, as valuable bovines too were offered. (Cf. the relative values of livestock in Michael Heltzer, *Goods, Prices and the Organization of Trade in Ugarit* [Wiesbaden, 1978], pp. 21, 86–7.) The economic reality was that, although individually less valuable, cattle, especially small cattle, were the basis of the livestock economy, and their fertility far more important than that of any of the larger, in Israel unclean, species such as the equids. Unblemished first-born belonging to clean species were irredeemable. Like first-fruits, the first-born of the essential livestock species constituted an essential token offering intended to guarantee the prosperity of the remainder of the herd and harvest.

APPENDIX 3

The identification of scaleless fish or even of fish in general with snakes is well documented. In much of Africa, there is as a result of this identification widespread aversion to eating any fish. "As a rule . . . it is said that the fish is not eaten because it is a snake, or is at least 'closely related' to the latter. In exceptional cases it is said that the fish is a lizard" (Sture Lagercrantz, "Forbidden Fish", *Orientalia Suecana* 2 [1953], p. 7). In Mesopotamia, the *girītu* (MURRA), "catfish", was perhaps avoided on the same grounds (A. Salonen, *Die Fischerei im alten Mesopotamien* [Helsinki, 1970], p. 185–7, following B. Landsberger *MSL* viii. 2, p. 89). The Akkadian word *girītu* passed into Arabic as *jirrīṭ*, and is compared to Persian *mārmāhi*, "snake fish" (E.W. Lane, *An Arabic-English Lexicon* [London, 1863–93], p. 404). Akkadian *kuppû*, an eel or eel-like fish (goby?), is determined alike by MUŠ, the sign for snake, and by KU_6, that for "fish". The equation at least of the eel and the snake is also found sporadically in Muslim texts (M. Cook, "Early Islamic Dietary Law", *Jerusalem Studies in Arabic and Islam* 7 [1964], p. 242). According to al-Jāḥiẓ, "Everything living in the water with fish and resembling snakes, such as the moray (Ar. *mārmāhī*) and the eel (Ar. *ʾinklīs*), [is] all of two sorts, one of which is the offspring of snakes modified by the influence of the nature of the country and the water, and the other is the progeny of fish and snakes . . . they were all snakes originally. They interbreed since fish are kindred of nature to these snakes . . ." (*Kitāb al-Ḥayawān* [Cairo, 1323–25], II 44.4–45.1, trans. William Wilson, *Al-Jāḥiẓ and Arabic Zoology* [Ph.D. Diss. University of Utah, 1965], p. 118). It was widely held in the classical world that the *muraena* eel mated with a viper (literature cited in Pauly-Wissowa, "muraene"). Indeed, in Latin the generic term for eel, *anguilla*, is derived from the word for snake, *anguis*. For further examples of the equation especially of scaleless fish with snakes see J. Scheftelowitz, *ARW* 14 (1911), pp. 358ff. For this analogy at least there is thus ample evidence, albeit none from Israel itself. But, given the general paucity of information about all animals and especially marine life in the biblical period, this lack is hardly significant.

The two criteria for clean aquatic life – fins and scales – potentially exclude a great number of marine and fresh-water animals. It is likely, however, that the priests were concerned only with those commonly encountered by most Israelites. In practice, then, the scope of their investigation would be limited to those animals found in inland streams and lakes (e.g. eels and catfish). Although incapable of proof, my suspicion is that the dietary law had primarily these few species in mind. The creators of the dietary law had but limited information about the multitude of unclean marine creatures to be found off the coasts.

In the case of fish proper, the primary factor in the determination of uncleanness was the analogy between scaleless or finless fish and snakes. In the case of the crustaceans, if they were known or considered, this analogy is unlikely to have been at work. There is reason to suppose, for example, that the crab may have been linked to terrestrial šĕrāṣîm, either because it also moves on land or else on the basis of appearance. The latter seems to be the more likely reason in the case of shrimps (for crab, shrimp and mussels in inland waters cf. F.S. Bodenheimer, *Animal Life in Palestine* [Jerusalem, 1935], pp. 441, 442, 446). We can document such analogical processes in other Near Eastern cultures. Alongside the common Akkadian word for crab, *kušû*, there is *eribû* = BURU^{KU_6} (lX), lit. "locust fish", as well as *erib nāri* (BURU$_5$ ÍD^{KU_6}), or *erib tāmti*, "shrimp?" (see Salonen, s.v.). This term *eribû* also calls to mind the Arabic ʾarbiyān, which denotes several crustaceans such as the crab (R. Dozy, *Supplément aux dictionnares Arabes* I [Leiden, 1881], p. 17). The Arabic sources cited by Dozy themselves define ʾarbiyān as a "sea locust", using the common term for locust, *jarād*. *jarād al-baḥr* is now a common term for crayfish (so, e.g., H. Wehr). The Syriac cognate ʾarbītāʾ also means "sea crab" (I. Löw, "Aramäische Fischnamen", in *Orientalische Studien Theodor Nöldeke z. siebz. Geburtstag gewidmet* [Giessen, 1906], p. 551). If in Israel too it was the locust that was the terrestrial analogue of animals such as the crab, then in theory it would have been possible to argue that crabs, shrimp and the like were also clean. Alternatively, however, crustaceans could simply have been dismissed as unclean on the basis of the fish paradigm, which overrode all other considerations The only conclusion that I would draw from these latter examples is that similarities of appearance or behavior between sea creatures and those of the land were not lost on the peoples of the Near East, and that the principle of analogy is by no means far-fetched. In fact, it can

be demonstrated in a large number of bird and fish names and
determinatives in Akkadian and Sumerian.

APPENDIX 4

If, as I have argued, the list of birds is complete, then we have
a means of testing the assumption that the rationale for the exclusion
of birds is based on their eating habits. If the number of carrion and
predatory birds likely to have been known to the Israelites is about
the same as the number of species listed in Lev. xi, then my
assumption has probably been verified. Of the nearly 350 bird species
in Palestine (listed in H.B. Tristram's *Survey of Western Palestine*
[London, Committee of the Palestine Exploration Fund, 1885],
Fauna and Flora, pp. 30–139), about one third may feed on rodents
or small vertebrates. (Convenient, brief descriptions of the diets of the
species listed by Tristram may be found in the *Encyclopaedia Britannica*.)
Not all these species would have been familiar or even known to
Israelites living in the central highlands. The shore birds (Scolopa-
cidae), for example, 18 members of which are found in Palestine, were
probably relative unknowns. It is also a fact that Israelites did not
sharply distinguish between members of some families, such as the
Falconidae (see further below). In practice, then, the number of
distinct predatory or carrion species identified by Israelite zoologists
would certainly have been far lower. I believe that we may get an
approximate but much more realistic figure by comparing the
number of such birds known in later sources. Of the 85 bird species
mentioned in the Talmud, about 37 belong to the meat-eating
category (cf. the list in L. Lewysohn, *Die Zoologie des Talmuds*
[Frankfurt, 1858], pp. 159–218). This figure includes the 20 of Lev.
xi. A somewhat larger number, 51 by my count, was known to
Palestinian Arabs questioned by G. Dalman ("Arabische Vogel-
namen von Palästina und Syrien", *ZDPV* 36 [1913], pp. 165–79).
(This figure includes only those species for which names are attested
in Palestine, and also takes account of the fact that several of the
names cover more than one species.) Even this number is probably
too high for biblical Israel, as it includes, for example, more sea birds
than Israel is likely to have known. We also know that the Israelites
did not sharply distinguish between members of the *Falconidae*, of
which 25 are found in Israel. The Arabs, who knew falcons well and
used them for hunting, still counted less than that. Only six species are
attested by Palestinian Arabic names. The Israelites, who did not use
the falcon, certainly knew even fewer species. A realistic number for
our test is therefore perhaps around 40.

It is now necessary to determine how many more species than the

20 which are named are covered by the list in Lev. xi. It is reasonable to suggest that the total number of birds subsumed under the four occurrences of *lĕmînēhû* cannot be larger than 20, that is, larger than the number of birds explicitly given by the list. This gives us 40 as the upper limit. The results of the test thus presented therefore accord well with the prevailing assumption that the criterion for the selection of birds was based on diet.

APPENDIX 5

The view that the use of meat was a concession to man's weakness was unambiguously expressed by U. Cassuto, *A Commentary On the Book of Genesis* I (Jerusalem, 1961), p. 58. "Apparently, the Torah seeks to convey that in principle man should refrain from eating meat . . . this was only a concession . . ." The same attitude seems to be implicit in A. Dillmann's treatment (*Handbuch der alttestamentlichen Theologie* [Leipzig, 1895], p. 366). G. von Rad's assessment is equivocal (*Theologie des Alten Testaments* I [Munich, 1957], p. 161). O. Eissfeldt's discussion (*Einleitung in das Alte Testament*[3] [Tübingen, 1964], pp. 245–6) must be mentioned, since his conclusions are so at odds with my own. In his opinion, there was, according to P, no sacrifice before Moses, and he bases this claim on the grounds that, if there had been sacrifice in pre-Mosaic times, its form would no doubt have contradicted that described in the Sinai Torah, and would therefore have been unacceptable to the priests. Eissfeldt further maintains that since meat-eating was not allowed in antediluvian times, sacrifice could scarcely have been possible. Neither of these arguments is convincing. First, there is too little P material in Genesis to allow one to conclude that in the priestly view of history sacrifice had played no role before Moses. What evidence we have suggests that if anything the opposite is more likely the case. P would have had no reason to deny the narrative accounts of Abel's, Noah's and the Patriarchs' sacrifices. If they were offered in a way different from that described in Mosaic Torah, why should that matter? The priests, like the author(s) of the J narrative, no doubt recognized that the Patriarchs, for example, did things which were later proscribed (e.g. married within the prohibited degrees of consanguinity). The point is that they felt no need to impose on the Patriarchs a way of life that was thought to have come into being only with Moses. Had they done so, our text would likely have been "cleaned up" to make Abraham out to be a perfect follower of Mosaic law. The fact that later editors were content to leave in the contradictions probably indicates that they found nothing shocking in them.

A weightier argument in favor of Eissfeldt's view would be that

according to souce analysis, in the account of the flood attributed to
P, Noah takes only two of each clean animal with him into the ark,
whereas in J he takes seven. In this P account, therefore, sacrifice
would seem to have been impossible. The story of Noah's sacrifice in
Gen. viii 20ff. is thus not without reason attributed to J, despite the
fact that it comes between two P passages (*vv.* 14–19 and ix 1–17).

It is nevertheless possible to imagine how P could have conceived of
Noah's sacrifice. What Noah offers as his ᶜōlâ was likely the crop of
yearlings born during the voyage. Noah enters the ark according to
priestly dating on the 17th day of the second month (vii 11), and
leaves it a year later on the 14th day of the same month (viii 14). By
the time Noah's animals enter the ark many of them will already have
been several months pregnant, according to traditional breeding
patterns. Sheep, for example, typically begin conceiving in Adar, the
12th month, and give birth after a gestation period of five months
(Feliks, *Encyclopaedia Judaica* 14, col. 333). Despite the fact Noah takes
only two adults with him into the ark, it is therefore possible that P too
had a sacrifice story.

Speculation aside, there is in any event independent evidence that
P knew of (though in this case it could no longer accept) traditional
sacrifices. Lev. xvii 5 refers to sacrifices which the Israelites had been
accustomed to perform in the countryside. Indeed, the priests could
scarcely have failed to conclude from the fact that other nations had
also long practiced sacrifice that sacrifice was an ancient institution
among all peoples.

Eissfeldt's second point, that sacrifice and vegetarianism would
have been considered incompatible, is more easily dealt with. It
ignores that fact that all Mosaic sacrifices described in Genesis are
burnt offerings, whose flesh is entirely consumed: the worshipper gets
nothing. There is therefore no reason that vegetarianism and sacrifice
should have been regarded as incompatible.

I note finally that among the commentators I have read Ramban
alone seems to consider meat-eating as God's reward for good
behavior. In his comment on i 29, he says that Noah was given the
right to eat animal flesh because of his role in their rescue from the
flood.

APPENDIX 6

Though the subject is too involved for exhaustive discussion
here, I wish nevertheless to point out that the concern of Lev. xi
1–23 is with diet rather than impurity contracted by contact with
the animal's carcass, and that the issues of corpse-contamination
and diet can be radically separated. It is therefore possible that in

fact *vv.* 1–23 belong to an earlier historical stratum than *vv.* 24ff.

The reasons for treating *vv.* 1–23 as a conceptually independent entity are as follows. First, whereas in *vv.* 1–23 the primary and perhaps sole concern is with a prohibition of eating unclean animals, *vv.* 24–39 are entirely concerned with contamination from contact with their carcasses, and with the steps necessary to eliminate such impurity. Since *vv.* 24–39 introduce an entirely new subject, we would expect them to begin with the rules for the treatment of impurity contracted by contact with the carcasses of the animals discussed in *vv.* 4–7. But in fact the rules for purification given in *vv.* 24ff. are not said to cover the four animals discussed in *vv.* 4–7. What makes this asymmetry especially significant is the fact that so much emphasis was placed on just these four in the initial statement of the dietary law. In contrast, *vv.* 24ff. deal with those animals which are excluded on the basis of the criteria of *v.* 3 but which are not specifically mentioned because there is no possible ambiguity about their uncleanness. One explanation of this striking asymmetry would be that *vv.* 24–31 were added as a supplement in order to anticipate a possible misunderstanding in the earlier text, namely, that from *v.* 8 one could perhaps have concluded that only contact with the carcasses of the four animals specified in *vv.* 4–7 conveyed impurity. However, the author of *vv.* 24–31 obviously recognized that, if contact with the carcass of one of these four species makes one impure, then so does that with any of the animals implicitly excluded by *v.* 3, that is, all land animals which lack cloven hooves and which are not ruminants. Since *v.* 8 does not make this clear, our author is at pains to spell it out. Thus, *v.* 26 deals with large non-ruminants with hooves which are not cloven (e.g. the equids), *v.* 27 covers large non-ruminants without hooves, and *v.* 29 deals with those small land animals which lack hooves and which are not ruminants. Given the secondary nature of *vv.* 24–31, we must reckon with the possibility that they are in fact not a mere afterthought but a contribution from another hand.

Be that as it may, *vv.* 24–38 do more than merely clarify a point of potential misunderstanding in the earlier law. *V.* 8 simply forbids Israelites from touching the carcass of an unclean animal. As already noted, nothing is said about what, if anything, one could or should do if one were to become unclean through such contact, necessary though such information would be. In other words, *vv.* 2–8 seem only to be enunciating general principles. I would therefore argue that the law is effectively saying, "You shall not eat the flesh of these animals or even touch their carcasses". What *vv.* 24–38 have in mind is something quite different. Here, it is assumed that people will be handling the carcasses of these animals. Such contact would of course be a practical necessity. If, for example, one owned an ass, and woke up one morning to find that it had died during the night, the animal would have to be disposed of, and, as far as religious scruples allowed, made use of. There would be any number of such problems. The question, then, for the priests was: granted that you do not use the unclean animal's carcass for food, what sort of impurity is conveyed by contact with it, and how can it be eliminated? *Vv.* 24–38 provide answers to these questions.

Significantly, however, nothing is ever said about the nature of the impurity contracted by eating the flesh of an unclean animal. This is perhaps the most important reason for subordinating the prohibition of touching to that of eating, as I did in rendering *v.* 8, in effect, "You shall not eat their flesh or even touch their carcasses". Compare Eve's elaboration of God's commandment not to eat the forbidden fruit: ʾāmar ʾĕlōhîm lōʾ tōʾkĕlû mimmennû wĕlōʾ tiggĕʿû bô (Gen. iii 3).

The last mention of carcass contamination (*vv.* 39–40) is not unreasonably regarded by many as an even later addition to Lev. xi than *vv.* 24–38, as it would seem to vitiate the distinction between the carcasses of clean and unclean animals (so. e.g. Milgrom). There is, however, an alternative understanding of the text (suggested to me by Professor David Wright), according to which *vv.* 39–40 are of a piece with *vv.* 24–38. This reading is schematically illustrated in the following figure:

VERSE	CATEGORY TREATED
Vv. 2–3, 8	General guidelines for all land animals.
Vv. 4–7	Exceptional cases which meet one but not both of the above criteria for cleanness.
UNCLEAN *Vv.* 9–23	Air-borne and marine *šĕqāṣîm*: animals which are forbidden as food, but whose carcasses do not contaminate. *tĕšaqqĕṣû** refers only to eating their flesh.
Vv. 24–38	Land animals disqualified by the criteria of *vv.* 2–3, but which lack both the criteria of cleanness.
CLEAN *Vv.* 39–40	Clean animals; those which may be eaten *as long as they are properly slaughtered* (cf. Lev. xvii). If they die a natural death, or are killed by other animals, their carcasses become unclean.

Vv. 41–5: SUMMARY (H)

* Milgrom has suggested in his seminar on Lev. xi that there is perhaps a distinction between the terms *šeqes* and *ṭāmēʾ*, the former indicating simply prohibition as food; the latter the contraction of impurity through contact with the carcass.

This schematization highlights some important features of Lev. xi. First, the concern with carcass contamination is a constant for all land animals, regardless of their being clean and unclean. In other words, it is totally independent of the issue of cleanness. If so, it is properly analogous to (though not identical with) the problem of human corpse contamination (cf. Num. xix). (Birds, fishes and insects do not come in for consideration as land animals, and do not contaminate, except as food.) The dietary law may therefore be analysed without any reference to the issue of corpse contamination. (Hence my remarks above pp. 180–1.)

Second, *vv.* 9–23 clearly interrupt what would be the logical sequence of categories if Lev. xi were a unitary composition with a single organizing principle. Presumably, all those animals unclean as food whose carcasses contaminate would be treated together, then unclean animals whose carcasses do not contaminate (fish, birds), and finally clean animals, which are not properly slaughtered. *Vv.* 9–23 would belong, then, immediately before *vv.* 39–40. If, however, *vv.* 2–23 are treated as an independent unit, then the placement of *vv.* 9–23 is unobjectionable. *Vv.* 2–23, then, are arguably not only conceptually but also historically independent of *vv.* 24–40. Another possible indication that *vv.* 2–23 and *vv.* 24ff. come from different hands is the use of *běhēmâ* in *vv.* 2 and 26 respectively. In the former, this term includes every kind of land animal; it and not *ḥayyâ* (*v.* 2b) is the more general term. *V.* 26, however, restricts the use of *běhēmâ* to the equid class, while *ḥayyâ* applies to all (wild?) beasts which go on all fours (*v.* 27).

In sum, then, we have good grounds for divorcing our analysis of the dietary law from the issue of carcass contamination. The prohibition of *v.* 8 forbids touching, but probably does so primarily to stress the absoluteness of the prohibition of eating. Whatever the historical relationship among the parts of this text, the issues of dietary prohibition and carcass contamination are typologically speaking radically separable, and arise from different concerns. The concern which led to the creation of the dietary law has nothing to do with the usual categories of uncleanness, to which corpse contamination belongs.

This independence is also clearly seen in the way Deuteronomy treats these issues. If it does not actually antedate the addition of *vv.* 24–40 in the priestly tradition, the Deuteronomic version at least ignores these verses, for it leaves off with Lev. xi 23. It mentions *něbēlâ*, but only by way of a prohibition of eating. Like Lev. xi, Deuteronomy is formulating a dietary law that is independent of a system of impurities, for which Deuteronomy would generally seem to have no

use. Dt. xiv, even if it had the entire text of Lev. xi before it, perceived
that the issues of diet and corpse contamination can be separated
from each other without doing violence to either. What distinguishes
Dt.'s version from that of Leviticus is simply the degree to which it
goes out of its way to make the law easily applicable. In contrast to
Lev. xi, for example, it provides a list of licit land animals that is
clearly designed to make the application of the law as unambiguous
as possible (vv. 4ff.). In the interest of easy and systematic reference, it
also collects together other diet-related laws from several sources.
Thus, unlike Lev. xi, it includes (v. 21) the prohibition of cooking
a kid in its mother's milk (< Ex. xxiii 19). The mention of něbēlâ itself
is probably from outside Lev. xi (cf. Ex. xxiii 30). (On this score Dt.
xiv is actually at odds with P. Cf. Lev. xvii 15–16.) Even the law of the
tithe, which follows Deuteronomy's diet law (vv. 22ff.), may perhaps
have been put here because it has to do with diet, for, in contrast to P,
Dt. allows the worshipper to consume his own tithe (cf. Lev. xxvii
30–3; Num. xviii 21–32). But, at the same time that it ignores
impurity contracted through contract, Deut. consistently uses the
term ṭāmēʾ, even where Lev. xi uses šeqeṣ. For Deuteronomy at least,
this term did not involve the notion of communicable impurity; it is
rather a term of opprobrium.

   The relative dating of Deut. xiv and Lev. xi is problematic. P is
generally placed later than D. But against the earlier dating at least of
Deut. xiv, one must consider the cogent arguments of W.L. Moran
("The Literary Connection between Lev. 11, 13–19 and Deut. 14,
12–18", CBQ 28 [1966], pp. 271–7). In the case of the birds, the
priority of Lev. xi seems likely. It has also been observed that ch. xiv is
stylistically untypical of Dt. (so e.g. S.R. Driver, Deuteronomy [3rd
edn, Edinburgh, 1902], p. 163; Eissfeldt, Einleitung,³ p. 300), which
makes it all the more probable that its source is in fact nothing other
than Lev. xi 1–23. What we cannot yet say with certainty is whether
Deuteronomy simply chose to ignore Lev. xi 24ff. or whether in the
version it was following these verses were not present.

"YAHWEH IS ONE": THE TRANSLATION OF THE SHEMA

by

R.W.L. MOBERLY

Durham

One of the fundamental theological statements of the OT is Deut. vi 4, the Shema. It is notable, however, that while the importance of the verse is not in doubt, its interpretation is a matter of continuing and unresolved debate. Much of the debate revolves around disagreement as to the translation of the Hebrew, whose possible different renderings give rise to significantly different meanings. It is the thesis of this article that the disagreement about translation can in fact be satisfactorily resolved. If the thesis is correct it will not of itself resolve all the problems of interpretation, since the proposed translation raises particular interpretative difficulties of its own; but it will provide the necessary foundation on which any true interpretation must be built.

The Hebrew text of Deut. vi 4 reads: *šᵉmaᶜ yiśrā³ēl yhwh ³ĕlōhênû yhwh ³eḥād*. It is generally agreed that *šᵉmaᶜ yiśrā³ēl* is unproblematic and should be rendered "Hear, O Israel" (cf. Deut. ix 1, xx 3), serving as an introduction to what follows. The problem of translation centres on the fact that in the next four words *yhwh ³ĕlōhênû yhwh ³eḥād* there is no verb, and therefore a verb must be supplied by the translator. The natural assumption is that this verb should be the verb "to be", for it is a common idiom of Biblical Hebrew to use verbless clauses whose construction is that of noun and predicate juxtaposed and related by an implied verb "to be".[1] Further, it is also a natural assumption that the tense of the verb is present, since no other tense is suggested by the context[2] and Hebrew tends to indicate past or future by the specific

---

[1] On noun-clauses see GK §§ 140, 141.

[2] A future sense was given to the second part of the verse by Rashi who interpreted it "canonically" in the light of the wider context of Zeph. iii 9 and Zech. xiv 9 to give the sense that the Lord who is now God of Israel alone will in future be the one God of all the earth (A.M. Silbermann [ed.], *The Pentateuch with the Commentary of Rashi: Deuteronomy* [Jerusalem, 1973], p. 37).

inclusion of *hāyâ* or *yihyeh*.[3] If, then, one is to understand the verb "is", the crucial question is precisely where in the sentence it should be understood.

To put the same point differently, the question is how much of the sentence is subject and how much is predicate. What precedes the verb that the translator must supply will be the subject and what follows the verb will be the predicate. But the division between subject and predicate can be put at any point in the sentence. The four words of the clause offer three possible positions in which the verb can be understood; and if the verb is understood in the first position then it can also be understood in the third, thereby making a sentence with two subjects and two predicates. There are thus four basic alternatives:[4]

(i)   *yhwh – ʾĕlōhênû yhwh ʾeḥād:* "Yahweh is our God, Yahweh alone".[5]
(ii) *yhwh ʾelōhênû–yhwh ʾeḥād:* "Yahweh our God is one Yahweh".[6]
(iii) *yhwh ʾĕlōhênû yhwh – ʾeḥād:* "Yahweh our God, Yahweh is one".
(iv) *yhwh-ʾĕlōhênû yhwh–ʾeḥād:* "Yahweh is our God, Yahweh is one".[7]

If one examines these four renderings (with their variations), two basic differences among them become apparent. First, if *yhwh* is subject and *ʾĕlōhênû* is predicate, as in (i) and (iv), then we have a statement about the relationship between Yahweh and Israel, while if *ʾĕlōhênû* is part of the subject and not the predicate, as in (ii) and (iii), then we have a statement about the nature or character of Yahweh. Secondly, (i) is different from all other renderings in translating *ʾeḥād* as "alone" rather than "one". It is not absolutely necessary that if *yhwh* is subject

---

[3] Cf. GK § 141 *f, g, i.*

[4] Cf. e.g. S.R. Driver, *Deuteronomy* (3rd edn, Edinburgh, 1902), pp. 89–90. It should be noted that yet other renderings have been proposed. For example, F.I. Andersen suggests "Our one God is Yahweh, Yahweh" (*The Hebrew Verbless Clause in the Pentateuch* [Nashville, 1970], p. 47), while M. Dahood suggested "Obey, Israel, Yahweh. Yahweh our God is the Unique" (L.R. Fisher [ed.], *Ras Shamra Parallels* I [Rome, 1972], p. 361). These may perhaps best be described as syntactically adventurous. The present argument with regard to the more common renderings will apply equally to these.

[5] A variant, which avoids giving the unusual sense "alone" to *ʾeḥād* is "The LORD is our God, one LORD" (*New English Bible*). This variant seems to make better sense with the title "LORD" than with the proper name Yahweh.

[6] This was the rendering of the LXX: κύριος ὁ Θεὸς ἡμῶν κύριος εἷς ἐστιν. In this form the text is cited in Mk xii 29. One modern liturgical rendering of this is "The Lord our God is the only Lord" (*The Alternative Service Book 1980* [Cambridge, 1980], p. 120). Although this is an attractive rendering, it depends on the implications of the title "Lord" and would be less meaningful if the proper name Yahweh were substituted.

[7] Or "Yahweh is our God, Yahweh is 'One'", if *ʾeḥād* is taken as a name or title (C.H. Gordon, "His Name is 'One'", *JNES* 29 [1970], pp. 198–9).

and the rest of the sentence predicate that ʾeḥād should be rendered "alone" (see n. 5), but "alone" makes better sense than "one" and is therefore widely adopted.

Given these two basic differences, there is a general tendency to regard the four alternatives as essentially reducible to two: either "Yahweh is our God, Yahweh alone", which states the exclusive relationship between Yahweh and Israel, or "Yahweh our God, Yahweh is one" which states the oneness of Yahweh. The first rendering is generally preferred by modern scholars,[8] while the second was generally preferred in traditional Jewish usage,[9] and still has some modern advocates.[10]

With regard to these two alternatives, two observations would, I think, command a wide consensus. The first is that it is not possible to make a definitive choice between the two renderings, because each is an acceptable translation of the Hebrew. It is common practice in modern translations of the OT that, whichever rendering is chosen in the text, at least one alternative, and sometimes all three alternative options, are noted in the margin as possibilities.[11] Secondly, the rendering "Yahweh is our God, Yahweh alone" is more obviously in keeping with the central concerns of Deuteronomic covenant theology than is a statement about the oneness of Yahweh whose precise sense is not immediately apparent and which is all too easily interpreted in the light of the monotheistic concerns of later periods. The obviously appropriate sense of "Yahweh alone" is recognized even by those who do not think it is the correct rendering (see Janzen [n. 10], p. 281).

Despite the obvious appropriateness of "Yahweh is our God, Yahweh alone", and despite the fact that it is preferred by a majority of modern scholars, I shall argue that it cannot be the correct translation because of a simple fact of Hebrew idiom.

The translation "Yahweh is our God, Yahweh alone" involves two crucial judgements about the Hebrew. The first is that it is possible to render ʾeḥād as "alone". It is this that has most often been called in

---

[8] See e.g. S.D. McBride, "The Yoke of the Kingdom", *Interpretation* 27 (1973), esp. pp. 274, 293; P.D. Miller, "The Most Important Word: The Yoke of the Kingdom", *Iliff Review* (1984), pp. 17–29; J.D. Levenson, *Sinai & Zion* (Minneapolis, 1985), p. 82; and, more tentatively, A.D.H. Mayes, *Deuteronomy* (Grand Rapids and London, 1979), p. 176.

[9] See e.g. L. Jacobs, *A Jewish Theology* (London, 1973), p. 21

[10] See e.g. J.F.A. Sawyer, "Biblical Alternatives to Monotheism", *Theology* 87 (1984), p. 175; J.G. Janzen, "On the most important word in the Shema (Deuteronomy vi 4–5)", *VT* 37 (1987), pp. 280–300.

[11] So the *Revised Version, Revised Standard Version, Jerusalem Bible, New International Version*, though not the *NEB*.

question, because it involves giving ʾeḥād a sense that is otherwise apparently unparalleled in the OT. Although the usage of ʾeḥād is not our primary concern, it is still necessary briefly to consider the point.

A.D.H. Mayes, for example (n. 8), cites five passages in support of the meaning of ʾeḥād as "alone": Isa. li 2; Ezek. xxxiii 24, xxxvii 22; Zech. xiv 9; 1 Chr. xxix 1. But in fact none of these is a clear example, and in all of them ʾeḥād probably retains its basic meaning of numerical singularity. In both Isa. li 2 and Ezek. xxxiii 24 there is a numerical contrast between Abraham who was but one and the large number of his descendants. In Ezek. xxxvii 22 the point is that Israel shall be one nation with one king as opposed to two nations with two kings, again a numerical contrast. Zech. xiv 9 is apparently a citation of Deut. vi 4 and raises problems similar to those of Deut. vi 4; it will be argued below that it probably uses ʾeḥād as a predicate in a numerical sense.

1 Chron. xxix 1 is the most problematic instance. The Hebrew of v. 1aß reads: šᵉlōmōh bᵉnî ʾeḥād bāḥar-bô ʾĕlōhîm naᶜar wārāk. It is customary to render this "Solomon my son, whom alone God has chosen, is young . . . ",[12] a rendering advocated or accepted by most commentators.[13] It depends on two assumptions. First, it assumes that ʾeḥād should be construed with bāḥar on the basis of the idiomatic peculiarity of Chronicles to omit the relative ʾăšer.[14] Secondly, it assumes a contextual linkage with 1 Chron. xxviii 4–5, the point being that Solomon alone of David's many sons was chosen by Yahweh. Yet both these assumptions may be questioned, and an alternative construal is probably preferable. First, it is unnecessary to assume the idiomatic omission of ʾăšer. It makes good sense to take ʾeḥād with šᵉlōmōh bᵉnî: "Solomon my son is but one man (ʾeḥād having a sense similar to that in Isa. li 2; Ezek. xxxiii 24); Yahweh has chosen him when he is but an inexperienced youth". Secondly, the contextual contrast is not with David's other sons as in xxviii 4–5, which in the context of ch. xxix is irrelevant, but with the large number of Israelites whom David is addressing. The point is that because Solomon is but one man (and young and inexperienced), he needs all the help he can get from the many people of Israel, who should therefore contribute generously to the project.

It remains the case, therefore, that the objection to rendering ʾeḥād as "alone" has not been met. But although the objection is strong it

---

[12] So RV, RSV, JB: cf. NEB.
[13] See e.g. W. Rudolph, Chronikbücher (Tübingen, 1955), p. 190; H.G.M. Williamson, 1 and 2 Chronicles (Grand Rapids and London, 1982), p. 183; R. Braun, I Chronicles (Waco, Texas, 1986), p. 277.
[14] See S.R. Driver, Introduction to the Literature of the OT (9th edn, Edinburgh, 1913), p. 537; cf. GK § 155 d).

has not generally been considered decisive since, despite the lack of other clear examples of such usage, many scholars have thought that the sense yielded is so good that it justifies taking ʾeḥād in an otherwise unparalleled sense.

There is, however, a second crucial judgement involved in the translation "Yahweh is our God, Yahweh alone". This is that it is possible to take ʾĕlōhênû as the predicate of yhwh. It is this that, to the best of my knowledge, has received remarkably little attention.[15] Yet it is, I suggest, the decisive issue.

A survey of Deuteronomic usage[16] (excluding, for the moment, Deut. vi 4) reveals the following statistics.[17] Throughout Deuteronomy the divine name yhwh and the epithet ʾĕlōhîm in one form or other are frequently juxtaposed. Most frequently, 300 times in all, yhwh is juxtaposed with ʾĕlōhîm with a first person plural suffix, ʾĕlōhênû, or with second person singular or second person plural suffix, ʾĕlōhekā, ʾĕlōhêkem, the three of which are largely interchangeable in Deuteronomic idiom.[18] In 12 further instances yhwh is juxtaposed to other forms of ʾĕlōhîm (first person singular suffix, third person singular suffix, and the construct with ʾābôt, itself with various suffixes). In all these 312 instances where yhwh and ʾĕlōhîm are juxtaposed, the two words are always in apposition. ʾĕlōhîm is always used descriptively, i.e. "Yahweh our/your God", and never predicatively, i.e. "Yahweh is our/your God". (If ʾĕlōhîm is the predicate of yhwh it is not directly juxtaposed, but occurs in the form hāʾĕlōhîm and is separated by the insertion of hûʾ [Deut. iv 35, 39, vii 9; cf. 1 Kgs viii 60]). If this is consistent Deuteronomic idiom in 312 instances, it provides strong support for the contention that in the 313th instance, i.e. Deut. vi 4, the same idiom should be discerned. In Deut. vi 4, therefore, yhwh ʾĕlōhênû must be rendered "Yahweh our God", not "Yahweh is our God", and the verse must be a statement about the oneness of

---

[15] The idiomatic point that is discussed here is mentioned by N. Lohfink in his discussion of Deut. vi 4, but its implications for the debate about translation are not fully spelt out ("ʾechadh" in G.J. Botterweck, H. Ringgren [ed.], *Theological Dictionary of the Old Testament* I [Grand Rapids, 1977], pp. 196–7 = *Theologisches Wörterbuch zum Alten Testament* I [Stuttgart, 1973], cols 213–14).

[16] For present purposes it is unnecessary to distinguish between different compositional levels within Deuteronomy as there is a consistency of usage in this regard throughout the book.

[17] The survey is based on the MT. There is some variation in other manuscript traditions because in some of the instances where yhwh appears in the MT without ʾĕlōhîm juxtaposed there is a tendency to conform to the common idiom by adding ʾĕlōhîm; see *BHS* at e.g. Deut. vi 12, 18, ix 18.

[18] It would be otiose to cite all the references here. Simply within Deut. vi (apart from v. 4) the idiom occurs in vv. 1, 2, 5, 10, 13, 15, 16, 17, 20, 24, 25.

Yahweh and not about the exclusive relationship between Yahweh and Israel.

Admittedly, one might attempt to lessen the force of the statistics by arguing, as is often done, that the formula *yhwh ʾĕlōhênû yhwh ʾeḥād* originally existed independently as a cultic formula prior to its present inclusion within Deuteronomy,[19] and may have meant "Yahweh is our God . . . " in that context. But even if this be allowed as a possibility (and by the nature of the case it must remain hypothetical), it must still be asked how the Deuteronomist intended the words to be understood, given the consistency of usage elsewhere. One could reasonably expect some indication of distinctive usage, were that intended, such as the wording *yhwh hûʾ ʾĕlōhênû*. Given the absence of any such marker there is no reason to suppose that the usage of *yhwh ʾĕlōhênû* in Deut. vi 4 is in any way different from that elsewhere in the book.

If we return now to the translation of the Shema as a whole, we are left with the two alternatives "Yahweh our God, Yahweh is one" and "Yahweh our God is one Yahweh". Between these it is more difficult to choose, but it is also less important as their meaning is similar. Two factors, however, suggest that the former is preferable. First, the recognition of the consistent idiom of conjoining *yhwh* with a form of *ʾĕlōhîm* may explain the otherwise slightly puzzling resumptive use of *yhwh* as subject before the predicate.[20] If the writer wished to use *ʾeḥād* as a predicate of *yhwh* and say *yhwh ʾeḥād* (and if there was a pre-existing cultic formula it was surely simply these two words), but also wished to introduce the divine name in his customary idiomatic way, then it was the idiomatic but intrusive use of *ʾĕlōhênû* that necessitated a resumptive use of *yhwh*.

Secondly, and more importantly, there is Zech. xiv 9, which is apparently the sole citation of Deut. vi 4 elsewhere in the OT. The text of *v. 9b* reads: *bayyôm hahûʾ yihyeh yhwh ʾeḥād ušᵉmôʾeḥād*. Although it raises problems of its own, only two points need be mentioned here. First, the text apparently envisages the eschatological fulfilment of Deut. vi 4, which had perhaps by then already become a recognized confession of faith. As such it represents the earliest surviving interpretation of Deut. vi 4. Although one cannot be sure that by the time of Zech. xiv 9 the Shema had not undergone some shift in meaning from its usage in Deut. vi 4, there is no good reason to

---

[19] E.g. McBride (n. 8), p. 297 and n. 51; Lohfink (n. 15), p. 197.
[20] S.R. Driver (n. 4) commented that "no sufficient reason appears for the resumption of the subject by the second 'Jehovah'".

suppose that any interpretative shift took place. All the material in Zech. xiv is deeply rooted in Zion traditions and shows resistance, not accommodation, to the non-Jewish world, be it Persian or Hellenistic, and so there is no reason to suppose reinterpretation in the light of wider cultural change. With due caution, therefore, it is reasonable to use Zech. xiv 9 in interpreting Deut. vi 4. Secondly, the most natural interpretation of the syntax of *yihyeh yhwh ʾeḥād* is that *ʾeḥād* is predicate to *yhwh* as subject (and similarly *uš^emô ʾeḥād*). It is this predicative use of *ʾeḥād* in Zech. xiv 9 that most strongly suggests a similar use in Deut. vi 4.

I conclude, therefore, that the Shema cannot legitimately be rendered "Yahweh is our God, Yahweh alone", but should best be translated "Hear, O Israel: Yahweh our God, Yahweh is one". It is not, therefore, a statement about Israel's exclusive relationship with Yahweh, although that exclusive relationship is indeed presupposed by the words "Yahweh our God". Rather, it is a statement about Yahweh; though precisely what it means to say that Yahweh is "one" is an issue to which I hope to return on another occasion.

CONCERNING RETURN TO EGYPT:
DEUTERONOMY XVII 16 AND XXVIII 68
RECONSIDERED

by

DAVID J. REIMER

Oxford

The Deuteronomic law concerning the king (Deut. xvii 14–20) contains an unusual prohibition. After prohibiting the multiplication of horses, the law proceeds:

> *wᵉlōʾ-yāšîb ʾet-hāʿām miṣraymâ lᵉmaʿan harbôt sûs wyhwh ʾāmar lōʾ tōsîpûn lāšûb badderek hazzeh ʿôd* (xvii 16aβ-b)
> And he shall not return the people to Egypt in order to multiply horses, for Yahweh has said, "You shall never return in this way again."

Later in the book, at the end of the curses of ch. xxviii, this prohibition is re-echoed as a curse itself:

> *wᵉhĕšîbᵉkā yhwh miṣrayim boʾŏniyyôt badderek ʾăšer ʾāmartî lōʾ tōsîp ʿôd lirʾōtāh* (xxviii 68a)
> And Yahweh will bring you back to Egypt in boats, in the way of which I said, "You shall never again see it."

Clearly, these two verses are related, and the similarities apparent: the initial use of the root *šwb*; the concern with *miṣrayim;* the inclusion of a "concrete detail" (xvii 16: *lᵉmaʿan harbôt sûs*; xxviii 68: *boʾŏniyyôt*); the reference to a quotation using *ʾmr*; the inclusion of *badderek*; the quotation formulated as *lōʾ* + hiphil of *ysp* + infinitive + *ʿôd*.

Still, there are several differences of detail which may be noted:

xvii 16	xxviii 68
– formulated as prohibition	– formulated as threat
– quotation attributed to Yahweh	– quotation attributed to Moses
– the people are never again "to return" (*lāšûb*) to Egypt	– the people are never again "to see" (*lirʾōtāh*) it (Egypt? "the way"?)
– the king does the returning	– Yahweh does the returning
– *badderek* is inside the quotation	– *badderek* is outside the quotation

- 2nd person references in   - formulated in 2nd person
  plural   singular

The primary purpose of this article is to clarify the relationship between these two verses. What is their relative status? Is one dependent on the other for its entry into the text, or are they contemporary? What is the referent for the quotation, or does one exist? The further question of the individual "concrete details" will be briefly addressed at the end of the article.

Several suggestions have been put forward concerning the referent for the quotations which are said to be known by the reader. Opinion forms into two camps: those who do not find a referent and those who do. Belonging to the former are G. von Rad;[1] G. Seitz, who believes the tradition has not "passed on" (*nicht überliefert*) the word of Yahweh in xvii 16,[2] or "documented" (*nicht belegen*) the "Jahwewort" [sic] of xxviii 68;[3] and A.D.H. Mayes, who says these pronouncements are not preserved. But in connection with xvii 16, Mayes alludes to Hos. viii 13 and ix 3 giving the impression that one tradition may lie behind the passages in both Deuteronomy and Hosea.[4] M. Weinfeld parallels xvii 16 to Hos. viii 13 and xxviii 68 to Hos. xi 5, but without comment. He points out the common interest in the "menace" of returning to Egypt but does not attempt to elucidate the relationships between various texts.[5]

Firmly in the latter camp, of those who do find referents for the quotation, are N. Lohfink and his pupil D.E. Skweres, who speculates that xxviii 68 relies on xvii 16, but immediately states that it is more probable that they both quote some previously known material.[6] After brief analysis, he suggests Ex. xiv 13 as the basis of xxviii 68. There, Moses encourages the people not to fear the pursuing Egyptians: *kî ʾǎšer rᵉʾîtem ʾet-miṣrayim hayyôm lōʾ tōsîpû lirʾōtām ᶜôd ᶜad-ᶜôlām*. While Ex. xiv 13 may also provide the source for xvii 16, he hesitates over the change of *rʾh* and *šwb* in the "infinitive" positions,

---

[1] *Deuteronomium* (Göttingen, 1964), p. 126 (= *Deuteronomy: A Commentary* [London and Philadelphia, 1966], p. 176).

[2] "Das Jahwewort, auf das hier angespielt wird und an das auch 28, 68 noch einmal erinnert, ist uns nicht überliefert", *Redaktionsgeschichtliche Studien zum Deuteronomium* (Stuttgart, 1971), p. 233.

[3] P. 302: "Das Jahwewort, das in v68 zitiert wird, ist ausserhalb des Dt. nicht zu belegen. Nur Dt. 17,16b beruft sich darauf."

[4] "No word of Yahweh on the subject has been preserved, though a reference to it is given also in 28:68, and its existence would add greatly to the impact of Hos. 8:13; 9:3": *Deuteronomy* (London and Grand Rapids, 1981), p. 272, and cf. p. 358.

[5] *Deuteronomy and the Deuteronomic School* (Oxford, 1972), p. 168.

[6] *Die Rückverweise im Buch Deuteronomium* (Rome, 1979), p. 193.

and further suggests Ex. xiii 17 as the referent for xvii 16 where *šwb* does appear (p. 194).

Lohfink, in dialogue with Skweres, deals only with xvii 16 and rejects the suggestion from Exodus because neither is a divine order or pronouncement. In addition, Ex. xiv 13 does not include the "decisive" (*entscheidende*) *word šwb*.[7] Lohfink's alternative is Hos. xi 5, previously noted by Weinfeld. The first part of that verse reads: *lōʾ yāšûb ʾel-ʾereṣ miṣrayim*. Lohfink argues that this is a better proposal since it has the advantage of employing *šwb* as well as being a divine pronouncement.[8]

Lohfink's own suggestion is also beset with problems, as he himself recognizes. Chief of these is the text critical problem whether *lōʾ* should be retained as the initial word of Hos. xi 5 or emended to *lô* and read as the final word of Hos. xi 4 (cf. the LXX). Even if one retains the MT, so at odds is it with the rest of Hosea that appeal is made to the so-called "asseverative *lōʾ*" to avoid the problem.[9] As it stands in the MT, Hos. xi 5 contradicts an otherwise consistent attitude towards Egypt in the book of Hosea, especially viii 13 and ix 3 where Ephraim is returned to Egypt in punishment. Among the English versions the emendation is accepted by the *Revised Standard Version*, *The New English Bible* and *Today's English Version*.[10] Further, there are important points where Hos. xi 5 and Deut. xvii 16 fail to connect: the construction is dissimilar; neither the hiphil of *ysp* nor the particle *ʿōd* is employed in Hos. xi 5. Even if *lōʾ* was already in the text "used" by Deuteronomy, these difficulties strong militate against accepting Lohfink's proposal.

Skweres's suggestion that Ex. xiv 13 is the referent for Deut. xxviii 68 holds merit. The coincidences are striking:

Deut. xxviii 68a *lōʾ tōsîp ʿôd lirʾōtāh*
        Ex. xiv 13b *lōʾ tōsîpû lirʾōtām ʿôd ʿad-ʿôlām*

Both are pronouncements of Moses. Variations are minor: the verb number differs, but Skweres notes that change in number is attested even with inner-Deuteronomic quotations.[11] Of greater import is that

---

[7] "Hos. xi 5 als Bezugstext von Dtn. xvii 16", *VT* 31 (1981), p. 227.

[8] However, for the link between this passage and Hosea see already J. Wellhausen, *Die Composition des Hexateuchs und der historischen Bücher des Alten Testaments* (3rd edn, Berlin, 1899), Nachträge, p. 358.

[9] See F.I. Andersen and D.N. Freedman, *Hosea: A New Translation with Introduction and Commentary* (Garden City, 1980) pp. 583–4.

[10] See also the *New International Version* where the *lōʾ* is retained, but the verse is formulated as a rhetorical question to render the same sense as the emended text.

[11] P. 194 and n. 871. He cites Deut. xviii 16 and v 25 as examples.

Exodus speaks of never again seeing "the Egyptians" while Deuteronomy is concerned with "the way". Nor is Exodus concerned with
"returning" to Egypt as is the case in Deuteronomy.[12] Still, the
coincidence is too great for these differences to be dissuasive.

Ex. xiv 13 is thus a plausible referent for Deut. xxviii 68. Deut. xvii
16, however, has no satisfactory referent. Neither Ex. xiii 17 nor Hos.
xi 5 corresponds to a great enough degree to enable one to argue that
they are quoted in Deut. xvii 16. After discussing the relationships of
xvii 16 and xxviii 68 to their respective pericopes another proposal
will be put forward.

Deut. xvii 14–20

The Deuteronomic law concerning the king is composed of a brief
protasis (v. 14) and a lengthy apodosis (vv. 15–20). The protasis is
formulated with 2nd person singular verbs, and begins with the "if
you ... " form familiar in the Deuteronomic code. The apodosis
continues with 2nd person singular address. It allows the installation
of a king of Yahweh's choosing (v. 15a) who is of native Israelite stock,
a regulation which is stated both positively and negatively (v. 15b).
With this, a series of stipulations follow, formulated in the 3rd person
singular: socio-economic concerns are dealt with in vv. 16–17; and
matters in the moral-religious sphere in vv. 18–20.

Each of the five stipulations that addresses the socio-economic
concerns follows the pattern of $l\bar{o}^\circ$ + 3rd singular verb. (i) The king
shall not "multiply" for himself horses (v. 16aα); (ii) he shall not send
the people back to Egypt to multiply horses (v. 16aβ); (iii) he shall not
"multiply" for himself wives (v. 17aα); (iv) his heart shall not turn
away (v. 17aβ); and (v) he shall not "greatly multiply" for himself
silver and gold (v. 17b). In this final stipulation, the objects precede
the verb, varying the order of the four preceding stipulations, and
forming a bracket for the sequence. The second stipulation (v. 16aβ),
an expansion of the initial limitation of multiplying horses, is itself
expanded in v. 16b, with a quotation from Yahweh legitimizing the
prohibition concerning return to Egypt. The quotation itself uses the
2nd person plural ($l\bar{o}^\circ$ $t\bar{o}s\bar{i}p\hat{u}n$) and is preceded by a 2nd person plural
form ($l\bar{a}kem$).

With $w^e h\bar{a}y\hat{a}$ of v. 18, a transition is made to the moral-religious
sphere. The formulation is now positive rather than negative. The

---

[12] Skweres notes and dismisses these points.

king is required to write and read a "copy of the law" (*vv.* 18aα, 19aβ), and the presence of the Levitical priest is required (*v.* 18bβ). Three infinitive clauses given the rationale. The king will learn: (i) to fear Yahweh his God; (ii) to keep "the words of this Torah"; and (iii) to do these statutes. In the final case, the object precedes the infinitive. Thus the pattern: inf.-obj., inf.-obj., obj.-inf. emerges, the final clause providing a sense of closure. Two further negative regulations are placed on the character of the king in *v.* 20a; a motivation clause appears in *v.* 20b.

Scholarly opinion varies as to which elements are to be considered secondary, and layers are clearly discernible even if the fine distinctions remain hazy.[13] The shift to religious interest and the onset of Deuteronomic phraseology mark out *vv.* 18–20 as a later layer than *vv.* 15–17. However, with Deuteronomic phrases embedded in the protasis (*v.* 14a), this does not rule out the possibility that *vv.* 18–20 belong in the law which first appeared in the Deuteronomic code.[14] The ties of vocabulary and interest between *v.* 17aβ and *v.* 20a suggest the assignment of this clause in *v.* 17 to the same layer as *vv.* 18–20. With the formulation of the law in the 2nd person singular, the secondary status of *v.* 16aβ-b is also implied, given its use of the plural and its expansionary character. This would leave a sequence of three *lōʾ yarbeh* clauses (*vv.* 16aα, 17aα, 17b) forming the kernel of the stipulations, each of which is pithy in formulation and coherent in content. Legitimation of the institution of kingship, then, appears in *v.* 15, given divine selection and native citizenship.[15]

Thus *v.* 16aβ-b appears to be loosely attached to its context. The stipulations against multiplying horses, wives and money are general in character, not tied to a particular time or setting. Attempts have been made to link this series to a particular king, notably Solomon,[16] but the caution of Mayes is well taken: " . . . the aim of building up an effective army of horses and chariots was undoubtedly pursued by

---

[13] See the summary in R.P. Merendino, *Das Deuteronomische Gesetz* (Bonn, 1969), p. 172.

[14] The concern exhibited in *v.* 20a for the brethren is related to that of *v.* 15 and draws it more strongly into the basic layer than *vv.* 18–19. It may be assigned to the same hand that brought *v.* 17a into the text in an attempt to bring some "religious" content into a context where it is in short supply.

[15] The redundancy of language between *v.* 15a and *v.* 15bα, as well as the logical problem of reconciling divine choice (*v.* 15aβ) and dynastic succession (*v.* 20bβ), suggests further literary critical problems in this passage, but these are unrelated to the purposes of this analysis.

[16] E.g. Weinfeld: "If there is any negative tendency in the law of the king in Deuteronomy it is not directed towards the monarchy as such but against a specific king. Solomon's sins are echoed in this law" (p. 168).

more than one king ... and it must remain doubtful that a particular individual is in view".[17] The temptations covered in the *lōʾ yarbeh* series are not tied exclusively to a single monarch in ancient Israel: while some kings are notable for their excess, that by itself does not change the general character of this series.

In this "timeless" context appears *v.* 16aβ-b. It is secondary, as was noted above, and it has a sense of concreteness. Why the concern with Egyptian horses? Was this a common temptation in the same way that amassing wealth or harem-building was? No – it seems that there is a *Tendenz* at work which is specific to to this situation. Given that this pericope is Deuteronomic in origin and that this particular element is secondary to the original layer, the likely date for its appearance is early in the exilic age. The possibilities for the historical background of this prohibition will be considered below.

Deut. xxviii 58–68

Deut. xxviii is a lengthy chapter comprising the conditional blessings and curses which conclude the Deuteronomic code. They have been subject to much expansion, and it would appear that *vv.* 58–68 are secondary to the core of blessings and curses. This section is marked off from the preceding by a new conditional introduction (*ʾim lōʾ tišmōr laʿăśôt ...*) and by its own distinctive flavour.

The protasis of *v.* 58 renews the conditional formulation interrupted by *vv.* 47–57 which recounted the disasters brought about by disobedience. The condition in *v.* 58 is formulated in the 2nd person singular and rests on two things: they are to be careful "to do (*laʿăśôt*) all the words of this Torah"; and "to fear (*lǝyirʾâ*) this glorious and awesome name". The "Torah" is described as "the writings of this book" which suggests Deuteronomy is already in written form when this section is formulated.[18]

The apodosis divides into two sections: 1. *vv.* 59–61 are curses of sickness and disease; 2. *vv.* 64–8 are concerned with life away from the land. *Vv.* 62–3 describe the outcome of the plagues (*v.* 62) and forecast God's pleasure in destruction (*v.* 63). These two verses are composed

---

[17] P. 272. Mayes extrapolates this to include the stipulations concerning wives and wealth.

[18] It is interesting to note that the concerns expressed in this protasis reflect many of the concerns which appear in xvii 18–19, where the king is instructed "to fear (*lǝyirʾâ*) Yahweh his God, to keep (*lišmōr*) all the words of this Torah, and these statutes to do them (*laʿăśōtām*)" (*v.* 19b).

in the 2nd person plural with Deuteronomic catch phrases in the 2nd person singular (*vv.* 62b, 63bβ). The two sections (*vv.* 59–61, 64–8) comprise a series of six verbs, three in each section, describing the actions Yahweh will take if his people are disobedient (*vv.* 59a, 60a, 61b, 64a, 65b and 68a). In five of six cases Yahweh is the explicit subject, *v.* 60a being the exception.

The first series of three is tied closely together by the use of the terms *makkâ* and *ḥŏlî* which appear in both *vv.* 59b and 61a. A rare word for "disease" is used in *v.* 60a, *madwēh*, found only twice in the Hebrew Bible, both times in Deuteronomy. The objects are placed in front of the verb in *v.* 61; thus *vv.* 59–61 have a chiastic structure, symmetrical around *v.* 60.

> *wᵉhiplāʾ yhwh ʾet-makkōtᵉkā wᵉʾēt makkōt zarᶜekā*
> *makkōt gᵉdōlôt wᵉneʾĕmānôt*
> *woḥŏlāyim rāᶜîm wᵉneʾĕmānîm.*
> *v.* 60 *gam kol-ḥŏlî*
> *wᵉkol-makkâ ʾăšer lōʾ kātûb bᵉsēper hattôrâ hazzōʾt*
> *yaᶜlēm yhwh ᶜālekā ᶜad hiššāmᵉdāk*

This tight unit is followed by a 2nd person plural verb, no longer describing Yahweh's activity, but rather detailing the effects of sickness and plague (*v.* 62a) and the reason behind it (*v.* 62b). The 2nd person plural is carried into *v.* 63 which states God's willingness to destroy: just as Yahweh was pleased (*wᵉhāyâ kaʾăšer-śāś yhwh*) to do good and increase his people, so he will be pleased (*kēn yāśîś yhwh*) to destroy and exterminate his people. The structure is perfectly parallel. *V.* 63b is in the same vein as *v.* 62a; it describes the outcome of God's destructive activity.

The second series of three verbs is concerned with life away from the land, for Yahweh will scatter (*wehĕpîṣᵉkâ*) them among the nations (*v.* 64a). There they will find no relaxation nor rest, and their quality of life will be destroyed (*v.* 65b). The adjectives describing *lēb ᶜênayim* and *nepeš* in *v.* 65b are all rare: *raggāz* and **dᵉʾābôn* are both *hapax legomena*, while *killāyôn* occurs only twice.

The shift from describing Yahweh's activity to describing its results occurs again in *vv.* 66–7. Unlike *vv.* 62–3, these verses are formulated in the 2nd person singular. The word *ḥayyekā* begins and ends *v.* 66, while *v.* 66b is closely connected to *v.* 67. There the notion of "fearing night and day" is expanded by two sets of doublets:

> 67a *babbōqer tōʾmar mî-yittēn ᶜereb*
>   *ûbāᶜereb tōʾmar mî-yittēn bōqer*
> 67b *mippaḥad lᵉbābᵉkā ʾăšer tipḥād*
>   *ûmimmarʾēh ᶜênekā ʾăšer tirʾeh*

With *lēb* and *ᶜayin* in both *v.* 65b and *v.* 67b a mild inclusio is formed, tying together the already tight structures of *vv.* 65b–67.

In *v.* 68a, the final threat of punishment is tabled: Yahweh will return (*wehĕšib'kā*) his people to Egypt in boats, thus reversing what Moses had said to them, that "you will never see it (Egypt) again". This is subject to expansion in *v.* 68b, where the outcome is described using a verb in the 2nd person plural: they will try to sell themselves as slaves, but there will be no buyers.

Since Deut. xxviii 58–68 is marked by a number of unusual words and phrases, the Deuteronomic phraseology stands out in even greater contrast. However, the typical language is embedded in the composition, and so, although the passage is of late origin, the style is not an indicator of a precise date. Layering, such as that found in the law of the king, is not readily apparent. *V.* 65a is dependent on *v.* 64, and *v.* 65b follows well on *v.* 65a in terms of content. The coherent structure of *vv.* 65b–67 was noted above. Nothing inherent in *v.* 68a suggests a secondary status in relation to the pericope. Indeed, it follows the regular pattern for the series of verbs, and in theme hearkens back to that of *v.* 60 where "all the diseases of Egypt" will be brought back to them (*wᵉhēšib*) by Yahweh.

Thus *v.* 68a appears at home in its context. The mention of the peculiar and concrete detail *boᵓŏniyyôt* distinguishes it from the general nature of most of the curses in this pericope: sickness, disease, scattering, weakness and fear. It is possible that its concreteness suggests some reflection of historical experience. This will be discussed below. In any case, we are again brought into the exilic period. Closer identification will be examined after a comparison of xxviii 68a to xvii 16aβ-b.

A brief summary of the pertinent information from the structural analysis will help put these two passages in relief.

It was found that xvii 16aβ-b was loosely attached to its context; the reference to Egypt was not occasioned by anything in the pericope; it alone was in the 2nd person plural, the law as a whole being formulated in the 2nd and 3rd person singular. In the discussion preceding the structural analysis, no adequate referent for the embedded quotation was found.

On the other hand, xxviii 68a appeared at home in its surroundings, concerns with Egypt having already surfaced in xxviii 60a. It followed the pattern of the backbone of the apodosis: *waw* + (hiphil) perfect + explicit subject Yahweh. Second person references were singular. It was earlier found (following Skweres) that Ex. xiv 13 was the word of Moses to which the quotation refers.

Given this situation, is the reverse of Skweres's tentative suggestion possible, that xvii 16 is dependent on xxviii 68? Once this "quotation" appears as a word of Moses in the context of the actions of Yahweh, it is reasonable to see this then transported to the context of xvii 16 as a word of Yahweh. Alternatively, the action of Yahweh in xxvii 68 becomes the word of Yahweh in xvii 16. The threat of punishment in xxviii 68 prepares the ground for return to Egypt to be an evil to avoid, i.e. a prohibition in xvii 16. The evil that Yahweh will bring upon his disobedient people as a curse is not to be voluntarily undertaken by the king. Both xxviii 68 and xvii 16 are concerned with *hadderek*, but xvii 16 seems to shift the sense from "way" as a means in a concrete sense, to "way" as a fashion or manner in an abstract sense. The 2nd person plural form of xvii 16 suggests a date later than the singular form of xxviii 68.[19] The switch from *lirʾōtāh* to *lāšûb* is due to demands of context.

A movement of this kind, from word of Moses to word of Yahweh, is described by M. Fishbane in connection with "pseudepigraphic" inner-biblical legal exegesis.[20] Fishbane depicts a three-stage process:

> ... First, each element of the human legal *traditio* is legitimated by its transformation into a part of the authoritative divine *traditum* given to Moses; second, Moses is thereby transformed from the mediator of specific revelations to the mediator of whatever was spoken in his name, or taught as part of his teaching; and third, the word of YHWH becomes as comprehensive as the *traditum* itself ... (p. 258).

The terms are slightly shifted in our case. We are not dealing with a piece of legal exegesis which has received "dignification and elevation" by the move from Moses as mediator to Yahweh as source. Nonetheless, the dynamic is similar. In the charged political atmosphere surrounding the collapse of Judah, the words of Moses that Yahweh's people should never again see the Egyptians (Ex. xiv 13) took on deeper significance, first as an evil to be avoided in the curses of Deut. xxviii 68, then as a prohibition in Deut. xvii 16, where the avoidance of Egypt is fully legitimized as a command of Yahweh.

The political atmosphere served as the impulse for this transformation. In his article discussed above (n. 7), Lohfink points to the polemic of "der babylonischen gegen die ägyptische Golah" preserved in the book of Jeremiah as the likely setting for the varying

---

[19] The relation of the 2nd person singular to the plural in Deuteronomy is still debated. G. Minette de Tillesse, in "Sections 'tu' et sections 'vous' dans le Deutéronome", *VT* 12 (1962), pp. 29–87, argues that the singular sections are earlier than the plural. This is not a hard-and-fast rule, however, and it is noted here with caution.

[20] In *Biblical Interpretation in Ancient Israel* (Oxford, 1985), pp. 257–60.

attitude toward Egypt which he finds in Hosea. Although his main proposition was rejected, this observation is valuable and makes sense of the presence of xxviii 68 and xvii 16 in their respective passages. The pro-Babylonian and anti-Egyptian polemic has most often been seen in terms of the pro-Babylonian outlook of the Deuteronomistic History.[21] The prohibitions discussed in this article draw attention to the anti-Egyptian side of that struggle.

A brief review of the pertinent Jeremiah traditions shows there is more to be found in this vein. Jeremiah is full of prophecies giving divine sanction to the aggression of the Babylonians (Jer. xxi 1–10, xxii 24–5, xxv 9, etc.). The opposition to this stance is graphically documented in the confrontation between Jeremiah and Hananiah in Jer. xxvii–xxviii. Through this episode, two factions appear which may be characterized as pro-Babylonian and anti-Babylonian. Opposition to Egypt is seen in other texts. In Jer. xxiv 8 in the vision of the good and bad figs, the "bad figs" are defined as "Zedekiah the king of Judah and his princes and the remnant of Jerusalem who remain in this land and those dwelling in the land of Egypt". The account of the events surrounding the assassination of Gedaliah also sheds light on the attitude toward Egypt. In Jer. xlii the group around Yohanan seeks guidance from Jeremiah: should they remain in the land or flee? Jeremiah tells them to stay, condemning them if they should go to Egypt: "Yahweh has spoken to you, remnant of Judah, 'You shall not go to Egypt'" (Jer. xlii 19a).[22] Later, in Egypt, Jeremiah condemns the Jews who have come to Egypt to the same fate that befell Jerusalem "so that none of the remnant of Judah who have come to live in Egypt shall escape or survive or return to the land of Judah" (Jer. xliv 11–14).

The tradition forbidding reliance on Egypt was an old one, going back to the fall of the northern kingdom. "Woe to those who go down to Egypt for help and rely on horses ... but do not look to the Holy One of Israel", cries Isaiah (xxxi 1). This was equally meaningful at the collapse of the southern kingdom. Preserved in Ezekiel is the statement "and [Egypt] shall never again be the reliance of the house of Israel, recalling their inquity when they turn to them for aid" (xxix 16). This is precisely the situation which would produce such rhetorically loaded verses as Deut. xvii 16 and xxviii 68.

---

[21] See e.g. C.T. Begg, "The Significance of Jehoiachin's Release: A New Proposal", *JSOT* 36 (1986), pp. 49–56.

[22] This passage itself may be another use of the topos developed in Deut. xvii 16, xxviii 68. The content is similar, and the language rings closer to that of Deuteronomy than Exodus (xiv 13).

This leads us to a brief discussion of the "concrete details": *lᵉmaᶜan harbôt sûs* in xvii 16; and *bo⁾ŏniyyôt* in xxviii 68.

In the previous discussion it was posited that xvii 16aβ-b made its appearance in the text early in the exilic period. The kernel of the law, the three *lō⁾-yarbeh* stipulations, was seen to be general in character, but a special interest can be seen at work in the expansion of *v.* 16aβ-b. Is any tradition preserved which may connect with this particular concern of multiplying horses and Egypt? As noted above, there had been a long stream of tradition which counselled against military ties with Egypt. Scholars have found evidence for such ties going back to the time of Psammetichus I,²³ and involvement of Judean mercenaries in Egypt may even have continued into Zekekiah's reign, coincident with that of Psammetichus II.²⁴ Ezek. xvii 15 may provide some evidence in relation to Deut. xvii 16aβ-b. Ezek. xvii tells the fable of the eagles, the cedar, and the vine, and records the interpretation. The fable, in *vv.* 1–10, has been dated to the period of Zedekiah's reign before the final siege of Jerusalem.²⁵ But the interpretative passage seems to presuppose the fall of the city, and so is to be dated some time after 586,²⁶ i.e., roughly contemporary with the Deuteronomy text. The fable in itself is an indication of the pro-Babylonian and anti-Egyptian polemic existing at this time. The two eagles represent Nebuchadnezzar of Babylon and Hophra of Egypt. The wayward vine is Zedekiah. Part of the interpretation declares:

> But [Zedekiah] rebelled against [Nebuchadnezzar] by sending (*lišlōaḥ*) ambassadors to Egypt that they might give him horses and a large army. Will he succeed? Can a man escape who does such things?
>
> (Ezek. xvii 15)

The verbal coincidences between the texts are not great, but the relationship is not a textual one, but is temporal and thematic. In Ezek. xvii 15, it is Zedekiah's ambassadors (*mal⁾ākā(y)w*) who are sent to Egypt, not the "people" (*hāᶜām*) as in Deut. xvii 16. But as Kraeling pointed out, *hāᶜām* designates some specific group, not the whole nation ([n. 23], p. 44). It is plausible to suppose that Zedekiah's

---

²³ See E.G. Kraeling, *The Brooklyn Museum Aramaic Papyri. New Documents of the Fifth Century B.C. from the Jewish Colony at Elephantine* (New Haven, Conn., 1953), pp. 43–4.

²⁴ Cf. M. Greenberg, "Ezekiel 17 and the Policy of Psammetichus II", *JBL* 76 (1957), pp. 304–9, esp. p. 307.

²⁵ W. Zimmerli puts the date during the years 592–591, these being the dates in Ezek. viii 1 and xx 1. He thinks this is adequate, although no "compelling arguments can be brought in demonstration of it", *Ezechiel 1* (Neukirchen-Vluyn, 1969), p. 379 (= *Ezekiel 1* [Philadelphia, 1979], p. 361).

²⁶ Zimmerli, p. 384 (E. tr., p. 364); also J.W. Wevers, *Ezekiel* (London, 11969), p. 136.

ambassadors were negotiating an exchange of mercenaries for horses and further military aid. In general terms, the pro-Babylonian and anti-Egyptian polemic brings the concern against going to Egypt to the fore, and the activity of Zedekiah was a concrete situation which needed to be addressed.

The specific setting for xxviii 68 with its reference to "boats" remains elusive. The matter has received recent attention from D.G. Schley.[27] On the basis of the annals of Assurbanipal, Schley dates this text to the first half of the 7th century B.C. The annal recounts how twenty-two kings, the king of Judah among them, marched as vassals against Egypt; their route included a sea journey (*ANET*, p. 294). But this does not tie the curses of Deut. xxviii 58–68 to a contemporary date. The journey as it appears in Deuteronomy, to be sold as slaves, does not correspond to a military expedition with a powerful aggressor.[28] Nor does the annal provide the only possible explanation for the curse. More evidence has recently come to light which may suggest that the backdrop to this problem had been of long standing, such as that for the trade for horses. N. Avigad published a seal impression of Judean provenance depicting a sailing ship which he dated to the 8th–7th century B.C.[29] M. Görg offered an interpretation of this seal, in which the seal owner is identified with "ägyptenfreund-licher Kreise" in Judah or Jerusalem.[30] The name "Oniyahu" ("my ship is Yahweh") is related to corresponding Egyptian names using "Amun". It is possible that this understanding gives us another glimpse of relations between Judah and Egypt. On this reading, xxviii 58–68 reflects an ironic reversal of the situation hoped for by co-operative ties with Egypt: instead of prosperity there will be misery, and the boats that symbolized their trade will deal in slavery. Although the pro-Babylonian and anti-Egyptian polemic is well attested, this particular aspect of it with the interpretation it provides for our text remains speculative, as do other attempts to tie this verse down to a single historical backdrop.

---

[27] "'Yahweh will cause you to return to Egypt in ships' (Deuteronomy xxviii 68)", *VT* 35 (1985), pp. 369–72; and the literature cited there.

[28] On the connection with slavery see S.R. Driver, *A Critical and Exegetical Commentary on Deuteronomy* (3rd edn, Edinburgh, 1902), p. 319. Driver used other texts as well: Ezek. xxvii 13; Joel iii 6; Amos i 19.

[29] "The script represents the semi-cursive formal Hebrew of the 8th-7th century B.C. at its best. It exhibits no special key letters that could provide a closer date": "A Hebrew Seal Depicting a Sailing Ship", *BASOR* 246 (1982), pp. 59–62 (p. 59). Note also seal impressions from the Persain period (from Persepolis) depicting war galleys in M. - C. de Grave, *The Ships of the Ancient Near East (c. 2000–c. 500 B.C.)* (Leuven, 1981), pp. 74–5, pl. XLVI 106–7; cf. Avigad, p. 62, n. 4.

[30] "'Mein Schiff ist Yhwh'. Zur Dekoration eines hebräischen Siegels", *Biblishe Notizen* 25 (1984), pp. 7–9 (p. 9).

To summarize: the primary purpose of this article was to clarify the uncertain relations between the prohibitions aganst return to Egypt found in Deut. xvii 16 and xxviii 68. It was argued that the word of Moses in Ex. xiv 13, with its assurance that Yahweh's people would never again see *miṣrayim* was quoted in Deut. xxviii 68 with new effect. Return to Egypt became an evil to be avoided. Another transformation took place when Deut. xvii 16 used xxviii 68 and gave full legitimation to the prohibition as a word of Yahweh. In short, Deut. xvii 16 depends on xxviii 68, which in turn depends on Ex. xiv 13. A secondary purpose was to examine the historical background of the concrete details included in the prohibitions. Although the impulse which gave rise to them cannot be precisely dated, the pro-Babylonian and anti-Egypt polemic of the exilic period is the most likely backdrop. In this polemic, and in these prohibitions, long standing positive attitudes towards Egypt were opposed.[31]

[31] I am indebted to Professor P.E. Dion of the University of Toronto for his critical comments on an earlier draft of this article.

THE CREED OF DEUTERONOMY XXVI REVISITED

by

DWIGHT R. DANIELS

Hamburg

It would be difficult to overestimate the importance of the "short historical creed" for the theological work of Gerhard von Rad. Discovered in 1938, it remained a creative force in his presentation of OT theology.[1] Von Rad's concern in his 1938 monograph was to pose the question of the final form or genre of the Hexateuch. Why do the hexateuchal sources treat the particular span of Israelite history that they do? In pursuing this question von Rad came across the "short historical creed" of Dt. xxvi 5b–9 with its primary parallels in Dt. vi 20–4 and Josh. xxiv 2b–13. These historical summaries recount basically the same events recounted in the Hexateuch, with two significant differences. The summaries mention neither history prior to the patriarchs nor the covenant at Sinai. From this he argued that the Exodus-Conquest tradition and the Sinai tradition were originally independent. He associated the Sinai tradition with the feast of booths and covenant renewal at Shechem and the Exodus-Conquest tradition with the feast of weeks celebrated at Gilgal. It was the Yahwist who first combined the traditions in his literary work. He also developed the patriarchal traditions in the light of the resulting combination and prefaced the primeval history. In this manner von Rad accounted for the current form of the hexateuchal sources.

In his own investigation of the Pentateuch, M. Noth accepted von Rad's basic thesis, though with one significant difference. On the basis of the parallels in J and E he argued that much of the innovation

---

[1] *Das formgeschichtliche Problem des Hexateuchs* (Stuttgart, 1938) = "The form-critical Problem of the Hexateuch", in *The Problem of the Hexateuch and other essays* (London, 1984), pp. 1–78, and his *Theologie des Alten Testaments* I (Munich, 1957), pp. 13–15 = (⁸1982), pp. 17–20 = *Old Testament Theology* I (Edinburgh, London and New York, 1962), pp. 3–5.

which von Rad had attributed to the Yahwist must already have been present in a common *Grundlage* (G) lying behind both J and E.[2]

The ensuing critique of von Rad's thesis took on two basic forms: discussion of the original independence of the Exodus-Conquest and Sinai traditions, and the age and nature of such historical creeds.[3] A. Weiser argued that the differing characters of the Exodus-Conquest tradition as the revelation of the divine essence and the Sinai tradition as the revelation of the divine will were not due to their belonging to different festivals but to their being separate parts of a single festival of covenant renewal. This he deduced from Josh. xxiv where both historical recital and law form part of the covenantal ceremony.[4] Weiser's basic position found significant support in the discovery of the parallels between Israel's covenant tradition and the treaty tradition of the ancient Near East.[5] These treaties usually include a historical prologue which precedes the obligations defined in the body of the treaty. The Exodus-Conquest tradition (creed) was compared with the historical prologue and the Sinai tradition with the treaty stipulations, and on these grounds the traditions were seen to be firmly bound to one another.[6]

As for the second line of criticism, von Rad had noted the presence of Deuteronomic phraseology in the creed of Dt. xxvi 5b–9 but chose not to determine the actual extent of this "retouching". On this score he was duly criticized by L. Rost, who undertook such an investigation. He held that only the statement "a perishing Aramean was my father, and now behold, I bring the first fruits of the ground which you, Yahweh, have given me" was in fact old, the rest being

---

[2] *Überlieferungsgeschichte des Pentateuch* (Stuttgart, 1948), pp. 40–4 = *A History of Pentateuchal Traditions* (Englewood Cliffs, New Jersey, 1972 = Chico, California, 1981), pp. 38–41.

[3] G. Wallis, "Die geschichtliche Erfahrung und das Bekenntnis zu Jahwe im Alten Testament", *ThLZ* 101 (1976), cols 801–16, also lists criticism of the term "credo" or "creed" as an appropriate name for the genre (cols 808–9). The term "historical summary" is often substituted as broader and hence applicable to all the relevant texts, whereas "creed" covers primarily the situation in Dt. xxvi. Since this passage is the focus of the present study, I retain von Rad's terminology for purposes of simplicity.

[4] *Einleitung in das Alte Testament* (Göttingen, 1957), pp. 72–85.

[5] Cf. G. Mendenhall, "Law and Covenant in Israel and the Ancient Near East", *BA* 17 (1954), pp. 26–46, 49–76.

[6] So e.g. K. Baltzer, *Das Bundesformular* (Neukirchen, 1960); W. Beyerlin, *Herkunft und Geschichte der ältesten Sinaitradition* (Tübingen, 1961); J.N.M. Wijngaards, *The Formulas of the Deuteronomic Creed* (*Dt. 6/20–23: 26/5–9*) (Tilburg, 1963); H.B. Huffmon, "The Exodus, Sinai and the Credo", *CBQ* 27 (1965), pp. 101–13.

a Deuteronomic expansion.[7] W. Richter, though accepting Rost's results, approaches the problem from a different angle. He examines all the texts in which the formulae which comprise the creed occur "under the particular aspect of the gradual system building of the Israelite faith".[8] He comes to the conclusion that the combination of these formulae stands at the end of the tradition-historical process and not at the beginning. The creed is a summary of more extensive traditions.

B.S. Childs also advocates this view. Examining the content of Deuteronomic formulae employed with reference to the Exodus, he argues that initially the "bringing out" from Egypt and the "signs and wonders" were broad in meaning. When the tetrateuchal traditions of the "event at the sea" entered, the "signs and wonders" were specifically identified with the plagues and the "bringing out" referred specifically to the departure from Egyptian territory. If this analysis is correct, then, so Childs, it calls into question, or at least does not support, von Rad's thesis concerning the formation of the Hexateuch. "More likely, therefore, is the alternative hypothesis that these chapters are basically Deuteronomic abbreviations of fuller traditions."[9]

The summary hypothesis has become influencial and is naturally adopted by those arguing for a late date for the pentateuchal sources.[10] But the articles in which this theory is developed are not without their problems. Richter's conception of a creed as merely the combination of set formulae is suspect, and it may reasonably be questioned if the term "gradual system building" does not lend a certain inevitability to the results. Neither does his study consider the implications of the fragmentary nature of the transmission of Israel's traditions in the OT. Childs's comments are cursory, and it is not at all apparent why a shift in the content of Deuteronomic phraseology should indicate a Deuteronomic origin for the creed. All that Childs's study can suggest is that the current form of Dt. xxvi

---

[7] "Das kleine geschichtliche Credo", in *Das kleine Credo und andere Studien zum Alten Testament* (Heidelberg, 1965), pp. 11–25.

[8] "Beobachtungen zur theologischen Systembildung in der alttestamentlichen Literatur anhand des 'kleinen geschichtlichen Credo'", in *Wahrheit und Verkündigung*, Fs. M. Schmaus (Munich, 1967) I, pp. 175–212, quotation p. 178.

[9] "Deuteronomic Formulae of the Exodus Traditions", *SVT* 16 (1967), pp. 30–9, quotation p. 39.

[10] So e.g. J. Van Seters, *In Search of History* (New Haven, Conn., and London, 1983), pp. 229, 336.

8 comes from the period prior to the shift, but not that this form is original.

This brings us back to Rost's study. Subsequent studies have not tended to confirm his analysis. Thus, R.P. Merendino, G. Waßermann and N. Lohfink have all argued that the extent of Deuteronomic language in Dt. xxvi 5b–9(10) is far less extensive than Rost claimed.[11] Merendino and Waßermann consequently maintain, as had von Rad before them, that the creed is older than its present literary context, whereas Lohfink nevertheless retains Rost's hypothesis of the creed's development.

This brief presentation of the history of research, which makes no pretension of being comprehensive,[12] suffices to indicate that several issues remain disputed. It is not the intention of this study to explore all of them, but rather to re-examine the pivotal text of the discussion – the "short historical creed" of Dt. xxvi. The study poses two questions. First, is the creed a Deuteronomic composition or can a pre-Deuteronomic form be detected? In this connection only those expressions or phrases which are attested in Deuteronomy with sufficient frequency to be meaningful and either exclusively in or with significant preponderance over aganst attestations outside Deuteronomy will be accepted as Deuteronomic. Secondly, should a pre-Deuteronomic form be reconstructed, then what is the age of this form? In what period of Israel's history is it likely to have been composed? The study will then conclude with some implications of the results for pentateuchal studies.

The Original Form of the Creed[13]

The expression "a perishing/wandering[14] Aramean was my father" is unique in the OT and hence cannot be considered Deuteronomic. The remainder of *v.* 5 is generally formulated, with two exceptions.

---

[11] R.P. Merendino, *Das deuteronomische Gesetz* (Bonn, 1969), pp. 346–71; G. Waßermann, "Das kleine geschichtliche Credo (Deut. 26, 5ff.) und seine deuteronomische Übermalung", *Theologische Versuche* II (1970), pp. 27–46; N. Lohfink, "Zum kleinen geschichtlichen Credo' Dtn 26,5–9", *ThPh* 46 (1971), pp. 19–39.

[12] The reader is referred to the article of Wallis (n. 3).

[13] In the following familiarity with the Hebrew text is assumed and hence transliteration only occasionally given. The translation is based in large part on the *RSV*.

[14] The exact connotation of *ꜣbd* in this passge is disputed, but need not be decided here. On the issue see M.A. Beek, "Das Problem des aramäischen Stammvaters (Deut. XXVI 5)", *OTS* 8 (1950), pp. 193–212, esp. pp. 199–201; H. Seebass, *Der Erzvater Israel* (*BZAW* 98; Berlin, 1966), p. 4; Waßermann (n. 11), p. 30.

The phrase "few in number" occurs elsewhere only in Dt. xxviii 62, so that the infrequency of the phrase prohibits considering it Deuteronomic. Similarly, the combination *gôy gādôl ᶜāṣûm wārāb*, "a great, mighty and populous nation", is found only here. "Great nation" occurs also in Gen. xii 2, xxi 18, xlvi 3; also in Ex. xxxii 10 and Dt. iv 6–8 (3 times; cf. also *ᶜam gādôl* "great people" in Dt. i 28, ii 10, 21, ix 2). "Mighty nation" is attested in Dt. ix 14; Isa. lx 22; Joel i 6; Mic. iv 3, 7; Zech. viii 22; and the combination "a great and mighty nation" in Gen. xviii 18; Num. xiv 12 (both J). "Populous nations" is a relatively frequent phrase concentrated in texts of the outgoing pre-exilic era and later (only possible earlier occurrences in Mic. iv 2, 11), whereas the singular is attested only in the combined (comparative) formulation "a mighty and populous nation" in Dt. ix 14 (formulations with *ᶜam* are by comparison more evenly distributed), to which may be compared "a populous and mighty people" in Joel ii 2. The poetic structure of the creed (see below) indicates that the line is overloaded, and, given the distributions enumerated above, it would seem that the alliterative *gôy gādôl* "great nation" is original, the adjectives "mighty and populous" being secondary additions (cf. Merendino [n. 11], p. 353).

The hiphil of *rᶜᶜ* is common, and in application to the "harsh treatment" in Egypt it occurs in Ex. v 23 (J); Num. xx 15 (JE), and the piel of *ᶜnh* for the affliction in Egypt is found elsewhere only in Ex. i 11–12; Gen. xv 13. Neither usage is Deuteronomic.[15] Likewise "hard bondage" is not attested elsewhere in Deuteronomy. It is found twice in P (Ex. i 14, vi 9), but this hardly justifies branding *v.* 6b secondary.[16]

There is nothing uniquely Deuteronomic about "crying to Yahweh", which occurs only here in Deuteronomy (cf. Ex. viii 8, xiv 10, 15, xv 25, xvii 4, xxii 22, 26; Num. xii 13, xx 16; Josh. xxiv 7). The phrase "the God of our fathers" occurs elsewhere only in Ezra vii 27; 1 Chr. xii 18; 2 Chr. xx 6, but is paralleled by the frequent designation "the God of your/their fathers", a favorite of Deuteronomy (i 11, 21, iv 1, vi 3, xii 1, xxvii 3, xxix 24) but also attested in Exodus (iii 13, 15, 16, iv

---

[15] Waßermann (n. 11), p. 32, considers "and they oppressed us" to be "suspicious" because it is explanatory. But a degree of redundancy in a piece of poetry is hardly suspicious.

[16] *Contra* Rost (n. 7), p. 12; Waßermann, (n. 11), p. 32; and with Lohfink (n. 11), p. 29.

5),[17] so that Lohfink is certainly correct when he states that the formula is "neither exclusively nor originally Deuteronomic".[18] The remainder of *v.* 7 evidences no characteristically Deuteronomic language. However, the trilogy of nouns for the oppression in Egypt again overloads the line, so that it may reasonably be suspected that the latter two were added by the same hand detected in *v.* 5b.[19]

In *v.* 8 the general statement "and Yahweh brought us out of Egypt" is followed by a series of adverbial prepositional phrases. "With a strong hand" is found in the pentateuchal sources (Ex. iii 19, vi 1; Num. xx 20), whereas "outstretched arm" is not attested prior to Deuteronomy, which is then of course true for the combination of the two phrases, which is found four other times in Deuteronomy (iv 34, v 15, vii 19, xi 2; cf. ix 26, 29). "Great terror(s)" in connection with the Exodus is attested elsewhere only in Dt. iv 34, xxxiv 12; Jer. xxxii 21; and the "signs and wonders" in Dt. iv 34, vi 22, vii 19, xxix 2, xxxiv 11; although both "signs" (Ex. iv, viii 19, x 1–2) and "wonders" (Ex. iv 21) are known to other sources. The evidence thus indicates that all the prepositional phrases of *v.* 8aβb are Deuteronomic additions. There is general agreement on this point.

The expression "this place" is not only common in Deuteronomy but also throughout the OT, and so is not specifally Deuteronomic. Also, Yahweh's giving the land cannot be considered Deuteronomic since the phrase is frequent in the patriarchal narratives, albeit as a promise awaiting fulfillment (cf. also Josh. xxiv 13). Similarly, the formula "a land flowing with milk and honey" is a favorite in Deuteronomy (vi 3, xi 9, xxvi 15, xxvii 3; cf. xxxi 20), but also occurs in Ex. iii 8, 17, xii 5 (Dtr supplement?), xxxiii 3; Num. xiii 27, xvi 13–14. The appositional phrase, therefore, need not be a Deuteronomic addition.[20]

The results of the foregoing analysis indicate the shape of the

---

[17] Some scholars consider Ex. iii to be late because it ostensibly presupposes the genre of the prophetic call (e.g. H.H. Schmid, *Der sogenannte Jahwist* [Zürich, 1976], pp. 19–43), but on this see the more differentiating remarks of W.H. Schmidt, *Exodus* (Neukirchen, 1977), pp. 123–9, and on the expression "the God of your/their fathers" pp. 130–1. Cf. also "the God of your father" Gen. xxvi 24, xxviii 13, xxxi 42, 53, xxxii 10, xliii 23, xlvi 1, 3, 1 17; Ex. iii 6, xv 2, xviii 4.

[18] (N. 11), p. 29. The choice of the first person plural suffix in Dt. xxvi 7 is necessitated by the context.

[19] Similarly, Waßermann (n. 11), p. 32, citing Ex. iii 7.

[20] *Contra* Merendino (n. 11), p. 355, offering no reasons. Waßermann (n. 11), p. 34, considers it "suspicious" for familiar reasons (see n. 15), but still reckons it to the *Grundform*, albeit in parentheses. For Lohfink (n. 11), p. 30, it is a Deuteronomic formula already found in the old pentateuchal sources.

pre-Deuteronomic short historical creed to be as follows:

5   A perishing/wandering Aramean was my father,
    and he went down to Egypt.
And he sojourned there with a few people;
    and he became there a great nation.
6   And the Egyptians treated us harshly and afflicted us,
    and laid upon us hard bondage.
7   And we cried to Yahweh,
    the God of our fathers.
And Yahweh heard our voice,
    and saw our affliction.
8   And Yahweh brought us out of Egypt,
9   and he brought us to this place.
And he gave us this land,
    a land flowing with milk and honey.
10 And now, behold:
    I bring the first fruits of the ground
    which you have given me, Yahweh.

The resulting text displays good *parallelismus membrorum*. Only *v.* 10 presents modest difficulties. But if the first two words (of the Hebrew) are bracketed out as anacrusis, a feature not inappropriate at such a weighty juncture, then this verse can also be taken as poetic.

As already mentioned, Rost considered the original confession to be limited to the statement "a perishing Aramean was my father, and now behold, I bring the first fruits of the ground which you, Yahweh, have given me". His argument is twofold. First, his investigation of the language of the creed led him to the conclusion that *vv.* 6–9 are a unified Deuteronomistic addition whose closest parallels are in the framework speeches of Deuteronomy and in Baruch's biography of Jeremiah and which is therefore to be dated to this period (Rost [n. 7], pp. 12–14). But as shown above, the Deuteronom(ist)ic component of these verses is restricted. Secondly, he argues that the first person singular suffix in *v.* 5 ("my father") corresponds to the first person singular in *v.* 10, whereas *vv.* 6–9 are composed in the first person plural. However, the juxtaposition of *v.* 5 and *v.* 10a is unsatisfactory because of the mention of Jacob's descent into Egypt and growth to a great nation there. The reference to these events requires a mediatory text explaining how the bringer of the first fruits came into possession of the land when his ancestors were previously in Egypt. Such a text is of course present in *vv.* 6–9, and so the corresponding portion of *v.* 5b must be taken with these verses (Rost, pp. 14–19). It should be pointed out, however, that the problem arises only after *vv.* 6–9 are removed. If these verses (in their pre-Deuteronomic form) are not removed, and in fact there is no reason to remove them,[21] then a well-constructed and well-conceived text remains. When Lohfink nevertheless attempts to explain why a "Deuteronomic" addition in *vv.* 5b–9 displays so little Deuteronomic language ([n. 11], pp. 30–3), it is because he has accepted Rost's result without adequately questioning the supporting argumentation. And this turns out to be flawed. There are hence no grounds for doubting the unity of the pre-Deuteronomic creed in Dt. xxvi 5b–10a.

We turn now to the question of the *Sitz im Leben* of the creed. The creed itself indicates that it was recited upon presentation of the first fruits (*v.* 10a), and this is also the testimony of its present context. The form of the ritual genre has been shown to be a series of short sentences connected with *waw*-perfect verbal forms.[22] Such verbal forms are found in the framework of the creed, but the sentences are hardly short. However, the relative clauses of *vv.* 2–3 contain stock Deuteronomic phraseology such as "the land which Yahweh your God gives you" (*vv.* 1, 2) and "(the place) which Yahweh your God will choose to make his name dwell there" (*v.* 2) or presuppose the fictional setting of the book, as in "and when you come into the land" (*v.* 1) and "(the priest) who will be in those days" (*v.* 3). The remainder of *vv.* 1–4, however, displays no specifically Deuteronomic language. A doublet to *v.* 4b has been seen in *v.* 10bα, leading some to argue that *v.* 10b is older because the bringer himself lays down the basket rather than the priest.[23] However, *vv.* 10bβ–11 bring an interpretative summation of the foregoing, and there is no reason to dissociate *v.* 10bα from them. Although it is actually the priest who physically places the basket before the altar of Yahweh, it can also be said of the cultic participant who has the priest perform the act for him that he

---

[21] The shift to the first person plural in *v.* 6 is understandable since the speaker identifies himself with the people Israel after recounting its birth. The return to the first person singular in *v.* 10a also presents no problems since it is an individual who presents the first fruits. The reason why the recitation begins with a first person singular (suffix) is not immediately apparent, but neiter can a compelling argument be given as to why this cannot be so. The reason may lie, however, in the fact that the speaker has already made a declaration in the first person singular (*v.* 3, see below) and so continues in this person when he resumes his speech. The argument of Lohfink (n. 11), p. 23, that the singular "father" (*v.* 5) clashes with the plural "(God of our) fathers" (*v.* 7) carries no weight since it was only one father, Jacob, who descended into Egypt and grew to become Israel.

[22] See R. Rendtorff, *Die Gesetze in der Priesterschrift* (Göttingen, ²1963), and K. Koch, *Die Priesterschrift von Exodus 25 bis Leviticus 16* (Göttingen, 1959).

[23] So e.g. A. Bertholet, *Deuteronomium* (Freiburg i.B., Leipzig and Tübingen, 1899), p. 80; C. Steuernagel, *Das Deuteronomium* (Göttingen, 1923), p. 144.

placed the basket before Yahweh. Such a summation is not part of the ritual genre, and so the same hand that made the additions in *vv.* 1–4 is probably also responsible for *vv.* 10*b*–11. The pre-Deuteronomic introduction to the creed may hence be reconstructed as follows:

> 2 You shall take from the first fruits of the ground.
> You shall put (them) in a basket.
> You shall go to the sanctuary.
> 3 You shall come to the priest.
> You shall say to him,
> > "I declare today to Yahweh your God
> > that I have come into the land."
> 4 The priest shall take the basket from your hand.
> He shall place it before the altar of Yahweh your God.
> You shall respond and say before Yahweh your God, ...

Underlying the current form of Dt. xxvi 1–11 there is thus a pre-Deuteronomic regulation concerning the presentation of the first fruits which includes the recitation of the creed on this occasion.

The Age of the Creed

This being the case, the question arises as to the approximate period in which the creed originated. The obvious *terminus post quem* is Israel's presence in the land presupposed by the creed. On the other end, the creed is currently embedded in a portion of Deuteronomy commonly considered to have been part of Proto-Deuteronomy. Proto-Deuteronomy is to be dated some time around 700 B.C., and this provides an initial *terminus ante quem* for the pre-Deuteronomic form identified above.

The creed itself offers little that can be used for dating the creed. Only the designation of the ancestor as a "perishing/wandering Aramean" can be evaluated in this connection, and to do this Israel's relations with the Arameans must be examined.[24]

Relations between the Israelites and the Arameans in the monarchic period were anything but peaceful. David was confronted with the expansive policy of Hadadezer, king of Aram-Zobah, which naturally clashed with his own efforts to expand his empire. In the decisive battle David was able to defeat the Aramean coalition and incorporate

---

[24] For what follows see conveniently B. Mazar, "The Aramean Empire and its Relations with Israel", BA 25 (1962), pp. 98–120; and more extensively M.F. Unger, *Israel and the Arameans of Damascus* (London, 1957).

its territory into his kingdom (2 Sam. viii 3–8, x 1–19). However, a certain Rezon, son of Eliada, formerly of Hadadezer's army, assumed command of a "marauding band" operating out of Damascus and no doubt stirring up trouble in this part of the realm. During Solomon's reign he was proclaimed king in Damascus, becoming Solomon's adversary because "he abhorred Israel" (1 Kings xi 23–5).

Following the breakdown of the Davidic-Solomonic empire, this Aramean state no doubt expanded its influence, for we find Ben-Hadad I exploiting hostilities between Israel and Judah, apparently as part of a policy of divide and conquer (1 Kings xv 16–20). By the time of Ahab the "wrangling between Israel and Aram-Damascus (had) turned into a protracted war" (Mazar [n. 24], p. 106), which included an unsuccessful siege of Samaria and an Israelite victory a year later (1 Kings xx). Ahab's leniency toward his defeated foe may have been prompted by his perception of the coming Assyrian threat (Mazar, p. 114). In any event, Israel and Damascus joined forces (along with others) for the battle of Qarqar (853 B.C.). The coalition was successful, staving off for the time being further Assyrian advances, but the alliance between Samaria and Damascus proved to be a shotgun wedding, and the marriage lasted at best three years. At this time Jehoshaphat, king of Judah, induced Ahab to assist him in wresting Ramoth-gilead from Aramean control. The expedition was a failure that cost Ahab his life (1 Kings xxii 1–4, 29–40), and the city remained contested throughout the reign of his son Jehoram (2 Kings ix 14–15).

Hazael's policy towards his southern neighbors was no less aggressive than that of his predecessor. He took Gilead and Bashan in Transjordan (2 Kings x 32–3), and on another occasion exacted tribute from Jerusalem (2 Kings xii 17–18). Hazael was succeeded by his son Ben-Hadad, concerning whom 2 Kings xiii 25 reports that "three times Joash defeated him and recovered the cities of Israel". Jeroboam II again made Damascus a dependency of Israel (2 Kings xiv 28), but this was probably so only during his reign (so Unger [n. 24], p. 95). In any case Rezin, king of Damascus, appears as a fully equal partner of Pekah, king of Israel, in the Syro-Ephraimite war, which issued in the end of the Aramean kingdom of Damascus and its incorporation into the Assyrian empire (2 Kings xvi 5–9).

This brief scan of the relations between Israel and the Arameans in the monarchic period shows that they were characterized by belligerence and rivalry throughout the entire period. At no time in this period does it appear likely that the Israelites would have been inclined to emphasize their Aramean ancestry. On the contrary, one would expect this fact to be discreetly ignored rather than given prominence at the beginning of a creed. The monarchic period may therefore reasonably be excluded as the age of the creed's origin.

When one turns to the pre-monarchic era, the picture changes dramatically. The only mention of animosity with the Arameans is in Judg. iii 7–11. Here it is stated that Cushan-rishathaim, king of Aram-naharaim, oppressed Israel for eight years until Yahweh raised up Othniel to deliver Israel. Unfortunately, the historical evaluation of this text is extremely difficult, including the possibility that Cushan was an Edomite.[25] Yet even if the text is taken at face value, the encounter remains an isolated episode. In the time of Jephthah the Israelites served the Baals and Ashtaroth of Aram (and others, Judg. x 6), and then we do not hear of the Arameans again until the time of David, except perhaps to say that the Danites had no dealings with them when they migrated to the north.[26] Israelite relations with the Arameans, such as existed, were thus for the most part peaceful at this time, and the Israelites would have had no cause to suppress their Aramean heritage. The most probable date for the pre-Deuteronomic form of the creed is therefore the pre-monarchic period.[27]

These results indicate that in this period Israelite tradition identified or at least closely associated the ancestors of Israel with the Arameans. Such a close relationship is of course reflected in the genealogies of Genesis in which Aram appears (Gen. x 22–3, xxii 20–4; cf. also xxv 20) and especially in Jacob's dealings with Laban the Aramean (Gen. xxviii 5, xxxi 20, 24). Outside the OT, the Arameans first appear on the stage of world history with certainty as the Aḥlamu-Arameans against whom Tiglath-pileser I (1115–1077) waged so many campaigns.[28] Aḥlamu are attested as far back as the 18th century B.C.,[29] but unfortunately the exact nature of the relationship between the Aḥlamu and the Aḥlamu-Arameans is not clear. We are hence left with two basic options: either Israel's ancestors are to be associated with Aramean migrations in the second

---

[25] So e.g. H.W. Hertzberg, *Die Bücher Josua, Richter, Ruth* (Göttingen, 1953), pp. 163–4; J. Gray, *Joshua, Judges and Ruth* (London and Edinburgh, 1967), pp. 213–15.

[26] A portion of the LXX textual transmission (cf. G.F. Moore, *Judges* [Edinburgh, 1895], p. 392) reads at Judg. xviii 7 μετὰ Συρίας prompting some to emend ᵓādām to ᵓārām here and in v. 28; cf. e.g. K. Budde, *Das Buch der Richter* (Tübingen, 1897), p. 119; Hertzberg (n. 25), p. 236, n. 1; R.G. Boling, *Judges* (Garden City, New York, 1975), p. 263; J.A. Soggin, *Judges* (London and Philadelphia, 1981), p. 273.

[27] Rost (n. 7), p. 19, also dates his old formula to the period of the judges, so that our disagreement is confined to the scope of the old formula.

[28] Cf. H.W.F. Saggs, *The Might That Was Assyria* (London, 1984), pp. 61–6.

[29] R. de Vaux, *Histoire ancienne d'Israël* (Paris, 1971), p. 195 = *The Early History of Israel* (London and Philadelphia, 1978), p. 202.

half of the second millennium B.C.[30] or the association with the
Arameans may be anachronistic and have been induced by the
location of patriarchal origins in a region where the Arameans later
settled and rose to prominence.[31] The issue is a complex one and goes
beyond the scope of the current study.[32] For present purposes it
suffices to place the statement within a broader historical context and
point out possible ramifications.

Implications for Pentateuchal Studies

The investigation has confirmed the (undemonstrated) contention
of von Rad that "this prayer (= Dt. xxvi 5b–9) is very much older,
both in form and content, than the literary context into which it has
since been inserted".[33] But this study has neither proved nor
disproved his hypothesis of hexateuchal origins (nor was it intended
to do so). It is still conceivable that such condensed presentations of
Israel's early history are summaries abstracted from more extensive
sources. These summaries cannot, however, be restricted to the late
pre-exilic period, but are attested as early as the pre-monarchic era.
On the summary hypothesis this in turn would mean that more
extensive sources must also have been present at this time. In either
case the conclusion appears unavoidable that an overarching and
integrating conception of her early history was already present in
Israel prior to the monarchy.[34]

---

[30] So S. Herrmann, *Geschichte Israels in alttestamentlicher Zeit* (Munich, ²1980), pp.
63–81 = *A History of Israel in Old Testament Times* (London, ²1981), pp. 41–55.
[31] So J. Bright, *A History of Israel* (Philadelphia and London, ²1972), pp. 89–90.
[32] See de Vaux (n. 29), pp. 194–201; E. tr., pp. 200–9, for discussion and literature.
[33] "Form-Critical Problem" (n. 1), p. 4 = "Formgeschichtliches Problem", pp.
3–4. The prayer actually includes *v.* 10a as well.
[34] After the manuscript had gone to the printer, the article of
S. Kreuzer, "Identität in den Anfängen. Die alttestamentlichen Bekenntnisse zur
Frühgeschichte Israels", in H.H. Schmid (ed.), *Mythos und Rationalität* (Gütersloh,
1988), pp. 134–48, came to my attention. He apparently follows Rost's thesis
regarding an old confession only in *vv.* 5, 10. He holds the intervening text to be
"significantly younger", only to speak in the next paragraph of "an older Exodus
confession" based on Num. xx (cf. C. Carmichael, "A new view of the origin of the
Deuteronomic Credo", *VT* 19 [1969], pp. 273–89). The combination of the two
confessions is Deuteronomic (p. 142). However, as indicated above, there is no reason
to divide the pre-Deuteronomic creed, and in my opinion a dependence on Num. xx
is not compelling since there are many differences. Also, the possibility that
dependence, if any, is in the other direction is not considered.

INDEXES

AUTHORS CITED

Abel, F.M.   48–50, 70, 173
Aberbach, M.   150, 156
Abou Assaf, A.   23
Abrahams, I.   27
Ackroyd, P.R.   6
Adler, E.N.   49
Aharoni, Y.   57, 60, 162, 170
Albertz, R.   112
Albright, W.F.   51, 70, 188, 197
Alexander, T.D.   131–48
Allen, L.C.   114
Alt, A.   49, 67–8, 71
Anati, E.   167–72, 174
Andersen, F.I.   137, 142–3, 210, 219
Anderson, A.A.   114
Anderson, B.W.   18, 109, 149
Andreasen, M.–E.A.   73
Antin, P.   71
Astruc, J.   142
Avigad, N.   228

Baentsch, B.   173
Bailey, C.   170
Baker, J.A.   11
Baltzer, K.   232
Barnabé (Meistermann — see p. 71),
   Le Père   46, 50, 68, 71
Barr, J.   23
Barth, K.   22, 24
Bartlett, J.R.   173
Barton, J.   128
Baumgartner, W.   5–6
Beek, M.A.   234
Begg, C.T.   226
Benzinger, I.   53
Bertholet, A.   238
Beyerlin, W.   232
Bietak, M.   165, 167
Bird, P.   14
Blacker, C.E.   35
Blum, E.   106, 111
Bodenheimer, F.S.   192, 201
Boling, R.G.   241
Boomershine, T.E.   13
Bordreuil, P.   23
Botterweck, G.J.   5, 105, 213
Brandenstein, W.   38, 40

Bratsiotis, N.P.   5
Braun, R.L.   212
Brenner, A.   13
Briggs, C.A. and E.G.   56
Bright, J.   242
Brugsch, H.   161–2
Bryant, D.T.   21, 28
Budd, P.J.   117
Budde, K.   6, 25, 29, 241
Burns, D.E.   13
Buttrick, D.G.   110

Carmichael, C.M.   242
Cassuto, U.   1–4, 27, 31, 36, 38, 140,
   203
Cazelles, H.   162, 165–6
Childs, B.S.   15, 25, 31, 151, 233
Clédat, J.   162–3
Clines, D.J.A.   12–13, 22, 30
Coats, G.W.   12, 131, 134, 145, 147
Conrad, E.W.   32
Cook, M.   200
Crenshaw, J.L.   113
Cross, F.M.   18, 125, 150–1
Culley, R.C.   13, 132
Cuntz, O.   162

Dahood, M.J.   117, 210
Dalman, G.   190, 202
Daniels, D.R.   231–42
Davidson, R.   105
Davies, G.I.   45, 73, 161–75
Davies, P.R.   2
Davies, T.W.   56
Davis, S.   188
Day, J.   73
Delitzsch, Franz   1–4, 115
Dhorme, E.P.   6, 38
Dillmann, A.   19, 26, 29, 36, 131, 135,
   142, 146, 173, 203
Dion, P.–E.   13, 229
Doeller, J.   183
Donner, H.   162, 165
Doré, J.   76–7, 90, 102
Dorst, J.   19
Dothan, M.   162, 169
Dougherty, R.P.   96

Douglas, Mary   177–82, 186, 188, 192,
   194–6, 198–9
Dozy, R.   201
Driver, S.R.   2–4, 26, 36, 114, 134,
   136, 141–2, 208, 210, 212, 214, 228
Dunn. J.D.G.   103

Edwards, J.W.   22
Ehrlich, A.B.   109
Eichhorn, J.G.   142
Eichrodt, W.   11, 110
Eissfeldt, O.   150, 161–2, 203–4, 208
Elias, N.   178
Elliger, K.   198
Emerton, J.A.   18, 45–71, 73–102
Engel, H.   162
Erbt, W.   53, 61, 71
Evans, C.D.   73
Ewald, G.H.A.   173

Feliks, J.   190, 204
Finkelstein, I.   161, 163
Firmage, E.B.   177–208
Fishbane, M.   128, 225
Fisher, L.R.   210
Fitzmyer, J.A.   49, 71
Fohrer, G.   11, 134, 141, 162
Franceschini, A.   50
Frazer, J.G.   187
Freedman, D.N.   219
Frerichs, E.S.   106
Fueck, J.   162

Gadd, C.J.   42
Galbiati, E.   77, 89, 102
Gammie, J.G.   49, 52–8, 61, 63–5, 71
Gane, R.   177
Gaster, M.   48–9
Gaster, T.H.   48
Gaston, L.   106–7, 110
Gelston, A.   130
Gerstenblith, P.   171
Geus, C.H.J. de 170
Gispen, W.H.   1, 2
Glueck, N.   167, 173, 175
Görg, M.   228
Goodman, M.   48
Gordon, C.H.   210
Gotteri, N.   9
Graf, K.H.   131
Grant, A.M.   2
Grave, M.–C. de   228
Gray, J.   241
Greenberg, M.   227
Gross, H.   22
Gunkel, H.   1–4, 19, 22, 25, 94,
   114–15, 117, 121, 131, 134–6, 138, 141
Gunn, D.M.   13

Hahn, F.   103, 115
Hahn, J.   151
Hallo, W.W.   73
Hanson, P.D.   150
Haran, M.   172, 186
Harris, M.   192, 194
Hass, G.   188
Hauser, A.J.   13
Heidland, H.W.   109
Heinisch, P.   36
Heltzer, M.   199
Hendel, R.   31
Hengel, M.   117
Herrmann, S.   242
Hertzberg, H.W.   6, 46, 53, 71, 241
Herzfeld, E.E.   37
Hess, R.   1–15
Hilberg, I.   71
Hölscher, G.   40
Hoffner H.A.   38
Holl, K.   71
Holladay, C.R.   48
Holzinger, H.   135, 173
Horowitz, W.   35–43
Horton, F.L.   56, 71
Huffmon, H.B.   232
Humbert, P.   22

Jacob, B.   106, 109
Jacobs, L.   211
Janzen, J.G.   211
Jenks, A.   151, 158
Jepsen, A.   105, 145
Jeremias, A.   53–4, 71
Jirku, A.   6
Jobling, D.   3, 13
Johnson, M.D.   4
Jónsson, G.A.   22

Kaiser, O.   104
Kempson, R.M.   9
Kennett, R.H.   150
Kenyon, Kathleen M.   171
Kikawada, I.M.   12–13
Kilmer, A.D.   32
Kirkland, J.R.   50, 52–5, 57–60,
   63, 65–8, 71
Kirkpatrick, Patricia G.   86
Kittel, G.   109
Klein, R.W.   130
Klopfenstein, M.A.   162
Klostermann, A.   6
Knudtzon, J.A.   6, 67
Koch, K.   238
Kockert, M.   106
Koehler, L.   5–6, 22, 192
König, E.   137, 141–2
Koenig, J.   174

Kornfeld, W. 199
Kraeling, E.G. 25, 31, 227
Kraus, H.-J. 114, 117
Kraus, S. 190
Kreuzer, S. 242
Kuenen, A. 131

Labuschagne, C.J. 138
Lagarde, P. de 49
Lagercrantz, S. 200
Lagrage, M.J. 173
Lambert, W.G. 35, 42
Landersdorfer, S. 49, 53–4, 61–3, 66, 71
Landsberger, B. 200
Lane, E.W. 200
Langdon, S. 42
Lehming, S. 155
Leimbach, K.A. 6
Levenson, J.D. 106, 111, 211
Levine, B.A. 106
Lewysohn, L. 202
Lichtenstein, M. 145
Lie, A.G. 39
Lods, A. 59
Löw, I. 201
Loewe, M.A.N. 35
Loewenstamm, S.E. 155
Lohfink, N. 104, 110, 119, 213–14, 218–19, 234–6, 238
Lussier, E. 2
Lyon, D. 39
Lyons, J. 7–8

McBride, S.D. 211, 214
McCarter, P.K. 6, 158
McCurley, F.R. 14
Macdonald, J. 48–9
McEvenue, S.E. 134, 136, 138
Mackay, C. 52–6, 58–60, 71
Marks, J.H. 17
Martin, J. 25
Martin, J.D. 2
Mayes, A.D.H. 211–12, 218, 222
Mazar, A. 188
Mazar, B. 239–40
Meek, T.J. 150
Meistermann — see Barnabé (Meistermann), Le Père
Mendenhall, G.E. 232, 236
Merendino, R.P. 221, 234
Meshel, Z. 163
Mettinger, T.N.D. 22
Meyers, Carol L. 15
Milgrom, J. 177, 182, 184, 188, 192, 195
Milik, J.T. 52
Millar, F. 48
Millard, A.R. 23, 42, 148

Miller, J.M. 12, 21
Miller, P.D. 211
Minette de Tillesse, G. 225
Moberly, R.W.L. 103–30, 209–15
Möhlenbrink, K. 149, 151, 158
Moore, G.F. 241
Moran, W.L. 208
Morin, G. 71
Mras, K. 71
Muffs, Y. 82
Mussner, F. 22

Naidoff, B.D. 2
Neff, R.W. 138–9
Neiman, D. 38
Neusner, J. 106
Newing, E.G. 32
Nielsen, E. 64–6, 71
Niv, D. 164
Norin, S. 162
North, F.S. 150
Noth, M. 17–18, 33, 49, 131, 149, 157, 162, 165, 197–8, 231
Nyberg, H.S. 53, 65, 71, 83

O'Callaghan, R.T. 49
Ockinga, B. 23
O'Connor, M. 15
Oded, B. 38
Oeming, M. 106–7, 110
Olrik, A. 146
Oren, E. 163–7

Parker, J.F. 13
Parpola, S. 39
Patte, D. 13
Paul, S.M. 177
Perdue, L.G. 155
Porter, S. 7, 9
Poulsson, N. 25
Pritchard, J.B. 70
Procksch, O. 138, 141

Quinn, A. 12–13

Rad, G.von 1–2, 10, 17, 19, 21, 25, 31, 104, 108, 110–14, 121–3, 131, 203, 218, 231–4, 242
Rainey, A.F. 6
Redford, D.B. 131, 145
Reimer, D.J. 217–29
Rendtorff, R. 26, 112, 135, 137, 238
Richter, W. 233
Ringgren, H. 5, 11, 105, 213
Robinson, E. 51, 53, 71
Robinson, H.W. 59
Robinson, R.B. 5
Rosenzweig, F. 17

Rost, L. 232–5, 237–8, 241–2
Rothenberg, B. 162–3, 167, 170, 175
Rowley, H.H. 97
Rudolph, W. 173, 212
Ruppert, L. 138

Safren, J.D. 153
Saggs, H.W.F. 241
Salonen, B. 190, 200
Sanders, E.P. 109
Sawyer, J.F.A. 23–4
Sayce, A.H. 38
Schatz, W. 60, 71, 75, 87, 90–2, 97, 102
Scheftelowitz, J. 200
Schlatter, A. 53
Schley, D.G. 228
Schmid, H.H. 104, 110, 236, 242
Schmidt, W.H. 23, 236
Schmidtke, F. 38
Schottroff, W. 27
Schürer, E. 48
Scullion, J.J. 1, 21
Searle, J.R. 8
Seebass, H. 234
Segal, M.H. 145
Seitz, G. 218
Séligsohn, M. 49
Sellin, E. 84
Seybold, K. 105
Shea, W.H. 167
Silbermann, A.M. 209
Simons, J. 49, 163, 173
Skinner, J. 1, 3–4, 20-1, 25, 29, 38, 65, 71, 114, 131, 134, 136, 138, 141–2, 144, 146
Skweres, D.E. 218–20, 224
Smith, H.P. 6
Smith, R.H. 52, 54, 57, 71
Smolar, L. 150, 156
Soggin, J.A. 3, 241
Speiser, E.A. 2–3, 5, 19, 36, 109, 131, 133–4, 141–2
Stamm, J.J. 12
Stanley, A.P. 53–4, 71
Steck, O.H. 13, 27
Steuernagel, C. 238
Stevenson, W.B. 19
Stolz, F. 6
Strawson, P.F. 8
Streck, M. 41
Strus, A. 25
Sturdy, J.V.M. 23

Tal, A. 49
Tengström, S. 25

Trible, Phyllis 13
Thomas, D.W. 71
Thompson, T.L. 167
Tristram, H.B. 202
Tyrwhitt Drake, C.F. 51
Tsumura, D.T. 7

Ullmann, S. 9

Van Seters, J. 31, 77–8, 84–9, 91–102, 110, 127, 132, 135–9, 141–2, 145–7, 233
Vaux, R. de 74–5, 91–2, 98–9, 102, 173, 241–2
Vawter, B. 105, 134
Velde, C.W.M. van de 51, 71
Vermes, G. 48
Vermeylen, J. 152
Vriezen, Th. C. 11

Wächter, L. 68–9, 71
Wallace, H.N. 17–33
Wallis, G. 232
Walsh, J.T. 13
Warner, S.M. 146
Waßermann, G. 234–6
Weber, R. 50
Wehr, H. 201
Weinfeld, M. 177, 218, 221
Weiser, A. 117, 127, 232
Weiss, B. 195
Welch, J.W. 195
Wellhausen, J. 6, 131, 138, 149, 219
Wenham, G.J. 27, 31, 78, 80–4, 102, 106, 114, 147–8
Westermann, C. 1–5, 11, 21–2, 24–5, 29–31, 36, 38–9, 74, 76, 79, 87, 90–1, 97, 102, 108, 110, 112, 115, 131, 134, 136, 141–2, 144, 147–8
Wevers, J.W. 5, 227
Weyer, H. 162–3, 167
White, H.C. 13
White, J.B. 73
White, Marsha 149–59
Whybray, R.N. 131, 146
Wijngaards, J.N.M. 232
Wildberger, H. 22
Wilkinson, J.D. 50
Williamson, H.G.M. 45, 73, 212
Wilson, R.R. 4
Wilson, W. 200
Winckler, H. 6, 39, 53–4, 61, 71
Wiseman, D.J. 148
Wit, C. de 163
Wolff, H.W. 11, 27, 103
Wright, D. 177, 206

Wright, G.E.   66, 71, 156

Zakowitz, Y.   153
Ziegler, J. 50

Zimmerli, W.   75, 91, 102, 131, 134, 141, 227
Zlotowitz, M.   106

REFERENCES

Biblical

Genesis

i	1, 4, 9–12, 14–15
i–v	1–15
i 1–ii 3	20–2, 24, 33
i 1–ii 4	10, 12, 18
i 5, 8, 10	20
i 20, 21	180
i 25	29
i 26	2, 19–20, 22, 29
i 26–7	4, 11–12, 33
i 26–8	14, 19–20, 23
i 26–ii 15	5
i 27	1–2, 4, 19–20
i 27–8	19
i 29	196, 204
i 30	196
ii	1–3, 5, 9–11, 14–15
ii–iii	2, 11
ii–iv	7, 13, 22
ii–ix	2
ii ff.	11
ii 4–20	15
ii 4–25	10–11
ii 4–iii 24	12–13
ii 4–iv 26	18, 21–4, 33
ii 5	2
ii 5 ff.	3
ii 7, 8	1–2
ii 15	1–3
ii 16, 18–19	1–2, 5
ii 20	1–3, 5, 15, 29
ii 21	1–2
ii 21–4	14
ii 21 ff.	2
ii 22	1
ii 23	1, 5
ii 25	1
iii	2, 4–5, 11, 14–15, 31–2
iii 3	206
iii 5	23
iii 6	31
iii 8	1
iii 9	1–2
iii 12	1, 5
iii 16–19	21, 24, 27, 29, 33
iii 17	3, 5, 26
iii 17–19	26
iii 20	1, 5, 20
iii 21	3, 5
iii 22	1–2, 31
iii 22–4	23
iii 24	1–2
iv	2, 4–5, 10, 12, 20, 28–9
iv 1	1–2, 4–5, 20
iv 1–24	21–2
iv 1–v 2	4
iv 2	20
iv 4	196
iv 17	20
iv 17–24	20–1, 26
iv 17–26	21, 24
iv 23–4	28
iv 25	2, 4–5, 9
iv 25–6	20–1
iv 26	4, 21–3, 140
v	4, 9–12, 19–22, 29, 33
v 1	2, 4–5, 12, 19–20, 24, 33
v 1–2	13, 19–21, 24
v 1–3	10, 14, 19, 22–4, 30
v 1–8	21
v 1–28	19
v 1–32	18–19, 24–5, 28–30, 32
v 1–vi 8	18, 21, 33
v 2	4–5, 19–20, 22
v 2–3	20
v 3	5, 11, 19–22
v 3–5	2, 12, 20
v 3–28	21, 24
v 4	5
v 4–5	20
v 5	5
v 18–20	49
v 28	24
v 29	19, 24–9, 33
v 30–2	19, 21, 24
v 32	21, 30
vi 1	29–32
vi 1–2	31
vi 1–4	19, 29–32
vi 1–8	19, 29–30
vi 2	30
vi 3	31–2
vi 5	28–31
vi 5–8	19, 24, 28–30, 32–3
vi 5–13	30
vi 6	28–9
vi 7	29–30, 33
vi 9	30, 124
vi 9–12	32
vi 9–13	30
vi 9-ix 29	18, 25, 30
vi 10	21, 30
vi 11–13	30
vi 19	29
vii 1	124
vii 8	29
vii 11	204
vii 22	29
viii 1	28
viii 14–19	204
viii 17	29, 180
viii 19–20	29
viii 20–2	26
viii 20 ff.	196, 204
viii 21	26–7
viii 21–2	24, 29
ix 1	14
ix 1–17	204
ix 2–3	196
ix 6	22–3
ix 7	180
ix 16	120
ix 20	26–7
ix 20–1	25–7
x	35–43
x 2–4	38
x 2–5	35, 42
x 3–4	38
x 4–5	36
x 5	35–6, 38, 42–3
x 6–20	35
x 10	38, 40
x 20	35–6

x 21–31   36
x 22   21
x 22–3   241
x 24–5   21
x 29, 32   36
x 31   35–6
x 32   35
xi 1–9   32
xi 10–17   21
xi 10–26   19
xi 26–7   21
xi 30   135
xii–xiv   119
xii 1–3   104, 119
xii 1–4   118
xii 2   235
xii 3   27, 129
xii 6   63, 104
xii 6–7   63
xii 7   119
xii 10–20   135
xii 17   135
xiii 7   96, 104
xiii 14–17   106, 118–19
xiv   45, 48, 63–4, 73–102
xiv 1   77
xiv 1–2   89
xiv 1–9   73, 79, 87–8, 91, 93
xiv 1–11   74, 76–7, 80–1, 84–5, 87, 90–1, 94
xiv 1–12   84
xiv 1–17   94
xiv 2   74, 77, 88, 92
xiv 3   74, 88
xiv 4–7   77
xiv 5   60, 92, 94
xiv 5–6   92
xiv 7   61, 74, 88, 92, 170
xiv 8   74, 77, 88, 92
xiv 9   38, 77
xiv 10–11   74, 79, 81, 87, 91, 102
xiv 10–12   77
xiv 11   80–1, 89
xiv 12   74, 77, 80–1, 85, 89
xiv 12–16   80, 87
xiv 12–17   74, 76, 86–7, 91
xiv 12–24   76–7, 94
xiv 12 ff.   80–1
xiv 13   61, 74, 79–80, 89, 92, 96, 137

xiv 13–14   77
xiv 13–16   84–7
xiv 14   74, 79, 89
xiv 14–16   74
xiv 15   80
xiv 15–16   76
xiv 16   74, 79, 81, 85, 89
xiv 17   46, 51, 60, 62, 70, 74, 76–8, 81, 83–6, 88, 90–1
xiv 17–19   83
xiv 18   83–4
xiv 18–20   45–71, 74–9, 82–4,, 90–1, 97–9, 101
xiv 19–20   77, 83
xiv 20   76–9, 81, 84, 90
xiv 21   74, 77–8, 80–1, 83, 91
xiv 21–3   78–9, 86–8, 91
xiv 21–4   74, 76, 84–6, 90, 94
xiv 22   74, 77–9, 84, 90
xiv 22–3   89
xiv 22–4   80
xiv 23   74, 77, 80, 84–5, 90
xiv 24   77, 80–2, 85, 87, 137
xv   103, 112, 119–20, 127–8
xv 1   105
xv 1–6   104, 107, 112
xv 1 ff.   145
xv 2   138
xv 2–3   105
xv 3   138
xv 4–5   105, 118–19
xv 6   103–30
xv 7–21   119
xv 13   235
xv 18   104, 119–20, 128–9
xv 18–20   95
xvi   131–48
xvi 1   134–7, 145
xvi 1–16   132, 139–40, 147
xvi 2   132, 134–7, 145
xvi 3   134–7, 140
xvi 3–4   137
xvi 4   132, 136
xvi 4–14   134
xvi 5   134, 137, 145
xvi 6   132–4, 137–8, 145

xvi 6–14   132
xvi 7   133–4, 148
xvi 7–8   138
xvi 7–14   138
xvi 8   134, 138, 145
xvi 9   133–4, 138–9, 146, 148
xvi 9–10   138
xvi 9–12   139
xvi 10   134, 138–9, 146, 148
xvi 11   134, 138, 148
xvi 11–12   138–9
xvi 11–14   138
xvi 13   134, 148
xvi 13–14   140
xvi 15   20, 134, 140, 143
xvi 15–16   134, 146
xvi 15–xviii 15   144
xvi 16   134, 140, 143, 145–6
xvii   120, 128, 139, 143–4, 146–7
xvii 2   139
xvii 3   138–9
xvii 6   138
xvii 7   120, 138
xvii 9   138–9
xvii 10   144
xvii 10–14   143
xvii 15   138–9
xvii 16   139
xvii 20   146
xvii 24–5   145–6
xviii   144
xviii 5   82
xviii 14   143
xviii 16–33   124
xviii 17–18   104
xviii 18   235
xx 18   136
xxi   131–48
xxi 1   141–2
xxi 1–2   141, 143, 144
xxi 1–7   140–2, 144, 146–7
xxi 1–21   132, 139, 141, 146
xxi 2   141–4, 146
xxi 2–3   143
xxi 2–5   141–2
xxi 3   20, 141, 143, 146
xxi 3–5   141
xxi 4   143–4

xxi 5	141, 143, 145–6	xxxvii–l	145	xiv 31	105
xxi 6	138, 141–2, 144	xxxvii 4	61	xv 2	236
xxi 6–7	141, 144	xxxvii 35	65	xv 25	235
xxi 6–21	141, 144	xxxviii 3	140	xvii 4	235
xxi 7	138, 141–2, 144	xxxviii 15	121	xviii 4	236
xxi 8	141	xxxix 1	5	xviii 7	174
xxi 8–21	131, 140–1,	xl 4	142	xviii 12	149
	144–7	xlii 5, 7, 13, 29, 32	136	xix 9	105
xxi 9–10	132, 146	xliii 23	236	xix 24	149
xxi 10	133, 144	xliv 8	136	xx 5	125
xxi 11–14	132	xliv 18	158	xxii 22, 26	235
xxi 12	144	xlv 26	105	xxiii 19	208
xxi 12–13	144–5	xlvi 1	236	xxiii 23, 28	96
xxi 13	144–6	xlvi 3	145, 235–6	xxiii 30	208
xxi 14	133, 144–6	xlvii 26	145	xxiv 1	149
xxi 14–19	132	xlviii 22	63	xxiv 4	168
xxi 15–16	144–5	l 17	236	xxiv 9, 14	149
xxi 17	144	l 24–5	142	xxv 30, 31 ff.	186
xxi 18	144–6, 235			xxix 18	186
xxi 19	133, 144–5	*Exodus*		xxix 37	184
xxi 20	144–5	i–xiii	171	xxxii	149–55, 157–9
xxi 20–1	133	i 11–12, 14	235	xxxiii–xxxiv	152
xxii	63, 103, 106,	ii 14	5	xxxii 1–4	154
	128–9	iii	236	xxxii 1–6	151, 153–5
xxii 1	103	iii 6–7	236	xxxii 2–3	153
xxii 1–14	127	iii 8	96, 236	xxxii 4–5	152
xxii 11	145	iii 13, 15–16	235	xxxii 4–6	154, 156
xxii 12	103	iii 17	96, 236	xxxii 6	155
xxii 14	104	iii 19	236	xxxii 8	151, 156
xxii 15	145	iv	236	xxxii 10	235
xxii 15–18	126–9	iv 1	105	xxxii 20	157
xxii 20–4	241	iv 5	235–6	xxxii 21–4	155
xxv 1–10, 13–15	153	iv 8	105	xxxii 24	155
xxv 20	241	iv 21	236	xxxii 25–9	155, 157
xxvi 19	64, 127	v 1, 4, 20	149	xxxii 26–9	155
xxvi 24	236	v 23	235	xxxii 30–4	156–7
xxvii 19	27	vi 1	236	xxxiii 2	96
xxviii 5	241	vi 9	235	xxxiii 3	236
xxviii 12 ff.	145	vi 14–27	151	xxxiii 8, 10	174
xxviii 13	236	vii 28	180	xxxiv 7	125
xxxi 15	121	viii 8	235	xxxiv 9	123
xxxi 20, 24	241	viii 19	236	xxxiv 11	96
xxxi 42, 53	236	ix 27	149	xxxiv 19–20	199
xxxii 10	236	x 1–2	236	xxxiv 20	199
xxxiii 9	82	x 3, 8, 16	149		
xxxiii 18	45–7, 49, 52–4,	xii 5	236		
	61, 64, 66–9	xiii 1–2	199	*Leviticus*	
xxxiii 20	63	xiii 5	96	i 9, 13, 17	186
xxxiv	66	xiii 11–16	199	ii 1–2, 4, 9	186
xxxiv 21	61, 64	xiii 13	199	ii 11	189
xxxv 1–4	153	xiii 17	219–20	iii 5	186
xxxv 1–10	150	xiv 1–xv 21	161	v 2–3	184
xxxv 4	143	xiv 2, 9	161	vi 8	186
xxxv 6	136	xiv 10	235	vi 11	184
xxxv 10	20	xiv 13	218–20, 224–6,	vi 14	186
xxxv 13–15	150		229	vii 18	107, 110, 116,
xxxv 15	20	xiv 15	235		122

xi   177–9, 181, 183–4,
     187, 191, 194, 197,
     202–3, 206–8
xi 1   187
xi 1–23   181, 184,
     204–5, 208
xi 2   207
xi 2–3   206
xi 2–8   205
xi 2–23   207
xi 3   185, 187–9, 205
xi 4–7   188–9, 205–6
xi 4–8   188
xi 8   205–7
xi 9   197
xi 9–23   206–7
xi 10   179
xi 21   180, 192
xi 22   192
xi 23   192, 207
xi 24–31   205
xi 24–38   205–6
xi 24–39   205
xi 24–40   207
xi 24 ff.   205, 207–8
xi 26   205, 207
xi 26–30   188
xi 26 ff.   188
xi 25   188, 205, 207
xi 29   188, 205
xi 39–40   206–7
xi 41–5   184, 206
xii–xv   182–4
xv 31   181, 184
xvi 29   183
xvii   197
xvii 4   107, 110
xvii 5   204
xvii 8, 10, 12–13, 15   183
xvii 15–16   184, 208
xviii 26   183
xix 7   110
xx   189
xx 2   183
xx 17–25   184
xx 25   189
xxi 1–4   184
xxi 6, 8   186
xxi 9   5
xxi 11–12   184
xxi 17, 21–2   186
xxii 22   193
xxii 25   186
xxiii 13, 18   186
xxiv 2–9   186
xxvii 26 ff.   199
xxvii 30–3   208

Numbers
xii   149, 152, 157–9
xii 1   157
xii 2   157–8
xii 2–9   157
xii 6–8   157–8
xii 10–15   157
xii 11   158
xii 13   235
xiii 21   57
xiii 26   172
xiii 27   236
xiv 11   105
xiv 12   235
xv 1–12   186
xv 26, 29–30   183
xvi 13–14   236
xvi 30   65
xviii 21–32   208
xviii 27   107, 110
xviii 30   107
xix   182–4, 207
xix 10   183
xx   242
xx 1   172
xx 12   105
xx 15–16   235
xx 20   236
xx 27–8   173
xxii 1   171
xxiii 7   161
xxiv 16   99
xxv   117, 120, 125
xxv 1   57
xxv 6–13   114
xxv 13   117–18, 120,
     125
xxvi 58   151
xxxi 16   125
xxxii 38   57
xxxiii   172
xxxiii 1–49   165, 172–5
xxxiii 10–11   170
xxxiii 30, 36–41   173
xxxiii 38   173–4
xxxiii 49   57

Deuteronomy
i–ii   173
i 2   170
i 11   235
i 19   170, 173
i 19–25   172
i 20   170
i 21   235
i 28   235
i 34–40   172

i 44   170
ii 1   173
ii 1–3   172
ii 3, 8   173
ii 10   235
ii 10–11   92, 94
ii 20–1   92
ii 21   235
ii 29   173
iv 1   235
iv 3   125
iv 6–8   235
iv 34   236
iv 35, 39   213
v 7   124
v 25   219
vi 1–2   213
vi 3   235–6
vi 4   209–15
vi 5, 10, 12–13,
     15–18, 20   213
vi 20–4   231
vi 22   236
vi 24   213
vi 25   123–4
vii 1   96
vii 9   213
vii 19   236
ix 1   209
ix 2, 14   235
ix 18   213
ix 23   105
x 6   173
xi 9   236
xi 29   63
xii 1   235
xii 1–14   156
xii 5   156
xiv   208
xiv 4 ff., 21, 22 ff.   208
xvii 14   220–1
xvii 14–20   217, 220
xvii 15   220–1
xvii 15–17   221
xvii 15–20   220
xvii 16   217–29
xvii 16–17   220
xvii 17   220–1
xvii 18   220–1
xvii 18–19   221
xvii 18–20   220–1
xvii 19–20   221
xviii 16   219
xx 3   209
xx 17   96
xxiv 13   109, 115, 123–4
xxvi 1   238

xxvi 1–4   238–9
xxvi 1–11   239
xxvi 2–3   238
xxvi 5   235–8, 242
xxvi 5–10   231–42
xxvi 6   235, 238
xxvi 6–9   237–8
xxvi 7   236, 238
xxvi 8   236
xxvi 10   237–8, 242
xxvi 10–11   238–9
xxvi 15   236
xxvi 42   235
xxvii 3   235–6
xxviii 1–14   124
xxviii 11   63
xxviii 47–58   222
xxviii 58–68   222, 224,
                  228
xxviii 59   223
xxviii 59–61   222–3
xxviii 60   223–4
xxviii 61–2   223
xxviii 62–3   222–3
xxviii 64   223–4
xxviii 64–8   222–3
xxviii 65   223–4
xxviii 65–7   224
xxviii 66–7   223
xxviii 67   223–4
xxviii 68   217–29
xxix 2   236
xxix 23   92–3
xxix 24   235
xxxi 20   236
xxxiii 9   155
xxxiii 19   46
xxxiv 11   236

Joshua
ii 1   57
iii 1   57
iii 10   96
iv 20–3   174
viii 33   63
ix 1   96
x 1, 3   51
xii 8   96
xii 17   57
xiii 17   57
xv 9–10   57
xv 27   173
xv 60   57
xvi 8   57
xvii 8   57
xviii 14   57
xxi 13–19   152

xxi 25   61
xxii 7   57
xxii 17   125
xxiv   232
xxiv 2–13   231
xxiv 7   235
xxiv 11   96
xxiv 13   236

Judges
iii 5   96
iii 7–11   241
vi 13   158
vi 24   61
viii 24–6   153
viii 37   59
ix 4   59
ix 9   186
ix 13   25, 186
ix 27   58
ix 46   59
x 6   241
xviii 7   241
xviii 28   57
xix 11   60
xx 27–8   152

1 Samuel
i 13   121
i 24   186
i 26   158
ii 27–36   152
ii 35   158
iii 10–14   152
iii 11–14   125
vi 21   57
vii 1–2   57
ix 4   53
x 3   186
xii 6–8   107
xx 26   183
xxi 5   183
xxi 5–7   186
xxvii 12   105

2 Samuel
viii 3–8   240
x   6
x 1–19   240
x 6   5, 57
x 8   5
xi 4   183
xvi 1–8   58
xviii 18   51, 62
xix 20   107, 122–3
xxii 24–5   122

xxiii 5   120
xxiv 24   82

1 Kings
iii 17, 26   158
viii 60   213
x 7   105
xi 23–5   240
xii   63, 151–2
xii 26–33   156
xii 28   151–2
xii 28–33   154
xii 31   151
xii 32–3   152
xv 16–20   240
xx   240
xxii 1–4   240

2 Kings
v   183
vii 3 ff.   183
ix 14–15   240
x 32–3   240
xii 17–18   240
xiii 25   240
xiv 28   240
xvi 5–9   240
xvii 20–3   157
xxiii 15–18   156

Isaiah
iii 21   153
xi 1–9   124
xi 7   196
xi 11   37
xxi   95
xxiii 2, 6   38
xxvii 9   123
xxix 17   121
xxxi 1   226
xxxii 1–8   124
xxxii 15   121
xxxii 15–20   124
xli 2, 6   41
xli 8   127
xli 10   107
xlv 23   106
xlvi 13   107
li 1–2   127
li 2   212
li 6   107
liii 1   105
liii 4   121
liii 11   122
lvi 1   123
lx 22   235

Jeremiah
ii 10 — 38
x 25 — 22
xii 6 — 105
xxi 1–10 — 226
xxii 24–5 — 226
xxiii 5–6 — 124
xxiv 8 — 226
xxv 9 — 226
xxv 22 — 37, 41
xxvii–xxviii — 226
xxxi 29–30 — 124
xxxiii 15–16 — 124
xl 14 — 105
xli 5 — 45, 66
xlii — 226
xlii 19 — 226
xliv 11–14 — 226
xlviii 3 — 57
xlviii 5 (LXX) — 45, 66–7

Ezekiel
xiv 12–20 — 124
xvi 5 — 53, 60
xvii — 227
xvii 1–10, 15 — 227
xviii — 122, 124
xviii 9 — 110
xxv 9 — 57
xxvi 15–18 — 37
xxvii 6 — 38
xxvii 7 — 38
xxvii 12–15 — 39
xxvii 13 — 228
xxix 16 — 162, 226
xxx 6 — 162
xxxiii 24 — 127, 212
xxxvii 22 — 212
xxxix 6 — 39
xl 7, 16 — 186
xlvi — 75
xlvii 1–11 — 52

Hosea
viii 13 — 218–19
ix 3 — 219
ix 4 — 186
xi 4 — 219
xi 5 — 218–20
xi 8 — 91
xi 10 — 125

Joel
i 6 — 235
ii 2 — 235
ii 7 — 5
iii 6 — 228

Amos
i 19 — 228

Micah
iv 2-3, 7, 11 — 235
vi 4–5 — 107
vi 5 — 57
vii 5 — 105

Zephaniah
iii 9 — 22, 209

Zechariah
viii 22 — 235
xiv — 215
xiv 9 — 209, 212, 214–15

Malachi
i 7, 12 — 186

Psalms
i — 122
vii 17 — 107
vii 18 — 100
xviii 24–5 — 122
xxii 31–2 — 107
xxiv 4–5 — 124
xxvii 4 — 55
xxxi 2 — 107
xxxii 2 — 107, 122–3
xlviii 3 — 101
xlviii 5–7 — 56
l 1 — 100
lxix 28–9 — 122
lxxii — 123
lxxiii 11 — 99
lxxvi — 57, 59–60, 70
lxxvi 3 — 45–6, 51, 55–7, 70
lxxvii 10–11 — 99
lxxviii 7–8, 17, 19 — 100
lxxviii 22 — 105
lxxviii 35 — 99
lxxviii 41, 56 — 100
lxxxii 1, 6 — 100
civ 15 — 25
cv 8–11 — 120
cv 30 — 180
cvi — 127
cvi 12, 24 — 105
cvi 28–31 — 117, 125
cvi 30 — 114, 117
cvi 30–1 — 116, 119
cvi 31 — 107–8, 114–18, 120–3, 125
cvi 46–7 — 127
cvii 11 — 99

cx — 51, 55–7, 59–60, 70, 98, 100–1
cx 2 — 45, 100
cx 4 — 45, 98, 100–1
cxix 66 — 105
cxxx 3–4 — 123
cxxxii 6 — 57

Job
i 21 — 65
xiii 24 — 121
xix 15 — 121
xxxiii 10 — 121
xl 15–23 — 188
xl 30 — 190
xli 19, 24 — 121

Proverbs
xiv 15 — 105
xvi 6 — 123
xxvii 14 — 107, 122
xxxi 6–7 — 25

Lamentations
ii 6 — 55
iii 35, 38 — 100
iv 2 — 121

Esther
x 1 — 37, 41

Ezra
vii 27 — 235
ix 1 — 95–6

Nehemiah
ii 20 — 109
ix 8 — 96, 107
xiii 16 — 190

1 Chronicles
i 7 — 38
i 42 — 173
v 8 — 57
vi 25 — 61
xii 18 — 235
xii 2i -8 — 151
xvi 15–18 — 120

2 Chronicles
viii 7 — 96
ix 6 — 105
xx 6 — 235
xx 20 — 105
xxvi 16 ff. — 75
xxviii 4–5 — 212
xxix 1 — 212

xxxii 15   105
xxxvi 15   55

Mark
xii 29   210

John
iii 23   45, 50–1

Romans
iv   103, 108
iv 3   195

Galatians
iii   103, 108, 129
iii 6   105

James
ii 14–26   103, 129
ii 23   105

Revelation
xx 9   53

Apocrypha and Pseudepigrapha

Judith
iv 4   45, 54, 67

1 Maccabees
ii 52   103

Letter of Aristeas
146   190

Jubilees
v 1   31
xxx   45, 48, 54, 61, 66, 67

Qumran

Genesis Apocryphon
XX 13   47
XXII 16, 21   78

Josephus

Jewish War
VI, § 438   47

Antiquities
I, §§ 180–1   47
VII, § 243   51, 62

Rabbinical Sources

M. Ḥullin
III 6   190

B. Sanhedrin
63a   151

B. Ḥullin
36b   191
59b   187